WAVES OF PROTEST

Social Movements Since the Sixties

edited by
JO FREEMAN
and
VICTORIA JOHNSON

ROWMAN & LITTLEFIELD PUBLISHERS, INC.
Lanham • Boulder • New York • Oxford

ROWMAN & LITTLEFIELD PUBLISHERS, INC.

Published in the United States of America
by Rowman & Littlefield Publishers, Inc.
4720 Boston Way, Lanham, Maryland 20706

12 Hid's Copse Road
Cumnor Hill, Oxford OX2 9JJ, England

British Library Cataloguing in Publication Information Available

Library of Congress Cataloging-in-Publication Data

Waves of protest : social movements since the sixties / edited by Jo
    Freeman and Victoria Johnson.
        p.   cm. — (People, passions, and power)
    Includes bibliographical references and index.
    ISBN 0-8476-8747-3 (cloth : alk. paper). — ISBN 0-8476-8748-1
(pbk. : alk. paper)
    1. Social movements—United States—History.   I. Freeman, Jo.
II. Johnson, Victoria.   III. Series.
HN59.W34   1999
303.48'4'0973—dc21   98-51041
                                                                 CIP

Printed in the United States of America

∞ ™ The paper used in this publication meets the minimum requirements of
American National Standard for Information Sciences—Permanence of Paper
for Printed Library Materials, ANSI/NISO Z39.48–1992.

Contents

Part Three: Consciousness

Part Four: Strategy and Tactics

Part Five: Decline

Copyright Acknowledgments

Carol M. Mueller. Reprinted here with minor revisions by permission of Yale University Press.

Chapter 10: Copyright © 1999 by David G. Bromley and Diana Gay Cutchin.

Chapter 11: Copyright © 1977, 1999 by Jo Freeman. Originally published in *The Dynamics of Social Movements,* ed. Mayer N. Zald and John D. McCarthy (Cambridge, Mass.: Winthrop, 1979), as "Resource Mobilization and Strategy: A Model for Analyzing Social Movement Organization Actions." Reprinted under its current title in *Social Movements of the Sixties and Seventies,* ed. Jo Freeman (New York: Longman, 1983). Reprinted here with minor revisions.

Chapter 12: Copyright © 1999 by Victoria Johnson.

Chapter 13: Copyright © 1999 by David S. Meyer. An early version of this paper was presented at the annual meeting of the American Political Science Association in Chicago, September 2, 1992, and at the NYU seminar on Protest, Power, and Politics, in October 1995.

Chapter 14: Copyright © 1983, 1999 by J. Craig Jenkins. Expanded and revised from the version originally published in *Social Movements of the Sixties and Seventies,* ed. Jo Freeman (New York: Longman, 1983).

Chapter 15: Copyright © 1983 by Frederick D. Miller. Originally published in *Social Movements of the Sixties and Seventies,* ed. Jo Freeman (New York: Longman, 1983).

Chapter 16: Copyright © 1983 by Doug McAdam. Originally published in *Social Movements of the Sixties and Seventies,* ed. Jo Freeman (New York: Longman, 1983).

Chapter 17: Copyright © 1977 by Sage Publications, Inc. Originally published in *Journal of Black Studies* 18 (1977): 13–28. Reprinted in *Social Movements of the Sixties and Seventies,* ed. Jo Freeman (New York: Longman, 1983). Reprinted here with permission of Sage.

All photographs copyright © 1999 by Jo Freeman, except "Operation Rescue" photograph on p. 219, copyright © by Victoria Johnson.

Preface

The decade of the 1960s was one of those rare periods that transform society. It was a decade that spilled over into the seventies and eighties. Its effects are still rippling through some of our more remote social bayous even as the reaction to those effects dominates the societal center. The sixties was marked, above all, by public discontent organized into protest movements.

While protests are common in our history, there have been three periods since our country's founding in which wave after wave of protests have reshaped our policies, priorities, and values. The first of these were the moral reform movements, particularly abolition and temperance, which preceded our Civil War. The second were the populist and progressive movements between 1890 and 1920 that sought to curb corruption in politics and the economic power of corporations. The sixties movements and their progeny were the third.

While each period has its own theme, there are some common characteristics. They last roughly twenty to thirty years. While there are a few major movements that set the tone of the period, there are many minor ones that vary the theme and bring its ideas to people who might otherwise be unaffected. There is always a backlash. Social movements generate countermovements, and sometimes they also spawn government repression. Countermovements can limit the reach of social movements; they can also mobilize new populations and stimulate new movements. At the end of the period there are new institutions, new interest groups, and different policies and priorities than there were before, though these are not always the ones the initial movements aimed to attain.

This book is about American movements and countermovements of the third wave.

The civil rights movement that began in the late fifties was the first of the sixties movements, and it set the tone and style for what was to come. Organized by and for southern blacks, the civil rights movement nonetheless sought a reaffirmation of such basic American values as equal rights and individual dignity. This reaffirmation by a movement that targeted as its enemy a practice—segregation—typical of a region that itself was stigmatized by the rest of the nation made it easy for a population still appalled by the atrocities of Hitler's Germany to view the movement's achievements as a goal and not a threat. It was not until black protest "went north" that serious national opposition appeared.

In the meantime, the civil rights movement captured the imagination of a public jaded by a decade of conformity, particularly the post–World War II generation attending college. The young people who found an answer to President John F. Kennedy's call to "ask what you can do for your country" through participation in the civil rights movement began to apply the concepts and values they had learned from that movement to other segments of society. These values were initially expressed in the Port Huron Statement, adopted in 1962 by the Students for a Democratic Society. It urged "the establishment of a democracy of individual participation governed by two central aims: that the individual share in those social decisions determining the quality and direction of his life; that society be organized to encourage independence in men [sic] and provide the media for their common participation. . . ."

SDS went through many changes before finally self-destructing in 1969, but the values expressed in the Port Huron Statement did not die with it. These values emphasized the politicization of society, individual fulfillment, and the legitimation of dissent in a sharp break with the previous era's stress on privatization and conformity. Such a change proved enduring even while conservatives organized their own movements in reaction to the successes of the sixties and seventies.

Politicization and individual fulfillment as values probably had their greatest effect in the women's movement, which expressed them in the phrase "the personal is political" and acted them out in ways that began to violate fundamental American institutions such as patriarchy. Although this movement began in the sixties, it did not become public until 1970, and in the decade of the seventies it reached its peak and greatest influence. More than any other movement of the past two decades, it deprivatized what had heretofore been perceived as personal problems.

Although the sixties is viewed as the decade of protest, it was really the seventies that saw the greatest flowering of movements on a wide variety of issues. As waves of protest spread throughout our society, new segments of the population picked up the banner of social change. Gays and lesbians, animal rights activists, and the disabled were just some of the many identities that appeared in order to demand new laws, attitudes, and practices. Indeed "identity" took on new meaning, resulting in highly organized groups distinct from traditional economic "interests."

But when protests grew larger and more frequent, publicity waned. Four marches on Washington between 1960 and 1980 drew more than one hundred thousand participants: a civil rights march in 1963, an antiwar demonstration in 1969, an ERA march in 1978, and an antinuclear march in 1979. While accurate figures aren't available, there were probably more marches and demonstrations in the seventies than the sixties.

The eruption of movements in the seventies testified to the success of the sixties movements in several ways. First, the sixties movements legitimated dissent itself. Protesters are no longer stigmatized as subversive; at worst they are dismissed as troublemakers. Second, the use of mass demonstrations and even civil disobedience was perceived as effective. Participants may have seen few immediate benefits from their actions, but they attracted the attention of many others who had neither the skills nor the knowledge to use the traditional methods of political insiders. Last, but hardly least, the gains achieved in the sixties stimulated a backlash.

The sixties movements were largely from the Left. Those of the seventies, eighties, and nineties were from the Right as well as the Left, and other movements were unclassifiable on a Left–Right spectrum. The initial targets of the countermovements were issues that were publicly prominent: busing, the Equal Rights Amendment, and abortion. Soon added were opposition to civil rights for gays, affirmative action, environmental regulation, health and safety programs, and immigrants, legal and illegal. In the eighties and nineties the Christian Right, which had sporadically resisted the changes demanded by the movements of the sixties and seventies, organized into a politically cohesive and permanent opposition.

By the end of the twentieth century the third wave of protests had long worn out, and even the countermovements had lost steam and direction. The third wave left in its wake new values, new priorities, new organized groups, and new political alignments. It also left new conflicts, but ones that would be fought through the courts and the legislatures rather than on the streets. Protest slipped from the headlines to the back pages. It remains for another era, another generation of idealists, to see protest as the best route to change.

Introduction

One of the most difficult problems in analyzing social movements is defining exactly what a social movement is. Participants generally know that they are part of a movement, but movements are so diverse that it is difficult to isolate their common elements and incorporate them into a succinct definition. Virtually all movement theorists have differing definitions. Nonetheless, there are some common themes and elements that recur in case studies and theoretical analyses, although not always with a common emphasis.

Spontaneity and structure are the most important elements. Scholars writing from the collective behavior perspective emphasized the spontaneity present in fads, crowds, panics, riots, and social movements, with the latter merely a more organized version of these similar phenomena. Little attention was paid to how movements became organized, or how the type of organization affected the movement's goals and participants. Resource mobilization theorists critiqued this perspective, emphasizing the importance of structure to understand social movements. They downplayed spontaneity, sometimes to the point of viewing all movement actions as deliberate and calculated.

It is much more useful to think of all the many forms of social action as existing along a continuum. At one end are those forms marked by their contagious spontaneity and lack of structure, such as fads, trends, and crowds. At the other end are interest groups whose primary characteristic is a well-developed and stable organization often impervious to spontaneous demands from their members. In the middle are social movements that, however diverse they may be, exhibit noticeable spontaneity and a describable structure, even if a formal organization is lacking. It is difficult to identify the exact amount of structure necessary to distinguish a social movement from a crowd or trend, and often harder to distinguish a social movement organization from an interest group, but those distinctions are crucial. It is the tension between spontaneity and structure that

1

gives a social movement its peculiar flavor. When one significantly dominates the other, what may one day be, or may once have been, a social
movement, is something else.

Conceptualizing a social movement as the middle of a continuum does
not mean there is a natural progression from the spontaneous end to the
organized one, as "natural history" theorists postulate. As some of the
case studies in this book illustrate, the organization can exist before the
movement. While it is unusual for a highly formalized organization to
become a social movement organization, it is even more unusual for a
totally unorganized mass to become one.

A social movement has one or more core organizations in a penumbra
of people who engage in spontaneous supportive behavior that the core
organizations can often mobilize but less often control. When there is
spontaneous behavior with only embryonic organization, there may be
a premovement phenomenon awaiting the right conditions to become a
movement, but there is no movement per se. When the penumbra of
spontaneous behavior has contracted to no more than the core organizations, or has not yet developed, there is also no movement. An organization that can mobilize only its own members, and whose members mobilize only when urged to action by their organization, is lacking a key
characteristic of movements. Regardless of whether structure or spontaneity comes first, or if they appear simultaneously, the important point is
that both must exist.

In addition to structure and spontaneity other important elements
shape the form and content of a social movement. Whether all are necessary to make a movement is open to debate. But they are so prevalent that
they cannot be overlooked.

Of utmost importance is consciousness that one is part of a group with
whom one shares a particular concern. Individuals acting in response to
common social forces with no particular identification with one another
may be setting a trend, but they are not part of a movement. It was said
by sixties activists that "the movement is a state of mind." As Roberta
Johnson demonstrates in her analysis of the disabled, it is a common state
of mind and a sense of identification with others who hold similar views
that make possible the common acts of movement participants, even
when they are out of communication with each other. Government agents
in the 1960s often attributed concurrent eruptions of protest on the campus as the result of some underlying control by agents of a well-organized
subversive group. The real culprit was the press, which by publicizing the
actions of students on one campus gave new ideas for actions to students
with a common state of mind on other campuses. The spontaneous activities that subsequently occurred may not yet have been a movement, but

they drew upon the common consciousness that was later forged into a movement.

Alternatively, a movement can create consciousness. The desire to do this by spreading the movement's message is another key component. This missionary impulse is not limited to social movements, but when it is lacking, it usually indicates that the movement has been successfully repressed or is stagnating. It may also mean that what ought to be a movement has never become one. There is a reason social movements are called "movements." Without the missionary impulse they do not move.

The message carried is another important element—some would say the most important. Highly developed movements usually embody their message in an elaborate ideology that may antedate the movement or be constructed by it. Such an ideology has several parts. It specifies discontents, prescribes solutions, justifies a change from the status quo, and may also identify the agents of social change and the strategy and tactics they are to use. Not all movements have a complete ideology, nor is one necessary. What is necessary is identification of a problem, and a vision of a better future. These alone can create a belief system of extraordinary power.

It has become common to use the term "movement" for two different phenomena, and this can cause some confusion in understanding what a movement is. "Movement" is used initially for the mobilization and organization of large numbers of people to pursue a common cause. It is also used for the community of believers that is created by that mobilization. The first of these is a short-term phenomenon. Movements always decline. But when movements cease, the community that was created often continues. It may even survive until the next wave of movement activity, and may (or may not) provide resources and ideas for a new generation of movement activists. When reading about the "movement" it is important to understand whether mobilization or community is the topic because the questions asked will have different answers.

* * *

The sixties transformed the study and analysis of social movements. Previously, social movements was a subfield within the framework of collective behavior. While not all those grounded in this tradition agreed on what a social movement was, or what the key elements of analysis ought to be, they did share a common distaste, often subtle, for movements and their participants. By and large these writers came of age politically and academically in the thirties and forties when the prevalent movements were extremist in nature. Fascism, communism, and other totalitarian movements shaped their perception of social movements and the questions they considered central to their analyses. The literature of this period was focused on the psychology of movement participation. It looked for the sources of discontent, analyzed the motives of participants, parsed their ideology, and critiqued their leadership.

Movement scholars writing in the seventies and eighties were influenced by the movements of the sixties and seventies. Unlike the previous generation, most of these writers were sympathetic to the movements they studied. Many had been participants, or had friends who were involved. Consequently, they asked very different questions, ones of more immediate interest to movement participants. Their core concerns—access to resources, political opportunity, organization, and strategy—are reflected in some of the chapters of this book. The "resource mobilization" school looked on movement participation as a rational decision calculated to obtain specific goals. It downplayed the role of ideology and grievances in favor of examining actions. Scholars asked "who did what" rather than "why."

During the 1980s and 1990s the pendulum swung. Analysts asked "how" political opportunities or access to resources led to collective action. Ideology was restored to explain how grievances were translated into actions, and movement culture became a core concern. The construction of meaning and the manipulation of symbols became crucial to explaining mobilization, and to assessing movement success or decline.

Much of the research on what we call "consciousness"—movement ideology, culture, and collective identity—has been influenced by European "New Social Movement" theorists. They proposed that the search for identity distinguishes the movements of the 1970s and 1980s from earlier class-based movements. Movement participation is seen as a way to question all aspects of the social order, from government to interpersonal relationships to organization.

In 1983 Jo Freeman published a collection of articles on *Social Movements of the Sixties and Seventies*. The authors in that book were largely from the "resource mobilization" school. Their chapters revealed its diversity of approaches as well as its commonality of concerns. This book, published sixteen years later, retains the best of those articles, some of which have become classics in the literature. A couple have been revised and updated. Most remain as they were. To these have been added new chapters reflecting the change in theoretical approaches as well as the new social movements. Thus this book is not only about movements, but is part of an intellectual movement in the study of social movements. It illuminates the changes in the questions asked by scholars over the past forty years.

Part One Introduction

How movements start is addressed in the first chapter. Jo Freeman believes that movements most readily begin from preexisting co-optable communication networks. These can be galvanized into a new movement by a crisis, or mobilized by organizers seeking to create a movement. To illustrate how this happens, she relies on studies of the civil rights movement, SDS, and both branches of the women's liberation movement to show the interplay of structure and spontaneity, rational calculation and collective identity.

Roberta Johnson illuminates the importance of microstructural factors by asking why the disabled organized into a social movement in some cities but not in others. She concludes that the crucial conditions were a change of consciousness, preexisting social networks, and legitimation and facilitation by political elites.

Eric Hirsch looks at political solidarity to explain recruitment and commitment. Analyzing a student protest at Columbia University, he finds that individuals will sacrifice themselves for a cause when there is consciousness-raising, collective empowerment, polarization, and group decision-making.

James Jasper compares two recruitment strategies used by animal rights activists. He finds that social networks can be tapped for friends and family but that strangers are more readily mobilized by moral shocks. When a movement wants to reach beyond its readily available networks, it must use emotion and ideas, conveyed through books, direct mail, and other impersonal means, to persuade people to join and to act.

1

On the Origins of Social Movements

Jo Freeman

Most movements have inconspicuous beginnings. The significant elements of their origins are usually forgotten or distorted by the time a trained observer seeks to trace them out. Perhaps this is why so much theoretical literature on social movements concentrated on causes (Gurr 1970, Davies 1962, Oberschall 1973) and motivations (Toch 1965, Cantril 1941, Hoffer 1951, Adorno et al. 1950), while the "spark of life" by which the "mass is to cross the threshold of organizational life" (Lowi 1971, 41) has received scant attention.

From where do the people come who make up the initial, organizing cadre of a movement? How do they come together, and how do they come to share a similar view of the world in circumstances that compel them to political action? In what ways does the nature of its sources affect the future development of the movement?

Before answering these questions, let us first look at data on the origins of four social movements prominent in the sixties and seventies: civil rights, student protest, welfare rights, and women's liberation. These data identify recurrent elements involved in movement formation. The ways in which these elements interact, given a sufficient level of grievances, would support the following propositions.

Proposition 1: The need for a *preexisting communications network* or infrastructure within the social base of a movement is a primary prerequisite for "spontaneous" activity. Masses alone do not form movements, however discontented they may be. Groups of previously unorganized indi-

viduals may spontaneously form into small local associations—usually
along the lines of informal social networks—in response to a specific
strain or crisis. If they are not linked in some manner, however, the protest does not become generalized but remains a local irritant or dissolves
completely. If a movement is to spread rapidly, the communications network must already exist. If only the rudiments of a network exist, movement formation requires a high input of "organizing" activity.

Proposition 2: Not just any communications network will do. It must be
a network that is *co-optable* to the new ideas of the incipient movement.
To be co-optable, it must be composed of like-minded people whose backgrounds, experiences, or locations in the social structure make them receptive to the ideas of a specific new movement.

Proposition 3: Given the existence of a co-optable communications network, or at least the rudimentary development of a potential one, and
grievances, one or more precipitants are required. Here, two distinct patterns emerge that often overlap. In one, a *crisis* galvanizes the network
into spontaneous action in a new direction. In the other, one or more persons begin *organizing* a new organization or disseminating a new idea.
For spontaneous action to occur, the communications network must be
well formed or the initial protest will not survive the incipient stage. If it
is not well formed, organizing efforts must occur; that is, one or more
persons must specifically attempt to construct a movement. To be successful, organizers must be skilled and must have a fertile field in which to
work. If no communications network already exists, there must at least be
emerging spontaneous groups that are acutely attuned to the issue, albeit
uncoordinated. To sum up, if a co-optable communications network is already established, a crisis is all that is necessary to galvanize it. If it is
rudimentary, an organizing cadre of one or more persons is necessary.
Such a cadre is superfluous if the former conditions exist, but it is essential if they do not.

The Civil Rights Movement

The civil rights movement has two origins, although one contributed significantly to the other. The first can be dated from December 7, 1955,
when the arrest of Rosa Parks for occupying a "white" seat on a bus stimulated both the Montgomery bus boycott and the formation of the Montgomery Improvement Association. The second can be dated either from
February 1, 1960, when four freshmen at A & T College in Greensboro,
North Carolina, sat-in at a white lunch counter, or from April 15 to 17,
when a conference at Shaw University in Raleigh, North Carolina, resulted in the formation of the Student Nonviolent Coordinating Commit-

tee (SNCC). To understand why there were two origins one has to understand the social structure of the southern black community, as an incipient generation gap alone is inadequate to explain it.

Within this community the two most important institutions, often the only institutions, were the church and the black college. They provided the primary networks through which most southern blacks interacted and communicated with one another on a regular basis. In turn, the colleges and churches were linked in a regional communications network. These institutions were also the source of black leadership, for "preachers" and "teachers" held the main status positions in black society. Of the two, the church was by far the more important; it touched on more people's lives and was the largest and oldest institution in the black community. Even during slavery there had been an "invisible church." After emancipation, "organized religious life became the chief means by which a structured or organized social life came into existence among the Negro masses" (Frazier 1963, 17). Furthermore, preachers were more economically independent of white society than were teachers.

Neither of these institutions represented all the segments of black society but the segments they did represent eventually formed the main social base for supplying civil rights activists. The church was composed of a male leadership and a largely middle-aged, lower-class female followership. The black colleges were the homes of black intellectuals and middle-class youth, male and female.

Both origins of the civil rights movement resulted in the formation of new organizations, despite the fact that at least three seemingly potential social movement organizations already existed. The wealthiest of these was the Urban League, founded in 1910. It, however, was not only largely restricted to a small portion of the black and white bourgeoisie but, until 1961, felt itself to be "essentially a social service agency" (Clark 1966, 245).

Founded in 1909, the National Association for the Advancement of Colored People (NAACP) pursued channels of legal change until it finally persuaded the Supreme Court to abolish educational segregation in *Brown v. Board of Education.* More than any other single event, this decision created the atmosphere of rising expectations that helped precipitate the movement. The NAACP suffered from its own success, however. Having organized itself primarily to support court cases and utilize other "respectable" means, it "either was not able or did not desire to modify its program in response to new demands. It believed it should continue its important work by using those techniques it had already perfected" (Blumer 1951, 199).

The Congress of Racial Equality (CORE), like the other two organizations, was founded in the North. It began in 1942 as the Chicago Committee of Racial Equality, which was composed primarily of students at the University of Chicago. An off-shoot of the pacifist Fellowship of Reconciliation, its leaders were middle-class intellectual reformers, less prominent and more alienated from the mainstream of American society than the founders of the NAACP. They regarded the NAACP's legalism as too gradualist and ineffective, and aimed to apply Gandhian techniques of non-violent direct action to the problem of race relations in the United States. A year later, the Chicago Committee joined with a half dozen other groups that had emerged across the country, mostly under the encouragement of the F.O.R. to form a federation known as the Congress of Racial Equality. (Rudwick and Meier 1970, 10)

CORE's activities anticipated many of the main forms of protest of the civil rights movement, and its attitudes certainly seemed to fit CORE for the role of a major civil rights organization. But though it became quite influential, at the time the movement actually began, CORE had declined almost to the point of extinction. Its failure reflects the historical reality that organizations are less likely to create social movements than be created by them. More important, CORE was poorly situated to lead a movement of southern blacks. Northern-based and composed primarily of pacifist intellectuals, it had no roots in any of the existing structures of the black community, and in the North these structures were themselves weak. CORE could be a source of ideas, but not of coordination.

The coordination of a new movement required the creation of a new organization. But that was not apparent until after the Montgomery bus boycott began. That boycott was organized through institutions already existing in the black community of Montgomery.

Rosa Parks's refusal to give up her seat on the bus to a white man was not the first time such defiance of segregation laws had occurred. There had been talk of a boycott previously, but after local black leaders had a congenial meeting with the city commissioners, nothing happened—on either side (King 1958, 37–41). When Parks, a former secretary of the local NAACP, was arrested, she immediately called E. D. Nixon, at that time the president of the local chapter. He not only bailed her out but informed a few influential women in the city, most of whom were members of the Women's Political Council (WPC). After numerous phone calls between their members, it was the WPC that actually suggested the boycott and E. D. Nixon who initially organized it (King 1958, 44–45).

The Montgomery Improvement Association (MIA) was formed at a meeting of eighteen ministers and civic leaders the Monday after Parks's conviction and a day of successful boycotting, to provide ongoing coordination. No one then suspected that coordination would be necessary for over a year, with car pools organized to provide alternative transportation for seventeen thousand riders a day. During this time the MIA grew slowly to a staff of ten in order to handle the voluminous correspondence, as well as to provide rides and keep the movement's momentum going. The organization, and the car pools, were financed by $250,000 in donations that poured in from all over the world in response to heavy press publicity about the boycott. But the organizational framework for the boycott and the MIA was the church. Most, although not all, of the officers were ministers, and Sunday meetings with congregations continued to be the main means of communicating with members of the black community to encourage them to continue the protest.

The boycott did not end until the federal courts ruled Alabama's bus segregation laws unconstitutional late in 1956—at the same time that the state courts ruled the boycott illegal. In the meantime, black leaders throughout the South had visited Montgomery, and out of the discussions came agreement to continue antisegregation protests regularly and systematically under the aegis of a new organization, the Southern Christian Leadership Conference (SCLC). The NAACP could not lead the protests because, according to an SCLC pamphlet, "during the late 50s, the NAACP had been driven out of some Southern states. Its branches were outlawed as foreign corporations and its lawyers were charged with barratry, that is, persistently inciting litigation."

On January 10, 1957, over one hundred people gathered in Atlanta at a meeting called by four ministers, including Martin Luther King Jr. Bayard Rustin drew up the "working papers." Initially called the Southern Leadership Conference on Transportation and Nonviolent Integration, the SCLC never developed a mass base even when it changed its name. It established numerous "affiliates" but did most of its work through the churches in the communities to which it sent its fieldworkers.

The church was not just the only institution available for a movement to work through; in many ways it was ideal. It performed "the central organizing function in the Negro community" (Holloway 1969, 22), providing both access to large masses of people on a regular basis and a natural leadership. As Wyatt Tee Walker, former executive director of SCLC, commented, "The Church today is central to the movement. If a Negro's going to have a meeting, where's he going to have it? Mostly he doesn't have a Masonic lodge, and he's not going to get the public schools. And the church is the primary means of communication" (Brink and Harris 1964, 103). Thus the church eventually came to be the center of the voter registration drives as well as many of the other activities of the civil rights movement.

Even the young men and women of SNCC had to use the church, though they had trouble doing so because, unlike most of the officers of SCLC, they were not themselves ministers and thus did not have a "fraternal" connection. Instead they tended to draw many of their resources and

people from outside the particular town in which they were working by utilizing their natural organizational base, the college.

SNCC did not begin the sit-ins, but came out of them. Once begun, the idea of the sit-in spread initially by means of the mass media. But such sit-ins almost always took place in towns where there were black colleges, and groups on these campuses essentially organized the sit-in activities of their communities. Nonetheless, "CORE, with its long emphasis of nonviolent direct action, played an important part, once the sit-ins began, as an educational and organizing agent" (Zinn 1964, 23). CORE had very few staff in the South, but there were enough to at least hold classes and practice sessions in nonviolence.

It was SCLC, however, that was actually responsible for the formation of SNCC, although it might well have organized itself eventually. Ella Baker, then executive secretary of SCLC, thought something should be done to coordinate the rapidly spreading sit-ins in 1960, and many members of SCLC thought it might be appropriate to organize a youth group. With SCLC money, Baker persuaded her alma mater, Shaw University, to provide facilities to contact the groups at centers of sit-in activity. Some two hundred people showed up for the meeting, decided to have no official connection with SCLC beyond a "friendly relationship," and formed the Student Nonviolent Coordinating Committee (Zinn 1964, 32–34). It had no members, and its fieldworkers numbered two hundred at their highest point, but it was from the campuses, especially the southern black colleges, that it drew its sustenance and upon which its organizational base rested.

"The Movement"

The term "the Movement" was originally applied to the civil rights movement by those participating in it, but as this activity expanded into a general critique of American society and concomitant action, the term broadened with it. To white youth throughout most of the sixties, "the Movement" referred to that plethora of youth and/or radical activities that started from the campus and eventually enveloped a large segment of middle-class youth. The term also refers to "the student movement" and "the New Left." The campus was a natural communications network for students and intellectuals. But it was a large place, for the most part, so at least in the beginning the basic units had to be smaller and the ties between them more definitive than was necessary once the movement was more developed.

In the late 1950s liberal and socialist groups of students on different campuses formed new organizations. SLATE appeared at Berkeley,

POLIT at Chicago, and VOICE at Ann Arbor, Michigan. Student journals, such as *New University Thought* and *Studies on the Left*, modeled after the *New Left Review* in London, began publishing. Several crises prompted other student organizations to form. The Bay of Pigs fiasco led to Fair Play for Cuba chapters. The Berlin crisis in the summer of 1961, the resumption of nuclear testing, and the push for a massive civil defense program resulted in the Student Peace Union and student chapters of SANE (O'Brien 1969, 4–5). These groups were not themselves a student movement, merely the student branches of "adult" organizations (Haber 1966, 35–36). They were inspired to reach beyond their origins by the southern sit-ins of 1960. "[T]he sit-ins served as a mechanism for bringing . . . students together for the first time for practical interaction over political issues" and disrupted "the prevailing pattern of political apathy" (Flacks 1970, 1).

In 1960, Students for a Democratic Society (SDS) was just one of several national student political groups. It had recently changed its name from the Student League for Industrial Democracy (SLID), but still remained the relatively insignificant youth affiliate of an aging social democratic clearinghouse for liberal, pro-labor, anti-communist ideas. What put life into this moribund group were two University of Michigan students, Al Haber and Tom Hayden. In the late spring of 1960 Al Haber organized a conference on Human Rights in the North, "which began SDS's long association with SNCC and recruited some of the young people who subsequently became the 'old guard' SDS leadership" (Kissinger and Ross 1968, 16).

After the conference, the United Auto Workers donated $10,000 to SDS, which used the money to hire Haber as an organizer. He corresponded widely, mimeographed and mailed pamphlets, gave speeches, and generally made contacts with and between others (Sale 1973, 35). Both Hayden and Haber argued that the different issues on which activists were working were interconnected, that a movement had to be created to work for broad social change, that the university was a potential base and agency in a movement for social change, and that SDS could play an important role in this movement (O'Brien 1969, 6). Despite this potential, SDS "remained practically non-existent as an organization in the late 1960-to-1961 school year. Then, in the summer of 1961, the 14th Congress of the National Student Association was held in Madison, Wisconsin. . . . It was regional and national meetings of NSA which first brought together Northern white radicals" (Kissinger and Ross 1968, 16). In 1962 SDS broke away to stand by itself.

What followed were years of hard organizing effort, stimulated by civil rights activity and campus protests (Sale, 1973). In the early years SDS had many competitors for the affections of students, but none in the form of organizations claiming to represent students as students. The others were largely youth groups of national liberal and socialist organizations. SDS's activities were never confined solely to the campus, and usually sought to channel student activity to the support of other movement efforts. But its formation does illustrate once again the pattern found elsewhere (Haber 1966, 35).

The National Welfare Rights Organization

The welfare rights movement is an excellent example of movement entrepreneurship and government involvement in movement formation. If ever a movement was *constructed*, this one was. The building blocks of its construction were the Great Society antipoverty programs and the plethora of black and especially white civil rights workers who were left "unemployed" with that movement's decline (Piven and Cloward 1971, 321). Many local welfare protest groups originated in antipoverty agencies in order to get more money for the poor. Many others came out of community organizations formed by liberal church groups and urban civil rights activists a few years before. These groups were widely scattered throughout the country and not linked by any communications mechanism.

The entrepreneur who linked them in order to create a movement was George Wiley, a former chemistry professor and civil rights activist who left CORE after losing his bid to become national director. Attracted to the idea of organizing welfare recipients by a pamphlet written by Columbia social work professor Richard Cloward, later published in *The Nation*, Wiley organized the Poverty/Rights Action Center in Washington in May 1966. The P/RAC office opened on a $15,000 budget soon after a conference on the guaranteed annual income at the University of Chicago. Organized by three social work students, it brought together organizers and representatives of welfare groups, community organizations, and poverty workers. Although not specifically invited, Wiley came and was given a place on the conference program. When the participants seemed receptive to his ideas, Wiley announced to the press that there would be national demonstrations on June 30 in support of an Ohio march for adequate welfare already being organized by the Cleveland Council of Churches (Piven and Cloward 1977, 288–91).

Wiley volunteered his new organization to coordinate the national support actions. Drawing upon his contacts from the civil rights movement and those he met at the conference, his "support activities" were highly successful.

On the morning of June 30, when they finally reached Columbus, the forty marchers were joined by two thousand recipients and sympathizers from other towns in Ohio. On the same day in New York two thousand recipients massed in front of City Hall to picket in the hot sun. . . . Groups of recipients in fifteen other cities . . . also joined demonstrations against "the welfare." (Piven and Cloward 1971, 323)

This action was followed by a national conference of one hundred people in August that elected a coordinating committee to plan a founding conference for the National Welfare Rights Organization (NWRO). "The organizers were members of Students for a Democratic Society, church people, and most prominently, VISTA and other antipoverty program workers" (Piven and Cloward 1977, 291–92).

VISTA volunteers continued to be the NWRO's "chief organizing resource" (Piven and Cloward 1971, 329). But they were not the only resource supplied by the government.

If the NWRO developed as a by-product of federal intervention in the cities, it later came to have quite direct relations with the national government. In 1968, the outgoing Johnson Administration granted NWRO more than $400,000 through the Department of Labor, a sum roughly equivalent to the total amount raised from private sources after the organization was formed. . . . Federal officials were aware that the money would go toward strengthening local relief groups. (Piven and Cloward 1971, 329–30)

In effect, the federal government was supporting a social movement organization whose purpose was to extract more money from state and local governments.

This intimate connection between the federal government, the NWRO, and recipient groups lasted only a few years. The NWRO eventually faced organizational problems it was unable to surmount, and antipoverty programs were dismantled by the Nixon administration (Piven and Cloward 1977). But while they lasted, local recipient groups were forged into a movement by experienced civil rights activists and government-funded volunteers under the direction of a single well-trained organizer with an entrepreneurial instinct.

The Women's Liberation Movement

Women are not well organized. Historically tied to the family and isolated from their own kind, only in the late nineteenth century did women in this country have the opportunity to develop independent associations of their own. These associations took years and years of careful organizational work to build. Eventually they formed the basis for the suffrage movement of the early twentieth century. The associations took less time to die. Today the Women's Trade Union League, the General Federation of Women's Clubs, the Women's Christian Temperance Union, not to mention the powerful National American Woman's Suffrage Association, are all either dead or a pale shadow of their former selves.

As of 1960, not one organization of women had the potential to become a social movement organization, nor was there any form of "neutral" structure of interaction to provide the base for such an organization. Only the National Woman's Party remained dedicated to feminist concerns, and it was essentially a lobbying group for the Equal Rights Amendment, which few outside Washington, D.C., had ever heard of. The 180,000-member Federation of Business and Professional Women's Clubs might have provided a base. Yet, while it steadily lobbied for legislation of importance to women, as late as "1966 it rejected a number of suggestions that it redefine . . . goals and tactics and become a kind of 'NAACP for women' . . . out of fear of being labeled 'feminist' " (Hole and Levine 1971, 81). Before any social movement could develop among women, there had to be a structure to bring potential feminist sympathizers together.

What happened in the 1960s was the development of two new communications networks in which women played prominent roles that allowed, even forced, an awakened interest in the feminist ideas. As a result, the movement actually has two origins, from two different strata of society, with two different styles, orientations, sets of values, and forms of organization. The first of these will be referred to as the "older branch" of the movement, partially because it began first and partially because it was on the older side of the "generation gap" that pervaded the sixties. Its most prominent organization is the National Organization for Women (NOW), which was founded in 1966. The "younger branch" consisted of innumerable small groups engaged in a variety of activities whose contact with one another was always tenuous (Freeman 1975, 50).

The forces that led to NOW's formation were set in motion in 1961 when President John F. Kennedy established the President's Commission on the Status of Women at the behest of Esther Petersen, then director of the Women's Bureau at the Department of Labor. Its 1963 report, *American Women,* and subsequent committee publications documented just how thoroughly women were denied many rights and opportunities. The most significant response to the activity of the President's Commission was the establishment of some fifty state commissions to do similar research on a state level. The presidential and state commission activity laid the groundwork for the future movement in two significant ways. (1) It unearthed ample evidence of women's unequal status and in the process convinced many previously uninterested women that something should be done. (2) It created a climate of expectations that something would be done. The women of the presidential and state commissions who were exposed to these influences exchanged visits, correspondence, and staff, and met with one another at an annual commission convention organized by the Women's Bureau. They were in a position to share and mutually reinforce their growing awareness and concern over women's issues. These commissions created an embryonic communications network.

During this time, two other events of significance occurred. The first was the publication of Betty Friedan's *The Feminine Mystique* in 1963. A quick best-seller, the book stimulated many women to question the status quo and some women to suggest to Friedan that an organization be formed to do something about it. The second event was the addition of "sex" to Title VII of the 1964 Civil Rights Act, prohibiting employment discrimination. The Equal Employment Opportunity Commission (EEOC) refused to seriously enforce the "sex" provision. A rapidly growing feminist coterie within the EEOC concluded that "sex" would be taken more seriously if there were "some sort of NAACP for women" to put pressure on the government. They talked to the women they thought could organize such a group.

On June 30, 1966, these three strands of incipient feminism came together, and NOW was tied from the knot. At that time, government officials running the Third National Conference of Commissions on the Status of Women, ironically titled "Targets for Action," forbade the presentation of a suggested resolution calling for the EEOC to treat sex discrimination with the same consideration as race discrimination. The officials said one government agency could not be allowed to pressure another, despite the fact that the state commissions were not federal agencies. The small group of women who desired such a resolution had met the night before in Friedan's hotel room to discuss the possibility of a civil rights organization for women. Not convinced of the need, they chose instead to propose the resolution. When conference officials vetoed it, they held a whispered conversation over lunch and agreed to form an action organization "to bring women into full participation in the mainstream of American society now, assuming all the privileges and responsibilities thereof in truly equal partnership with men." The name NOW was coined by Friedan, who was at the conference doing research on a book. When word leaked out, twenty-eight women paid five dollars each to join before the day was over (Friedan 1967, 4).

By the time the organizing conference was held the following October 29 and 30, over three hundred men and women had become charter members. Instead of organizational experience, what the early NOW members had was experience in working with and in the media, and it was here that their early efforts were aimed. As a result, NOW often gave the impression of being larger than it was. It was highly successful in getting in the press; much less successful in either bringing about concrete changes or forming an organization. Thus it was not until 1970, when the national press simultaneously did major stories on the women's liberation movement, that NOW's membership increased significantly (Freeman 1975, 85–87).

In the meantime, unaware of and unknown to NOW, the EEOC, or the state commissions, younger women began forming their own movement. Here, too, the groundwork had been laid some years before. The different social action projects of the sixties had attracted many women, who were quickly shunted into traditional roles and faced with the self-evident contradiction of working in a "freedom movement" but not being very free. No single "youth movement" activity or organization is responsible for forming the younger branch of the women's liberation movement, but together they created a "radical community" in which like-minded people continually interacted or were made aware of one another. This community provided the necessary network of communication and its radical ideas—the framework of analysis that "explained" the dismal situation in which radical women found themselves.

As early as 1964 papers had been circulated on women, and individual temporary women's caucuses had been held (see Hayden and King 1966). But it was not until 1967 and 1968 that the groups developed a determined, if cautious, continuity and began to consciously expand themselves. At least five groups in five different cities (Chicago, Toronto, Detroit, Seattle, and Gainesville, Florida) formed spontaneously, independently of one another. They came at an auspicious moment, for 1967 was the year in which blacks kicked whites out of the civil rights movement, student power was discredited by SDS, and the New Left was on the wane. Only draft resistance activities were on the increase, and this movement more than any other exemplified the social inequities of the sexes. Men could resist the draft. Women could only counsel resistance.

At this point, there were few opportunities available for political work. Some women fit well into the secondary role of draft counseling. Many didn't. For years their complaints of unfair treatment had been forestalled by movement men with the dictum that those things could wait until after the revolution. Now these political women found time on their hands, but still the men would not listen.

A typical example was the event that precipitated the formation of the Chicago group, the first independent group in this country. At the August 1967 National Conference for New Politics a women's caucus met for days, but was told its resolution wasn't significant enough to merit a floor discussion. By threatening to tie up the convention with procedural motions the women succeeded in having their statement tacked to the end of the agenda. It was never discussed. The chair refused to recognize any of the many women standing by the microphone, their hands straining upward. When he instead called on someone to speak on "the forgotten American, the American Indian," five women rushed the podium to demand an explanation. But the chairman just patted one of them on the head (literally) and told her, "Cool down, little girl. We have more important things to talk about than women's problems."

The "little girl" was Shulamith Firestone, future author of *The Dialectic of Sex* (1971), and she didn't cool down. Instead she joined with another Chicago woman she met there, who had unsuccessfully tried to organize a women's group that summer, to call a meeting of the women who had halfheartedly attended those summer meetings. Telling their stories to those women, they stimulated sufficient rage to carry the group for three months, and by that time it was a permanent institution.

Another somewhat similar event occurred in Seattle the following winter. At the University of Washington an SDS organizer was explaining to a large meeting how white college youth established rapport with the poor whites with whom they were working. "He noted that sometimes after analyzing societal ills, the men shared leisure time by 'balling a chick together.' He pointed out that such activities did much to enhance the political consciousness of the poor white youth. A woman in the audience asked, 'And what did it do for the consciousness of the chick?'" (Hole and Levine 1971, 120). After the meeting, a handful of enraged women formed Seattle's first group.

Subsequent groups to the initial five were largely organized rather than formed spontaneously out of recent events. In particular, the Chicago group was responsible for the formation of many new groups in Chicago and in other cities. Unlike NOW, the women in the first groups had years of experience as trained organizers. They knew how to utilize the infrastructure of the radical community, the underground press, and the free universities to disseminate women's liberation ideas. Chicago, as a center of New Left activity, had the largest number of politically conscious organizers. Many traveled widely to left conferences and demonstrations, and most used the opportunity to talk with other women about the new movement. Despite public derision by radical men, or perhaps because of it, young women steadily formed new groups around the country.

Analysis

From these data there appear to be four essential elements involved in movement formation: (1) the growth of a preexisting communications network that is (2) co-optable to the ideas of the new movement, (3) a series of crises that galvanize into action people involved in a co-optable network, and/or (4) subsequent organizing effort to weld the spontaneous groups together into a movement. Each of these elements needs to be examined in detail.

Communications Network

The four movements we have looked at developed out of already existing networks within their populations. The church and the black college were the primary institutions through which southern blacks communicated their concerns. In the North the church was much weaker and the black college nonexistent, perhaps explaining why the movement had greater difficulty developing and surviving there. The Movement, composed primarily of white youth, had its centers on the campus because this was where that constituency could readily be found. Nonetheless, campuses were too large and disconnected for incipient movement leaders to find each other. Instead they fruitfully used the national and regional conferences of the National Student Association (NSA) to identify and reach those students who were socially conscious. The welfare rights movement, much more than the others, was created by the conscious efforts of one person. But that person had to find constituents somewhere, and he found them most readily in groups already organized by antipoverty agencies. Organizers for the national movement, in turn, were found among former civil rights activists looking for new directions for their political energies.

The women's liberation movement, even more than the previous ones, illustrates the importance of a network precisely because the conditions for a movement existed before a network came into being, but the movement didn't exist until afterward. Analysts of socioeconomic causes have concluded that the movement could have started anytime within a twenty-year period. Strain for women was as great in 1955 as in 1965 (Ferriss 1971). What changed was the organizational situation. It was not until new networks emerged among women aware of inequities beyond local boundaries that a movement could grow past the point of occasional, spontaneous uprisings. The fact that two distinct movements, with two separate origins, developed from two networks unaware of each other is further evidence of the key role of preexisting communications networks as the fertile soil in which new movements can sprout.

Co-optability

A recurrent theme is that not just any communications network will do. It must be one that is co-optable to the ideas of the new movement. The Business and Professional Women's (BPW) clubs were a network among women, but having rejected feminism, they could not overcome the ideological barrier to new political action until after feminism became established. Similarly, there were communications networks among students other than that of the NSA, for example fraternities and athletic associations. But these were not networks that politically conscious young people were likely to be involved in.

On the other hand, the women on the presidential and state commissions and the feminist coterie of the EEOC were co-optable largely because their immersion in the facts of female status and the details of sex discrimination cases made them very conscious of the need for change. Likewise, the young women of the "radical community" lived in an atmosphere of questioning, confrontation, and change. They absorbed an ideology of "freedom" and "liberation" far more potent than any latent antifeminism might have been.

NSA does not appear to have been as readily co-optable to the Movement as the new women's networks were to feminism. As an association of student governments, its participants had other concerns besides political ones. But while it didn't transform itself, it was a source of recruitment and a forum for discussion that gave the early SDS organizers contacts on many campuses.

Exactly what makes a network co-optable is harder to elucidate. Pinard (1971, 186) noted the necessity for groups to "possess or develop an ideology or simply subjective interests congruent with that of a new movement" for them to "act as mobilizing rather than restraining agents toward that movement." The diffusion of innovation studies point out that new ideas must fit in with already established norms for changes to happen easily. Furthermore, a social system that has as a value "innovativeness" (as the radical community did) will more rapidly adopt ideas than one that looks upon the habitual performance of traditional practices as the ideal (as most organized women's groups did in the fifties). People who have had similar experiences are likely to share similar perceptions of a situation and to mutually reinforce those perceptions as well as their subsequent interpretation. A co-optable network, then, is one whose members have had common experiences that predispose them to be receptive to the particular new ideas of the incipient movement and who are not faced with structural or ideological barriers to action. If the new movement can interpret these experiences and perceptions in ways that point out channels for social action, then participation in a social movement becomes the logical thing to do.

The Role of Crises

As our examples have illustrated, similar perceptions must be translated into action. This is often done by a crisis. For blacks in Montgomery, this was prompted by Rosa Parks's refusal to give up her seat on a bus to a white man. For women who formed the older branch of the women's movement, the impetus to organize was the refusal of the EEOC to enforce the sex provision of Title VII, precipitated by the concomitant refusal of federal officials at the conference to allow a supportive resolution. For younger women there were a series of minor crises.

While not all movements are formed by such precipitating events, they are quite common, as they serve to crystallize and focus discontent. From their own experiences, directly and concretely, people feel the need for change in a situation that allows for an exchange of feelings with others, mutual validation, and a subsequent reinforcement of innovative interpretation. Nothing makes desire for change more acute than a crisis. Such a crisis need not be a major one; it need only embody collective discontent.

Organizing Efforts

A crisis will only catalyze a well-formed communications network. If such networks are embryonically developed or only partially co-optable, the potentially active individuals in them must be linked together by someone. This is essentially what George Wiley did for local recipient groups and what SDS organizers did with the contacts they made in NSA and on campuses. "Some protest may persist where the source of trouble is constantly present. But interest ordinarily cannot be maintained unless there is a welding of spontaneous groups into some stable organization" (Jackson et al. 1960, 37). In other words, people must be organized. Social movements do not simply occur.

The role of the organizer in movement formation is another neglected aspect of the theoretical literature. There has been great concern with leadership, but the two roles are distinct and not always performed by the same individual. In the early stages of a movement, it is the organizer much more than any leader who is important, and such an individual or cadre must often operate behind the scenes.

The importance of organizers is pervasive in the sixties movements. Dr. King may have been the public spokesperson of the Montgomery bus boycott who caught the eye of the media, but it was E. D. Nixon who organized it. Certainly the "organizing cadre" that young women in the radical community came to be was key to the growth of that branch of the women's liberation movement, despite the fact that no "leaders" were produced (and were actively discouraged). The existence of many leaders but no organizers in the older branch of the women's liberation movement readily explains its subsequent slow development. The crucial role of organizers in SDS and the National Welfare Rights Organization was described earlier.

Other organizations, even the government, often serve as training centers for organizers and sources of material support to aid the formation of groups and/or movements. The civil rights movement was the training ground for many an organizer of other movements. The League for Industrial Democracy financed SDS in its early days, and the NSA provided indirect support by hiring many SDS organizers as NSA staff. The role of the government in the formation of the National Welfare Rights Organization was quite significant.

From all this it would appear that training as an organizer or at least as a proselytizer or entrepreneur of some kind is a necessary background for those individuals who act as movement innovators. Even in something as seemingly spontaneous as a social movement, the professional is more valuable than the amateur.

References

Adorno, T. W., et al. 1950. *The Authoritarian Personality.* New York: Harper & Row.

Blumer, Herbert. 1951. "Social Movements." In *New Outline of the Principles of Sociology,* ed. A. M. Lee. New York: Barnes and Noble.

Brink, William, and Louis Harris. 1964. *The Negro Revolution in America.* New York: Simon and Schuster.

Cantril, Hadley. 1941. *The Psychology of Social Movements.* New York: Wiley.

Clark, Kenneth B. 1966. "The Civil Rights Movement: Momentum and Organization." *Daedalus* 95, no. 1 (Winter): 239–67.

Davies, James C. 1962. "Toward a Theory of Revolution." *American Sociological Review* 27, no. 1: 5–19.

Ferriss, Abbott L. 1971. *Indicators of Trends in the Status of American Women.* New York: Russell Sage Foundation.

Firestone, Shulamith. 1971. *The Dialectic of Sex.* New York: Morrow.

Flacks, Richard. 1970. "The New Left and American Politics: After Ten Years." Paper presented at the American Political Science Association convention, September.

Frazier, E. Franklin. 1963. *The Negro Church in America.* New York: Schocken.

Freeman, Jo. 1973. "The Origins of the Women's Liberation Movement." *American Journal of Sociology* 78, no. 4 (January): 792–811.

———. 1975. *The Politics of Women's Liberation.* New York: Longman.

Friedan, Betty. 1963. *The Feminine Mystique.* New York: Dell.

———. 1967. "NOW: How It Began." *Women Speaking* (April): 4, 6.

Gurr, Ted. 1970. *Why Men Rebel.* Princeton: Princeton University Press.

Haber, Robert A. 1966. "From Protest to Radicalism: An Appraisal of the Student Movement: 1960." In *The New Student Left,* ed. Michael Cohen and Dennis Hale. Boston: Beacon Press, 34–42.

Hayden, Casey, and Mary King. 1966. "A Kind of Memo." *Liberation* 9, no. 2 (April): 35–36.

Hoffer, Eric. 1951. *The True Believer.* New York: Harper & Row.

Hole, Judith, and Ellen Levine. 1971. *Rebirth of Feminism.* New York: Quadrangle Books.

Holloway, Harry. 1969. *The Politics of the Southern Negro.* New York: Random House.

Jackson, Maurice, et al. 1960. "The Failure of an Incipient Social Movement." *Pacific Sociological Review* 3, no. 1: 40.

King, Martin Luther, Jr. 1958. *Stride Toward Freedom.* New York: Harper & Row.

Kissinger, C. Clark, and Bob Ross. 1968. "Starting in '60: Or From SLID to Resistance." *New Left Notes* (10 June).

Lowi, Theodore J. 1971. *The Politics of Discord.* New York: Basic Books.

Oberschall, Anthony. 1973. *Social Conflict and Social Movements.* Englewood Cliffs, N.J.: Prentice-Hall.

O'Brien, James. 1969. *A History of the New Left, 1960–68.* Cambridge, Mass.: New England Free Press.

Pinard, Maurice. 1971. *The Rise of a Third Party: A Study in Crisis Politics.* Englewood Cliffs, N.J.: Prentice-Hall.

Piven, Frances Fox, and Richard Cloward. 1971. *Regulating the Poor: The Functions of Public Welfare.* New York: Pantheon.

———. 1977. *Poor People's Movements: Why They Succeed, How They Fail.* New York: Pantheon.

Rudwick, Elliott, and August Meier. 1970. "Organizational Structure and Goal Succession: A Comparative Analysis of the NAACP and CORE, 1964–1968." *Social Science Quarterly* 51 (June): 9–24.

Sale, Kirkpatrick. 1973. *SDS.* New York: Random House.

Toch, Hans. 1965. *The Social Psychology of Social Movements.* Indianapolis: Bobbs-Merrill.

Zinn, Howard. 1964. *SNCC: The New Abolitionists.* Boston: Beacon Press.

2

Mobilizing the Disabled

Roberta Ann Johnson

There have always been large numbers of people with disabilities living in the United States. By the late 1970s, there were approximately 30 million.[1] There have always been some charitable and service organizations to meet some of the needs of some disabled people, and particularly since the 1960s, the number of disabled organizations has grown rapidly as the bureaucracy of government service agencies has expanded. But until the 1970s there had never been a large and effective social movement that bridged the gap between different disabilities, spanned the coasts, and continually spawned groups who prodded for disabled rights and services as what Jenkins and Perrow call groups acting in "insurgent" fashion.[2] With so many disabled people, why was there no social movement of the disabled?

To understand the longtime absence of a general social movement we must look to the one area in the United States where a social movement of the disabled was most visible and strong: Berkeley, California. This chapter focuses on what was unique in the Berkeley experience, as well as on more general factors that work to encourage the mobilization of the disabled.

Legislative Background

That there has not been a general social movement of the disabled does not mean there has not been legislation to provide "services for the handicapped." There has. The main thrust of the congressional acts, however, was not civil rights but vocational rehabilitation, and judging from the dates of the major acts, the congressional aim seems to have been largely one of accommodating returning wounded GIs. In fact, accommodating the returning soldier was the specific purpose of the first bills introduced in Congress in 1917 and 1918 and the Smith-Sears Act (P.L. 178), which passed and was signed by President Woodrow Wilson in 1918. The first of a series of rehabilitation acts, Smith-Sears included provisions for the industrially handicapped as well. Each client was eligible for training, counseling, and placement services. In 1935 the program became permanent with the passage of the Social Security Act.

World War II brought the next major changes in the rehabilitation program (P.L. 73–113). Medical, surgical, and other restorative services were authorized, and for the first time, the bill included the mentally ill and mentally retarded.

During the Korean peace talks, Congress passed P.L. 83–565, which improved the financial arrangements of matching moneys to induce states to improve their programs. And in 1968, as the Vietnam War escalated, Congress passed P.L. 89–333, which was designed to expand and enlarge public programs for the handicapped. Services were again expanded in 1967 and 1968 (P.L. 90–341), but it was not until the 1973 Vocational Rehabilitation Act (P.L. 93–112) that there was a major change in legislative philosophy.

The major achievement of this act was not more vocational rehabilitation, although an important feature of the act included services for the severely handicapped, but that it included a significant, far-reaching, and potentially revolutionary commitment to the rights of the disabled. The revolution was wrought in a one-sentence section of the bill, Section 504, which read: "No otherwise qualified handicapped individual in the United States, shall solely by reason of his handicap, be excluded from the participation in, be denied the benefits of, or be subjected to discrimination under any program or activity receiving Federal financial assistance."

The wording of Section 504 paralleled the language of Section 601 of Title VI of the 1964 Civil Rights Act and Title IX of the 1972 Education Amendments Act. And like these sections, its passage did not guarantee implementation and compliance.

It is important to note that Section 504 was not heralded as groundbreaking civil rights legislation. In fact, congressional supporters avoided such a focus for fear it would turn the more conservative members of Congress against the bill. All the press attention and debate seemed to be riveted on the struggle between the Nixon White House and Congress over spending. In fact, President Richard Nixon vetoed the bill twice

(Congress passed the third, cut version), and a *Washington Post* editorial characterized its unfortunate history by saying, "All in all this appears to be a meritorious bill which has become a pawn in the bitter struggle between an obstinate Congress and an equally stubborn President."[3]

The small part of the news coverage that focused on the bill's content, rather than on its political or financial aspects, was generally condescending in tone and not infused at all with a civil rights perspective. For example, Senator Hubert Humphrey reacted to the Nixon veto: "It's just a goddamn outrage. It's a day of infamy for the White House. It's an example of the President ganging up on the lame, the sick, the blind and the retarded."[4] And Representative John Brademas, House manager of the bill, said about the impending vote to override the presidential veto that he didn't believe there were many congresspeople who "would want to vote *against the crippled* more than once in a session."[5]

That is not to say that there was no lobbying pressure from the physically disabled and their supporters. Thirty-five organizations lobbied to override Nixon's veto including the AFL/CIO, UAW, Easter Seals, and state mental health departments.[6] There were some demonstrations in New York City, and in the District of Columbia, more than two hundred people with disabilities, most of them from the annual meeting of the President's Committee on Employment of the Handicapped and the United Cerebral Palsy Association, held a day-long protest ending with a candlelight vigil at the Lincoln Memorial.[7] And although there was a *Washington Post* article that in passing touched on the "rights" of the disabled by warning that it was "time to stop treating the disabled as 'second rate citizens,' "[8] civil rights was not part of the congressional debates and was never raised as an issue during the hearings.[9] At this time, although some of the disabled saw their cause as a civil rights one, most people did not.

During 1975 and 1976, the Office for Civil Rights of the Department of Health, Education, and Welfare delayed implementing Section 504 regulations, first with an inflationary impact study and then with countless meetings with groups across the country including ten town meetings held in May and June 1976.[10] Even after HEW composed a final form for Section 504 "regs" (as they were later called), the secretary of HEW did not sign them, ignoring a federal court order to do so.[11]

Under the Carter administration, HEW did not move any faster. HEW Secretary Joseph Califano delayed signing the implementing regulations so that his staff could rewrite them.[12] In February and March 1977, when it became clear that more than cosmetic changes were being considered by HEW, disabled groups started to plan action[13] to prevent Califano from building "loopholes, waivers and exemptions"[14] into the regulations.

The Takeover

The American Coalition of Citizens with Disabilities (ACCD), an umbrella lobbying group representing forty-five groups and based in Washington, D.C., was created in 1974 by people attending the annual meeting in Washington of the President's Committee on Employment of the Handicapped. The American Council of the Blind, the National Association of the Deaf, Paralyzed Veterans of America, the Center for Independent Living, the National Paraplegic Foundation, and disabled student programs of colleges and universities from across the country were some of the early groups affiliated with ACCD.[15] The American Council of the Blind had a particularly important role to play in the beginning, at times even representing ACCD.

It was not until October 1975 that there was enough money collected from the membership to pay for a director. Frank Bowe, the first director, thought it was of primary importance to establish ACCD's presence in Washington. Until 1977, the organization's primary goals were to seek funding by applying for federal contracts and grants, to appear before congressional committees to testify on legislation, and to develop membership by recruiting organizations to join.

In March 1977 ACCD threatened political activities nationwide in a letter to President Jimmy Carter. In the letter ACCD gave Secretary Califano a deadline of April 4, 1977, to sign the regulations "to bring his line agencies on-board and to begin preparation of an extensive compliance/enforcement program."[16] Groups of disabled people across the country were asked to prepare for protest demonstrations.

The Berkeley Center for Independent Living (CIL) spearheaded the creation of a "504 Emergency Coalition" in the Bay Area, which included the Independent Living Project in San Francisco and thirty or so disabled and supporting groups. By late March the Northern California Emergency Coalition was already explicitly threatening protest demonstrations and sit-ins.

Demonstrations were scheduled to take place on April 5 at HEW buildings in ten different cities.[17] The demonstrations either failed (like the one in New York where only six people showed up to demonstrate) or were small and short-lived. The sit-ins held in Washington, D.C., and Denver lasted one day; the one in Los Angeles had very few participants, but lasted three days.

In Washington, D.C., 300 disabled people, most of them from the immediate area, demonstrated, and 50 to 75 people (estimates vary) remained overnight in HEW offices on the sixth floor where Secretary Califano's office was located.[18] The General Services Administration wanted to oust the Washington demonstrators, but Califano and other HEW officials insisted that "no force" be used. Instead, the demonstrators were starved out.[19] The next day, having been allowed only one cup of coffee and a doughnut, those who sat-in decided to leave as a group rather than trickle out, and a "band of blind, deaf or otherwise disabled" demonstrators left the HEW building after twenty-eight hours of occupation.[20] The Washington demonstrators had neither community support nor support from government officials.

In Denver, 150 people showed up to demonstrate, while others blocked the intersection at 18th and Stack Streets to coincide with the demonstration. Coverage on the noon news encouraged more people to join. Taking their directions from the Washington-based ACCD, when the Denver demonstrators heard that San Franciscans and Washington demonstrators were planning to stay overnight, the Denver folks got bedding and medication, and fifty-two stayed. At 9 P.M. they let the news media into the building, and the 10 P.M. news included coverage of the sit-in.

The next morning, the Denver group left the building at about the same time the Washington demonstrators did. In Denver they called their demonstration a success because, according to one of the more active participants, Janet Dorsey, the sit-in had opened up important communication lines with regional HEW officials. When the demonstrators left the building, they held a press conference and then attended debates in the state legislature on a disabled civil rights bill that just happened to be scheduled for that day.[21]

The Los Angeles sit-in lasted three days. Preparation began in March at meetings attended by a handful of people and held at the Westside Center for Independent Living. On April 5, between forty and fifty demonstrators showed up for a scheduled rally outside the HEW building, and approximately fifteen disabled people entered the building for a sit-in. The demonstrations had some support from local church groups, and food was provided by friends of those who were sitting-in. They had some political support as well. The second night, before the federal employees left the building, officials threatened that the disabled demonstrators would be removed by police. Congressman Tony Bielensen, of the 23rd Congressional District, gave the demonstrators a haven in his office in HEW, preventing any police action. Ed Roberts, director of California's Rehabilitation Department, was also there, giving support. Nevertheless, the Los Angeles demonstrators did not have general community support, nor did they have complete support from disabled groups. The California Association of Physically Handicapped, for example, refused to get involved in the struggle. During the week, no new people joined the sit-in, no new community support was forthcoming, and the sit-in did not generate a growing momentum.[22] They left the building on Friday, April 8, announcing:

> When we left the demonstration, we did not have the organizational support
> to provide food and medical supplies over the weekend, when the doors
> would be closed to all people coming in and out. Friday afternoon all dis-
> abled people and supporters were denied access to the building. There were
> no attendants for the severely disabled demonstrators, and at that time we
> could get none into the building for the weekend. These restrictions, im-
> posed on us suddenly, were a complete policy reversal by the Federal Secur-
> ity Officers.[23]

In San Francisco, the experience of the demonstrators was quite different. Strategy meetings were held in March at Berkeley's Center for Independent Living. Numerous northern California organizations of disabled
persons were represented in their coalition,[24] and the demonstrators had
the support of important community groups and businesses as well. Flyers went out, with the CIL logo prominent at the top, advertising a noontime demonstration to be held at the San Francisco HEW building "to demand signing of Federal antidiscrimination regulations for the disabled."
Hundreds of the disabled and their supporters demonstrated outside,
and hundreds entered the building. Approximately 150 did not leave
when the building officially closed at 5 P.M.

The Salvation Army was there with food, coffee, and blankets for the
first night. The Delancy Street Foundation, a well-established, politically
important ex-prisoner organization, knew in advance about the San Francisco takeover and was also there providing food on the first day of the
sit-in.[25] By the third day, the Black Panthers were providing food and endorsing the demonstrators' goals in their newspaper; the local Safeway
was supplying food and medicine;[26] and a Hispanic group, the Mission
Rebels, was providing hot breakfasts. Labor organizations, including
many AFL/CIO–affiliated unions, in particular the International Association of Machinists, the Teamsters, and the International Longshoremen's
Association, gave their support to the demonstration. The Federal Workers Union, including many employees in the HEW building, gave support
and assistance, as did Werner Erhard of est, who visited and contributed
money. Gay groups, like the Butterfly Brigade, assisted the demonstrators
by smuggling in walkie-talkies and toiletries. As one demonstrator put it,
"The thing that was neat was it was disabled folks from all over working
together and it was also nondisabled support up the kazoo."[27]

The demonstrators at first planned only to stay overnight, then only
over the weekend, but plans can change. The San Francisco demonstrators vowed they would not leave HEW until Califano signed the Section
504 regulations. Judy Heumann, one of the demonstration leaders, remembers the decision to stay:

> I think what was the deciding factor for us staying in the building was the
> fact that the other demonstrations were failing and that the group in Wash-

ington was starved out and so a lot of us here began to feel like we had the strongest base and that we wanted to continue what was going and that we were the only ones left to do it. So it wasn't like a frolicksome, you know . . . it's OK so we'll stay, it was much more strategy of why are we staying. . . .[28]

California officials and politicians spoke out on behalf of the demonstrators. On April 8 Joe Maldonado, the HEW regional director, called Califano to urge him to sign the regulations. On April 9 Ed Roberts, director of the state's Rehabilitation Department, urged approval. California's secretary of health, Mario Obledo, followed suit on April 10.[29]

By April 12, Congressman Phillip Burton expressed his support for the 150 demonstrators who remained at HEW. Burton openly criticized Califano, and on April 15, Burton and Representative George Miller arranged to hold congressional hearings on the proposed regulations right there at the site of the sit-in.[30]

Attention and political support grew. California Congressman Tom Bates of Berkeley sent Califano a letter with the signatures of forty-six state assembly people supporting the demonstrators' demands, and endorsements came from Assemblyman Willie Brown, San Francisco Mayor George Moscone, and the San Francisco Board of Supervisors. The *San Francisco Chronicle* carried at least one story a day about the demonstration, as did the television news.

By April 18, Moscone had obtained hoses to rig up showers at the city's expense, as well as mats, towels, soap, and cream for chair sores at the city's expense, and while HEW Commissioner Maldonado caused some delays—at one point saying, "We're not running a hotel here," and warning he'd have Moscone arrested—by the second week of the demonstration the city had even installed showers.[31]

As the sit-in continued, the San Francisco demonstrators selected a group of eighteen (mostly the CIL leadership), who went to Washington on April 19 to lobby in person. They brought with them more endorsements, including a San Francisco Board of Supervisors' resolution urging Califano to sign and the official endorsement of Obledo.[32]

The demonstrators carried with them other Bay Area support. The ABC TV San Francisco affiliate, KGO, sent a reporter and photographer to Washington to accompany the group. The International Association of Machinists organized a banquet at its Washington headquarters, provided the demonstrators with drivers, and rented a Hertz truck to transport the disabled around Washington. In fact, the union attached a "504" sign to the truck, and when Hertz people saw the logo on the truck on a television program, they asked for the truck back. The Machinists refused.[33]

The San Francisco representatives were not allowed into the HEW building. "Two dozen deaf, blind, and mentally retarded demonstrators," the *Washington Post* wrote, "many of them in wheelchairs, turned away from HEW by armed guards, were demanding to see Califano."[34] Instead, they continued their demonstrations outside, including an all-night vigil and candlelight prayer service in front of Califano's home.[35]

The demonstrators never spoke personally with either Califano or Carter but they did have two meetings with Stuart Eizenstat, assistant to the president in domestic affairs.[36] They also persuaded Senator Alan Cranston to write to Califano, urging him to sign the regulations.[37] When the demonstration was over, the protesters called their attempts to contact the administration "a tremendous success." Said one of the leaders, "We raised a lot of consciousness back in Washington. We got the support of more than thirty Congress persons. We were able to talk to all kinds of people."[38]

Finally, on Thursday, April 28, 1977, day 24 of the San Francisco sit-in, Secretary Joseph A. Califano Jr. signed "the regs." He issued an eleven-page announcement for immediate release. It began,

> For decades, handicapped Americans have been an oppressed and, all too often, a hidden minority, subjected to unconscionable discrimination, beset by demoralizing indignities, detoured out of the mainstream of American life and unable to secure their rightful role as full and independent citizens.
>
>   Today I am issuing a regulation, pursuant to Section 504 of the Rehabilitation Act of 1973, that will open a new world of equal opportunity for more than 35 million handicapped Americans—the blind, the deaf, persons confined to wheelchairs, the mentally ill or retarded, and those with other handicaps.[39]

Jubilant, the demonstrators went home to California. Two days later, all the demonstrators left the San Francisco HEW building, flanked by politician friends, and supporters, feeling victorious. They held a well-publicized rally attended by hundreds. Said Kitty Cone, "What we have done is shown the country that disabled people can carry on a fight—to the highest levels of government. In the process we have gained a whole lot of self-respect."[40]

The Protest

Michael Lipsky defines "protest activity . . . as a mode of political action oriented toward objection to one or more policies or conditions, characterized by showmanship or display of an unconventional nature, and undertaken to obtain rewards from political or economic systems while working within the systems."[41] Since so few disabled people were involved in the "protest activity" just described, it seems, in retrospect, a great miracle that they achieved their goal. One factor was that the goal was specific and "achievable." Another was that they "successfully activated," to use Lipsky's model, "third parties," creating bargaining resources.

But there is a more fundamental issue to be addressed here. The real question is how and why, in 1977, Bay Area disabled people seemed to suddenly burst on to the public arena so much more effectively than in any other area, with a well-articulated collective goal and with a vision larger than that of their disability-specific organizations. Their protest did not succeed because of shared interest or "potential" shared interest. As Jenkins so aptly puts it, "common interests do not collective action make."[42] The protest was just the tip of the iceberg. A social movement had already been congealing in the Bay Area, and thus the events of April 1977 were merely a catalyst to protest activity.

What laid the foundation for a social movement of the disabled was the development of an independent living philosophy—a consequence of independent living programs (ILP) that had developed and grown in California. The programs consisted of "nonresidential service centers controlled by disabled individuals that enable persons with diversified disabilities to live in integrated settings within their own communities . . . independence [did] not mean doing things physically alone. It mean[t] being able to make independent decisions. It is a mind process not contingent on a 'normal' body."[43] The movement for independence was called unique. One journalist described it as a search "for the means to give each person not only equality but as much control as possible over his or her life."[44] Judy Heumann candidly described the importance of ILP in her life when she spoke to congresspeople holding hearings in 1978 on the Vocational Rehabilitation Act:

> I had polio when I was 1½ years old, and I am a severely disabled individual. I grew up in New York City, and I lived there for 25 years. I liked New York but the environment there demanded a lifestyle of dependency. In order for me to make the advances that I wanted to with my life, I learned to manipulate my environment to the best of my ability. There was no formal support system.
>
> In 1973, I was contacted in New York by Ed Roberts and urged to apply to graduate school at the University of California, Berkeley, and to get involved in a program he called CIL. . . . I decided that I would come out for one week as an experiment to see the situation for myself. I was what people in California might describe as "blown away."
>
> I came to Berkeley, was met at the airport by a disabled friend, driving a van with a hydraulic lift. I stayed in a home that was accessible and was given a loaner electric wheelchair to use, and I was assisted with personal care needs by a paid attendant.

> My life quickly began to change. I was in charge of my own activities, getting up when I wanted, going to bed when I wanted, taking a shower when I wanted and the like. All these things may appear small to you, but for me it was the first time that my handicap did not completely control my life. I decided to stay in California.[45]

During the 1970s, the Bay Area became "the nation's capital for the handicapped" with proportionately more severely disabled people than anywhere else in the country. Berkeley became the "unwilling" center of the disabled movement with the establishment of the Center for Independent Living in 1972.[46] CIL grew "from a staff of eleven, working in a two bedroom apartment funded by one federal grant, to an organization staffed by 117 people supported by more than 21 different contracts with an annual budget of around $900,000."[47] The development of an independent living philosophy was essential for birthing a social movement of the disabled—not only because of its emphasis on pride and autonomy for the disabled but because it took disabled people out of their isolation and brought them together in large numbers. Three elements were required for a social movement of the disabled, and these were prevalent in Berkeley, California, in quantities and forms not available elsewhere: (1) a change of consciousness, (2) preexisting social networks, and (3) legitimation and facilitation by political elites.

A Change of Consciousness

A change of consciousness was the biggest hurdle for the disabled. What was required for the disabled to become a social movement was nothing short of a redefinition of themselves. Traditionally they had been dealt with in a paternalistic way and had accepted gratefully bureaucratic gifts coming from "on high." They were seen as unfortunate people—"poor crips," as some of the demonstrators mockingly described it. Disability was stigmatized as shameful; the disabled were seen, and felt themselves to be, dependents on charitable society. With this self-image, there could never be a social movement, for the felt dependency inhibited the sense of efficacy a movement required and the stigmatized view of self discouraged identification with other disabled people. A change of consciousness was necessary. There were three parts to the change of consciousness necessary for a disabled social movement: (1) destigmatization, (2) group identification, and (3) the development of feelings of efficacy.

Destigmatization was a vital first step. A new self-image required feeling pride about a condition seen as shameful and often ugly. The following description of a summer camp for disabled children illustrates vividly the abhorrent qualities attached to the disabled:

The woods and paths of Camp Wiggin were accustomed to troops of running feet and the noise of children at play. With these children there was
only silence. Parents unfolded wheelchairs, and carefully lifted their children
into them. In procession, they wheeled the children—about 120 in all—
toward us waiting counselors. They would be under our care for the next
two weeks.

What do you say to a parade of children who move toward you only by
the energy of their parents: children with swollen heads, or sightless eyes, or
bodies without arms or legs; children drained of expression, pallid in color
and spirit. They seemed old for their age, yet without visible life, crumbled
and stuffed into wheelchairs, covered with blankets to ward off, not the cold,
but the sight of disfigurement.[48]

Not only did the disabled have to develop a positive self-image but they
had to identify with others who were disabled. The second shift in consciousness, group identification, was also difficult because there is a psy-
chic cost in identifying with crippled people in a culture that emphasizes
youth and beauty and allows some disabled to blend in and "mainstream." The problem of group identification existed for other social
movements based on an immutable characteristic. But disability is more
stigmatizing than any other characteristic, even race.[49] Demonstrations
have functioned for stigmatized groups to reduce the felt differences between members. For example, Alice Walker remembers the 1963 civil
rights March on Washington in the following way: "I felt my soul rising
from the sheer force of Martin King's eloquent goodness . . . whatever the
Kennedy Administration may have done, or not done, had nothing to do
with the closeness I felt that day to my own people."[50] In much the same
way, for many disabled people, the persistent San Francisco sit-in and its
success in 1977 marked a change in their consciousness of group identification or, as one woman put it, "started her awareness."[51]

Connection with others was not only psychologically harder but physically more difficult than with other groups. In general they experienced
more isolation than the suburban housewife separated from other women
or the closeted homosexual in smalltown America. Not only did they
rarely come in contact with other disabled people but many of the disabled had less contact with *anyone* because of their disabilities. Exceptions, like the deaf community, were people who had so much contact
with each other that they knew no one else. This ingrown contact tended
to prevent their wholesale participation in and identification with a general disability movement. The deaf, for example, were used to identifying
with their group alone, and many did not see themselves as "physically
disabled."[52]

Additionally, many of the disabled "subcultures," as the demonstrators called them, had made advances on their own. Organizations such as

the National Federation of the Blind were not enthusiastic about coalescing with others because they had their own history of accommodating legislation.[53] Gary Gill is most candid about how his identification as a blind person was transformed to identification with the disabled movement at the 504 takeover:

> For me [the takeover] was great. Up to that point, I was working somewhat in the blind community . . . but when I got in the building . . . slowly, you know how realizations climb up from the gut to the brain, slowly I had to realize that hey, there's some other stuff going on here. . . . I saw all these folks in chairs and I learned a little finger spelling and started working with deaf folks and it was just neat to see that as a group we could do stuff.[54]

Another way in which consciousness was changed was by labeling the disabled demands as a civil rights struggle. Although not originally seen as civil rights legislation, implementation of 504 was portrayed by the ACCD as a civil rights issue, and the leaflets disseminated by CIL for the San Francisco demonstration demanded "equal rights for the disabled."

After the Bay Area sit-in started, the disabled protesters repeatedly connected their struggle to other civil rights struggles. At one of their early meetings with the press the demonstrators focused on the tone of media coverage and expressed their concern that the event be covered as a civil rights issue to get them "to stop focusing on 'this is how so and so gets put to bed' " coverage, according to Heumann.[55] "This is the age of civil rights and liberation," one demonstrator declared. "We have had the black man's [sic] rights, gay rights, women's rights and now it is disabled rights."[56] Another demonstrator, referring to Rosa Parks and the black civil rights movement, said, "I don't want to move to the front of the bus, I just want to be able to get on it."[57] During the sit-in, supporting organizations like the Black Panthers and politicians like Congressman Phillip Burton also used the civil rights perspective in their endorsements. Some, like Assemblyman Willie Brown, even referred to the 1970s as the "era" for "the rights of the handicapped and the disabled."[58] The press quickly picked up the connection.[59]

The disabled used more than civil rights rhetoric. They used its *method*—the sit-in—and its *chant*—"We shall overcome."[60] Not surprisingly, the press was soon referring to disabled leaders as "the new militants,"[61] their demonstration as a "most poignant civil rights demonstration,"[62] and the 1973 Vocational Rehabilitation Act as their "first major Civil Rights Act."[63] Even Califano, when he finally signed the regulations, referred to them as opening "an era of civil rights in America,"[64] and President Carter one month later vowed that "we are committed to guaranteeing the civil rights of the disabled."[65]

Thus the civil rights perspective provided a philosophical basis for takeover. By linking the disabled with other civil rights movements it also helped legitimize their demands as well as normalizing and dignifying a stigmatized group. Most important, the civil rights perspective created a unifying theme that all the distinct and separate disabled people could rally around.

The third prerequisite for a change in consciousness was the development of feelings of efficacy. Piven and Cloward call efficacy the essential transformation of consciousness. It is required before people who are ordinarily fatalistic can assert their rights.[66] The idea of independent living was a key to the development of feelings of efficacy.

The idea of independence and self-help was romanticized by the press during the San Francisco sit-in. One journalist described day three, "Amid the chanting and singing there were touching scenes of wheelchair demonstrators who still had the use of their arms feeding those who were too disabled to help themselves,"[67] and the new philosophy connected with the est vision of Werner Erhard who said, when he visited the protesters, "It's moving and inspiring to see these people take charge of their own lives."[68]

When the disabled began to feel more self-sufficient, it enabled them to move from a recipient role to that of actor. This was clearly illustrated during the sit-in. As one paraplegic protester proclaimed, "I slept on the floor last night and I'll stay here until the bill is law. It's hard for people like us to do something like this. But we believe enough in our cause to put up with inconvenience."[69] Another boasted, "The movement was begun by the disabled and run by and for the disabled."[70] It was only in Berkeley where all three changes of consciousness—destigmatization, group identification, sense of self-efficacy—were occurring in a large-scale way.

Preexisting Social Networks

It was also only in Berkeley that social networks were well enough developed to make a strong, autonomous, community-based movement of disabled people possible. Many social scientists have described the importance to social movements of already existing social networks.[71] Among the disabled, the primary social networks were within their own disabilities. Gary Gill's candid description of his involvement in the sit-in illustrates the importance of, and his dependence on, his own social network: the blind community. For him, the patronizing local coverage of the sit-in got him to act and activate his network:

> That night I watched the news . . . it was the Channel 2 News . . . they were particularly not good this night . . . the guy comes on and says . . . these blind

so and so's, these crippled up so and so's, what are they trying to do, they already got welfare, I mean, are they asking for more charity, they already got rehabilitation. . . . Well, I had a quantum reaction to that, kinda' like a bad smallpox vaccination . . . so my wife and I started gathering blind folks because we're tied in, somewhat, to the blind network at that time, and a bunch of us went over.[72]

It was a spontaneous reaction, but it would have died in the bud without the already existing social network to activate.

In no other city was there such a large proportion of disabled residents visible and interfacing with each other and with other members of the community. In no other city did you have so many disabled people living, not isolated in their parents' homes or rest homes, but living in the community and connected to organizations for service as well as for social life.

The importance of Berkeley's networks is illustrated by contrasting it with other cities. A civil rights–oriented disabled group had formed in New York City in 1970 when Judy Heumann was denied the right to teach in public school. It had sponsored demonstrations in support of the passage of the Vocational Rehabilitation Act. Yet in 1977 disabled people were not mobilized. Heumann suggests it was because the activists of the early seventies had left and the organizations were only "political" organizations without a service component,[73] which, for a disabled person, makes the ties to the organization much stronger. The service component generated social connections. In 1977 the disabled in New York City were not sufficiently socially connected with one another or with the greater community to have a successful sit-in. Consciousness may have been there, but social networks were not.

In Los Angeles, two Independent Living Centers and a fairly large number of deaf people participated in the HEW sit-in. Yet there wasn't a large range of disabled organizations involved in the demonstration and sit-in, and although there was some local church support, there wasn't the range of community support the Berkeley disabled experienced. Food in Los Angeles was supplied by supportive friends, not by supportive organizations. For Doug Martin, who was then head of the Northside Independence Center, the most crucial difference between L.A. and the Bay Area was geography. The sheer size of L.A. prevented physical connections among L.A.'s disabled; Berkeley's small size and street use made such connections possible.[74]

There were social networks among the disabled in Denver, but they lacked a history of aggressive autonomous activity, and they lacked the ability, in 1977, to act independently of ACCD directives. The coalition of demonstrators was described by one of its members as "loose and informal." It was made up of people from the Cerebral Palsy Center, members of the Commission on the Disabled, the Governor's Council on the Disabled, Atlantis Community (a CIL-type group started in 1974), and others.

In Washington, the home of ACCD, there was nowhere near the same level of networking with the community that there was even in Denver. Although large numbers of the disabled participated in the District demonstration and sit-in, the demonstrators had not created the necessary bonds with community groups so that they could be nurtured by their community's food and supplies and bolstered by their community's encouragement, support, and political endorsements.

Elite Legitimation and Facilitation

Another factor that contributed to the disabled forming a social movement was elite legitimation and facilitation. The prime example of elite legitimation was the passage of the 1973 Vocational Rehabilitation Act itself. The inclusion of Title V and especially the development of the 504 section had a profound effect on the goals and aspirations of disabled people.

It was precisely what Piven and Cloward describe happened with the passage of section 7a of the 1933 National Industrial Recovery Act, which provided employees the right to organize and bargain collectively. This gave the workers "an elan, a righteousness that they had not had before."

> The impact on workers was electrifying. It was as if incipient struggles had now been crowned with an aura of what Rudé called "natural justice." Felt grievances became public grievances, for the federal government itself had declared the workers' cause to be just.[75]

Likewise, the federal government facilitated the movement when it declared the disabled cause to be a just one in 1973.

What was different for the disabled was that the passage of the 1973 law was a cause and not a consequence of a general disabled movement and struggle. As Heumann describes it:

> The '64 Civil Rights Act was the culmination of years and years of work. Striving towards the '64 Civil Rights Act was also an organizing tool, for the movement. Now, with the '73 act substantially the work, in my opinion, that was done on it was done by the key legislators themselves. There was . . . no street action, there was no national uniform letter-writing campaign . . . so it was put through so you kind of picked up ownership of it after it was through. . . . I think that has been detrimental . . . in as much as you've had

to give it to the disabled population and make them own it and accept pride in what it is and then fight for it.[76]

The real danger was that the government's generosity would work against a social movement, for paternalistic welfare feeds a welfare mentality and militates against a move from recipient to actor. As Turner suggests, "Individuals and groups who are totally dependent upon a dominant group are those least likely to challenge the propriety of their situation."[77] Thus, the government's paternalistic generosity might have *undermined* a social movement of the disabled had there been no four-year delay in the signing of the "regs." Instead, the government legitimized a goal and then ignored it, thus forcing the disabled to struggle, and the struggle created consciousness. (This is analogous to the effect the sex provision of Title VII had on the women's movement.)

The Bay Area was the only place in which elite legitimation happened on a grand scale. Public officials seemed to be tripping over one another in the rush to endorse the disabled cause. However, the government not only helped legitimize a social movement of the disabled,[78] it also facilitated its development. It provided numerous town meetings and conferences,[79] recruited supporters, developed leaders, facilitated corporate action, gave information, and provided funding. In fact, the federal government played the facilitator role even *before* the 1973 act was passed. The 1973 Washington vigil held in support of the bill was made up mainly of participants from a federally sponsored annual conference, the President's Committee on Employment of the Handicapped.

After the 504 regulations were signed in 1977, the federal government continued to facilitate the movement. First, the law gives the movement focus; as one participant candidly admits, "The direction of the movement is overseeing that laws are enforced."[80] Second, the federal government funds the movement. A nationwide 504 training program, designed to teach disabled people their rights under Section 504, has reached five thousand disabled people in the West and Midwest and eight thousand in the rest of the country.[81] In fact, the 504 training workshops have become a means of movement recruitment. As one 504 training participant describes it,

> One of the big things now is getting disabled folks to know they have these rights . . . all these 504 trainings all over the country . . . we teach them what their rights are, we also teach them how to organize and become radical. That's the hidden agenda. We teach them how to do coalition work which means to coalesce with other folks with other disabilities.[82]

Furthermore, in 1978, a year after the 504 regulations were signed by Secretary Califano, amendments to the 1973 Rehabilitation Act were passed.

They provided for the establishment of Independent Living Programs throughout the country, as well as for the strengthening of state protection and advocacy systems for disabled individuals.

The federal government legitimizes and facilitates the social movement of the disabled, but the government did not cause the movement. The movement blossomed in the Bay Area because of the aggressive support of local officials against a backdrop of independent living ideology that was vital for a change of consciousness and because an extensive communication network was strongly in place and ready to be activated. The federal government merely contributed to the development of a social movement but the contribution was important.

The Vocational Rehabilitation Act of 1973 legitimized a vision of social integration for the disabled. The government's delay in implementing the law stimulated the demonstrations and sit-in and helped integrate the disabled into the tradition of civil rights struggles. Standing out as a measure of that success is the fact that in Berkeley and the surrounding Bay Area, police paddy wagons are wheelchair accessible.

Notes

This chapter was written by Dr. Johnson in her private capacity. No official support or endorsement of the Office for Civil Rights or the Department of Education is intended or should be inferred. Judith Bell, a student at the University of California, Santa Cruz, provided research assistance for this chapter.

1. Steven V. Roberts, "Putting a Price Tag on Equality," *New York Times* (23 June 1978), 1.

2. J. Craig Jenkins and Charles Perrow, "The Insurgency of the Powerless: Farm Worker Movements (1946–1972)," *American Sociological Review* 42 (April 1977): 249.

3. Caspar W. Weinberger, "The Rehabilitation Veto: An Administrative View," *Washington Post* (4 April 1973), A19; confirmed by Reese Robrahn, executive director of American Coalition of Citizens with Disabilities, telephone interview, 10 March 1981.

4. Spencer Rich, "Senate Fails by Four Votes to Kill Veto," *Washington Post* (4 April 1973), A1.

5. Richard L. Lyons, "Hill Again Passes Pocket-Vetoed Bill," *Washington Post* (16 March 1973), A1. Italics added.

6. Rowland Evans and Robert Novak, "They've Given Up on Mr. Gray," *Washington Post* (25 March 1973), C7.

7. "Vigil Ends Protest by Handicapped," *Washington Post* (4 May 1973), C2.

8. Ralph Craib, "PUC Member Tells of Her Outrage: HEW Protesters Talk about It," *San Francisco Chronicle* (15 April 1977), 10.

9. According to the executive director of American Coalition of Citizens with Disabilities, Reese Robrahn, the civil rights issue was avoided by the bill's spon-

sors so as not to alienate the more conservative but supportive members of Congress.

10. For a list of the meetings, see "Twenty-two Meetings Set on Proposed Bias Ruling" *Washington Post* (16 July 1976), A10.

11. "Mathews Hesitates at Order for Rules to Aid Handicapped," *Washington Post* (19 January 1977), C12; according to Reese Robrahn, executive director of American Coalition of Citizens with Disabilities, colleges and universities spearheaded the opposition to implementation using the cost issue.

12. James D. Whitaker, "Carter Broke Promises Say Handicapped," *Washington Post* (8 January 1977), 43.

13. In their call for action, the Northern California Emergency Coalition wrote: "it is now more than one month since the Secretary's announcement and we have now been informed that the task force review will not be completed for another few weeks. Furthermore, it is now clear that many of the substantive provisions in the regulations that were developed after exhaustive negotiations by HEW with beneficiaries and recipients of federal funds alike, are being reconsidered for purposes of major revision. We are dismayed by this apparent breach of faith and feel the time may have come for us to begin to take action." Frank C. Bowe, executive director, ACCD, Center for Independent Living, Inc., letter announcing the 5 April noontime demonstration at San Francisco HEW, p. 3.

14. Joseph Whitaker, "Handicapped Gather at HEW to Agitate for Rights Enforcement," *Washington Post* (6 April 1977), B8.

15. Joyce Jackson, "History of ACCD," to Board of Directors, ACCD (unpublished paper), June 1981.

16. Frank G. Bowe, letter to President Carter from the American Coalition of Citizens with Disabilities, Inc.

17. The ten cities were Washington, D.C., Boston, Seattle, New York, Atlanta, Philadelphia, Chicago, Dallas, San Francisco, and Denver. Joseph Whitaker, "Handicapped Plan Protest at HEW Offices in Ten Cities," *Washington Post* (30 March 1977), A3.

18. Whitaker, "Handicapped Gather." Estimates of numbers vary. See also "SF Demonstration: HEW Protest by Handicapped," *San Francisco Chronicle* (7 April 1977), 9.

19. According to Reese Robrahn, present director of ACCD, based on the advice given to them by the NAACP and other groups, the demonstrators simply didn't anticipate that they would be denied food. Telephone interview, July 1981.

20. Michael Grieg, "Disabled Protestors Continue Sit-In at HEW Office Here," *San Francisco Chronicle* (7 April 1977), 9.

21. Interview with Janet Dorsey, Denver disabled activist and demonstrator, 26 March 1981.

22. Telephone interview with Doug Martin, former director of the Westside Center for Independent Living, 12 August 1980.

23. Quoted in the San Francisco 504-Coalition news release of 9 April 1977.

24. The following, from Bowe's letter to Jimmy Carter (n. 16), is a partial list of organizations and their representatives making up the 504 Emergency Coalition: Paralyzed Veterans of America; Gray Panthers; American Council of the Blind of

California; AID Retarded Citizens; Catholic Social Services Hearing Impaired Program; Silent Strength; Center for Independent Living; Lighthouse for the Blind; Community Arthritis Project; Diane Schechter of the Committee for Equal Access to Parks and Forests; United Cerebral Palsy; Margaret Emory of the Mental Health Consumer Concerns of Alameda County; Association of the Physically Handicapped, California; Senior Citizens Centers; Physically Disabled Students Program; Mark Randol, Secretary, Hemophilia Foundation of Northern California; Adult Independence Development Center; Jim Pechin, Coordinator, Disabled Paralegal Advocate Program; Swords to Plowshares Veterans Organization; Herbert Levine, Director, Employment Project for the Physically Handicapped; John King, Director, United Cerebral Palsy Foundation; Coalition of Veterans for Human Rights; Flower of the Dragon Veterans Rights Organization; Disabled People's Legal Resource Center; United Paraplegics of Berkeley.

25. Delancy Street was involved with CIL in the planning of the demonstration and sit-in because Delancy Street was a substance-abuse organization (alcohol, narcotics) and the 504 regulations included drug abusers and alcoholics in their list of disabilities. There were rumors that a revised version of the regulations might exclude these groups so it was in Delancy Street's interest to keep up the pressure on Califano against major revisions. Interview with Karen Parker, consultant, Center for Independent Living, Berkeley, and former San Francisco Aid for Retarded Citizens, 1 August 1980.

26. "Panthers Back Handicapped Demonstrators," *San Francisco Chronicle* (8 April 1977), 38.

27. Interview with Gary Gill, 504 consumer advocate trainer, Berkeley, California, 9 May 1980.

28. Interview with Judy Heumann, senior deputy director, Center for Independent Living, Berkeley, California, 1 August 1980.

29. "Panthers Back Handicapped"; "Handicapped Rights Plea," *San Francisco Chronicle* (9 April 1977), 38; A. Fumiko Nakao, "State Rehab Chief Joins the Protest," *San Francisco Chronicle* (10 April 1977), A7.

30. "Phillip Burton Backs HEW Protestors," *San Francisco Chronicle* (12 April 1977), 5.

31. Alex Abella, "Mayor Blasts HEW on Sit-in," *San Francisco Chronicle* (18 April 1977), 9.

32. "Handicapped Spurn Offer by HEW Chief," *San Francisco Chronicle* (19 April 1977), 7.

33. Interview with Karen Parker, consultant at Center for Independent Living, Berkeley, California, and former San Francisco Aid for Retarded Citizens, 1 August 1980.

34. "Handicapped Take Protest to Washington," *San Francisco Chronicle* (20 April 1977), 6.

35. Ibid.

36. Carol Pogaser, "The Disabled: Through with Silence and Shame," *San Francisco Chronicle* (24 April 1977), Al.

37. "Handicapped Take Protest"; Joseph Whitaker, "Handicapped Protest Turned Away at HEW," *Washington Post* (23 April 1977), B5.

38. Kitty Cone, quoted in "Handicapped Return from Washington," *San Francisco Chronicle* (28 April 1977), 3.

39. Joseph A. Califano Jr., *HEW NEWS* (28 April 1977).

40. "The Handicapped Will End Their Sit-in at Noon," *San Francisco Chronicle* (30 April 1977), 2.

41. Michael Lipsky, "Protest as a Political Resource," *American Political Science Review* (December 1968): 1145.

42. J. Craig Jenkins, "The Dynamics of Mobilization: The Transformation of a Constituency into a Movement." Paper presented at the annual meeting of Society for the Study of Social Problems, Chicago (4 September 1977), 5.

43. Judy Heumann, senior deputy director, Center for Independent Living, Berkeley, California, statement, *Hearings Before the Subcommittee on Select Education of the Committee on Education and Labor,* House of Representatives, 95th Cong., 2nd sess., April 1978, 78.

44. Georgie Anne Geyer, "Moving Back into Society," *Washington Post* (25 July 1977), A21.

45. Heumann, *Hearings,* 77.

46. Geyer, "Moving Back into Society."

47. Phil Draper, executive director, Center for Independent Living, Berkeley, California, statement in *Hearings,* 214; also see *New York Times* (17 April 1977) for a description of CIL.

48. Ron Jones, "The Acorn People," *Psychology Today* (June 1977), 70.

49. John Gliedman, "The Wheelchair Rebellion," *Psychology Today* (August 1979), 99.

50. Alice Walker, "Ten Years After the March on Washington: Staying Home in Mississippi," *New York Times Magazine* (26 August 1973), 9.

51. Interview with Joyce Jackson, counseling coordinator, Community Resources for Independent Living, Hayward, California, 30 May 1980.

52. Ibid.

53. The American Council of the Blind was one of the founding organizations of ACCD. Examples of disability-distinct legislation are the Randolph-Sheppard vending stands for the blind enacted in 1936 and the 1938 Wagner O'Day Act for federal government purchase of blind-made products. Also, see note 12 for the large number of organizations that represent particular kinds of disabilities as an illustration of the degree of separation between the disabilities.

54. Gill interview (n. 27). Italics added.

55. Heumann interview (n. 28).

56. Steven Handler Klein, quoted in Craib, "PUC Member Tells of Her Outrage."

57. Pogaser, "The Disabled: Through with Silence and Shame."

58. Assemblyman Willie Brown, "The Disabled in the 70s," *Phoenix* (12 May 1977), 6 (San Francisco State University).

59. *New York Times* (17 April 1977).

60. Pogaser, "The Disabled: Through with Silence and Shame."

61. Myra MacPherson, "Newly Militant Disabled Waging War on Discrimination," *Washington Post* (9 May 1977), A2.

62. Ralph Craib, "Emotional Plea for Handicapped. Hearing at Protest Site," *San Francisco Chronicle* (16 April 1977), 5.

63. Myra MacPherson and Joseph D. Whitaker, "Handicapped Rights Rule Is Signed," *Washington Post* (29 April 1977), Al.

64. Ibid.

65. "Carter's Promise to Disabled," *San Francisco Chronicle* (24 May 1977).

66. Frances Fox Piven and Richard A. Cloward, *Poor People's Movements* (New York: Vintage Books, 1979), 3–4.

67. Michael Grieg, "S. F. Handicapped Sit-In Grows," *San Francisco Chronicle* (8 April 1977), 6.

68. Nakao, "State Rehab Chief Joins the Protest."

69. Grieg, "Disabled Protestors Continue."

70. Pogaser, "The Disabled: Through with Silence and Shame."

71. Jo Freeman; see chapter 1 of this book.

72. Gill interview (n. 27).

73. Heumann interview (n. 28).

74. Martin interview (n. 22).

75. Piven and Cloward, *Poor People's Movements*, 113. 1 am grateful to Professor G. William Domhoff, University of California, Santa Cruz, for pointing out the similarity with the industrial workers example.

76. Heumann interview (n. 28).

77. Ralph H. Turner, "The Sense of Injustice in Social Movements," *Proceedings of the South Western Sociological Association,* Dallas, Texas (April 11–13, 1968), 124.

78. See Gary T. Marx, "External Efforts to Damage or Facilitate Social Movements: Some Patterns, Explanations, Outcomes, and Complications," in *The Dynamics of Social Movements,* ed. Mayer N. Zald and John D. McCarthy (Cambridge, Mass.: Winthrop, 1979), 96.

79. The following is a list of town meetings held in 1976. August 3: Newark and Albuquerque. August 5: Richmond and Denver. August 10: Pittsburgh and Syracuse. August 13: Manchester, N.H., and Raleigh, N.C. August 17: Portland, Ore., and Anchorage. August 24: Little Rock and Honolulu. August 26: Los Angeles, Phoenix, and Birmingham. August 31: Miami, Kansas City, and Salt Lake City. September 2: Detroit and San Antonio.

80. Jackson interview (n. 51).

81. Heumann interview (n. 28).

82. Interview with Linda Gill, consultant, Center for Independent Living, Berkeley, California, 9 May 1980.

3

Sacrifice for the Cause: Group Processes, Recruitment, and Commitment in a Student Social Movement

Eric L. Hirsch

Early analyses of protest movement mobilization emphasized the irrationality of movement participation and argued that marginal, insecure people join movements because of a need for social direction. This approach has lost popularity because many movement participants are socially integrated and quite rational. A popular current approach, rational choice theory, counters by suggesting that movement participation is the result of individual cost-benefit calculations. But even the most elaborate individual incentive models cannot fully account for the manner in which group political processes influence movement participants to sacrifice individual interests in favor of a collective cause.

This chapter develops an alternative perspective on recruitment and commitment to protest movements; it emphasizes the importance of the development of political solidarity, that is, support for a group cause and its tactics. Mobilization can then be explained by analyzing how group-based political processes, such as *consciousness-raising, collective empowerment, polarization,* and *group decision-making,* induce movement participants to sacrifice their personal welfare for the group cause. Empirical support for this perspective comes from a detailed analysis of a Columbia University student movement that demanded that the university divest itself of stock in companies doing business in South Africa. The following discussion builds on the work of movement theorists (Gamson 1975;

Schwartz 1976; Tilly 1978; Gamson, Fireman, and Rytina 1982; McAdam 1982, 1986, 1988; Ferree and Miller 1985; Hirsch 1986, 1989; Rosenthal and Schwartz 1989)[1] and conflict theorists (Simmel 1955; Coser 1956, 1967; Edelman 1971; Kriesberg 1973; Sherif, Harvey, White, Hood, and Sherif 1988).

Impact of Group Processes

Consciousness-Raising

Potential recruits are not likely to join a protest movement unless they develop an ideological commitment to the group cause and believe that only noninstitutional means can further that cause. Consciousness-raising involves a group discussion where such beliefs are created or reinforced. It may occur among members of an emerging movement who realize they face a problem of common concern that cannot be solved through routine political processes. Or it may happen in an ongoing movement, when movement activists try to convince potential recruits that their cause is just, that institutional means of influence have been unsuccessful, and that morally committed individuals must fight for the cause. Effective consciousness-raising is a difficult task because protest tactics usually challenge acknowledged authority relationships. Predisposing factors, such as prior political socialization, may make certain individuals susceptible to some appeals and unsympathetic to others.

Consciousness-raising is not likely to take place among socially marginal individuals because such isolation implies difficulty in communicating ideas to others. And it is not likely to happen among a group of rational calculators because the evaluation of society and of the chances for change is often influenced more by commitment to political or moral values than by self-interest calculations (Fireman and Gamson 1979, Ferree and Miller 1985). Consciousness-raising is facilitated in nonhierarchical, loosely structured, face-to-face settings that are isolated from persons in power; in such *havens* (Hirsch 1989), people can easily express concerns, become aware of common problems, and begin to question the legitimacy of institutions that deny them the means for resolving those problems (Gerlach and Hine 1970, Rosenthal and Schwartz 1989).

Collective Empowerment

The recruitment and commitment of participants in a protest movement may also be affected by a group process called collective empowerment. While recruits may gain a sense of the potential power of a movement in consciousness-raising sessions, the real test for the movement comes at the actual protest site where all involved see how many are willing to take the risks associated with challenging authority. If large numbers are willing to sacrifice themselves for the movement, the chances for success seem greater; a "bandwagon effect" (Hirsch 1986) convinces people to participate in this particular protest because of its presumed ability to accomplish the movement goal. Tactics are more easily viewed as powerful if they are highly visible and dramatic and disrupt normal institutional routines.

Polarization

A third important group process is polarization. Protest challenges authority in a way that institutional tactics do not because it automatically questions the rules of the decision-making game. The use of nonroutine methods of influence also means that there is always uncertainty about the target's response. For these reasons, one common result of a protest is unpredictable escalating conflict. Each side sees the battle in black and white terms, uses increasingly coercive tactics, and develops high levels of distrust and anger toward the opponent (Kriesberg 1973, 170–73).

Polarization is often seen as a problem since it convinces each side that their position is right and the opponent's is wrong; this make compromise and negotiation less likely (Coleman 1957). Since it leads each side to develop the independent goal of harming the opponent, movement participants may lose sight of their original goal. Finally, escalation of coercive tactics by those in power can result in demobilization of the movement as individual participants assess the potential negative consequences of continued participation.

But if other group processes, such as consciousness-raising and collective empowerment, have created sufficient group identification, the protesters will respond to threats as a powerful, angry group rather than as isolated, frightened individuals. Under these circumstances, polarization can have a strong positive impact on participation (Coser 1956, 1967; Edelman 1971). The sense of crisis that develops in such conflicts strengthens participants' belief that their fate is tied to that of the group. They develop a willingness to continue to participate despite the personal risks because they believe the costs of protest should be collectively shared. Greater consensus on group goals develops because the importance of social factors in perception increases in an ambiguous conflict (Sherif et al. 1988); protesters become more likely to accept the arguments of their loved fellow activists and less likely to accept those of their hated enemy. Because of the need to act quickly in a crisis, participants also become willing to submerge their differences with respect to the group's tactical choices (Coleman 1957).

Group Decision-Making

Finally, group decision-making often plays an important role in motivating the continuing commitment of movement participants. Movements often have group discussions about whether to initiate, continue, or end a given protest. Committed protesters may feel bound by group decisions made during such discussions, even when those decisions are contrary to their personal preferences (Rosenthal and Schwartz 1989). Participation in a protest movement is often the result of a complex group decision-making process, and not the consequence of many isolated, rational individual decisions.

The Columbia Divestment Campaign: A Case Study

The importance of these four group processes—consciousness-raising, collective empowerment, polarization, and group decision-making—in recruitment and commitment in a protest movement is illustrated by the Columbia University divestment protest. In April 1985, several hundred Columbia University and Barnard College students sat down in front of the chained doors of the main Columbia College classroom and administrative building, Hamilton Hall, and stated that they would not leave until the university divested itself of stock in companies doing business in South Africa. Many students remained on this "blockade" for three weeks. This is a particularly good case for the analysis of movement recruitment and commitment because the majority of the participants in the protest had not been active previously in the divestment or other campus protest movements.

Protest actions of this kind can create problems for researchers because the organizers' need for secrecy often prevents the researcher from knowing of the event in advance. The best solution is to use as many diverse research methods as possible to study the movement after it has begun. I spent many hours at the protest site each day observing the activities of the protesters and their opponent, the Columbia administration. I also discussed the demonstration with participants and nonparticipants at the protest site, in classrooms, and at other campus settings; and examined the many leaflets, position papers, and press reports on the demonstration.

During the summer of 1985, I completed nineteen extended interviews, averaging ninety minutes each, with blockaders and members of the steering committee of the Coalition for a Free South Africa (CFSA), the group that organized and led the protest. The interviews covered the protester's political background, previous experience in politics and protest movements, his or her experiences during the three weeks of the protest, and feelings about the personal consequences of participation. All quotes are taken from transcripts of these interviews.

I also analyzed responses to a survey distributed to the dormitory mailboxes of a random sample of 300 Barnard and Columbia resident undergraduates during the third week of the protest. The 28-question survey assessed attitudes toward those on both sides of the conflict, the extent of the respondent's participation in the protest and in campus politics and social organizations, the respondent's general political values, and demographic information.

Of the 300 surveys, 181, or 60.3 percent, were returned. Given the situation on campus at the time and the fact that the semester was drawing to a close, it was difficult to increase the return rate through followup letters and questionnaires. If those who returned the questionnaires differed in a significant way from those who did not, survey results would be biased. However, it wasn't only divestment activists who returned the survey; a wide variety of opinions was expressed by respondents. Nine-tenths of respondents had not been active in the divestment movement prior to the blockade, and only about half favored divestment or felt that the blockade was justified when they first heard about it. A copy of the questionnaire and a summary of the results are available from the author upon request.

Consciousness-Raising

The Coalition for a Free South Africa (CFSA) was founded in 1981 to promote Columbia University's divestment of stock in companies doing business in South Africa. It was a loosely structured group with a predominantly black steering committee of about a dozen individuals who made decisions by consensus, and a less active circle of about fifty students who attended meetings and the group's protests and educational events. The group was nonhierarchical and nonbureaucratic and had few resources other than its members' labor. The CFSA tried to convince Columbia and Barnard students that blacks faced injustice under apartheid, that U.S. corporations with investments in South Africa profited from the low wages paid to blacks, that Columbia was an accomplice in apartheid because it invested in the stock of these companies, and that divestment would advance the anti-apartheid movement by putting economic and political pressure on the white regime of South Africa.

This consciousness-raising was done in a variety of small group settings, including dormitory rap sessions, forums, and teach-ins. Coverage of the CFSA's activities in the Columbia student newspaper and television reports on the violent repression of the anti-apartheid movement in South Africa increased student consciousness of apartheid and encouraged many students to support divestment.

Even in this early period, conflict between the CFSA and the Columbia administration affected the views of potential movement recruits. At first, the CFSA tried to achieve divestment by using traditional avenues of influence. In 1983, the organization was able to gain a unanimous vote for divestment by administration, faculty, and student representatives in the University Senate, but Columbia's Board of Trustees rejected the resolution. As one protester pointed out, that action was interpreted by many students as an indication that traditional means of influence could not achieve divestment:

> I remember in '83 when the Senate voted to divest. I was convinced that students had voiced their opinion and had been able to convince the minority of administrators that what they wanted was a moral thing. It hadn't been a bunch of radical youths taking buildings and burning things down to destroy. But rather, going through the system, and it seemed to me that for the first time in a really long time the system was going to work. And then I found out that it hadn't worked, and that just reaffirmed my feelings about how the system at Columbia really did work.

The result of CFSA's extensive organizing work was that many students were aware of the oppressed state of blacks in South Africa, the call for divestment by anti-apartheid activists, and the intransigence of the university president and trustees in the face of a unanimous vote for divestment by the representative democratic body at the university.

Collective Empowerment: The Initiation of the Blockade

In the next phase of the movement, the CFSA sponsored rallies and vigils to call attention to the intransigence of the trustees. Few students attended these demonstrations, probably because few supporters believed they would result in divestment. Deciding that more militant tactics were necessary, the CFSA steering committee began to plan a fast by steering committee members and a takeover of a campus building. The plan called for chaining shut the doors of the building and blocking the entrance with protesters; this, it was assumed, would lead to a symbolic arrest of a few dozen steering committee members and other hard-core supporters of divestment. The intent was to draw media coverage to dramatize the continuing fight for divestment.

Because they had worked hard on publicity, the steering committee of CFSA expected a large turnout for their initial rally, but fewer than two hundred students gathered at the Sundial in the center of campus on the morning of April 4. Speeches were made by a local political official, a representative of the African National Congress, several black South African students, and members of the CFSA steering committee. Many of those interviewed had been at the rally, but none felt that the speeches were any more or less inspiring than speeches they had heard at previous CFSA events.

At the conclusion of the speeches, nearly all of those present agreed to follow one of the CFSA steering committee members on a march around campus. Most expected to chant a few anti-apartheid and pro-divestment slogans and return to the Sundial for a short wrap-up speech. Instead, they were led to the steps in front of the already-chained doors at Hamilton Hall. The protesters did not understand at first why they had been led to this spot, and few noticed the chained doors.

The steering committee member then revealed the day's plan, stating that this group of protesters would not leave the steps until the university divested itself of stock in companies doing business in South Africa. At least 150 students remained where they were; no one recalls a significant number of defections. Within two hours, the group on the steps grew to over 250.

Why did so many students agree to participate in this militant protest? The CFSA steering committee did not have an answer. Student participation in their relatively safe rallies and vigils had been minimal, so they certainly did not expect hundreds to join a much riskier act of civil disobedience. According to one steering committee member:

> Needless to say, I was quite startled by the events of April 4. By noon, there must have been hundreds more people than I expected there would be. I was hoping for 50 people, including the hard core. We would all get carted off, and whatever obstacles were blockading the door would be cut, removed, or thrown up. That's what everyone was expecting. We would have a story written and the press would report that we had done this. Jesus Christ, what happened that day was absolutely mind boggling! I still haven't gotten over it.

It was hard for anyone to predict the high level of mobilization based on the prior actions and attitudes of the participants because so few had been active in the divestment movement prior to April 4. Only 9 percent of the random sample of students reported that they had been at least somewhat active in the divestment movement, yet 37 percent participated in blockade rallies and/or slept overnight on the steps of Hamilton Hall. In fact, these students did not know that they would join this militant protest until it was actually initiated.

It is unlikely that the decision to participate was due to a narrow individual cost-benefit analysis including such costs as the time involved and the definite possibilities of arrest and/or disciplinary action by the university. Regarding personal benefits, it is hard to see how any Columbia student could gain from the divestment of South Africa-related stock.

Rather, participation was due to a belief in the cause and the conviction that this protest might work where previous CFSA actions had failed. Consciousness-raising had convinced these students of the importance of divestment, but they had not participated in the movement because they did not believe its tactics would work. Once several hundred were in front of the doors, many demonstrators felt that such a large group using a dramatic tactic would have the power to call attention to the evils of apartheid and cause the university to seriously consider divestment:

> Often when I would see a rally, I'd think that here was a bunch of people huffing and puffing about an issue who are going to be ignored and things are going to go on just as they were before this rally. The fact that there were a couple of hundred people out there with the purpose of altering the way the University does business gave me the feeling that this would be noticed, that people would pay attention.

The belief in the potential power of the tactic was reinforced by the willingness of several leaders of the movement to sacrifice their individual interests to achieve divestment. Two black South African students who spoke at the rally faced the possibility of exile or arrest and imprisonment upon their return home. About half a dozen CFSA steering committee members had fasted for nearly two weeks simply to get a meeting with the university president and trustees; two of these students were eventually hospitalized. As one blockader testified:

> The fasters were doing something that personally took a lot of willpower for them, and that gave you a little extra willpower. To have to go into the hospital because you were off food for fifteen days and the Trustees won't even speak to you. It really made me angry at the Trustees, so I was determined that this was not something that was just going to whimper off. At least I was going to be there, and I know others felt the same way.

The leaders of the protest recruited participants by taking personal risks that demonstrated their own commitment to the cause and to this particular tactic; other students in the blockade ignored individual interests in favor of the cause as well.

> I do think it has something to do with the support of peers, just seeing that there were people who were willing to extend themselves and put their own

asses on the line. I guess it's the self-sacrifice aspect of it that appealed to me, that really drew my attention. These people were willing to sacrifice their own personal interests in a big way, or a larger way than usual. That's something that hit a chord with me. It was the degree to which people were willing to give up self-interest.

Another factor influencing participation may have been the fact that the protesters were not forced to decide to join the protest at all. Instead, they were led as a group to a position in front of the doors, unaware that this was an act of civil disobedience; the only decision to be made was whether or not to leave the protest. Although this was done because CFSA did not want to reveal its plans to campus security prematurely, the unintended consequence was to maximize participation; it was difficult for demonstrators to leave the steps because of the public example of self-sacrificing black South Africans and the fasters.

Of course, each protester had many less public opportunities to leave the protest during the three weeks after April 4. Most stayed, partly because of growing evidence of the power of this tactic. The protest soon gained the public support of a variety of groups locally and nationally, including Harlem community groups and churches, the Columbia faculty, unions on and off the campus, the African National Congress, and the United Nations. Students on other campuses engaged in similar protests. This support made the blockaders believe that their challenge to the authority of the Columbia administration was moral, necessary, and powerful. One blockader described this as being "part of something that was much larger than myself." Another suggested:

> One thing I believe now is that people in a grass-roots movement can actually have an impact, that we're not all completely helpless. I guess it was that sense of power that I didn't have before.

Polarization and Increased Commitment

Because the blockade was an unconventional attempt to gain political influence, the steering committee of CFSA was unable to predict how many would participate. For the same reason, they were unable to predict their opponent's reaction to their tactic. Based on the information they had on recent South African consulate and embassy protests, they assumed they would be arrested soon after the doors of Hamilton Hall were chained. As these expectations of a mostly symbolic arrest were communicated to the less politically experienced blockaders, a consensus developed that the blockade would be short-lived.

However, the administration did not order the arrest of the protesters. Instead, Columbia's president sent a letter to everyone at the university arguing that the students were "disruptive" and "coercive," and that they were trying to impose their will on the rest of the university. He suggested that "countless avenues of free speech" in the university community were open to them and that what they were doing was illegal, that divestment would probably hurt rather than help blacks in South Africa, and that the university was doing all it could to fight apartheid.

University officials began to videotape the protesters in order to prosecute them under university regulations on obstructing university buildings and disrupting university functions. They sent letters threatening suspension or expulsion to the members of the CFSA steering committee and a few others. Guarantees were given that those who reported for individual disciplinary hearings would be treated more leniently than those who did not. They also obtained a court order calling on participants in the blockade to cease and desist.

By threatening suspensions and expulsions, the administration had raised the stakes; the protesters felt much more threatened by these academic penalties than by symbolic arrests. There were other costs associated with participating in this protest, including dealing with the cold and freezing rain, missing classes, exams, and study time, and losing close relationships with nonblockaders. Ignoring these costs, the steering committee members who received letters refused to go to the disciplinary hearings, suggested that the administration was engaging in unfair selective prosecution, and reiterated their determination to remain in front of Hamilton Hall until the university divested.

Such actions were to be expected from the strongly committed CFSA steering committee. The surprise was that the less experienced majority of protesters also refused to be intimidated and remained on the blockade. They did so in part because of an example of self-sacrifice by one of their own. One of the politically inexperienced students, a senior with three weeks to go before graduation, received a letter threatening him with expulsion. Initially, he was scared:

> I was petrified, especially since Columbia has not been fun for me but rather painful. I really wanted to get out of here, and I was horrified by the thought that I would either have to come back to Columbia or go somewhere else and lose credits by transferring. My reaction was, "Why do they have to pick me? Why do I have to be the focal point of this whole thing?"

But he decided not to report for disciplinary action. He felt that he could not give in to his fears in the face of the sacrifices being made by the fasters and South African students.

> Listening to the commitment on the part of the steering committee people who had received letters made me feel bad that I even considered leaving

the blockade. One other factor was the fasters, the fact that there were South Africans involved in it, and that these people had more on the line than I did. I felt like I could not let these people down. I also felt that I was a sort of representative of a lot of people on the blockade and I felt I could not set a precedent by leaving and backing down.

His example was extremely important for the maintenance of commitment by the other inexperienced blockaders:

> They threatened (the blockader) with expulsion. It was sobering in a way. But it helped bond us together. It was stupid to do that because it just made people more furious, and it made people more resolved to stay. We just said we're not going to let him be expelled. We're all going to stick together in this.

The protesters responded to administration threats as a group, not as isolated individuals. Individual concerns about disciplinary actions were now secondary; each blockader saw her or his welfare as tied to the group fate. Paradoxically, the potential for high personal costs became a reason for participation; protesters wanted to be part of an important and powerful movement and they did not want fellow activists to face the wrath of the authorities alone. The night the threat of arrest was assumed to be greatest, Easter Sunday, was also the one night out of twenty-one with the greatest number sleeping out on the blockade. Soon after this, five hundred students signed a statement accepting personal responsibility for the blockade.

Collective Decision-Making and the End of the Blockade

Another group process that influenced participation in this protest was collective decision-making. Open-ended rap sessions among the blockaders, lasting up to four or five hours, were begun after administration representatives delivered the first disciplinary letters to the protesters. In all cases, a serious attempt was made to reach consensus among all those on the steps; votes were held on only a few occasions. One of the main questions was whether to continue the protest. This discussion was initiated by members of the CFSA steering committee because of their commitment to democratic decision-making, and because they understood that the blockaders would be more likely to continue the protest if they participated in a collective decision to do so. During the first two weeks of the protest, the consensus was to continue the blockade.

By the third week, though, some of the protesters began to feel that the protest should be ended. The sense of crisis had been dulled by the lack of action by the administration to back up their threats. It was now clear that there were no plans to call in the police to make arrests. As one block-ader put it, the "university's policy of waiting it out was becoming effec-tive." Also, an event can be news for only so long, and the image of Co-lumbia students sitting on the steps became commonplace. Diminishing television and print coverage reduced the collective belief in the power of this particular tactic. As one protester suggested:

> It was during the third week that I started spending nights at home and com-ing up in the morning. During the last week I probably spent three nights out [on the steps] and four nights at home. During that third week a kind of mood of lethargy hit, and it became a chorelike atmosphere. There was a lot of feeling that it was kind of futile to stay out there.

In the face of declining participation, long and heated discussions were held about ending the protest. Proponents of continuing the action ar-gued that protesters ought to honor their commitment to stay in front of the doors until Columbia divested. Those who advocated ending the pro-test argued that divestment was not imminent and that the blockade was no longer effective. As one protester put it:

> The blockade ended because a very thoughtful and carefully planned deci-sion was made. It was a question of what we could do that would be most effective for divestment. We decided that the blockade had done a lot, but at this point other things would be better, seeing how the administration was willing to sit us out.

On April 25, the blockade officially ended with a march into Harlem to a rally at a Baptist church. Five months later, the Columbia trustees divested.

Survey Results

Participant observation of the protest as well as extended interviews with the protesters revealed that certain group processes—consciousness-rais-ing, collective empowerment, polarization, and group decision-making—influenced recruitment to and motivated continuing participation in the blockade. Findings from the survey support this conclusion.[2]

One question on the survey asked the respondent to report on his or her level of involvement in the protest. Responses indicated that 18 percent completely avoided the demonstration, 44 percent stopped by out of curi-osity, 20 percent participated in the rallies supporting the blockade or fre-quently joined the demonstration during the daytime, and 17 percent spent at least one night sleeping on the steps.

Table 3.1 shows a multiple regression analysis with responses to the participation question as the dependent variable and a variety of possible correlates of participation as independent variables. The resulting equation explains 59 percent of the variance in participation. The single most important predictor is being politically liberal or radical, indicating that general ideological predisposition, not just commitment to the specific cause, has an important impact on protest participation. This is consistent with the findings of Walsh and Warland (1983) and Mueller and Opp (1986).

Another important factor associated with participation is the interaction effect between support for Columbia's divestment of all stock in companies doing business in South Africa and a belief that Columbia would divest as a result of the blockade.[3] This result indicates the importance of both consciousness-raising and collective empowerment processes in recruitment and commitment to protest; it shows that those who support the specific cause and believe in the power of the tactic to further that cause are likely to participate in a protest.

That participation is associated with a belief in the power of the collective tactic to further movement goals is given further support by the fact that those who felt that divestment would influence the policies of the South African government were more likely to join the movement. Finally, the equation shows an independent association of a declining opinion of the university president with participation, supporting the notion that a polarization process had an important effect on participation in the blockade.

TABLE 3.1
Regression between Level of Participation in the Blockade and Selected Independent Variables: Columbia University, 1985

Independent Variables	b	Beta
Conservative-liberal scale	.25	.32**
Support for divestment X effectiveness of blockade	.09	.24**
Personal expense caused by blockade justified?	.10	.15*
Opinion of university president declined	.18	.13*
Divestment will influence South African government?	.17	.14*
Extent of prior participation in divestment movement	.32	.09
Membership in campus political action organization	.09	.04
Number of campus organization memberships	−.01	−.01
First-year student	.05	.02
No religious affiliation	−.08	−.03
Constant	−.17	—

*$p<.05$ **$p<.01$
Note: $R^2 = .59$; N = 176.

A variety of other factors were entered in the equation to assess the propositions of rational choice and collective behavior theories. Those who felt that any personal expense or inconvenience suffered as a result of the blockade was justified were more likely to participate in the protest. In other words, participants were committed to the group cause and felt that personal costs suffered as a result of participation were justified. Other factors emphasized by resource mobilization theories of participation, such as prior participation in the divestment movement or in a political action group on campus, were not highly associated with joining the blockade. Propositions about the association between social marginality or a lack of values and recruitment to movements are not supported; being a first-year student, lacking a religious affiliation, and being a member of a small number of campus groups were not highly correlated with participation in the blockade.

Conclusion

Rational choice theories cannot explain why students joined and became committed to this protest action because group processes are not just the sum of individual preferences or predispositions. Such frameworks cannot easily account for why participants felt willing to accept the personal costs associated with this protest; it is contradictory to argue that students stayed on the blockade to enjoy the selective incentive of self-sacrifice. Recruitment and commitment to the blockade can only be understood through the analysis of how group discussions, empowerment, conflict, and decision-making led participants to a willingness to sacrifice self-interest in pursuit of a valued collective goal using a noninstitutional tactic.

Collective behavior theory is right about the importance of group-level processes in the mobilization of noninstitutional movements. But its proposition that protest originates in disorganized unrest certainly does not apply here. Years of well-organized activities by the CFSA were crucial in raising consciousness about the apartheid issue and on the need for noninstitutional means of influence to achieve divestment. The blockade itself was initiated only after two months of careful planning by the CFSA steering committee.

The blockaders were not just isolated individuals with preferences for divestment nor a set of confused, insecure people; rather, they were people who had been convinced by CFSA meetings that apartheid was evil, that divestment would help South African blacks, and that divestment could be achieved through protest. They joined the blockade on April 4 because it appeared to offer a powerful alternative to previously impotent demonstrations and because of the example of self-sacrificing CFSA leaders. The solidarity of the group increased after the administration's escalation of the conflict because group identification among the protesters was already strong enough so that they responded to the threat as a powerful group rather than as powerless individuals. Protesters remained at this long and risky protest partly because of the democratic decision-making processes used by the group.

This analysis of the 1985 Columbia University divestment protest indicates that useful theories of movement mobilization must include insights about how individual protesters are convinced by group-level processes to sacrifice themselves for the cause. This means asking new kinds of questions in movement research: What kinds of arguments in what kinds of settings convince people to support a political cause? Why did potential recruits decide that noninstitutional means of influence are justified and necessary? Under what circumstances is the example of leaders sacrificing for the cause likely to induce people to join a risky protest? Why do some tactics appear to offer a greater chance of success than others? Under what conditions do threats or actual repression by authorities create greater internal solidarity in a protest group? Under what conditions do threats or repression result in the demobilization of protest? What kinds of group decision-making processes are likely to convince people to continue to participate in a protest movement?

Generalizing from case studies is always difficult. Some aspects of student movements make them unusual, especially the ability of organizers to take advantage of the physical concentration of students on campuses. But the important impact of group processes on movement recruitment and commitment is not unique to the 1985 Columbia anti-apartheid movement. The development of solidarity based on a sense of collective power and polarization was also found in a Chicago community organization (Hirsch 1986). And these same group processes were crucial in the mobilization and development of the southern civil rights movement of the 1950s and 1960s. Consciousness-raising occurred in black churches and colleges. The collective power of protest was evident to those who participated in bus boycotts, sit-ins, freedom rides, and Freedom Summer. The movement relied heavily on the creation of polarized conflict between the white southern segregationist elite and black protesters to recruit participants to gain national media attention, and ultimately to force federal intervention to redress the social and political grievances of southern blacks (McAdam 1982, Morris 1984). Finally, two of the major mobilizations in the 1960s student movement—the Berkeley free speech movement in 1964 and the Columbia conflict in 1968—developed in a manner similar to the 1985 divestment movement (Heirich 1970, Avorn 1968).

Notes

I would like to thank Peter Oxman, Henry Glasheen, Lisa Ryan, Beth Roberts, and Allen Barton for working on the formulation and distribution of the random sample survey. Allen Barton, Mark Mizruchi, Michael Schwartz, and two anonymous reviewers read the manuscript and made useful suggestions for revision. I am grateful for research funds provided by the Council for Research in the Social Sciences of Columbia University. Finally, my special thanks to those participants in the blockade who agreed to be interviewed for this research.

1. I have elsewhere (1989) labeled this theoretical tradition "solidarity theory." Perrow (1979) calls those who emphasize the development of movement solidarity "resource mobilization I" theorists, but this term is better reserved for theories that emphasize the similarities between institutional and noninstitutional politics and are sympathetic to rational choice perspectives. Others working in this tradition have described it as "political process theory" (McAdam 1982), but until recently (McAdam 1986, 1988) this theory has generally emphasized macro-movement processes and ignored micromobilization. The best approach to further theoretical development in the field of social movements is to elaborate the connections between a macro-political process theory and a theory of micromobilization like the one described here.

2. A single cross-sectional survey cannot assess the importance of group processes. If one finds a political attitude to be highly correlated with participation in the blockade, how does one know whether the attitude caused participation or participation cause the attitude? This demonstrates the need for the qualitative methods of participant observation and extended interviews. Analysts should do baseline surveys to assess attitudes before a movement begins, as some analysts have done (Klandermans 1984; Klandermans and Oegema 1987; McAdam 1986, 1988). But as Walsh and Warland (1983) have pointed out, it is often difficult to predict the need for such baseline surveys before the outbreak of protest.

3. Klandermans's work (1984) inspired the use of an interaction term. Running the equation with the "support for divestment" question substituted for the interaction term results in an equation that explains 57 percent of the variance in participation. A similar result is obtained if only the question about whether Columbia would divest as a result of the blockade is included. If both questions are included and the interaction term omitted, the percentage of variance explained is 58 percent. In other words, the percent of variance explained is higher in the equation with only the interaction effect than with the main effects entered separately or together.

References

Avorn, Jerry. 1968. *Up Against the Wall: A History of the Columbia Crisis*. New York: Columbia Spectator Board of Associates.
Coleman, James. 1957. *Community Conflict*. New York: Free Press.
Coser, Lewis. 1956. *The Functions of Social Conflict*. New York: Free Press.

———. 1967. *Continuities in the Study of Social Conflict.* New York: Free Press.

Edelman, Murray. 1971. *Politics and Symbolic Action.* New York: Academic.

Ferree, Myra Marx, and Frederick D. Miller. 1985. "Mobilization and Meaning: Toward an Integration of Social Psychological and Resource Perspectives on Social Movements." *Sociological Inquiry* 55, no. 1 (winter): 38–61.

Fireman, Bruce, and William Gamson. 1979. "Utilitarian Logic in the Resource Mobilization Perspective." In *The Dynamics of Social Movements,* ed. Mayer N. Zald and John D. McCarthy. Cambridge, Mass.: Winthrop, 8–44.

Gamson, William. 1975. *The Strategy of Social Protest.* Homewood, Ill.: Dorsey Press.

Gamson, William, Bruce Fireman, and Steven Rytina. 1982. *Encounters with Unjust Authority.* Homewood, Ill.: Dorsey Press.

Gerlach, Luther P., and Virginia H. Hine. 1970. *People, Power, Change: Movements of Social Transformation.* Indianapolis: Bobbs-Merrill.

Heirich, Max. 1970. *The Spiral of Conflict: Berkeley, 1964.* New York: Columbia University Press.

Hirsch, Eric L. 1986. "The Creation of Political Solidarity in Social Movement Organizations." *Sociological Quarterly* 27: 373–87.

———. 1989. *Urban Revolt: Ethnic Politics in the Nineteenth Century Chicago Labor Movement.* Berkeley: University of California Press.

Klandermans, Bert. 1984. "Mobilization and Participation: Social-Psychological Expansions of Resource Mobilization Theory." *American Sociological Review* 49, no. 5 (October): 583–600.

Klandermans, Bert, and Dirk Oegema. 1987. "Potentials, Networks, Motivation, and Barriers: Steps Towards Participation in Social Movements." *American Sociological Review* 52, no. 4 (August): 519–31.

Kriesberg, Louis. 1973. *The Sociology of Social Conflicts.* Englewood Cliffs, N.J.: Prentice-Hall.

McAdam, Douglas. 1982. *Political Process and the Development of Black Insurgency.* Chicago: University of Chicago Press.

———. 1986. "Recruitment to High Risk Activism: The Case of Freedom Summer." *American Journal of Sociology* 92, no. 1 (July): 64–90.

———. 1988. "Micromobilization Contexts and Recruitment to Activism." *International Social Movement Research* 1: 125–54.

Morris, Aldon. 1984. *The Origins of the Civil Rights Movement.* New York: Free Press.

Mueller, Edward N., and Karl-Dieter Opp. 1986. "Rational Choice and Rebellious Collective Action." *American Political Science Review* 80, no. 2 (June): 471–87; Discussion (1987) 81, no. 2 (June): 557–64

Perrow, Charles. 1979. "The Sixties Observed." In *The Dynamics of Social Movements,* ed. Mayer N. Zald and John D. McCarthy. Cambridge, Mass.: Winthrop, 192–211.

Rosenthal, Naomi, and Michael Schwartz. 1989. "Spontaneity and Democracy in Social Protest." In *Organizing for Change: Social Movement Organizations in Europe and the United States,* ed. Bert Klandermans. Greenwich, Conn.: JAI Press, 33–59.

Schwartz, Michael. 1976. *Radical Protest and Social Structure: The Southern Farmers' Alliance and Cotton Tenancy, 1880–1890*. Chicago: University of Chicago.

Sherif, Muzafer, O. J. Harvey, B. Jack White, William R. Hood, and Carolyn W. Sherif. 1988. *The Robbers Cave Experiment: Intergroup Conflict and Cooperation*. Middletown, Conn.: Wesleyan University Press.

Simmel, Georg. 1955. *Conflict and the Web of Group Affiliations*. New York: Free Press.

Tilly, Charles. 1978. *From Mobilization to Revolution*. Reading, Mass.: Addison-Wesley.

Walsh, Edward J., and Rex H. Warland. 1983. "Social Movement Involvement in the Wake of a Nuclear Accident: Activists and Free Riders in the TMI Area." *American Sociological Review* 48, no. 4 (August): 764–80.

4

Recruiting Intimates, Recruiting Strangers: Building the Contemporary Animal Rights Movement

James M. Jasper

The animal rights movement in the United States was one of the fastest growing social movements of the 1980s, moving from obscurity at the beginning of the decade to the covers of most major news magazines by the end. The issue of fur coats, for example, was raised on television shows such as *Designing Women*, *L.A. Law*, even *Saturday Night Live*. From the comic strip *Doonesbury* to *U.S. News and World Report*, the movement was on people's minds. In the early 1980s hundreds of diverse new groups were founded, and later in the decade hundreds of thousands of people enrolled in them. The movement's visibility peaked in June 1990, when almost 30,000 activists came to Washington, D.C., for a "March for the Animals." After that, public protest subsided, to be replaced by lobbying and other interest group tactics.

The rapid growth of this movement offers a chance to examine one of the central questions of social movement theory: how members are recruited to an emerging movement. Once the movement has started, how are others persuaded to join it? And who joins, out of all those who hear about an issue? The relative importance of social networks, on the one hand, and ideas and meanings, on the other, is at the heart of debates over recruitment. I believe that the relative importance of these two factors varies across settings and movements. In particular, there seem to be two basic mechanisms for recruitment. One is through affective networks of friends and acquaintances. The other is through cultural messages transmitted by means of more anonymous media, which are necessary for recruiting strangers. Some social movements rely more on recruiting intimates, others on strangers.[1] Groups within a single movement may favor one pattern or the other, and a movement may move from one to the other over time.

The recruitment of strangers relies on the power of a movement's symbols to stimulate moral outrage. In some cases, moral shocks, purveyed by protest organizers, can reach unknown potential recruits as effectively as personal contact can mobilize friends and acquaintances. Moral meanings play a role in the recruitment of intimates, to be sure, but in the recruitment of strangers they are the central mechanism at work.

Theories of Recruitment

Theories of movement recruitment have evolved through three successive stages. The first asked what kinds of people join social movements; the emphasis was on the characteristics of individual participants. The second stage rejected individual-level explanations to focus on preexisting social networks and organizations. More recently the pendulum has swung back, toward a synthesis of individual and structural characteristics, with attention focused on the ideas and emotions transmitted through social networks. Let's examine each stage in turn.

Before the 1970s, social movement research was dominated by a "collective behavior" school primarily based on an image of protesters as swept up in crowds, acting in abnormal and sometimes irrational ways because of frustration with their individual circumstances. Some theories held that marginal and alienated members of society were most likely to join social movements (Kornhauser 1959); others pointed to those who were insecure or dogmatic (Adorno et al. 1950, Hoffer 1951). In "relative deprivation" theories, people joined movements in order to relieve the tension they felt from the gap between their current situation and what they thought their situation should be (Davies 1962, Gurr 1970). Such claims were usually demeaning to protesters, who were thought to be compensating for some sort of personal inadequacy, and subsequent empirical research did not support the image of protesters as more angry or alienated than others.

Problems like these helped inspire the "resource mobilization" paradigm that emerged in the early 1970s, shifting attention from what kinds of people protested to what kinds of structural conditions facilitated protest. Attitudes were dismissed as insufficient at best, for many people had the right attitudes but did not participate. As part of this new agenda, "biographical availability" was seen as necessary for participation: structural traits such as the lack of job, spouse, or children freed an individual for the time commitments of protest (McCarthy and Zald 1973, McAdam 1986). More importantly, a large number of researchers found that the best predictor of who will join is whether a person knows someone else already in the movement (Bolton 1972, Orum 1972, Snow 1976, Heirich 1977, Snow, Zurcher, and Ekland-Olson 1980). In many movements, a majority of participants are recruited this way (Snow et al. 1980). In other words, "co-optable communications networks" are the key structural condition for successful recruitment (Freeman 1973, 1983, this volume). In the extreme case of "bloc recruitment," organizers bring a social network almost intact into a movement (Oberschall 1973).

Different kinds of social networks can be used by social movements. Not all are political in origin or intent. Black churches were crucial for the emergence of the southern civil rights movement in the 1950s (Morris 1984); fundamentalist churches helped defeat the Equal Rights Amendment (Mansbridge 1986); and mosques facilitated the Iranian revolution (Snow and Marshall 1984). Networks developed for earlier political activities can also aid recruitment into a new movement—one reason that a history of previous activism makes someone more likely to be recruited (McAdam 1988). The clustering of movements in "protest cycles" makes this mutual support especially important, as one movement feeds into the next (Tarrow 1994). Because of these networks, prior activism and organizational memberships are important predictors of recruitment.

Some researchers, criticizing the network model as overly mechanical, have recently examined the messages transmitted across these networks. "For all the recent emphasis on macro-political or other structural 'determinants' of social movements, the immediate impetus to collective action remains a cognitive one" (McAdam, McCarthy, and Zald 1988, 713). Walsh (1981) described "suddenly imposed grievances": dramatic and unexpected events that highlight some social problem; in his case the Three Mile Island accident in 1979 alerted people to the risks of nuclear energy, giving a big boost to the antinuclear movement. Recruitment involves a cognitive shift for participants.

In this view, direct personal contacts are seen as important because they allow organizers and potential participants to "align" their "frames," to achieve a common definition of a social problem and a common prescription for solving it (Snow et al. 1986). In successful recruitment, organizers offer ways of seeing a social problem that resonate with the views and experiences of potential recruits. Snow and Benford (1992, 137) define a frame as "an interpretive schemata that simplifies and condenses the 'world out there' by selectively punctuating and encoding objects, situations, events, experiences, and sequences of actions within one's present or past environment." Networks are important because of the cultural meanings they transmit. Indeed, earlier work on the importance of networks (Snow et al. 1980) did not examine the effects of cognitive processes, much less argue that networks were more important than meanings as causal factors (Snow, Zurcher, and Ekland-Olson 1983). Networks and meanings are not rival explanations; they work together.

Snow and Benford (1988) distinguish three successive types of framing necessary for successful recruitment: *diagnostic,* in which a movement convinces potential converts that a problem needs to be addressed; *prognostic,* in which it convinces them of appropriate strategies, tactics, and targets; and *motivational,* in which it exhorts them to get involved in these activities. They argue that frames are more likely to be accepted if they fit well with the existing beliefs of potential recruits, if they involve empirically credible claims, if they are compatible with the life experiences of the audience, and if they fit with the narratives the audiences tell about their lives. Frames, in other words, must resonate with the salient beliefs of potential recruits.

But recruitment involves more than changes in cognitive beliefs about how the world works. Its moral and emotional dimensions are equally important. All the key concepts used to explain recruitment depend heavily on their emotional dynamics, even when they are theorized as purely cognitive (Jasper 1998). I have used the term "moral shock" to incorporate these other dimensions: moral shocks result from information or events that raise such a sense of outrage in people that they become inclined toward political action, with or without a network of contacts (Jasper and Poulsen 1995, Jasper 1997). These are usually public events, unexpected and highly publicized, like Walsh's "suddenly imposed grievances," but they can also be the experiences of individuals, such as the gradual discovery that one's drinking water has been contaminated by a local factory or waste site (Krauss 1989). Those who have been shocked often search out protest groups even if they have no friends or family who already belong to them, with moral shocks serving as the functional equivalent of social networks. Moral shocks do not arise only from suddenly imposed grievances. Organizers try hard to generate them through their rhetorical appeals. Finally, a moral shock involves far more than changing one's mind: it taps into moral sensibilities and involves powerful emotions.

The new synthesis pays more attention to what goes on inside people's heads (and hearts). Protest is no longer seen as a compensation for some lack, but part of an effort to impose cognitive meaning on the world, to forge personal and collective identities, to define and pursue collective interests, and to create or reinforce affective bonds with others. These are things that all humans desire and pursue. The underlying assumption, taken from resource mobilization, of a psychologically healthy protester, has in turn allowed researchers to study deviations from this norm, such as religious cults that coerce and manipulate potential recruits (Kilbourne and Richardson 1988). There is today considerable consensus that structural position in networks of transformations and cultural orientations (including cognitive, moral, and emotional) are equally important in recruitment. But there are also cases in which cultural messages can be used to recruit people in the absence of social networks, relying on moral shocks instead of personal contacts. This is what happened in the animal rights movement.

The History of Animal Protection

Although many individuals in early modern Europe had worried about cruelty to animals, the first organized movement to help nonhuman species began in England in the early nineteenth century. From 1800 to 1822, when an act finally passed, parliamentary bills were introduced to ban bull baiting, a common amusement in which a pack of dogs would attack bulls (or bears) with considerable bloody damage to both sides. Two years later an organization called the Society for the Prevention of Cruelty to Animals (SPCA) was formed, adding Royal to its name when Queen Victoria adopted the cause in 1840. The RSPCA was a favorite charity of the upper classes, who saw it as a way to civilize the working classes who abused cart and carriage horses in congested city streets. In the late 1860s similar organizations began to appear in all the major American cities outside the South, and states began to pass protective legislation. These groups addressed the suffering of animals in a wide range of practices: the abuse or starvation of pets by cruel owners, the use of carriage horses in extreme heat, the beating of such horses, cockfights, the inadequate anesthetization of animals in scientific experiments, and the conditions and transportation of animals raised for food. Their main tactic was humane education in the schools. After 1900, under the counterattack of scientists and with horses being replaced by motors, most of these humane societies focused on the treatment of pets. Until the 1980s they would be known primarily for their work in reducing cat and dog overpopulation.

Some of these groups, such as the American Society for the Protection of Animals, created in 1866, became large and wealthy. Others, such as Henry Salt's Humanitarian League of the 1890s, remained essentially the work of one person. Most of these older groups—especially those that have lasted—were driven by compassion for creatures seen as helpless victims, emphasizing animals' feelings more than their cognitive capacities. Although many groups represented only the idiosyncratic concerns of their founders, they usually appeared in waves that reflected widespread changes in public sentiment. For animal protection groups, the most recent surge began in the 1970s in Britain and the 1980s in the United States.

In the 1960s and 1970s a wave of new protest movements questioned basic aspects of modern societies, including large bureaucracies, corporate profits, unrestrained economic growth, the uses of science and technology, and various ways that individuals oppressed each other. There appeared a general sense that industrial societies hurt the powerless in many ways. In particular, environmentalists emphasized that nature was not ours to destroy at will, for it had moral rights of its own. They protested against the destruction of endangered species, whether elephants for their ivory or whales for their oil and blubber, as well as against interference with natural balances through practices such as trapping. With these concerns came an appreciation for complex patterns of animal cognition and communication as well as a concern for the fragile web of relationships among living beings. With the women's movement, many women began to recognize both big and little ways that they were taken advantage of, developing their own language for criticizing the major institutions of advanced capitalist societies. Feminism contributed a sensitivity to oppression, power, and exploitation, based on a recognition of mutual rights and responsibilities.

These movements affected how people thought about animals. In the late 1960s and early 1970s new groups were formed to aid wild animals, including baby seals that were hunted for their white fur, dolphins that were being killed in nets meant for tuna, and the wolf, which had been almost completely eliminated from the continental United States. Through generations of television specials, magazine articles, and books, most Americans had come to appreciate the complex mental capacities and deep emotional loyalties of these animals. They learned, for example, that gorillas and chimpanzees can communicate with humans by learning more than one hundred keyboard symbols; they even play jokes on their keepers. Many people began to feel uneasy at the destruction of these animals' natural habitats, and also at how other mammals were treated every day in modern societies.

The humane societies of one hundred years ago saw animal cruelty as aberrant and unusual; people trained in the movements of the sixties saw the same practices as systemic and widespread. They were troubled by the treatment of animals in laboratories and on modern "factory" farms, not simply with the problem of pet overpopulation. And they saw existing humane societies as timid in their protective efforts, more concerned with maintaining the support of wealthy patrons than with extending their activities on behalf of animals. Unlike many men and women with the same sentiments who were content to volunteer at local animal shelters, a small constellation of interested persons grew dissatisfied with traditional activities.

For these would-be activists, the works of several philosophers provided a language and ideology that seemed to crystallize their new concerns over the treatment of animals. Most influential was Peter Singer's *Animal Liberation* (1975), which denounced "speciesism" as a bias parallel to racism and sexism, arguing that because the pains and pleasures of many nonhumans were as intense as those of humans, they should not be ignored or discounted. The book also contained considerable evidence of animal suffering in scientific research and modern farming—two core institutional arenas largely ignored by animal welfare organizations. This publication energized these scattered citizens, providing them a "philosophy on which to hang our emotions, feelings, sentimentality—all the things we had thought were bad; it gave us an intellectual hat to put on our heads," as Joyce Tischler, cofounder of the Animal Legal Defense Fund expressed it (Jasper and Nelkin 1992, 93). Henry Spira, after taking a course from Singer in New York, organized a successful protest against cat experiments at the American Museum of Natural History in 1976–77.

These initial activists, inspired and trained by movements like ecology and feminism, founded a new generation of animal protection groups in the early 1980s. They were concerned with a wide range of animal abuses, including not only the issues raised by the first generation of humane societies but also practices in which the animals did not suffer any obvious physical harm, such as zoos, the use of fully anesthetized animals in research, the performances of animals in circuses, and the shearing of sheep for their wool. Some of the new activists attacked every instance of the domestication of animals as an infringement on these beings' deserved autonomy, including the keeping of pets (or "companion animals," in the phrase of activists more sympathetic to the practice). Thus a more radical animal "rights" movement developed alongside existing humane societies and animal "welfare" organizations; even the name of the new movement implied that animals were active subjects (with rights) rather than passive recipients of charity (in the humane tradition) or of good and bad treatment (as "welfare" seems to imply).

As in any vibrant movement, different groups used different tactics. The Animal Liberation Front (ALF), which began in Britain but was imported to the United States beginning in 1979, favored sabotage and laboratory break-ins, which not only "liberated" animals but also yielded notorious videotapes showing experimenters in an unfavorable light—tapes that outraged all who saw them and boosted recruitment. Even activists within the movement debated whether illegal tactics helped or hurt the movement's public image, especially after the FBI labeled the ALF "terrorist." People for the Ethical Treatment of Animals (PETA), the largest animal rights group in the United States with several hundred thousand paying members, used diverse tactics, especially those involving media attention, to improve its direct mail fund-raising and recruitment. For example, it sponsored a "barf-in" at the headquarters of cosmetics giant l'Oréal; protesters pretended to vomit into a large papier-mâché toilet because, they said, animal testing "made them sick." Older organizations, like the Humane Society of the United States, founded in 1954, also grew more radical under the influence of the new groups and ideas, although they continued their traditional practices of lobbying and education. In the 1980s as many as one million Americans joined or contributed to the radical new groups.

Even the first animal rights activists came to this issue by a different path from that most activists take. In general, we can see two broad patterns by which social movement activists are attracted to a new issue. In many cases, activists are already politically engaged, and they are drawn to a new cause because it is directly connected to their current ones. For example, they see links between civilian nuclear energy, plutonium proliferation, and nuclear weapons, and maybe extend their analyses to include capitalism, imperialism, racism, and sexism. Around 1984, for instance, the staff of California's Abalone Alliance, founded to oppose the Diablo Canyon nuclear reactor, were also fighting U.S. intervention in Central America, nuclear weapons, and government housing policies.

At the opposite extreme, some activists come to an issue entirely fresh. Some, for example, become environmental protesters when a hazardous waste dump is proposed for a site nearby, or they discover toxic chemicals in their water, or they face some other suddenly imposed grievance (Levine 1982, Walsh 1981, Krauss 1989, Gordon and Jasper 1996). In other cases well-intentioned employees become "whistleblowers" after making troubling discoveries about the companies they work for; they often end up becoming protesters (Bernstein and Jasper 1996). These people have a target thrust upon them through a moral shock, making them willing to protest, sometimes even to search out groups to join.[2] The animal rights movement lies somewhere between these two extremes of a logical progression from one cause to the next and the sudden shock of a new issue, with participants recruited both ways. Animal protection is partly related to other causes, especially environmentalism, but in some ways it remains unique. The first activists were *inspired* by feminism and environmentalism more than they were directly *extending* their principles. This remained true for later recruits: some came to the issue fresh, others through previous causes and networks.

Recruiting Intimates

One way organizers try to expand their groups is to recruit relatives, friends, and acquaintances, who might in turn bring in their own acquaintances. This is the mechanism described by scholars of protest movements, who found that most new recruits already knew someone in those movements. Because political goals are entwined with personal pleasures in the complex motivations behind protest, people easily join friends for an afternoon at a rally or march. They remind each other of the date, encourage each other to attend, share rides, and chat during lulls in the activities. People who might not attend by themselves would go with a friend, parent, or roommate. For instance, animal rights demonstrations that I attended always seemed to contain many teenage girls with their mothers in tow.

Social networks can be crucial when a new protest movement emerges out of a preexisting one, just as the peace movement of the early 1980s grew out of protest against civilian nuclear energy. This is most likely to happen when the themes and rhetoric of the new movement are similar to those of the older one, and it is one reason social movements tend to appear in waves. In many cases social ties were formed for political reasons from the start. In California, for instance, many affinity groups (clusters of ten to fifteen people who make collective decisions and attend protests together) moved intact from the Abalone Alliance, fighting the Diablo Canyon nuclear power plant, into the Livermore Action Group, fighting weapons production at the Lawrence Livermore Laboratory (Epstein 1991; Jasper 1997, chap. 8). Indeed, in countercultural networks like these, there is little difference between attracting leaders and recruiting rank-and-file members, as most participants are highly active, and "official" leaders are not allowed to emerge.

Because the animal rights movement addressed many of the issues of the existing animal welfare movement, organizers could recruit members of humane societies to the new animal rights groups. Those who volunteered at local pounds and shelters might be persuaded that visible political activities would help animals even more. The staffs of humane societies often became radicalized, whether or not their financial supporters did, and some joined the new animal rights groups. But early animal rights activists were not entirely successful at tapping into the networks of other protest movements, for example the enormous peace movement active in the early 1980s or the environmental movement, which had apparently related concerns.

In my own surveys of animal rights demonstrators in New York and Berkeley, I found that about one-third were recruited at least in part through preexisting political and social networks.[3] Respondents were asked what other political issues (past or present) had helped involve them in their current cause, and 90 out of 305 people (30 percent) wrote in other causes and movements. The most commonly mentioned were peace/disarmament (by 17 respondents), civil rights and racism (15), environmentalism (12), the women's movement (10), Vietnam (8), opposition to U.S. military intervention (7), and the antinuclear movement (6). Animal rights protesters were also asked what other causes they were *currently* involved in. The most common responses, in descending order, were environmentalism, the women's movement, peace/disarmament, human rights, opposition to U.S. military intervention, and the antinuclear movement. Their other political experiences, though, do not mean that they were recruited through networks from those other movements; some were drawn in by family and friends active in the emerging animal rights movement.

When asked to estimate the importance of a list of factors that might have involved them in the animal rights movement, roughly one-third of the protesters said that friends and family were "very important," one-third said these were "somewhat important," and one-third said "not important." However, 78 percent chose "other" and 72 percent selected "reading" as "very important" in involving them in the movement. Most of the responses written in as "other" involved reading, listening, and watching television.[4]

Organizers will not be able to persuade existing protesters and groups to become involved in a new issue if they cannot make a direct link to the causes about which existing groups care, or find comprehensive frames that could incorporate both causes. Despite their use of "rights talk," animal rights activists had trouble convincing people that if they cared about civil rights they should also care about animal rights, or even convincing those environmentalists who cared about wild animals that they should also care about domestic ones. These emerging animal rights activists would have happily used existing networks if they could have. But since they could not, they had to recruit strangers in order to expand their organizations.

Recruiting Strangers

The other way to recruit people to one's movement is by appealing to strangers—whether by going door-to-door (canvassing), setting up tables in airports and other busy places (tabling), or mailing brochures to people's homes (direct mail). Appeals are also made through public displays, for example in libraries, lectures open to the public, and—of course—advertising. Even those who simply adopt animals from shelters or take pets to veterinary offices often encounter animal rights literature there (Groves 1992). Certain institutions and settings are convenient arenas for recruiting strangers. Although the response rate of strangers to such appeals is very low—since most pay no attention or are not sympathetic—there are far more strangers out there than intimates. Even low response rates can yield large absolute numbers—potentially far more recruits than social networks can provide.

The technologies of direct mail have developed into a small but efficient industry. Direct mail "brokers" buy and trade lists of those who have contributed to other causes or have subscribed to certain magazines, so that they can target their audiences carefully on the basis of likely political sympathies. They test what kinds of envelopes and salutations are most likely to catch the reader's attention. Animal rights groups courted members of environmental groups such as Greenpeace and the World Wildlife Federation, who had already demonstrated their concern for animals. They needed to be persuaded that domestic animals needed help as much as wild ones. Greenpeace, which boasts millions of members worldwide who regularly contribute money, was the source of the lists that proved most effective for the new animal rights groups in their early direct mail appeals.

In the United States two of the most successful animal rights groups were founded primarily through direct mail appeals: People for the Ethical Treatment of Animals (PETA) and In Defense of Animals (IDA). After expanding slowly and locally during its first three years, PETA grew from 8,000 members in 1984 to more than 350,000 members by 1991. IDA attracted nearly 100,000 supporters during the same period. The literature of each group emphasized the dire needs of suffering animals but also the heroic efforts of the organization in fighting these abuses. A large network of financial supporters were fed information about the exploits of small groups of more dedicated activists who took risks, for example those who staged sit-ins, unfurled banners from cranes and laboratory buildings, or lobbied and brought lawsuits. Direct mail appeals must give readers a moral shock that rivets their attention, but also provide some hope of change. They must tout past accomplishments as evidence of a group's effectiveness without letting complacency dull their claims of urgency. Usually they expect strangers merely to donate money, not join picket lines.

Another group, Trans-Species Unlimited, tried to combine direct mail fund-raising with local grassroots activism. It hoped local chapters with regular meetings and activities would build an activist, participatory image that would help it raise funds. It could thereby attract both intimates *and* strangers. Only its New York chapter succeeded, however, launching a series of demonstrations against fur coats and vivisection that drew up to several thousand sympathizers at a time. But this chapter was so successful that it had little need for the national organization, and tensions developed between local and national leaders. Factional fighting eventually destroyed it. In its final effort to maintain a dual role, the national office of Trans-Species changed its name to Animal Rights Mobilization! (ARM!) and printed glossy brochures with an aggressive style. "ARM!" was printed as though it had been spray-painted on a wall, in an attempt to attract mail supporters who favored guerrilla tactics. This attempt failed, and ARM! collapsed, although different people later revived it. It is sometimes difficult to combine the recruitment of strangers and of intimates, perhaps because the two tend to join different kinds of groups.

Strangers on mailing lists can be persuaded to contribute money to a cause, but rarely their time. Only one-third of the street demonstrators I interviewed were pure strangers, with no effect of family and friends. Going to a demonstration or a meeting is difficult to fit into one's daily routines. But even when strangers do not show up in person, their contributions of money are vital for movements, especially when groups need to hire skilled professionals such as congressional lobbyists or boat pilots. Large numbers of paper "members" also give legitimacy and political wallop to groups. And such contributions are occasionally the beginning of a more serious time commitment.

Cities, with their dense populations, allow some appeals to strangers to be translated into active participation. Direct mail appeals are anonymous, and those contacted rarely do more than contribute money. But tabling involves a personal contact and conversation, and it shows that the activists and their recruits are—at least briefly—in the same place at the same time. In cities, they might be persuaded to come together at some other time: to attend a demonstration or rally. The sheer number of people who pass political tables on urban streets or suburban shopping malls increases the chance of fruitful contacts. Sometimes, then, the kind of movement that normally recruits intimates—those that encourage mass mobilization for intense activities rather than small bands of protesters supported by direct mail contributions—may also be able to recruit strangers through moral shocks. This happened in the New York group I surveyed.

Such personal contacts are undoubtedly stronger than impersonal information disseminated through the news media. Lofland (1966) called them, respectively, "embodied" and "disembodied" strategies of access (also see Thorne 1983). But disembodied strategies can be effective in recruiting strangers. Groves (1992, 47) showed that media publicity can substitute for intentional recruiting, recounting how one animal rights group was founded when the story of a lone activist was reported in a local newspaper. She was flooded with supportive mail. By responding to each letter she organized several local animal rights groups around her state. For a different social movement, Oberschall (1993, 232) argued that the media were crucial in 1960 for spreading sit-in strategies in the civil rights movement, when personal networks of black college students were not enough. For these disembodied channels to work, however, the moral message of an action or argument must be especially clear and compelling.

Sometimes moral shocks, administered by strangers, are a sufficient spur to activism. Animal rights demonstrators insisted on the importance of reading and viewing in their own recruitment. Almost all cited Singer's book as crucial to their own involvement. What they learned, and what they felt about what they learned, shocked them. A typical animal rights protester told me, "I remember my first photos of cats being tortured in experiments; it was at a table on Fifth Avenue in 1987. I didn't know anybody in the movement—in fact I thought they were a bunch of weirdos. But they were right about animal torture" (personal interview, March 1990). Moral shocks, conveyed through dramatic images, can do much of the work that friends do in quietly persuading those they know of the value of a new cause.

Changing Attitudes toward Animals

However members are recruited, the appeals of a new movement must resonate with broader cultural meanings in order to attract new recruits. At the broadest level, the animal rights movement could only have appeared in the aftermath of glacial changes in the way that citizens of modern societies encounter animals. Throughout most of their history, humans have treated animals in two simultaneous ways: as resources to be exploited, but also as pets to be treated with love and care. They have tenderly nurtured their lambs, then slaughtered them. They have doted on pet dogs, while stuffing cats into burlap sacks and setting them afire at carnivals. This balance between two attitudes, one instrumental and the other sentimental, has shifted in the countries of the industrializing West during the past several hundred years, with sentimental feelings toward animals gaining dominance. As the bourgeois family and home emerged in the sixteenth century, with love and affection partly replacing economic need as the glue holding the family together, pets were incorporated into this cozy circle. By the eighteenth century, many Europeans were giving their pets human names, writing epitaphs for them, and occasionally leaving them legacies. Except for cart and carriage horses, town dwellers gradually lost most instrumental contacts with animals. They hunted less, had fewer fields to plow, and raised fewer animals to slaughter (the exception being a few backyard chickens). Their main contact with animals was now with their pet dogs. As a result they were less likely to see animals primarily as resources, existing to serve economic ends. Animals could fulfill important emotional needs for humans, providing love and loyalty. In a long process extending over centuries, compassion replaced cruelty as the acceptable stance toward animals (Turner 1980, Thomas 1983, Serpell 1986, Ritvo 1987).

This rethinking of animals accelerated in nineteenth-century Britain and the United States, spreading across social class boundaries. With nature neutralized for most by industrialization and the growth of cities, reduced to a suburban garden and a pretty landscape painting, people could romanticize it as innocent and good, ignoring its cruelty and violence. Animals, accordingly, were seen not simply as like humans in their emotional capacities, but as superior. They were never duplicitous or unkind. They were innocent and helpless, perfect objects for the compassionate efforts of Victorian humane societies.

The recent animal rights movement added other important themes in framing animal issues. One was a critique of instrumentalism, defined as the reduction of living beings to the status of means, whether by large bureaucracies, profit-seeking corporations, or experts concerned only with new technologies. A second theme was the dissolution of boundaries distinguishing human and nonhuman cognitive abilities. Awareness of other species' ability to communicate, make decisions, and form permanent emotional attachments seemed to suggest that these beings not be considered mere raw materials for human projects. Underlying both sensibilities was the absence of formal religious beliefs, as most Christian denominations, for instance, claim biblical credence for human "sovereignty" over other species.

The new animal rights protesters had other traits that reflect these trends underlying modern pro-animal sentiments. Two-thirds of the new protesters were agnostics or atheists, in contrast to a very small percentage of Americans. More than half of my own respondents were unmarried, compared to one-third of adults nationwide. Almost all rank-and-file members had pets, although only half of the leaders of animal rights groups did (many of them thought that pets, even when called companion animals, were necessarily exploited because of their subordinate positions). These two facts would leave the respondents especially likely to bond emotionally with their animals. Two-thirds of participants were women, who have been disproportionately trained by culture and feminism to be especially attentive to innocent victims of power. Even though most were not active in other protest movements, the animal rights protesters I surveyed were politically similar to participants in other recent social movements. They were left of center: 34 percent claimed to be liberal, and 31 percent progressive or radical left. The movement's main magazine, *The Animals' Agenda*, had identical results—34 percent liberal and 32 percent radical—from its readers.[5] Anti-instrumental critiques of capitalism resonated with this political vision. Because of their backgrounds, these people were prepared to be shocked when they learned of certain treatments of animals.

Conclusion

The several steps in the growth of many movements are like concentric rings in a growing tree trunk. Once a few individuals have decided to commit their time and energy to a cause, they often begin by recruiting those closest to them. But they also try to attract strangers to the cause. Recruiting intimates and recruiting strangers require different activities and rhetorics.

Members of a protest movement can recruit acquaintances by building on common assumptions and political beliefs. They can refer to a wealth of symbols, feelings, and experiences shared over the years. In contrast, they must shock strangers, providing them with new and disturbing images and more extreme rhetoric in order to attract their attention. They need to exaggerate to get people to stop at a table or continue reading a direct mail solicitation. The recruitment of strangers thus highlights the importance of cultural meanings, moral visions, and strong emotions in the expansion of social movements.

Animal rights protesters were recruited heavily from strangers, but this was not the only social movement to grow this way. Many anti-abortion protesters joined their movement in response to the moral shock of *Roe v. Wade* in 1973. Luker (1984, 137) says, "More of the people we interviewed joined the pro-life movement in 1973 than in any other year, before or since; and almost without exception, they reported that they became mobilized to the cause on the very day the decision was handed down." Two-thirds of the anti-abortion activists in Luker's California sample were self-recruited in this way.[6]

Two different kinds of movements may result when recruitment depends primarily on one means or the other. The greater the time commitment and the risks required of participants, the greater the chance they will need to have preexisting emotional bonds with their fellow activists. At the least, they will have to build such loyalties quickly. Efforts to recruit strangers, in contrast, may require more extreme moralistic rhetoric that demonizes a movement's targets and opponents. This may make negotiation and compromise difficult. And in the absence of easily co-optable networks, early leaders may have to bear greater organizing costs in order to reach strangers.

Notes

1. This distinction is suggested in McCarthy (1987), who argues that new technologies such as direct mail can partly overcome the lack of preexisting organiza-

tion for an emerging movement. Cable, Walsh, and Warland (1988), studying the responses of several communities near the Three Mile Island nuclear accident, found that some protest groups formed around existing political and social networks, while others developed anew in direct response to the accident. For more on this contrast, see Jasper and Poulsen (1995).

2. On this "willingness," which may or may not find an outlet, see Jasper (1997, part two).

3. These figures come from surveys of two animal rights demonstrations in April 1988: 270 people responded at a New York City demonstration, and 35 people at the smaller Berkeley, California, demonstration (Jasper and Nelkin 1992, Jasper and Poulsen 1995). I combine these two samples in this discussion. Other data about movement participants, reported below, come from these, plus several surveys conducted of *Animals' Agenda* readers (Greanville and Moss 1985).

4. The list included "friends and family," "news media," "previous activism in other causes," "specific events," "things you have read," and "other," with blanks for respondents to specify or give examples. Respondents could check "very important," "somewhat important," or "not important" for each. Other students of the animal rights movement have similarly found a mix of those recruited through social networks and those recruited more anonymously: Groves (1992) interviewed a smaller sample of North Carolina activists; Sanders (1992, 95) studied the Cambridge Committee for Responsible Research (CCRR), a small Massachusetts group. Sanders found that of the 33 members he surveyed, 11 had first heard of CCRR through a friend, another 10 through other animal rights groups, and 12 through mailed literature, a public table, an advertisement, and a newspaper article.

5. *The Animals' Agenda*, May/June 1983, page 26.

6. Luker studied the early years of the anti-abortion movement, when many strangers were recruited, especially due to the shock of *Roe v. Wade* in 1973; in the 1980s there was considerable bloc recruitment through fundamentalist churches.

References

Adorno, T. W., Else Frenkel-Brunswik, Daniel J. Levinson, and R. Nevitt Sanford. 1950. *The Authoritarian Personality*. New York: Harper.

Bernstein, Mary, and James M. Jasper. 1996. "Interests and Credibility: Whistleblowers in Technological Conflicts." *Social Science Information* 35, no. 3 (September): 565–89.

Bolton, Charles D. 1972. "Alienation and Action: A Study of Peace Group Members." *American Journal of Sociology* 78, no. 3 (November): 537–61.

Cable, Sherry, Edward J. Walsh, and Rex H. Warland. 1988. "Differential Paths to Political Activism: Comparisons of Four Mobilization Processes After the Three Mile Island Accident." *Social Forces* 66, no. 4 (June): 951–69.

Davies, James C. 1962. "Toward a Theory of Revolution." *American Sociological Review* 27, no. 1 (February): 5–18.

Epstein, Barbara. 1991. *Political Protest and Cultural Revolution*. Berkeley: University of California Press.

Freeman, Jo. 1973. "The Origins of the Women's Liberation Movement." *American Journal of Sociology* 78, no. 4 (January): 792–811.

———. 1983. "On the Origins of Social Movements." In *Social Movements of the Sixties and Seventies*. New York: Longman, 8–30.

Gordon, Cynthia, and James M. Jasper. 1996. "Overcoming the 'NIMBY' Label: Rhetorical and Organizational Links for Local Protesters." *Research in Social Movements, Conflicts and Change* 19: 159–81.

Greanville, Patrice, and Doug Moss. 1985. "The Emerging Face of the Movement." *Animals' Agenda* 5, no. 2 (March/April): 10.

Groves, Julian McAllister. 1992. "Animal Rights and Animal Research." Unpublished Ph.D. thesis, University of North Carolina at Chapel Hill.

Gurr, Ted. 1970. *Why Men Rebel*. Princeton: Princeton University Press.

Heirich, Max. 1977. "Changes of Heart: A Test of Some Widely Held Theories of Religious Conversion." *American Journal of Sociology* 83, no. 3 (November): 653–80.

Hoffer, Eric. 1951. *The True Believer*. New York: New American Library.

Jasper, James M. 1997. *The Art of Moral Protest: Culture, Biography, and Creativity in Social Movements*. Chicago: University of Chicago Press.

———. 1998. "The Emotions of Protest: Affective and Reactive Emotions in and around Social Movements." *Sociological Forum* 13, no. 3: 397–424.

Jasper, James M., and Dorothy Nelkin. 1992. *The Animal Rights Crusade*. New York: Free Press.

Jasper, James M., and Jane Poulsen. 1995. "Recruiting Strangers and Friends: Moral Shocks and Social Networks in Animal Rights and Anti-Nuclear Protest." *Social Problems* 42, no. 4 (November): 493–512.

Kilbourne, Brock, and James T. Richardson. 1988. "Paradigm Conflict, Types of Conversion, and Conversion Theories." *Sociological Analysis* 50, no. 1 (Spring): 1–21.

Kornhauser, William. 1959. *The Politics of Mass Society*. Glencoe, Ill.: Free Press.

Krauss, Celene. 1989. "Community Struggles and the Shaping of Democratic Consciousness." *Sociological Forum* 4, no. 2 (June): 227–39.

Levine, Adeline Gordon. 1982. *Love Canal*. Lexington, Mass.: Lexington Books.

Lofland, John. 1966. *Doomsday Cult*. Englewood Cliffs, N.J.: Prentice-Hall.

Luker, Kristin. 1984. *Abortion and the Politics of Motherhood*. Berkeley: University of California Press.

Mansbridge, Jane. 1986. *Why We Lost the ERA*. Chicago: University of Chicago Press.

McAdam, Doug. 1986. "Recruitment to High-Risk Activism: The Case of Freedom Summer." *American Journal of Sociology* 92, no. 1 (July): 64–90.

———. 1988. *Freedom Summer*. New York: Oxford University Press.

McAdam, Doug, John D. McCarthy, and Mayer N. Zald. 1988. "Social Movements." In *Handbook of Sociology*, ed. Neil J. Smelser. Newbury Park, Calif.: Sage, 695–737.

McCarthy, John D. 1987. "Pro-Life and Pro-Choice Mobilization: Infrastructure

Deficits and New Technologies." In *Social Movements in an Organizational Society*, ed. Mayer N. Zald and John D. McCarthy. New Brunswick, N.J.: Transaction, 49–66.

McCarthy, John D., and Mayer N. Zald. 1973. *The Trend of Social Movements in America*. Morristown, N.J.: General Learning Press.

Morris, Aldon D. 1984. *The Origins of the Civil Rights Movement*. New York: Free Press.

Oberschall, Anthony. 1973. *Social Conflict and Social Movements*. Englewood Cliffs, N.J.: Prentice-Hall.

———. 1993. "The 1960 Sit-Ins: Protest, Diffusion and Movement Take-Off." In *Social Movements*. New Brunswick, N.J.: Transaction, 213–37.

Orum, Anthony M. 1972. *Black Students in Protest*. Washington, D.C.: American Sociological Association.

Ritvo, Harriet. 1987. *The Animal Estate*. Cambridge: Harvard University Press.

Sanders, Scott. 1992. "Encaging Science: Animal Activism in Cambridge, Massachusetts, 1985–1990." Unpublished B.A. thesis, Harvard University.

Serpell, James. 1986. *In the Company of Animals*. New York: Basil Blackwell.

Singer, Peter. 1975. *Animal Liberation*. New York: New York Review of Books Press.

Snow, David A. 1976. "The Nichiren Shoshu Buddhist Movement in America." Unpublished Ph.D. dissertation, U.C.L.A.

Snow, David A., and Robert D. Benford. 1988. "Ideology, Frame Resonance, and Participant Mobilization." *International Social Movement Research* 1: 197–217.

———. 1992. "Master Frames and Cycles of Protest." In *Frontiers in Social Movement Theory*, ed. Aldon D. Morris and Carol McClurg Mueller. New Haven: Yale University Press, 133–55.

Snow, David A., and Susan Marshall. 1984. "Cultural Imperialism, Social Movements, and the Islamic Revival." *Social Movements, Conflicts and Change* 7: 131–52.

Snow, David A., E. Burke Rochford Jr., Steven K. Worden, and Robert D. Benford. 1986. "Frame Alignment Processes, Micromobilization, and Movement Participation." *American Sociological Review* 51, no. 4 (August): 464–81.

Snow, David A., Louis A. Zurcher Jr., and Sheldon Ekland-Olson. 1980. "Social Networks and Social Movements: A Microstructural Approach to Differential Recruitment." *American Sociological Review* 45, no. 5 (October): 787–801.

———. 1983. "Further Thoughts on Social Networks and Movement Recruitment." *Sociology* 17, no. 1 (February): 112–20.

Tarrow, Sidney. 1994. *Power in Movement*. Cambridge: Cambridge University Press.

Thomas, Keith. 1983. *Man and the Natural World*. New York: Pantheon.

Thorne, Barrie. 1983. "Protest and the Problem of Credibility: Uses of Knowledge and Risk Taking in the Draft Resistance Movement of the 1960s." In *Social Movements of the Sixties and Seventies*, ed. Jo Freeman. New York: Longman, 101–14.

Turner, James. 1980. *Reckoning with the Beast*. Baltimore: Johns Hopkins University Press.

Walsh, Edward J. 1981. "Resources Mobilization and Citizen Protest in Communities Around Three Mile Island." *Social Problems* 29, no. 1 (October): 1–21.

Part Two

Organization

Part Two Introduction

All movements have some structure, but not all movements have major formal organizations that dominate and direct movement activity. For decades it was assumed that the ideal movement structure was one that applied the principles of bureaucracy, with centralization of decision-making, a specific division of labor, and rewards based on merit and expertise. Movements lacking these elements were viewed as defective.

In 1970 Luther Gerlach, in collaboration with the late Virginia Hine, challenged this view. The essence of their analysis appears in Gerlach's chapter comparing the environmental and Wise Use movements. He argues that the most common movement structure is segmentary, polycentric, and reticulate. It has several significant advantages over a centralized and bureaucratic organization or a movement dominated by one. These advantages include resistance to suppression; the possibility of multipenetration; and an increase in adaptive variation, system reliability, and competition.

Suzanne Staggenborg provides the contrasting approach. She argues that the professionalization of pro-choice movement organizations brought stability of funding, staffing, and continuity of programs not previously possible. While formal organizations rarely initiate action, they last longer than informal ones.

The movement of AIDS activists combined these approaches. Abigail Halcli shows how the most militant of these, ACT UP, forced institutions and formal movement organizations to become more responsive to people with AIDS. In the process she looks at the organizational tensions that led to the demise of ACT UP.

5

The Structure of Social Movements: Environmental Activism and Its Opponents

Luther P. Gerlach

In the late 1960s Virginia H. Hine and I examined the structure of several social movements. We found that the most common type of organization was neither centralized and bureaucratic nor amorphous, but one that was segmentary, polycentric, and reticulate (SPR) (Gerlach and Hine 1970, 1973; Gerlach 1971/1983).

- *Segmentary:* Composed of many diverse groups, which grow and die, divide and fuse, proliferate and contract.
- *Polycentric:* Having multiple, often temporary and sometimes competing leaders or centers of influence.
- *Reticulate:* Forming a loose, integrated network with multiple linkages through travelers, overlapping membership, joint activities, common reading matter, and shared ideals and opponents.

At the time, even movement participants did not fully appreciate the strengths of an SPR organization, believing that anything other than a centralized bureaucracy was either disorganized or an embryonic organization. Since then a consensus has emerged that SPR has many benefits, and not just for social movements. This chapter revisits and supplements our analysis. Although examples abound from many movements since the 1960s, I will feature examples from the environmental movement (once called the ecology movement), and the Wise Use (property rights) movement, which opposes the environmental activism. First we will examine each characteristic.

Segmentary

Movements have many organizationally distinct components that change through fission, fusion, and new creation. When we examined what we then called the "Participatory Ecology" movement in 1969–70, we found that movement groups included:

- Regional and local branches of bureaucratically structured national and international institutions that had been founded many years previously. These included the Sierra Club (1892), the Audubon Society (1905), the Wilderness Society (1935), the National Wildlife Federation (1936), and the Isaac Walton League (1922).
- Recently formed alternatives to these established institutions, notably the Environmental Defense Fund (1967), Friends of the Earth (1968), and Zero Population Growth (1968).
- A plethora of groups even more radical in ideology and/or tactics, with names such as the People's Architects, the Food Conspiracy, Ecology Action, Ecology Freaks, and Ecology Commandoes.
- A mushrooming array of small and local groups that people were forming in communities across the country to challenge the construction in their neighborhoods of power plants, jetports, dams, incinerators and other industrial facilities, and real estate development projects.

The ecology movement continued to move, to grow, to change, and to promote change. Sometime in the late 1970s people began to refer to it as environmentalism. In the late 1980s and early 1990s the European term "the Greens" became popular. Today, what is left is usually called the environmental movement or the Green movement.

Why Groups Divide

Some groups divide when their participants differ over ideology and tactics. Some deliberately spin off new cells. Others are created by new people inspired by movement ideology or provoked by similar conditions. We have identified four factors that contribute to this process of segmentation.

(1) *Personal power* is often a component of movement belief systems. In charismatic religious movements, participants believe that they can have

direct access to God and this will empower them. The environmental movement exhorts participants to "think globally, act locally," and not to be dissuaded by those who claim that there is not enough expert agreement to support action. In all of these movements, each individual and each small or local group feels the need to take the initiative to achieve those movement goals the person or group considers important. They don't wait to be asked. This helps produce divisions among persons and groups over ideology and tactics. It also motivates these participants to recruit others to support their competing ventures.

(2) *Preexisting cleavages* derived from socioeconomic differences, factionalism, and personal conflicts are often brought into a group and increase its fissiparous tendencies.

(3) *Competition* among movement members, especially leaders, for economic, political, social, and psychological rewards. Benefits include followers, media attention, influence, funds from foundations and government, and the satisfaction of knowing that they are advancing movement goals. Competition causes factions, realigns followers, and intensifies efforts to recruit new participants and broaden the base of support.

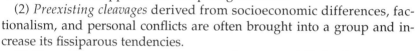

(4) *Ideological differences* are a major source of new groups. A strongly committed movement participant experiences an intensity of concern for ideological purity that people ordinarily feel only for threats to their personal or family well-being. Thus, for instance, environmental groups have regularly divided over disagreements about how much conventional culture and society must be changed to protect the environment, and how militant the tactics must be to achieve such changes. Some groups also split over how much to couple environmental protection with other issues, such as social reform or multinational corporations.

Most division occurs during the growth phase of a movement and contributes to its expansion, but it may occur at any time. Although they vary, new groups are often small and decentralized. Many make and implement decisions through consensus, while others are driven by strong individuals, if only temporarily. Sometimes existing organizations that are large and bureaucratic become movement groups, often undergoing profound changes in the process. Groups that are more likely to split pursue radicalism, reject authority, and/or reject organization. Despite its frequency, most groups are dismayed when they split. But some embrace it. Redwood Summer (RS) was launched by Earth First! in 1989–90 to protest the logging of California redwoods. Its coalition included peace and justice as well as environmental and local watershed management groups; soon it became a separate entity. Participants were expected to take what they learned back to their own states and form distinct groups beholden to no one but themselves (Pickett 1990, 8).

Having a variety of groups permits a social movement to do different things and reach out to different populations. Some of the participants in RS switched from protesting in the field to working for a referendum on protection of California forests. They then organized, temporarily, as the Environmental Protection Information Center (EPIC), which functioned essentially as a coordinator of a new array of groups working to get voter support for their proposal.

Sometimes movements beget countermovements, which are themselves segmentary. Environmental activism prompted the "Wise Use" or property rights movement. Loggers, mill workers, ranchers, farmers, miners, natural resource developers, snowmobile and dirt-bike riders, property owners, libertarians, populists, political conservatives, and some religious fundamentalists organized into many different and often localized groups. They include the Center for the Defense of Free Enterprise (CDFE), which takes a comprehensive approach to property use; the National Inholders/Multiple-Use Land Alliance, best known for demanding access to national parks and federal lands; the Blue Ribbon Coalition of recreation and off-road vehicle users in Pocatello, Idaho; the Women's Mining Coalition in Montana; the Pulp and Paper Workers Union; and the Pacific Legal Foundation in Sacramento, California. While coming from different places, they share the view that environmentalists and federal or state regulation of property in the name of ecosystem management threaten their interests. In the late 1980s and 1990s they organized against environmental legislation such as wetland protection and the Endangered Species Act. Instead they demanded multiple use of federal and state lands or the return of these lands to local or private ownership, with local management of natural resources.

Polycentric

Initially we termed these movements polycephalous because the movements we studied in the 1960s had many leaders, and these were not organized in a hierarchical chain of command. We changed the term to polycentric because movement participants since the 1960s often claim to have no leaders and are dismayed when a situational leader appears to be translating inspiration and influence into command. But whatever the attitude toward leadership, movements do have multiple centers of leadership.

While the press often picks out an individual to feature and quote, in reality it is rare for one person to be acknowledged by participants as *the* movement leader. Movement leaders are more likely to be charismatic than bureaucratic. People become leaders chiefly by inspiring and influencing others rather than by being chosen for their political or organizational skills. This leadership is usually situational, as leaders arise to cope with particular situations or episodic challenges in the life of a movement. Leaders must continue to prove their worth, and are often challenged by rivals.

In the 1970s Amory Lovins rose to prominence as an international leader in the movement to resist nuclear energy and to promote solar energy alternatives. In the late 1980s Dave Foreman became famous as the leader of direct action to stop logging of old growth forests, and Petra Kelly captured attention as the leader of the West German Greens and an international exponent of environmentalism. In the 1990s Ron Arnold, Alan Gottlieb, and Charles Cushman were recognized as founders and leaders of the Wise Use/property rights movement.

Although movement participants share common views, they also disagree. Different leaders reflect these disagreements. In the environmental movement many believe that economic growth is incompatible with saving the environment; others think that growth and development can be sustained through efficient and benign or "soft" technologies. Some believe militant direct action is necessary to force change, and others want to work peacefully within established rules. Even in the relatively small Redwood Summer some wanted to protest the U.S. action in the Persian Gulf War and attack big corporations, while others wanted to focus on stopping logging.

There is no one person or group able to make decisions that are binding upon all or even most of the participants in a movement. This makes negotiation and settlement difficult, if not impossible. Temporary leaders of a specific protest action may be able to reach agreement on concessions that will end the action, but they have no power to prevent anyone from returning at another time.

Reticulate

The diverse groups of a movement are not isolated from each other, but form an integrated network through nonhierarchical social linkages among their participants and through the understandings, identities, and opponents these participants share. These are interwoven to form a reticulate structure or network without any defined limit, through which information and ideas are exchanged.

Movement participants are not only linked internally, but with other movements whose participants share attitudes and values. Through these links a movement can draw material support or recruit new supporters. In the 1970s protesters of nuclear and fossil fuel power plants and lines formed alliances with organizations working to make and market solar and renewable energy technologies. In the 1980s environmentalists established relationships with feminist, labor, and civil rights organizations in order to overcome their image as urban elites. In the 1990s Wise Users have sought to expand beyond their rural and suburban bases in the West. They have joined with urban groups in eastern cities to oppose rent control laws, and allied with the political and religious right to elect conservatives to public office.

Linkages

(1) *Personal relationships* connect participants in different groups through kinship, marriage, friendship, neighborliness, and other associations. Even if groups split, the personal connections remain. Often an individual will participate in more than one group. Leaders are particularly active in networking. Indeed, one way to become and remain a leader is to recruit participants and to link groups together, that is, to become a node connecting many groups.

(2) *Communications technologies,* such as the telephone, radio and television talk shows, letters, newsletters, and membership magazines, allow individuals to extend their reach far beyond their own group. Since the mid-1980s e-mail and the Internet have been added to this repertoire. Individuals and groups reinforce and extend their relationships, consult with each other, and share information and interpretations. This helps them to coordinate their actions and act jointly, even over long distances.

(3) *Traveling evangelists and other visitors* provide living links in the movement network. They carry information across the network, from group to group, and build personal relationships with those they visit. In a general sense, evangelists are those who zealously spread the ideology of any movement, promoting its ideas, reinforcing the beliefs of participants, exhorting them to action, and helping them recruit newcomers and form groups, raise funds, and mobilize against opponents. Many are recognized leaders, who draw crowds when they visit different places. Some are ordinary participants who write about their travels and visits in movement newsletters. In the late 1960s and early 1970s students often traveled across the United States and western Europe by navigating movement networks, helped by local people who gave them contacts elsewhere.

(4) *Large gatherings* for conventions, conferences, workshops, and demonstrations allow participants to learn and share ideas, and to act on them. Through participation in gatherings, people not only learn movement ideology and demonstrate their commitment to the cause, they also make or reestablish relationships with each other. Conversely, mobilizing people to attend gatherings through their local groups reinforces movement linkages.

(5) *The Web* is aptly named. With the advent of the Internet, movement participants are now exchanging information and ideas through e-mail and Web sites. Many environment/ecology groups have Web sites (some are listed below) as does the Center for the Defense of Free Enterprise, a main coordinating node in the Wise Use network. Linkages vary from movement to movement, and some are specific to certain types of movements. Religious movements may hold revival meetings, but secular ones do not. Academic conferences are particular to movements with high concentrations of students or faculty. In the late 1960s and early 1970s participants in the anti-Vietnam War movement and later the ecology movement held "teach-ins" on college campuses. These gatherings, initially held to enable students and faculty to learn about the war or about environmental problems, also functioned to bring war protesters or ecology activists together to disseminate their messages across the country.

Integrating Factors

The segments in movement networks are also integrated by what they share or hold in common. These include a shared opposition and ideology. These factors complement each other and help constitute the culture of the movement.

Shared Opposition

The recognition or perception of an external opposition helps diverse movement groups to unite and to expand. A movement grows with the strength of its opposition, much as a kite flies against the wind. Opposition creates a sense of solidarity, a "we" against the "they." In many instances, movement participants see their cause as a small and heroic David against the Goliath of the establishment. As "underdogs," they must put aside their differences and work together.

When movements face countermovements, such as the environmental and Wise Use movements, each wages a propaganda war against the other, using the threat of one to mobilize the other. Environmentalists warn that opponents are growing in power, their leaders "want to destroy the environmental movement" (Western States Center 1993, 1), and their hidden supporters are the industrialists and developers who wish to exploit the environment for narrow economic gain. Wise Use theorists Arnold and Gottlieb argue in public addresses, in publications (Arnold and Gottlieb 1993, 53–77), and online (http://www.cdfe.org) that the environmental movement has close ties to government agencies and big foundations; a powerful combination requiring committed and united counteraction by the "citizen groups" sharing Wise Use ideas.

Both of these movements regularly research and "expose" each other. Wise User Charles Cushman alerts his National Inholders Association and Multiple-Use Land subscribers to environmentalist threats through his occasional newsletters. Barry Clausen, a private investigator hired by timber, mining, and ranching interests to investigate Earth First! wrote *Walking on the Edge: How I Infiltrated Earth First!* to expose it as an "eco-terrorist" organization that threatens the lives of loggers and miners and dupes ordinary environmentalists (Clausen 1994). Dave Mazza, a professional investigator and environmental activist, wrote about the connection between Wise Use and the Christian Right movements (Mazza 1993), while Carl Deal published *The Greenpeace Guide to Anti-Environmental Organizations* (1993). William Burke surveyed Wise Use activities in New England (1992), and the Wilderness Society commissioned MacWilliams Cosgrove Snider, a media and political communications firm, to study and report on the capabilities and limitations of the Wise Use movement (1993). Arnold and Gottlieb counter by claiming that the research was funded by a few private foundations not to advance understanding but only to destroy the movement.

Shared Ideology

Movement ideology operates on two levels. All participants share basic beliefs or core themes, which are sometimes articulated as slogans or aphorisms. The ecology movement used such concepts as ecosystem, interdependence, limited resources, renewable resources, spaceship earth, and no-growth economy. Wise Use has employed the concept of balance—harmonizing economy and ecology. At another level are a myriad of different interpretations and emphases on these themes. Disagreement may generate splits, but shared beliefs contribute to a sense of participating in a single movement. Sometimes these unifying tenets become master concepts that shape the discourse not only of movements, but of society as a whole. Once ecology passed into the popular lexicon the prefix "eco" became widely used to give new meaning to other words (e.g., ecofeminism). Sometimes beliefs or slogans change over time. Between the 1960s and the 1990s ecology became environmentalism, and after the Green movement became popular in Germany in the late 1970s and early 1980s, "green" became a synonym for both of these.

 Core beliefs can be shared because they are ambiguous and flexible, and they vary locally because they can be changed situationally. In 1972, biologist and early environmental evangelist René Dubos coined the term "thinking globally, acting locally" to warn that programs to protect the global environment cannot easily be translated everywhere into local actions but must be tailored to suit local ecological, economic, and cultural conditions (Dubos 1981). By the 1980s environmentalists had given the phrase multiple meanings. Some used it to encourage people to act locally on environmental problems in expectation that actions would combine to produce desirable global results. Some used it to imply that global exigencies override local ones. Some used it to claim that local actions serving local causes helped meet the challenge of global poverty and pollution (Gerlach 1991).

Adaptive Functions

The SPR style of organization supports rapid organizational growth in the face of strong opposition, inspires personal commitment, and flexibly adapts to rapidly changing conditions. It is highly adaptive for the following reasons.

(1) It prevents effective suppression by the authorities and the opposition. To the extent that local groups are autonomous and self-sufficient, some are likely to survive the destruction of others. This is also true of leaders; some will survive and even become more active and radical when others are removed, retired, or co-opted. For every group or leader eliminated, new ones arise, making movements look like the many-headed hydra of mythology. It is difficult to predict and control the behavior of the movement by controlling only some of these components. Even with suppression, burnout causes casualties. Having multiple groups limits the consequences of burnout. During the energy conflicts of the 1970s, when one group of power line protesters despaired of stopping line construction, another group took up the challenge.

(2) Factionalism and schism aid the penetration of the movement into a variety of social niches. Factionalism along lines of preexisting socioeconomic or cultural cleavages supplies recruits from a wide range of backgrounds, classes, and interests. Groups can be formed in many different sectors or communities. Redwood Summer and Earth First! recruited young adults who could afford to take personal risks. EPIC attracted Californians, mostly white, from the middle and upper classes, whose politics were more moderate. A few Native American tribes have organized to protect their rights to natural resources. Wise Use is much more diverse than environmentalism. It hosts groups of ranchers and farmers, loggers, miners, recreational vehicle users, and land developers. While some attract libertarians and free market advocates, others attract religious fundamentalists worrying that environmentalism is a type of neopaganism.

(3) Multiplicity of groups permits division of labor and adaptation to circumstances. The greater the differentiation of groups, the more likely the movement is able to offer something for every sympathizer to do to

further the movement's goals. In the environmental movement some groups take direct physical action to prevent loggers from cutting down redwoods in northern California or red and white pines in Minnesota, and other groups work with lawyers and public relations specialists to persuade courts and legislatures to block this logging. In Minnesota in 1997 and 1998, a group of Earth First! activists asked the founder of another group, Earth Protector, to use legal action to complement their direct demonstrations against logging in the Superior National Forest (Grow 1998). In northern California, opposition to logging old growth redwoods in the privately held Headwaters Forest has effectively included both the direct actions of Earth First! and the legal and legislative operations coordinated by EPIC. Wise Use has many segments: corporate and industry interests who contribute legal and financial resources, issue entrepreneurs who act as information clearinghouses and mobilizers of public responses, and individuals who worry that their way of life is threatened by environmental regulation (Switzer 1996, 1997).

(4) It contributes to system reliability. Failure of one part does not necessarily harm the other parts since these are not connected (Landau 1969). Instead, groups learn from failures and are free to disavow parts of the movement that fail. Just as one movement group is ready and able to take over the functions of another when it is no longer viable, so can a group disavow another if the latter's actions put the former at risk, or copy another if its actions prove successful.

(5) Competition between groups leads to escalation of effort. When one group or leader attracts more attention than another, the latter often steps up its activities to regain prominence. When a movement group threatens established institutions, they may respond by negotiating with a more moderate group. It will make gains for the movement and build outposts in the established order. Often, the more threatening group accuses the deal makers of selling out. This may motivate the latter to renew its militancy or to demand more from the establishment. The process repeats, opening new fronts while consolidating old gains. In the 1970s a leader of a Minnesota branch of a mainline environmental organization, the Isaac Walton League, urged legislators to pass a bill to establish the Boundary Waters as a Canoe Area Wilderness and exclude motorized travel by saying that if the "kids" do not see that they can protect the environment by working within the system, they will join radical groups that act more "on emotion." In an interview he said that he was motivated to lead this legislative action to prove wrong the young ecology activist who called him an "Uncle Tom" on conservation efforts.

(6) It facilitates trial and error learning through selective disavowal and emulation. Movement groups challenge established orders and conventional culture both in the ideas they espouse and in the tactics they use to

promote these ideas. Through trial and error come social and cultural forms that prove to be successful and adaptive. Because the groups are connected in a network of social relationships and information flows, knowledge about successes and failures flows rapidly from one group to another. While some environmental groups alienated loggers and millers, others sought to work with these loggers and millers by arguing that it was the big corporations who had depleted the forests of harvestable trees in order to make short-term profits. When the environmentalist call for no-growth was rejected by people because it appeared to threaten their economic opportunity and well-being, some environmental groups proposed the alternative idea of "sustainable development" through appropriate technology and resource management. When people worried about the consequences of not building more nuclear or fossil fuel energy facilities, proponents of solar energy took this as an opportunity to make and market solar technologies.

(7) It promotes striving, innovation, and entrepreneurial experimentation in generating and implementing sociocultural change. Environmental groups led the way in promoting the conservation of resources and recycling of waste. They developed new approaches to teaching about ecology; involved children and adults in monitoring water quality in lakes and rivers; helped to persuade government, foundations, and private firms to institutionalize new approaches; pushed industries to use less polluting and more resource efficient technologies; and pushed government to legislate environmental protection. By militantly resisting fossil and nuclear technologies and promoting the use of solar energy technologies, environmental groups have encouraged both government and private industry to rethink the future of nuclear energy (Gerlach 1978, 1979; Gerlach and Eide 1978). Since the 1980s, environmental groups across the world have taken the lead in warning governments and public bodies about the causes and risks of global climatic and other environmental change, and have done much to promote agreements among nations to reduce and control emissions into the atmosphere and oceans and other great bodies of water. Wise Use has both complemented and challenged the environmentalist agenda. Its demands for inclusion in decision-making has helped open the process and fostered a debate over how to balance environmental protection and economic development, and established the idea that development should be sustainable not only ecologically, but also socially and politically (Gerlach and Bengston 1994).

Conclusion

Social movements are segmentary, polycentric, and reticulate. This is a very effective form of organization. In particular it helps its participants to challenge and change the established order and to survive overwhelming opposition. It makes the movement difficult to suppress, affords maximum penetration of and recruitment from different socioeconomic and subcultural groups, contributes to system reliability through redundancy, duplication, and overlap, maximizes adaptive variation through diversity of participants and purposes, and encourages social innovation and problem solving.

References

Arnold, Ron, and Alan Gottlieb. 1993. *Trashing the Economy: How Runaway Environmentalism Is Wrecking America.* Bellevue, Wash.: Distributed by Merril Press.

Burke, William Kevin. 1992. *The Scent of Opportunity: A Survey of the Wise Use/ Property Rights Movement in New England.* Cambridge, Mass.: Political Research Associates, December.

Clausen, Barry, with Dana Rae Pomeroy. 1994. *Walking on the Edge: How I Infiltrated Earth First!* Olympia: Washington Contract Loggers Association, distributed by Merril Press.

Cushman, Charles. 1980s. National Inholders Association (NIA), *Multiple-Use Land Alliance (MULTA) Newsletter.* Bellevue, Wash.: Occasionally published since the early 1980s.

Deal, Carl. 1993. *The Greenpeace Guide to Anti-Environmental Organizations.* Berkeley, Calif.: Odonian Press.

Dubos, René. 1981. "Think Globally, Act Locally." In *Celebrations of Life.* New York: McGraw-Hill.

Environmental Protection Information Center (EPIC). 1997. *Wild California, A Newsletter of the Environmental Protection Information Center,* Spring, p. 2. P.O. Box 397, Garberville, CA 95542.

Gerlach, Luther P. 1971. "Movements of Revolutionary Change: Some Structural Characteristics." *American Behavioral Scientist* 14: 812–36. Abridged version in *Social Movements of the Sixties and Seventies,* ed. Jo Freeman. New York: Longman, 1983.

———. 1978. "The Great Energy Standoff." *Natural History* 87 (January).

———. 1979. "Energy Wars and Social Change." In *Predicting Sociocultural Change,* ed. Susan Abbot and John van Willigen. Southern Anthropological Society Proceedings #13. Athens: University of Georgia Press.

———. 1991. "Global Thinking, Local Acting: Movements to Save the Planet: Evaluation Review." *Special Issue: Managing the Global Commons* 15, no. 1 (February).

Gerlach, Luther P., and David Bengston. 1994. "If Ecosystem Management Is the Solution, What Is the Problem?" *Journal of Forestry* 92, no. 8 (August): 18–21.

Gerlach, Luther P., and Paul Eide. 1978. *Grassroots Energy,* 16-mm 27-minute, sound, color film. University of Minnesota Media Resources. Distributed by Penn State University film.

Gerlach, Luther P., and Virginia H. Hine. 1970. *People, Power, Change: Movements of Social Transformation.* Indianapolis: Bobbs-Merrill.

Gerlach, Luther P., and Virginia H. Hine. 1973. *Lifeway Leap: The Dynamics of Change in America*. Minneapolis: University of Minnesota Press.

Grow, Doug. 1998. "For Him, It's All Passion, No Profit: Activist Trying to Save Red Pines While Looking for a Place to Live." *Star Tribune*, 5 January, Metro/State, Minneapolis, p. B2.

Landau, Martin. 1969. "Redundancy, Rationality, and the Problem of Duplication and Overlap." *Public Administration Review* 24 (July/August): 346–58.

MacWilliams Cosgrove Snider (media, strategy, and political communications firm). 1993. *Report on the Wise Use Movement* (authors anonymous). Clearinghouse on Environmental Advocacy and Research, Center for Resource Economics, 1718 Connecticut Avenue, NW #300, Washington, D.C. 20009, for the Wilderness Society.

Mazza, Dave. 1993. *God, Land and Politics: The Wise Use and Christian Right Connection in 1992 Oregon Politics*. The Wise Use Public Exposure Project: Western States Center, 522 S.W. 5th Ave., Suite #1390, Portland, OR 97204; Montana AFL-CIO, P.O. Box 1176, Helena, MT 59624.

National Inholders Association (NIA). 1991. *Multiple-Use Land Alliance (MULTA)*, newsletter, Bellevue, Wash., 21 January, p. 1.

Pickett, Karen. 1990. "Redwood Summer." *Earth First! Journal* 11, no. 1 (1 November): 8.

Switzer, Jacqueline Vaughn. 1996. "Women and Wise Use: The Other Side of Environmental Activism." Paper delivered at the annual meeting of the Western Political Science Association, San Francisco, March 14–16.

———. 1997. *Green Backlash: The History and Politics of Environmental Opposition in the U.S.* Boulder: Rienner.

Western States Center. 1993. "Inside the 1993 Wise Use Leadership Project." *Western Horizons*, newsletter of the Wise Use Public Exposure Project's Grassroots Information Network, vol. 1, no. 3, Special Issue, September. Western States Center, 522 S.W. 5th Ave., Suite 1390, Portland, OR 97204, in collaboration with the Montana State AFL-CIO, P.O. Box 1176, Helena, MT 59624.

Web Addresses:

Center for the Defense of Free Enterprise—http://www.cdfe.org

Earth First!—http://www.envirolink.org/orgs/ef

The Environmental Protection Information Center—http://www.igc.org/epic/

Environment '97—http://www.environment97.org/framed/village/index.htm

Natural Resources Defense Council—http://www.nrdc.org/field/enashrae/html

Public Good Project—http://nwcitizen.com/publicgood

Sierra Club—http://www.sierraclub.org/human-rights

6

The Consequences of Professionalization and Formalization in the Pro-Choice Movement

Suzanne Staggenborg

As a result of the conceptual work of McCarthy and Zald (1973, 1977), the notion of the "professionalized" social movement is now firmly associated with the "resource mobilization" approach to collective action (cf. Jenkins 1983). They argue that professionalized movements are increasingly common as a result of increases in sources of funding for activists who make careers out of being movement leaders. In contrast to what they term "classical" movement organizations that rely on the mass mobilization of "beneficiary" constituents as active participants, "professional" social movement organizations (SMOs) rely primarily on paid leaders and "conscience" constituents who contribute money and are paper members rather than active participants. Importantly, this analysis suggests that social movements can be launched with adequate funding. "Entrepreneurs" can mobilize sentiments into movement organizations without the benefit of precipitating events or "suddenly imposed major grievances" (Walsh 1981) and without established constituencies.

McCarthy and Zald's analysis of professional movement organizations recognizes that there are different types of movement participants and different types of SMOs, which require different levels and types of participation. Although few theorists have expanded on the McCarthy-Zald analysis of professional movement organizations (exceptions are Cable 1984, Jenkins and Eckert 1986, Kleidman 1986, Oliver 1983), such conceptual development is important because different types of organizational structures and participants have consequences for movement goals and activities. Examination of the effects of organizational leadership and structure is relevant to debates over movement outcomes, such as those generated by Piven and Cloward's (1977) thesis that large formal movement organizations diffuse protest.

This chapter explores the consequences of professionalization in social movements by analyzing the impact of leadership and organizational structure in the pro-choice movement. My analysis is based on documentary and interview data gathered on the pro-choice movement (Staggenborg 1985) and focuses on a sample of thirteen pro-choice movement organizations—six national organizations and seven state and local organizations from Illinois and Chicago (see table 6.1). Documentary data cover the histories of the organizations from their beginnings to 1983.[1]

Fifty individuals were interviewed, including leaders and rank-and-file activists, who were active in the organizations during different periods. I analyze the changes in leadership and internal structures of the SMOs and the impact of these changes on the movement. In particular, I focus

TABLE 6.1
Sample of National and State/Local Pro-Choice SMOs

	Dates
National Organizations	
National Abortion Rights Action League (NARAL), formerly National Association for the Repeal of Abortion Laws (NARAL) until 1973	1969–
Religion Coalition for Abortion Rights (RCAR)	1973–
Zero Population Growth (ZPG)	1968–
National Organization for Women (NOW)	1966–
National Women's Health Network (NWHN)	1975–
Reproductive Rights National Network (R2N2)	1978–1984
State/Local Organizations	
National Abortion Rights Action League of Illinois (NARAL of Illinois), formerly Illinois Citizens for the Medical Control of Abortion (ICMCA) until 1975 and Abortion Rights Association of Illinois (ARA) until 1978	1966–
Illinois Religious Coalition for Abortion Rights (IRCAR)	1975–
Chicago-area Zero Population Growth (Chicago-area ZPG)	1970–1977
Chicago Women's Liberation Union (CWLU)	1969–1977
Chicago National Organization for Women (Chicago NOW)	1969–
Chicago Women's Health Task Force (CWHTF)	1977–1979
Women Organized for Reproductive Choice (WORC)	1979–

on changes in three major periods of the abortion conflict: the years prior to legalization of abortion in 1973; 1973 to 1976, when Congress first passed the Hyde Amendment cutoff of federal funding of abortion; and 1977–83 following the anti-abortion victory on the Hyde Amendment.

I begin by making some conceptual distinctions among three types of movement leaders and two major types of SMOs and then use these distinctions to classify the organizations by structure (see table 6.2). Next, I examine the impact of leadership on the formation of movement organizations and the formalization of SMOs. Then I examine the impact of formalization on the maintenance of SMOs, their strategies and tactics, and coalition work. Tables 6.3 through 6.6 summarize data for each SMO on the pattern of leadership and structural influence. More detailed case material illuminates processes under certain circumstances that may be more generalizable. Finally, I argue that the professionalization of social movements and activists does not necessarily help expand the social movement sector by initiating activities and organizations, but that professionalization and formalization importantly affect the structure and maintenance of social movement organizations, their strategies and tactics, and their participation in coalition work.

TABLE 6.2
Organizational Structures of Sample SMOs over Time

SMO	Pre-1973	1973–76	1977–83
National			
NARAL	informal	transition to formalized	formalized
RCAR		formalized	formalized
ZPG	informal	informal	transition to formalized
NOW	informal	transition to formalized	formalized
NWHN		informal	transition to formalized
R2N2			informal
State/Local			
ICMCA/ARA/ NARAL	informal	informal	formalized
IRCAR		informal	transition to formalized
Chicago-area ZPG	informal	(inactive)	(inactive)
Chicago NOW	informal	transition to formalized	formalized
CWLU	informal	informal	
CWHTF			informal
WORC			informal

Note: Details on organizational structures of sample SMOs are provided in tables 6.3 and 6.4.

Conceptual Distinctions

Types of Leadership in SMOs

With the professionalization of social movements and the availability of funding for staff positions, several types of leaders are found in SMOs (cf. McCarthy and Zald 1977, 1227; Oliver 1983, 163–64). *Professional managers* are paid staff who make careers out of movement work. Professional managers are likely to move from one SMO to another and from movement to movement over their careers (see McCarthy and Zald 1973, 15). Two types of *nonprofessional leaders* are *volunteer leaders* and *nonprofessional staff leaders*. Volunteer leaders are not paid.[2] Nonprofessional staff leaders are compensated for some or all of their time, but are not career activists. Rather, they serve as SMO staff for a short term and do not regard movement work as a career. As I argue below, there may be significant differences in orientation of leaders within this category based on whether the nonprofessional staff leader is temporarily dependent on the movement income for a living. Those who are dependent on the income may behave like professional managers in some respects, whereas those with other sources of income (or those willing to live at subsistence level) may behave more like volunteers. All three types of leaders are, by definition, involved in organizational decision-making. All three are also included in the category of *activists,* as are other nonleader members who are actively involved in the SMO as opposed to being paper members.

Paid leaders, then, may or may not be professionals in the sense of making careers out of movement work and, as Oliver (1983, 158) shows, may come from the "same pool" as volunteers. Of course, leaders who do not begin as movement professionals may become career activists. Both professional and nonprofessional leaders learn skills (e.g., public relations skills) that they can easily transfer from one organization to another and from one cause to another. Both professionals and nonprofessionals can serve as *entrepreneurs*—leaders who initiate movements, organizations, and tactics (cf. Kleidman 1986, 191–92). However, as I argue below, nonprofessional leaders are more likely to initiate movements (as opposed to SMOs) and tactics than are professionals.

Types of Movement Organizations

Changes in the structures of SMOs have occurred along with the professionalization of social movement leadership. In contrast to "classical" SMOs, which have mass memberships of beneficiary constituents, McCarthy and Zald (1973, 1977) argue that movement organizations with professional leadership have nonexistent or "paper" memberships and rely heavily on resources from constituents outside of the group(s) that benefit from movement achievements. Professional movement activists are thought to act as entrepreneurs who form such organizations by appealing to conscience constituents. The difficulty with this characterization of the structural changes in SMOs led by professionals is, as Oliver (1983) notes, that many such SMOs have both active and paper memberships. Similarly, organizations may rely on a mix of conscience and beneficiary constituents for resources.

An alternative characterization of structural differences in SMOs is based on differences in operating procedures. *Formalized* SMOs[3] have established procedures or structures that enable them to perform certain tasks routinely and to continue to function with changes in leadership. Formalized SMOs have bureaucratic procedures for decision-making, a developed division of labor with positions for various functions, explicit criteria for membership, and rules governing subunits (chapters or committees). For example, the formalized SMO may have a board of directors that meets a set number of times per year to make organizational policy; an executive committee of the board that meets more frequently to make administrative decisions; staff members who are responsible for contacts with the mass media, direct mail campaigns, and so forth; chapters that report to the national organization; and an individual rank-and-file membership. As I argue below, this type of SMO structure is associated with the professionalization of leadership. In contrast, *informal* SMOs[4] have few established procedures, loose membership requirements, and minimal division of labor. Decisions in informal organizations tend to be made in an ad hoc rather than routine manner (cf. Rothschild-Whitt 1979, 513). The organizational structure of an informal SMO is frequently adjusted; assignments among personnel and procedures are developed to meet immediate needs. Because informal SMOs lack established procedures, individual leaders can exert an important influence on the organization; major changes in SMO structure and activities are likely to occur with changes in leadership. Any subunits of informal SMOs, such as work groups or chapters, tend to be autonomous and loosely connected to one another. Informal organizations are dominated by nonprofessional, largely volunteer, leaders. The SMOs in my sample are classified by structure in table 6.2 based on the above criteria; details explaining the classifications are provided in table 6.3.[5] The major categories of formalized and informal SMOs are, of course, ideal types. In reality, some SMOs share elements of each type, often because they are in the process of changing structures. When SMOs formalize, they typically do so very gradually. Some SMOs look formalized on paper, but are informal in practice. Important differences also appear among SMOs within each of the two major categories (e.g., some are centralized and others decentral-

TABLE 6.3
Organizational Characteristics of Sample SMOs: Informal SMOs

SMO	Decision-making Structure and Division of Labor
Pre-1973 NARAL	informal control by small group of leaders on executive committee; board of directors representative of state organizations had no power; little division of labor
Pre-1977 ZPG	control by self-appointed board of directors; no participation by rank-and-file membership in national decision-making; division of labor between Washington lobbying office and California office
Pre-1973 NOW	elected board and officers; major decisions made by membership at annual conference; division of labor between administrative office, public information office, and legislative office
Pre-1977 NWHN	decision-making by informally recruited board of directors and five founders; informal division of labor
R2N2	decision-making initially done by membership at two annual membership conferences; later, regionally elected steering committee and annual membership conference; informal division of labor
ICMCA/ARA	informal decision-making by board and executive director; informal division of labor created by director as needed
Pre-1977 IRCAR	policy council of informally selected individuals active in member denominations; informal division of labor among small group of activists
Chicago-area ZPG	informal decision-making and division of labor among small number of activists and coordinator
Pre-1973 Chicago NOW	informal decision-making by board consisting of most active members; informal creation of committees by interested members
CWLU	decision-making by steering committee and in citywide meetings of membership; many experiments with structure, attempts to involve all members
CWHTF	informal decision-making and division of labor by small group of activists
WORC	changing structure consisting of steering committee and various issue and work committees; attempts to rotate tasks and include all members

Membership Criteria/Records	Connections to Subunits	Leadership
list of supporters rather than formal members, not formally maintained	loose connections to completely autonomous organizational members	volunteers and one nonprofessional staff director
dues-paying membership, but sloppy recordkeeping, little followup on members	loose connections to completely autonomous chapters	volunteers
dues-paying membership, lack of reliable membership records	very poor communication with chapters, lack of national-local coordination	volunteers
local organizations signed up by founders, no criteria for active involvement	loose connections to completely autonomous organizational members	volunteers
membership open to any organization sharing principles; no criteria for active involvement	difficulty integrating many organizational members into organization	volunteers and one staff coordinator
list of supporters rather than formal members	informal connection to autonomous "chapters" in other parts of state	volunteers and nonprofessional staff director
religious organizations in agreement with principles; no criteria for active participation	difficulty in involving subunits in organization	volunteer leaders and coordinator
no formal membership or records	loose connections to area chapters until they declined	volunteers
dues-paying membership	committees form and act independently	volunteers
list of supporters, dues initially voluntary, later required but not always collected; anyone active in workgroup or chapter was a "member"	loosely connected workgroups and chapters that were completely autonomous	volunteers and nonprofessional, part-time staff
exclusive "membership" of small group of friends	no subunits	volunteers
list of supporters; members include anyone who participates	typically not large enough for subunits; committees form and dissolve as needed	volunteers and one part-time nonprofessional staff

ized: cf. Gamson 1975). Nevertheless, the two major types of SMOs do differ from one another in important ways discussed below.

The Impact of Professional Leadership

The Initiation of Social Movements

Because professional movement activists can easily transfer their skills from one movement to another, McCarthy and Zald suggest that professional activists are likely to become entrepreneurs who start new organizations in which to work. If this is the case, an increase in movement careers should help to expand the social movement sector. Grievances can be manufactured by professional activists and SMOs, making the formation of social movements at least partially independent of overt grievances and environmental conditions (cf. Oberschall 1973, 158).

The McCarthy-Zald argument has been challenged on grounds of lack of evidence that professional managers and their SMOs originate insurgent challenges, although they may play a role in representing unorganized groups in more established interest group politics (Jenkins and Eckert 1986, 812). In the case of the civil rights movement, researchers have shown that informal indigenous SMOs initiated and led the movement (Morris 1984, Jenkins and Eckert 1986). In the case of the pro-choice movement, all of the SMOs in my sample that were active in the early movement were informal SMOs (see table 6.2). The leaders who initiated SMOs that formed in the period prior to legalization were all nonprofessional leaders, mostly volunteers (see table 6.3).

Professional managers may act as entrepreneurs in creating SMOs (as opposed to movements and collective action), but my data, together with cases from the literature, suggest that professionals are less likely than nonprofessionals to act as entrepreneurs. When professionals do initiate movement organizations, they are likely to be formalized rather than informal SMOs. Common Cause, for example, was initiated by a professional manager who created a formalized organization (see McFarland 1984). Many community organizations, which are often created by professional leaders, are also formally organized (see Delgado 1986). In my sample only the national Religious Coalition for Abortion Rights (RCAR) was initiated by individuals who might be called professional leaders; they included a staff member of the United Methodist Board of Church and Society. All of the other SMOs in my sample were initially organized by nonprofessional activists as informal SMOs (see tables 6.2, 6.3, and 6.4). Significantly, RCAR is also distinctive in that it originated as a formalized organization to mobilize existing organizations for institutionalized tactics (e.g., lobbying Congress) in a period when the movement as a whole was becoming more established.[6]

Given the lack of evidence that movement professionals initiate movements and informal SMOs, it is necessary to reconsider the relationship between the roles of movement "professional" and movement "entrepreneur." McCarthy and Zald suggest that, in response to the availability of resources, movement professionals become movement entrepreneurs, initiating movement activities and organizations because they are career activists looking for preferences to mobilize. Although no systematic evidence on the entrepreneurial activities of professional and nonprofessional leaders has been collected, my data indicate that the roles of "entrepreneur" and "professional" are, in some cases, distinct (cf. Roche and Sachs 1965).

An example of a nonprofessional entrepreneur in the abortion movement is Lawrence Lader, a writer and family planning advocate who published a book (Lader 1966) reporting on the large number of abortions being performed by licensed physicians in the United States and advocating legal abortion. After his research was published, Lader was inundated with requests for the names of doctors from women seeking abortions. He began to make referrals to women and then announced his referral service publicly as a strategy intended "to stir as much controversy and debate as possible while bringing the facts to the public" (Lader 1973, xi). Lader played a role in getting others to employ this strategy including the clergy who founded the Clergy Consultation Services on Abortion (see Carmen and Moody 1973). He later helped to found NARAL in 1969 and, more recently, founded another organization, the Abortion Rights Mobilization. Although remaining intensely interested in abortion and related family planning issues, Lader has not made a professional career out of his movement work; he continued to pursue his career as a writer while playing an entrepreneurial role in the movement.

Examples of nonentrepreneurial professionals in the pro-choice movement who have moved among established movement and political positions include Karen Mulhauser, an executive director of NARAL who became the executive director of Citizens Against Nuclear War after leaving NARAL in 1981. The NARAL director who succeeded her, Nanette Falkenberg, had previously been involved in union organizing work. In Illinois, the first professional leader of NARAL of Illinois was involved in community organizing work before taking the position of NARAL executive director and became a staff member of a political campaign after leaving NARAL.

These examples suggest that different factors may be responsible for the creation of two distinct roles. Movement entrepreneurs, the initiators of movement organizations and activities, may become paid activists who

TABLE 6.4

**Organizational Characteristics of Sample SMOs: Formalized SMOs
(including SMOs in transition to formalized structure)**

SMO	*Decision-making Structure and Division of Labor*
Post-1973 NARAL	decision-making by elected board of directors, executive committee; division of labor by function with paid staff as lobbyists, media experts, fundraisers, etc.
RCAR	decision-making by board of directors consisting of formal representatives of denominational members; division of labor by function using paid staff
Post-1977 ZPG	decision-making by board of directors and staff; division of labor by function using paid staff
Post-1973 NOW	decision-making by elected board and officers and delegates at national convention; division of labor by function using paid staff
Post-1977 NWHN	decision-making by formally elected board of directors; division of labor using paid staff
NARAL of Illinois	decision-making by board of directors elected on rotating basis; division of labor among committees using paid staff
Post-1976 IRCAR	formally elected policy council consisting of representatives from member denominations; creation of area units of activists
Post-1973 Chicago NOW	elected officers and board of directors; committees based on priorities screened by board and voted by membership; division of labor increasingly based on function using paid staff

Membership Criteria/Records	Connections to Subunits	Leadership
dues-paying membership, professional direct-mail techniques	formalized connections to affiliates; training and funds provided	professional leaders along with volunteer board
denominations that agree with principles; expectations of active involvement	financial support to affiliates that report activities annually to national organization	professional leaders together with volunteer board members
dues-paying membership, professional direct-mail; list of active members who participate in letter writing	some financial aid for chapter projects; formal guidelines for chapters developed	professional staff along with volunteer board
dues-paying individuals, professional direct mail; chapters	communication with chapters established as national organization expanded staff and increased finances; state and regional organizations created to further coordination	professional leaders
dues-paying membership, direct mail; attempts to actively involve organizational members	organization of first official chapters	professional staff together with volunteer board
dues-paying membership plus activists	committees created to perform needed tasks	professional director together with volunteer board
denominations agreeing with principles; attempts to encourage more active participation	more formalized ties to members and creation of formal area units	paid part-time director and volunteers
dues-paying members plus activists	committees tightly integrated into organization, no longer autonomous	professional staff and paid officers

benefit from the existence of the same resources that support professional managers, but they typically do not make careers out of moving from one cause to another and they may never find paid positions that suit them. Rather, they found movement organizations and initiate tactics for the same reasons that other constituents join them. That is, they have personal experiences and ideological commitments that make them interested in the particular issue(s) of the movement. They are also tied into the social networks and preexisting organizations structures that allow the movement to mobilize and are influenced by environmental developments (e.g., legalization of abortion in 1973) that make movement issues salient and provide opportunities for action (cf. Oliver 1983).

Professional managers, on the other hand, are not likely to be the initiators of social movements. They make careers out of service to SMOs and are often hired to come into SMOs that already have formal structures or are in the process of becoming formalized. Professional leaders are likely to care very much about the cause of the SMO—even if they aren't initially motivated out of particular concern for the issue(s) of the SMO. However, professionals' concerns with the particular causes of SMOs are part of their more general concern for a range of issues—the orientation toward social activism that made them choose a professional reform career.

Professionalization and the Formalization of SMOs

Not only are movement entrepreneur and professional distinct roles, but movement entrepreneurs and other nonprofessionals are likely to differ from professional managers in their organizational structure preferences. While McCarthy and Zald (1977) suggest that movement entrepreneurs create "professional" SMOs, my data support the argument that movement entrepreneurs prefer informal structures and may resist creation of formalized SMOs run by professional leaders. The professionalization of social movements (i.e., the rise of career leadership) is associated with the formalization of SMOs for two reasons: (1) professional managers tend to formalize the organizations that they lead; and (2) the SMOs that have the resources to hire professional managers are those with formalized structures.

Movement entrepreneurs prefer informal structures that enable them to maintain personal control. As the analogy to business entrepreneurs suggests, movement entrepreneurs are risk-takers (cf. Oliver 1983) who initiate movement organizations without certainty of success, just as capitalist entrepreneurs risk investment in new products. Like capitalist entrepreneurs, movement entrepreneurs are likely to be personally involved in the enterprise, desiring personal control over decision-making because they have taken the risks to establish an organization or movement. In contrast to the professional managers who bring skills to an organization and expect to operate within an established structure, movement entrepreneurs may try to prevent the creation of an organizational structure in which decision-making is routinized and, therefore, less subject to personal control.

The history of leadership in NARAL, which was founded in 1969 as the National Association for the Repeal of Abortion Laws, reveals that conflict between entrepreneurial leadership and formalization occurs in some circumstances. NARAL founders were not professional movement organizers in the sense of being career movement activists: rather, they were persons who had become dedicated to the cause of legal abortion as a result of their prior experiences, primarily in the family planning and population movements that provided the most important organizational bases for the rise of the single-issue abortion movement (see Staggenborg 1985). Because the decision-making structure was informal (see table 6.3), a movement entrepreneur who became chairman of the executive committee exerted a large amount of control over the organization; as he commented in a 1984 interview about his own style of leadership:

> Let's face it. . . . I don't believe in endless meetings, I like to make quick decisions. Maybe I acted unilaterally sometimes, although I was always careful to check with the executive committee. Some people objected to my calling [other members of the executive committee] and getting their approval on the phone. [But] we couldn't meet, we had to move fast, so I polled the exec committee around the country by phone. (Personal interview)

Although there were some disagreements among NARAL executive committee members' in the pre-1973 years, the informal decision-making structure seems to have worked fairly well at a time when the movement was very young, abortion was illegal in most states, and it was necessary to act quickly to take advantage of opportunities for action and to meet crises (e.g., the arrests of leaders involved in abortion referral activities).

After legalization, however, conflict over the decision-making structure occurred as NARAL attempted to establish itself as a lobbying force in Washington and to expand by organizing state affiliates. At this point, there was a power struggle within the organization between longtime leaders and entrepreneurs of NARAL and newer activists who objected to "power being concentrated in the hands of a few men in New York City" and who supported having persons "who are doing the work of the field—the State Coordinators" on the board (documents in NARAL of Illinois papers; University of Illinois at Chicago). The latter faction won a critical election in 1974 resulting in a turnover of leadership on the

NARAL executive committee. Although the executive committee remained the decision-making body of the organization, practices such as the use of proxy votes and phone calls to make important decisions were discontinued (personal interview with 1974 NARAL executive director), resulting in more formalized decision-making procedures that involved more activists at different levels. Another major change that occurred at this point was that for the first time the executive director and other paid staff became more important than the nonprofessional entrepreneurs as NARAL leaders. It was only with the defeat of movement entrepreneurs as organizational leaders that NARAL began to formalize and eventually grow into a large organization capable of acting in institutionalized arenas.[7]

If movement entrepreneurs interfere with the formalization of SMOs, as this case suggests, professional managers encourage formalization. While informal structures are associated with nonprofessional leadership, all of the organizations in my sample that have moved toward a more formal structure have done so under the leadership of professional managers (see tables 6.3 and 6.4). Although further study of the leadership styles of professional managers compared to nonprofessional SMO leaders is necessary, my data suggest some reasons why professional managers tend to formalize the SMOs they lead. Insofar as a bureaucratic or formalized structure is associated with organizational maintenance (Gamson 1975), professional leaders have a strong motivation to promote formalization: ongoing resources are needed to pay the salary of the professional manager. However, the motivation to promote financial stability is also shared by nonprofessional staff who are dependent on their income from the SMO position; moreover, it is possible to secure stable funding by means other than formalization. It is also important that professional managers are interested in using and developing organizing skills and expanding the SMOs they lead because this is what they do for a career. A formalized structure, with its developed division of labor, enables the professional manager to achieve a degree of organizational development not possible in informal SMOs.

The case of the Abortion Rights Association of Illinois (formerly Illinois Citizens for the Medical Control of Abortion and later NARAL of Illinois) reveals the role of professional leadership in the creation of organizational stability and bureaucracy. From 1970 to 1976, ICMCA/ARA was led by a nonprofessional director who was paid a small salary, but who volunteered much of her time and was often not paid on time because of financial problems of the organization. She was extremely effective, but did not create a structure such that others could easily carry on her work. Rather, organizational activities were carried out by force of her personality.[8] Moreover, volunteer efforts were channeled into instrumental tactics like lobbying, and little emphasis was placed on organizational mainte-nance activities such as fund-raising. When she resigned in early 1976, ARA entered a period of severe decline because of inept leadership and neglect of organizational maintenance.

A new director hired in 1978 was the first to develop a stable source of financial resources for the SMO. Although not a professional manager, the new director was highly motivated to secure funding because, unlike the previous directors, she was a graduate student who did not have a husband who made enough money to support her while she volunteered her time. She needed the money from the job and did not intend to work as a volunteer when there was not enough money to pay her salary (about $11,000 a year for part-time work) as had previous directors. Conse-quently, she set about trying to figure out how to bring a stable income to the organization. She eventually was able to do so by personally con-vincing the owners of a number of abortion clinics in the city to make monthly financial contributions to NARAL (personal interview with 1978–80 NARAL of Illinois director). Thus, it was important that the leader of Illinois NARAL was someone who, while not a career activist, did need to be paid and was therefore motivated to provide the organiza-tion with financial stability. However, the financial stability was based upon the personal appeal of the organization's director; the contributions from the clinics were received as a result of personal relationships with clinic owners established by the NARAL director. After she left NARAL and a new director replaced her in the fall of 1980, the organization lost these contributions and went through a period of budget tightening.

It was not until the first career professional took over leadership of NARAL of Illinois that the organization became more formalized and less dependent on the personal characteristics of its leaders. The director hired in 1980, who stayed with NARAL until 1983, was a young woman who had previously done community organizing work and who, unlike her predecessor, wanted a career in "organizing." She did not have any experience working on the abortion issue prior to being hired as the direc-tor of Illinois NARAL, but saw the job as a good experience for her, a way to develop her own skills and enhance her career objectives. Like other leaders, the professional manager was highly committed to the goals of the movement, both because of pro-choice views formed prior to direct-ing NARAL and because of her experiences in working with NARAL. But the professional director's orientation to her job led her to make impor-tant changes in the structure of the organization.

Until Illinois NARAL's first professional manager took over, the board of directors was selected from the same pool of longtime activists, many of whom were highly involved in other organizations like Planned Par-enthood and not very active in ARA/NARAL. Consequently, there was little division of labor in the organization and it was heavily reliant on the abilities of its executive director. When she was hired in 1980, the new director insisted that the board selection procedures be revised so that active new volunteer recruits could serve on the board and so that the terms of service on the board were systematically rotated. This procedure was implemented in 1980, resulting in a board composed of active volunteers along with some old board members who continued to serve on a rotating basis to provide experience to NARAL. The result was that a formal procedure for bringing new and active members into the structure of the organization was established for the first time. This change was important in making the organization less exclusively dependent on its executive director for leadership. It also made volunteers more available to the executive director for use in organizational maintenance activities, such as the NARAL "house meeting" program,[9] which provided an important source of funds to the SMO in the early 1980s. In Illinois NARAL and in other SMOs (see table 6.4), formalization occurred as professional managers took over leadership. Once a formalized structure is in place, SMOs are better able to mobilize resources and continue to hire professional staff (see below).

The Consequences of Formalization

The Maintenance of Social Movement Organizations

While informal movement organizations may be necessary to initiate movements, formalized SMOs do not necessarily defuse protest as Piven and Cloward (1977) argue; rather, they often perform important functions (e.g., lobbying) following victories won by informal SMOs (Jenkins and Eckert 1986, 827). And, while informal SMOs may be necessary to create the pressure for elite patronage, formalized SMOs are the usual beneficiaries of foundation funding and other elite contributions (Haines 1984, Jenkins 1985b, Jenkins and Eckert 1986). Consequently, formalized SMOs are able to maintain themselves—and the movement—over a longer period of time than are informal SMOs. This is particularly important in periods such as the one following legalization of abortion, when movement issues are less pressing and mobilization of constituents is more difficult.

Jenkins (1985b, 10) argues that one of the reasons that formalized SMOs are able to sustain themselves is that foundations prefer dealing with organizations that have professional leaders and "the fiscal and management devices that foundations have often expected of their clients." In the case of the civil rights movement, foundations "selected the new organizations that became permanent features of the political landscape" through their funding choices (Jenkins 1985b, 15). It is important to recognize, however, that this selection process is a two-way street. Formalized SMOs do not just passively receive support from foundations and other elite constituents; they actively solicit these resources. They are able to do so because they have organizational structures and professional staff that facilitate the mobilization of elite resources. Most importantly, professional staff are likely to have the know-how necessary to secure funding (e.g., grantwriting skills and familiarity with procedures for securing tax-exempt status).

The ability of formalized SMOs to obtain foundation funding is part of a broader capacity for organizational maintenance superior to that of informal SMOs. Paid staff and leaders are critical to the maintenance of formalized SMOs because they can be relied on to be present to carry out tasks such as ongoing contact with the press and fund-raising in a routine manner. A formalized structure ensures that there will be continuity in the performance of maintenance tasks and that the SMO will be prepared to take advantage of elite preferences and environmental opportunities (cf. Gamson 1975). Of course, volunteers might well have the skills to perform such tasks, and some informal SMOs do maintain themselves for a number of years, even in adverse environmental conditions (cf. Rupp and Taylor 1987). However, it is much more difficult to command the necessary time from volunteer activists on an ongoing basis. When informal SMOs do survive for many years, they are likely to remain small and exclusive, as was the case for the National Woman's Party studied by Rupp and Taylor (1987) and Women Organized for Reproductive Choice in my sample (see table 6.5).

The superior ability of formalized SMOs to maintain themselves is documented by the experiences of organizations in my sample (see tables 6.5 and 6.6). On the national level, all of the surviving pro-choice organizations have at least moved in the direction of formalization (see table 6.2). The one organization that did not do so, the Reproductive Rights National Network, was formed in a period of intense constituent interest in the abortion issue created by events such as passage of the Hyde Amendment cutoff of Medicaid funding of abortion in late 1976 and the election of Ronald Reagan as an anti-abortion president in 1980, but was unable to maintain itself after this period. On the local level, the movement industry declined in the period after legalization because of the lack of formalized SMOs (see tables 6.2 and 6.5). The exception was Chicago NOW, which was moving toward formalization but which was concentrating its energies on the Equal Rights Amendment rather than on the abortion issue. In the period after the environmental stimulus of the Hyde Amendment, the local pro-choice SMOs that became stable were those that began to formalize. Among informal SMOs, only Women Organized for Reproduc-

TABLE 6.5
Consequences of SMOs: Informal Organizations

SMO	Maintenance/Expansion/Decline
Pre-1973 NARAL	23 organizational members in states, 500–2,000 individual members, 1–2 staff, budgets of $30–70,000
Pre-1977 ZPG	high of 400 affiliates, 35,000 members in early 1970s; drop to about 60 affiliates, 8,500 members with budget of $350,000 in mid-70s
Pre-1973 NOW	initial membership of 1,200 individuals, 14 chapters; budget of $7,000 in 1967
Pre-1977 NWHN	initial participation of about 50 activists
R2N2	50–90 affiliates, high budget of $50,000; dissolution in 1984 due to lack of resources
ICMCA/ARA	active core of 30–35, part-time director, mailing list of about 700 contributors up until about 1976, when organization declined to about 60 paying members
Pre-1977 IRCAR	small core of activists; initial budget of $2,500, 8 denominational members, volunteer director through 1976
Chicago-area ZPG	high of about 11 area chapters, low of 3 and small core of activists in early 1970s; largely inactive after 1973 with exception of failed attempt to revive the organization in 1977
Pre-1973 Chicago NOW	about 20 active members, a few hundred paying members in early 1970s
CWLU	200–300 active members, numerous chapters and work groups, mailing list of 900 by 1971; greatly reduced active membership and number of chapters and work groups by mid-70s; formally dissolved in 1977
CWHTF	never more than about 15 active members, dissolved in 1979
WORC	high of about 30 active members in late 1970s, decline to about 10 active members in early 1980s; 100–150 paying members

Major Strategies and Tactics	*Coalition Work*
demonstrations, support for abortion referral services, coordination of state lobbying campaigns, encouragement of litigation	minor participation in short-lived coalitions
demonstrations, abortion referral work, state legislative lobbying, educational activities prior to 1973; congressional lobbying, educational work after 1973	staff support for congressional lobbying coalition after 1973
participation in demonstrations on abortion	minor participation in short-lived coalitions
support for local demonstrations	no active participation
demonstrations; grassroots organizing; petition campaign against Hyde Amendment; educational work	experienced great difficulty in attempts to participate in lobbying coalition, lack of communication with other SMOs in coalition
demonstrations, state legislative lobbying, encouragement of litigation, educational activities prior to 1973; continued state legislative lobbying, congressional letter-writing campaigns, educational work until decline in 1976	minor participation in largely unsuccessful pre-1973 coalition and short-lived 1977 coalition
participation in demonstrations; lobbying in state legislature, letter-writing campaigns to Congress, educational activities	no major coalition work
participation in ICMCA demonstrations, lobbying activities prior to 1973; inactive after early 1970s	minor participation in largely unsuccessful pre-1973 coalition; endorsement of coalition activities in 1977 prior to dissolving
participation in demonstrations, support for abortion referral work and support for ICMCA lobbying work by head of abortion committee	participation in short-lived coalitions
demonstrations, illegal abortion service, educational work prior to 1973; community organizing project to improve access to abortion after legalization, pickets and meetings to pressure providers, formation of Health Evaluation and Referral Service to rate abortion clinics and influence standards of service delivery; decline in activity by 1975–76	participation in largely unsuccessful attempts at coalition work prior to 1973
demonstrations, educational work to fight Medicaid funding cutoff in 1977	participation in short-lived coalition in 1977 characterized by a great deal of conflict
demonstrations, petition campaigns around Medicaid funding cutoffs and closing of public hospital abortion facility, educational work	experienced great difficulty in attempts to participate in Illinois Pro-Choice Alliance, eventually became inactive in coalition

TABLE 6.6
Consequences of SMO Structure: Formalized Organizations
(including SMOs in transition to formalized structure)

SMO	Maintenance/Expansion/Decline
Post-1973 NARAL	10,000 members, 4–8 staff, budget reaches $200,000 by 1976; 40 state affiliates, 140,000 members, 25 staff, budget reaches $3 million by 1983
RCAR	began with 24 organizational members, 13 affiliates, several staff, budget of $100,000; 31 organizational members and 28 affiliates, 8–10 staff and budget of $700,000 by 1983
Post-1977 ZPG	about 20 affiliates, 12,000 members, budget of $650,000
Post-1973 NOW	40,000 members, 700 chapters by 1974; budget of $500,000 by 1976; membership reaches 250,000, budget reaches $6,500,000 by 1983
Post-1977 NWHN	membership of 300 organizations, 13,000 individuals, budget of $300,000 by 1983
NARAL of Illinois	high of 200 active members, 4,000 paying members, budget of $80,000, full-time director and 3–4 part-time staff in early 1980s
Post-1976 IRCAR	mailing list of 600–15,000, 13 denominational members, part-time paid director, budget high of $10,000
Post-1973 Chicago NOW	about 500 paying members, budget of $10,000 in mid-1970s; about 50 active members, 3,000 paying members, budget of $175,000 by 1984

tive Choice (WORC) has survived and it has remained a small organization. Thus, on both the national and local levels, formalized SMOs have been stable organizations that helped to sustain the movement during lulls in visible movement activity brought about by environmental developments.

Not only do formalized SMOs help keep a movement alive in periods when constituents become complacent, such as that following legalization of abortion, but they are prepared to take advantage of opportunities for mobilization when the environment changes. In the late 1970s, when

Major Strategies and Tactics	Coalition Work
congressional lobbying, litigation from 1973 on; campaign work, PAC contributions, grassroots organizing beginning in late 1970s	began working in congressional lobbying coalition in 1973; leadership role in lobbying coalition by mid- to late 1970s
educational work, congressional lobbying since 1973; increased local organizing in late 1970s	began working in congressional lobbying coalition in 1973; leadership role in lobbying coalition by mid- to late 1970s
congressional lobbying	cooperation in letter-writing campaigns in response to alerts from coalition leaders
congressional lobbying work, educational work after 1973; political campaign work and PAC contributions by late 1970s	participation in congressional lobbying coalition
educational work; congressional testimony	participation in congressional lobbying coalition
legislative lobbying in late 1970s combined with political campaign work in early 1980s	participation in coalitions in late 1970s; leadership role in Illinois Pro-Choice Alliance
legislative lobbying, educational work; expansion of state organizing efforts in 1980s	participation in coalitions in late 1970s; increased role in 1980s
legislative lobbying and political campaigns work in late 1970s and 1980s	participation in lobbying coalition in late 1970s and 1980s

the anti-abortion movement scored its first major victories, including the cutoff of Medicaid funding for abortions, adherents and constituents were alerted by visible threats to legal abortion, and the ability of the pro-choice movement to mobilize was greatly enhanced. However, it was important not only that the environment was conducive to mobilization but also that the pro-choice movement had formalized organizations that were stable and ready for combat (cf. Gamson 1975). In NARAL, professional leaders were available with the skills and know-how necessary to form a political action committee, launch a highly successful direct mail drive, create an educational arm, obtain foundation grants, and organize state affiliates.

In contrast to the success of NARAL and other formalized SMOs in mobilizing resources (see table 6.6), informal movement organizations were not as prepared to take advantage of constituent concerns in the late 1970s. The Reproductive Rights National Network (known as R2N2), an informal SMO formed in the late 1970s, received a donation of money to undertake a direct mail campaign during this period, but the attempt to raise money and recruit activists in this manner was unsuccessful because activists in the organization's national office did not have the experience to carry out the program properly (personal interviews with 1980–83 R2N2 coordinator and steering committee member). There might have been local activists in the organization with direct mail skills who could have directed this campaign, but in this instance, and in others, the informal structure of the organization made access to such skills difficult to obtain. As one steering committee member commented in an interview, R2N2 suffered from "the classic leadership problem," the difficulty of trying to get people "to do what they are supposed to do," and the problem of "no one being around" to coordinate work that has long affected the "younger branch" of the women's movement (see Freeman 1975) of which R2N2 was a descendant. Ultimately, this structural problem led to the demise of R2N2 after the period of heightened constituent interest in abortion ended.[10]

Formalized SMOs, then, are able to maintain themselves during periods when it is difficult to mobilize support and are consequently ready to expand when the environment becomes more conducive. An important reason for this is that they have paid leaders who create stability because they can be relied on to perform ongoing tasks necessary to organizational maintenance. However, stability is not simply a matter of having paid activists: it is also important that formalized SMOs have structures that ensure that tasks are performed despite a turnover in personnel. It is the combination of formalized structure and professional leadership that facilitates organizational maintenance in SMOs.

Strategy and Tactics

While Piven and Cloward (1977) appear to be mistaken in their claim that formalized SMOs necessarily hasten the end of mass movements, their argument that formalization leads to a decline in militant direct-action tactics remains important. Formalization does affect the strategic and tactical choices of SMOs. First, formalized SMOs tend to engage in institutionalized tactics and typically do not initiate disruptive direct-action tactics. Second, formalized SMOs are more likely than informal SMOs to engage in activities that help to achieve organizational maintenance and expansion as well as influence on external targets.

Formalization and Institutionalized Tactics

The association between formalization and institutionalization of strategies and tactics occurs for two reasons: (1) As environmental developments push a movement into institutionalized arenas, SMOs often begin to formalize so they can engage in tactics such as legislative lobbying (cf. Cable 1984). Formalization allows SMOs to maintain the routines necessary for such tactics (e.g., ongoing contacts with legislators) through paid staff and an established division of labor. (2) Once SMOs are formalized, institutionalized tactics are preferred because they are more compatible with a formalized structure and with the schedules of professional activists. For example, institutionalized activities can be approved in advance; the amount and type of resources expended for such efforts can be controlled; and activities can be planned for the normal hours of the professional's working day.

The history of the pro-choice movement clearly reveals that formalization accelerated as environmental events forced the movement into institutionalized arenas. Prior to 1973, the movement to legalize abortion was an outsider to established politics. Although institutionalized tactics were employed in this period, no SMO confined its activities to institutionalized arenas: demonstrations and quasi-legal or illegal abortion referral activities were common tactics (see table 6.5).[11] After legalization in 1973, the arena for the abortion conflict switched to Congress and SMOs like NARAL began to formalize in order to act in that arena. After the Hyde Amendment was passed in 1976, the political arena became the primary battlefield for the abortion conflict, and formalization of SMOs within the movement accelerated. Although informal SMOs in my sample did engage in some institutionalized tactics, the organizations that sustained a heavy use of tactics such as legislative lobbying and political campaign work were most commonly formalized SMOs (see tables 6.5 and 6.6). It is possible for informal SMOs to engage in such tactics, but only as long as the leaders of the organization have the necessary know-how and other organizational resources. Formalized organizations are able to maintain such activities, despite changes in leadership, because of their structural division of labor.

Environmental forces and events, including countermovement activities, do place strong constraints on the tactics of SMOs. When environmental events call for nonroutine direct-action tactics, informal movement organizations typically play a critical role in initiating these tactics (Jenkins and Eckert 1986). In the case of the civil rights movement, for example, Morris (1984) shows that the formalized National Association for the Advancement of Colored People (NAACP) preferred to focus on legal and educational tactics, while informal SMOs were engaging in direct-action tactics. However, even the NAACP engaged in some direct-action tactics through its youth divisions at a time when it was clear that progress could only be made through tactics such as the sit-ins initiated by informal SMOs.

When formalized SMOs do engage in direct-action tactics, however, they are likely to be nondisruptive, planned versions of the tactics. NARAL's use of the "speak-out" tactic in the period following 1983 provides some evidence on this point. This was a period when the pro-choice movement was beginning to take the offensive in the legislative and political arenas, particularly after anti-abortion forces failed in their attempt to pass a Human Life bill through Congress in 1982 and the Supreme Court delivered a ruling in 1983 that struck down most of the restrictions on abortion that had been passed by state and local legislatures. The anti-abortion movement responded to these developments by forcing a switch away from the institutionalized arenas, in which pro-choice forces were beginning to gain the upper hand, to public relations tactics such as the film *The Silent Scream*.[12] As a result of media coverage that began to focus on the issue of fetal rights (cf. Kalter 1985), pro-choice organizations such as NARAL were forced to respond. NARAL chose to employ a version of the speak-out tactic originated by women's liberation groups in the late 1960s. Originally, the speak-out was a spontaneous type of public forum at which women spoke out about their experiences as women, relating their own stories about illegal abortions and so forth. NARAL's version of this tactic was a planned one; to focus media and public attention on women rather than on the fetus, NARAL asked women around the country to write letters about their experiences with abortion addressed to President Reagan and other elected officials and send the letters to NARAL and its affiliates. The letters were then read at public forums on a scheduled day. This case suggests that formalized organizations can switch from tactics in institutionalized arenas to other tactics when necessary, but the tactics they choose are likely to be orderly versions of direct-action tactics originated by informal SMOs.

Formalization and Organizational Maintenance Tactics

Not only are the tactics of formalized SMOs typically institutionalized, but they are also frequently geared toward organizational maintenance and expansion, in addition to more instrumental goals. This was certainly the case for NARAL and its affiliates, which embarked on a "grassroots organizing" strategy known as "Impact '80," intended to expand NARAL, and its political influence, in the late 1970s (see, for example, *NARAL News*, November 1978). It was also the case for NOW, which engaged in a number of high-profile tactics around abortion that were used in membership appeals in the 1980s (see, for example, *National NOW Times*, September/October 1979). In Chicago NOW, there was explicit discussion of the membership-expanding potential of the abortion issue in the late 1970s and early 1980s (personal interview with Chicago NOW executive director).

The experiences of organizations in my sample suggest that professional leaders play an important role in influencing organizations to adopt tactics that aid organizational maintenance. In several organizations, professional staff were responsible for undertaking direct mail campaigns that helped to expand the organization. In NARAL, an experienced director who took over in 1974 began a direct mail campaign that was later expanded by other professional leaders (personal interviews with 1974–75 and 1975–81 NARAL executive directors). In the National Women's Health Network (NWHN), an executive director succeeded in expanding organizational membership in the late 1970s through direct mail despite the concerns of nonprofessional leaders that direct mail would bring uncommitted members into the organization (personal interviews with NWHN board members). In Zero Population Growth (ZPG), a professional manager was responsible for reversing the decline in individual membership in the organization through direct mail after he finally convinced the nonprofessional leaders on the ZPG board to undertake the campaign (personal interview with 1976–80 ZPG executive director).

The case of Illinois NARAL is particularly valuable in revealing the role of professional leaders in advancing strategies that aid organizational expansion. In the early 1980s, the NARAL affiliate made important changes in its strategies and tactics, switching from an emphasis on legislative lobbying to heavy involvement in political campaign work. This switch was part of the national NARAL Impact '80 program, which began to be implemented by Illinois NARAL in 1979. However, it was not until the early 1980s, after a professional manager took over, that Illinois NARAL really became committed to the new tactics that included political campaign work and workshops to train volunteers, house meetings to recruit new members, and an "I'm Pro-Choice and I Vote" postcard campaign.

One reason why the switch in mobilization tactics occurred after 1980 was that the national NARAL organization had by this time become much better organized in implementing the grassroots organizing program through training and grants to local affiliates (see table 6.4). As the national organization became more formalized, it was able to extend more aid through its bureaucratic structure to affiliates and to exert more influence over their tactics. In fact, NARAL affiliates signed formal contracts in exchange for national funds to carry out programs in the early 1980s. The other reason was that there "were important differences in the state of the organization and in the orientations of the Illinois NARAL directors who served from 1978 to 1980 and from 1980 to 1983, which resulted in different strategies and tactics."

Because ARA was in a state of decline when she was hired in 1978 (see table 6.5), the new director spent much of her time in administrative tasks: securing funding, renewing contacts with members, and organizing the office. Because of her organization skills and attractive personal style, she was highly successful at reviving the organization. In doing so she used the skills of constituents but did not create a formalized organization. NARAL's strategies and tactics were determined solely by the pragmatic and instrumental approach of the 1978–80 executive director. Rather than concentrating on bringing large numbers of activists into the organization, she recruited volunteers with particular skills, including her friends, for specific tasks. Tactics were aimed less at gaining exposure for NARAL than at accomplishing specific objectives. For example, when a Chicago alderman moved to introduce an ordinance in the city council restricting the availability of abortions, the NARAL director worked to have the measure killed through quiet, behind-the-scenes maneuvers. In this instance and in lobbying work in the state legislature, she made use of the skills and influence of seasoned activists.

Because of her success with such tactics and her lack of concern with organization expansion, the 1978–80 director was not sold on the national NARAL Impact '80 program, which was intended to expand NARAL and make the organization a visible political force. In accordance with the national organization's wishes, she tried to implement the program, conducting a limited number of house meetings. But she remained unconvinced of their effectiveness, preferring more efficient methods of fundraising and recruitment. She had similar objections to other parts of the national NARAL grassroots organizing program. When I asked her about the political skills workshops, she replied:

> I refused to do those political skills workshops. I didn't have time, I said [to national NARAL], I'm doing the house meetings program—that's enough. I really just didn't think they were necessary—there are enough organizations like the League of Women Voters which do political skills training. From an organizational point of view, I guess it's good to do your own skills training to show that the organization is really involved. (Personal interview)

Although she recognized the organizational value of such tactics, this director was not primarily concerned with organizational expansion, but with more specific goals, such as defeating particular pieces of anti-abortion legislation. She was accustomed to using individual skills for this work rather than mobilizing large numbers of activists. When asked about campaign work, she replied:

> I do think the "I'm Pro-Choice and I Vote" [postcard campaign] was important in getting the message across to legislators and candidates in a public way. I put a lot of emphasis on [abortion] clinics for postcards because there was a ready-made setting for getting people to sign them. . . . As far as the campaign work, it was clear to me at the time that Reagan was going to be elected. It was too late in 1980 to make a difference. And, on the local level, there are already liberal groups . . . that almost always support pro-choice candidates anyway. I'm just not that much on duplicating efforts which I think NARAL is doing with the campaign work. (Personal interview)

As these comments indicate, the 1978–80 Illinois NARAL director preferred instrumental tactics rather than organizing tactics as a result of her background and experiences. She saw the house meetings as an inefficient way to raise money, and, while she recognized that political-skills workshops and campaign work were good for organizational visibility, she was not convinced of their effectiveness for achieving movement goals—her primary concern. She used the "I'm Pro-Choice and I Vote" postcards as a signal to legislators rather than as an organizing tool. Because of her influence, most of Illinois NARAL's activities during her tenure were instrumentally targeted at state legislators.

It was not until an executive director with experience in community organizing work and with ambitions for a movement career was hired in 1980 that the Illinois NARAL affiliate enthusiastically implemented the national NARAL grassroots organizing program. In contrast to her predecessor who had no interest in organizing per se, the new director was anxious to engage in "organizing" work to expand the local affiliate and eagerly began to develop the house meeting program that was part of the national NARAL organizing strategy. One of the reasons that she was successful in doing so was that, as described above, she created a more formalized organization. Whereas her predecessor had been reluctant to delegate certain tasks, including speaking at house meetings, the new director made heavy use of a division of labor that had not existed in the previously informal SMO. Aided by her past experience with community organizing she was highly successful at training volunteers to conduct house meetings and, with funds raised from the meetings and some financial aid from national NARAL, was able to hire an organizer to run the house meeting program, thereby increasing the division of labor in the SMO.

The new director's strategic approach was clearly influenced by her professional interest in organizing tactics. She used the NARAL house meeting program to raise money, but also as a means of bringing new activists into the NARAL organization. And just as the house meetings were used as an organizing tool, so were the NARAL postcards. As the NARAL director explained:

> The best thing about the postcards was that they gave us new contacts. We would set up tables in different places and people would come up and sign and say things like "I'm really glad someone is doing something about this issue." And then we'd say, "Would you like to get more involved?" We got a number of activists that way. We also got names for a mailing list. . . . So the postcards were good as a way of making contacts, a means of exposure for the organization. The actual effect of the postcards on legislators was, I think, minimal. I know some of the legislators never even opened the envelope; when we delivered an envelope full to Springfield, they'd just throw them away. (Personal interview)

Thus, Illinois NARAL employed tactics oriented toward organizational goals after moving toward formalization. This local case history suggests that professional leaders may be more likely than nonprofessional staff and volunteers to influence SMOs to engage in tactics that have organizational maintenance functions rather than strictly instrumental goals because they have organizational skills they want to use and develop.

Coalition Work

The formalization of social movement organizations also has implications for coalition work within movements. In my sample, formalized SMOs have played the dominant roles in lasting coalitions (see tables 6.5 and 6.6). Coalitions among formalized SMOs are easier to maintain than are coalitions among informal SMOs or between formalized and informal SMOs because formalized SMOs typically have staff members who are available to act as organizational representatives to the coalition and routinely coordinate the coalition work. Just as paid staff can be relied on to carry out maintenance tasks for SMOs, they can also be relied on to maintain contact with the representatives of other SMOs in a coalition. When all of the SMO representatives are paid staff, coordination is easiest. While volunteers can represent SMOs in coalitions, it is more difficult to keep volunteers in contact with one another and to coordinate their work, particularly in the absence of a formalized coalition organization with paid staff of its own. Thus, paid staff help to maintain coalitions, thereby lessening the organizational problems of coalition work (see Staggenborg 1986, 387).

The experiences of the Illinois Pro-Choice Alliance (IPCA), a Chicago-based coalition organization, reveal the impact of organizational structure on coalition work. Formalized movement organizations, including NARAL of Illinois and Chicago NOW, have played a major role in this coalition, while informal organizations, such as Women Organized for Reproductive Choice (WORC), have had a difficult time participating in the coalition. One past director of the Illinois Pro-Choice Alliance recognized this problem, commenting in an interview:

> There is a real difference between groups which have paid staff and the grassroots groups which are all volunteers. The groups with paid staff have a lot more opportunity to participate [in the coalition]—even trivial things like meeting times create problems. The groups with paid staff can meet in the Loop at lunch time—it makes it easier. Also . . . people from the grassroots groups tend to be intimidated by the paid staff, because as volunteers the grassroots people are less informed about the issue. Whereas, for the staff, it's their job to be informed, and they have the resources behind them. . . . I think too that the grassroots people have higher expectations about what can be done. They're volunteers who may have worked all day, then they do this in the evenings: they're cause-oriented and they expect more out of people and projects. Paid staff are the opposite in that they work on the issue during the day, and then want to go home to their families or whatever at night and leave it behind. They want to do projects with defined goals and time limits, projections as to the feasibility and all that. Not that paid staff are not committed people. I think it's good to have a balance between the grassroots and staffed groups. Without the grassroots people, I think things would be overstructured; with just the grassroots people, well, there's too much burnout among them. The staffers tend to last a lot longer. (Personal interview)

These perceptions are borne out by the difficulties of Women Organized for Reproductive Choice in trying to participate in the IPCA. WORC members interviewed also spoke of the problems that they had attending meetings at lunchtime in downtown Chicago, a time and place convenient for the staff of formalized SMO members of the coalition but difficult for WORC members, who tended to be women with full-time jobs in various parts of the city. Another reason for the difficulty is that the coalition has focused on institutionalized lobbying activities, tactics for which WORC members have neither the skills nor the ideological inclinations. Efforts by WORC to get the coalition to engage in a broader range of tactics, including direct-action tactics, have been unsuccessful. On the national level, the Reproductive Rights National Network had nearly identical problems participating in the Abortion Information Exchange coalition (see Staggenborg 1986). Formalized SMOs play an important role in maintaining coalitions, but they also influence coalitions toward narrower, institutionalized strategies and tactics and make the participation of informal SMOs difficult.

Conclusion

While professionalization of leadership and formalization of SMOs are not inevitable outcomes of social movements, they are important trends in many movements (cf. McCarthy and Zald 1973, 1977; Gamson 1975, 91). There is little evidence, however, that professional leaders and formalized SMOs will replace informal SMOs and nonprofessionals as the initiators of social movements and collective action. While systematic research on the influence of different types of movement leaders is needed, my data show that the roles of entrepreneur and professional manager are in some cases distinct. This is because environmental opportunities and preexisting organizational bases are critical determinants of movement mobilization; movement entrepreneurs do not manufacture grievances at will, but are influenced by the same environmental and organizational forces that mobilize other constituents. Contrary to the arguments of McCarthy and Zald (1973, 1977), nonprofessional leaders and informal SMOs remain important in initiating movements and tactics that are critical to the growth of insurgency (cf. McAdam 1983).

Professionalization of leadership has important implications for the maintenance and direction of social movement organizations. My data suggest that professional managers, as career activists, tend to formalize the organizations they lead in order to provide financial stability and the kind of division of labor that allows them to use and develop their organizational skills. Once formalized, SMOs continue to hire professional managers because they have the necessary resources. Contrary to the arguments of Piven and Cloward (1977), formalized SMOs do not diffuse protest but play an important role in maintaining themselves and the movement, particularly in unfavorable environmental conditions when it is difficult to mobilize constituents. Formalized SMOs are better able to maintain themselves than are informal ones, not only because they have paid staff who can be relied on to carry out organizational tasks, but also because a formalized structure ensures continuity despite changes in leadership and environmental conditions. Thus, a movement entrepreneur who prevents formalization by maintaining personal control over an SMO may ultimately cause the organization's demise. A movement that consists solely of informal SMOs is likely to have a shorter lifetime than a movement that includes formalized SMOs. Similarly, a coalition of informal SMOs has less chance of survival than a coalition of formalized SMOs.

While formalization helps to maintain social movements, it is also associated with the institutionalization of collective action. Formalized SMOs engage in fewer disruptive tactics of the sort that pressure government authorities and other elites to make concessions or provide support than do informal SMOs. Formalized SMOs also tend to select strategies and tactics that enhance organizational maintenance. Given the prominent role of professional managers in formalized SMOs, these findings raise the Michels ([1915] 1962) question of whether formalized organizations with professional leaders inevitably become oligarchical and conservative, as Piven and Cloward (1977) argue. Based on my data, I dispute the conclusion that formalized SMOs necessarily become oligarchical. In fact, many seem more democratic than informal SMOs because they follow routinized procedures that make it more difficult for individual leaders to attain disproportionate power. As Freeman (1973) argues, "structureless" SMOs are most subject to domination by individuals.

The tendency of formalized SMOs to engage in more institutionalized strategies and tactics than informal SMOs might be interpreted as a conservative development, given findings that militant direct-action tactics force elite concessions (cf. Jenkins and Eckert 1986). Informal SMOs, with their more flexible structures, are more likely to innovate direct-action tactics. However, the institutionalization of movement tactics by formalized SMOs does not necessarily mean that movement goals become less radical; an alternative interpretation is that movement demands and representatives become incorporated into mainstream politics. For example, the National Organization for Women is now an important representative of women's interests in the political arena. While the long-term implications of this phenomenon for the social movement sector and the political system require further investigation, it is certainly possible for formalized SMOs to exert a progressive influence on the political system.

Finally, my research raises the question of whether movements inevitably become formalized or institutionalized, as suggested by classical theories of social movements, which argue that movements progress through stages toward institutionalization (see Lang and Lang 1961, Turner and Killian 1957 for discussions of such stage theories). In the case of the pro-choice movement, there has clearly been a trend toward formalization. As Gamson (1975, 91) notes, there does seem to be a kernel of truth to theories that posit an inevitable trend toward bureaucratization or formalization. However, as Gamson also notes, "the reality is considered more complex" in that some SMOs begin with bureaucratic or formalized structures and others never develop formalized structure. Although neither Gamson nor I found cases of SMOs that developed informal structures after formalization,[13] such a change is conceivable under certain circumstances (e.g., if nonprofessional staff are hired to replace professional managers, a development most likely at the local level). Classical theories of the "natural history" of a movement focus on the institutionalization of a movement as a whole and ignore variations in the experiences of different SMOs within the movement. My research shows that SMOs vary in the ways in which they deal with internal organizational problems and changes in the environment. Formalization is one important means of solving organizational problems, particularly as SMOs grow larger; however, SMOs can also develop alternative structures. Important variations exist within the two broad categories of SMO structure that I have identified; further empirical research on leadership roles and SMO structures and their impact on organizational goals and activities is necessary.

Notes

The research for this chapter was supported by National Science Foundation Dissertation Grant No. SES-83 15574. Frank Dobbin, Carol Mueller, Rod Nelson, and two ASR reviewers provided helpful comments on earlier drafts of this chapter.

1. Manuscript collections used include the Women's Collection at Northwestern University, which contains newsletters and documents from NARAL, RCAR, ZPG, CWLU, ICMCA/ARA/NARAL of Illinois, and several coalitions; the papers of ICMA/ARA/NARAL and Chicago NOW at the University of Illinois, Chicago; the CWLU papers at the Chicago Historical Society; the Lawrence Lader papers at the New York Public Library; the public portions of the NARAL and NOW papers at the Schlesinger Library of Radcliffe College; and private papers provided by informants.

2. Volunteers may be "professionals" in the sense that they spend many years, perhaps a lifetime, doing movement work. However, they differ from professional managers in that they do not earn a living through movement work.

3. The term *bureaucratic* might be substituted for "formalized" (cf. Gamson 1975). However, I have used the latter because SMOs are never as bureaucratic as more established organizations such as corporations and government agencies (cf. Zald and Ash 1966, 329).

4. I have used the term *informal* to describe this type of SMO structure for want of a more positive label. The terminology of the existing literature on organizations and social movements is inadequate. The term *classical* used by McCarthy and Zald (1973, 1977) does not describe the structure of the SMO. The more descriptive term *grass roots* implies a mass membership base that may or may not be present in either "formalized" or "informal" SMOs. The term *collectivist* used by Rothschild-Whitt (1979) refers to a specific type of decision-making structure that is distinguished from "bureaucratic" organization; not all informal SMOs are collectivist. Freeman's (1979, 169) term *communal* or "small, local, and functionally

undifferentiated" organizations is inappropriate because not all informal SMOs are local organizations.

5. An appendix with further details on sample SMOs is available on request from the author.

6. The distinction between such formalized SMOs and interest groups or lobbies is not a sharp one (cf. Useem and Zald 1982). There is clearly a need for greater conceptual clarification of the differences between formalized SMOs and interest groups based on empirical research.

7. The conflict between entrepreneurial and professional roles also became apparent to me when I interviewed the anti-abortion leader Joseph Scheidler as part of another study. Scheidler helped to form several anti-abortion groups and was fired as executive director from two organizations for engaging in militant direct-action tactics without going through the proper organizational channels (see Roeser 1983). He finally founded his own organization in 1980, the Pro-Life Action League, in which he is unencumbered by bureaucratic decision-making procedures. As he told me in a 1981 interview:

> I don't like boards of directors—you always have to check with them when you want to do something and I was always getting in trouble with the board. So I resigned, or they fired me, however you want to put it, because they didn't like my tactics. . . . The Pro-Life Action League is my organization. I'm the chairman of the board and the other two board members are my wife and best friend. If I want to do something, I call up my wife and ask her if she thinks it's a good idea. Then I have two-thirds approval of the board! (Personal interview)

Additional examples of such conflict between the entrepreneurial and professional roles in the social movements literature can be cited. In the farmworker movement, there has been conflict over the leadership of Cesar Chavez, who attempted to maintain personal control over the United Farm Workers at a time when others wanted to create a more bureaucratic union structure (see Barr 1985; Jenkins 1985a, 204–6). In the gay rights movement, the "brash" activist Randy Wicker left the New York Mattachine Society to found "the Homosexual League of New York, a one-man organization designed to give him a free hand to pursue his own plans" (D'Emilio 1983, 158–59). In the environmental movement, Friends of the Earth founder David Brower was ousted from the organization after he failed in his attempts to maintain control over the SMO and prevent it from becoming formalized (Rauber 1986). And in Mothers Against Drunk Driving (MADD), there has been conflict over the role of MADD's entrepreneur, Candy Lightner, who has attempted to maintain personal control over a bureaucratizing organization (Reinarman 1985).

8. By all accounts this leader had an extraordinary ability to recruit volunteers for various tasks. As one of my informants explained, "She was really effective at getting people to do things. She would keep after you so that it was easier to do what she wanted rather than have her continue to bug you." Another activist concurred, "There was nothing like having her call you at 7 A.M. and tell you what you were going to do that day!" The problem of reliance on the personal characteristics of this director was later recognized by a board member who commented

that the problem with the longtime director was that she kept knowledge about the organization "in HER head" (document in private papers), making it difficult for her successor to assume control.

9. The "house meeting" tactic, which involved holding meetings in the homes of NARAL members or other interested persons, was a recruitment tool developed as part of a national NARAL grassroots organizing program.

10. The delay experienced by Women Organized for Reproductive Choice in obtaining the 501(c)(3) tax status that allows a nonprofit organization to obtain tax-deductible contributions also reveals the difficulties that informal SMOs have with organizational maintenance. Although there were several local Chicago foundations willing to fund organizations such as WORC, the SMO was unable to take advantage of these opportunities for some time because it had not obtained the necessary tax status. When I asked WORC's sole part-time, nonprofessional staff leader why the tax status had not been obtained, she replied that the delay occurred because she was the only one who knew how to apply for the status, but that she simply had not had the time to do it yet.

11. Abortion-referral activities were regarded by many activists as a militant means of challenging the system (see Lader 1973). In the case of women's movement projects such as the CWLU Abortion Counseling Service, there was an attempt to create an alternative type of organization as well as to serve the needs of women.

12. *The Silent Scream* attempted to use sonography to make its case that the fetus suffers pain in an abortion. The film was distributed to members of Congress and received a great deal of media attention, helping to shift the debate on abortion to "scientific" issues.

13. Although it never developed a structure that could be called formalized, one SMO in my sample, Women Organized for Reproductive Choice, did become even more informal as it became smaller.

References

Barr, Evan T. 1985. "Sour Grapes." *New Republic* 193 (25 November): 2–23.

Cable, Sherry, 1984. "Professionalization in Social Movement Organization: A Case Study of Pennsylvanians for Biblical Morality." *Sociological Focus* 17: 287–304.

Carmen, Arlene, and Howard Moody. 1973. *Abortion Counseling and Social Change*. Valley Forge, Pa.: Judson Press.

Delgado, Gary. 1986. *Organizing the Movement: The Roots and Growth of ACORN*. Philadelphia: Temple University Press.

D'Emilio, John. 1983. *Sexual Politics, Sexual Communities*. Chicago: University of Chicago Press.

Freeman, Jo. 1973. "The Tyranny of Structurelessness." *MS* 2 (July): 76–78, 86–89.

———. 1975. *The Politics of Women's Liberation*. New York: Longman.

———. 1979. "Resource Mobilization and Strategy: A Model for Analyzing Social

Movement Organization Actions." In *The Dynamics of Social Movements*, ed. Mayer N. Zald and John D. McCarthy. Cambridge, Mass.: Winthrop, 167–89.

Gamson, William A. 1975. *The Strategy of Social Protest*. Homewood, Ill.: Dorsey Press.

Haines, Herbert M. 1984. "Black Radicalization and the Funding of Civil Rights: 1957–1970." *Social Problems* 32, no. 1 (October): 31–43.

Jenkins, J. Craig. 1983. "Resource Mobilization Theory and the Study of Social Movements." *Annual Review of Sociology* 9: 527–53.

———. 1985a. *The Politics of Insurgency: The Farm Worker Movement in the 1960s*. New York: Columbia University Press.

———. 1985b. "Foundation Funding of Progressive Social Movements." In *Grant Seekers Guide: Funding Sourcebook*, ed. Jill R. Shellow. Mt. Kisco, N.Y.: Moyer Bell, 7–17.

Jenkins, J. Craig, and Craig M. Eckert. 1986. "Channeling Black Insurgency: Elite Patronage and Professional Social Movement Organizations in the Development of the Black Movement." *American Sociological Review* 51, no. 6 (December): 812–29.

Kalter, Joanmarie. 1985. "Abortion Bias: How Network Coverage Has Tilted to the ProLifers." *TV Guide* 33: 7–17.

Kleidman, Robert. 1986. "Opposing the Good War: Mobilization and Professionalization in the Emergency Peace Campaign." *Research in Social Movements, Conflicts and Change* 9: 177–200.

Lader, Lawrence. 1966. *Abortion*. Boston: Beacon Press.

———. 1973. *Abortion II: Making the Revolution*. Boston: Beacon Press.

Lang, Kurt, and Gladys E. Lang. 1961. *Collective Dynamics*. New York: Crowell.

McAdam, Doug. 1983. "Tactical Innovation and the Pace of Insurgency." *American Sociological Journal* 48, no. 6 (December): 735–54.

McCarthy, John D., and Mayer N. Zald. 1973. *The Trend of Social Movements in America: Professionalization and Resource Mobilization*. Morristown, N.J.: General Learning Press.

———. 1977. "Resource Mobilization and Social Movements: A Partial Theory." *American Journal of Sociology* 82: 1212–41.

McFarland, Andrew S. 1984. *Common Cause*. Chatham, N.J.: Chatham House.

Michels, Robert. [1915] 1962. *Political Parties*. New York: Collier.

Morris, Aldon D. 1984. *The Origins of the Civil Rights Movement: Black Communities Organizing for Change*. New York: Free Press.

NARAL of Illinois papers. Manuscripts Department, University of Illinois, Chicago, library.

Oberschall, Anthony. 1973. *Social Conflict and Social Movements*. Englewood Cliffs, N.J.: Prentice-Hall.

Oliver, Pamela. 1983. "The Mobilization of Paid and Volunteer Activists in the Neighborhood Movement." *Research in Social Movements, Conflicts and Change* 5: 133–70.

Piven, Frances Fox, and Richard A. Cloward. 1977. *Poor People's Movements*. New York: Vintage Books.

Rauber, Paul. 1986. "With Friends Like These." *Mother Jones* 11: 35–37, 47–49.

Reinarman, Craig. 1985. "Social Movements and Social Problems: 'Mothers Against Drunk Drivers,' Restrictive Alcohol Laws and Social Control in the 1980s." Paper presented at the Annual Meeting of the Society for the Study of Social Problems. Washington, D.C., August 23–26.

Roche, John P., and Stephen Sachs. 1965. "The Bureaucrat and the Enthusiast: An Exploration of the Leadership of Social Movements." *Western Political Quarterly* 8, no. 2 (June): 248–61.

Roeser, Thomas F. 1983. "The Pro-life Movement's Holy Terror."*Chicago Reader* 12 (44): 1, 14–24.

Rothschild-Whitt, Joyce. 1979. "The Collectivist Organization: An Alternative to Rational-Bureaucratic Models." *American Sociological Review* 44: 509–27.

Rupp, Leila J., and Verta Taylor. 1987. *Survival in the Doldrums.* New York: Oxford University Press.

Staggenborg, Suzanne. 1985. "Patterns of Collective Action in the Abortion Conflict: An Organizational Analysis of the Pro-Choice Movement." Ph.D. diss., Northwestern University.

———. 1986. "Coalition Work in the Pro-Choice Movement: Organizational and Environmental Opportunities and Obstacles." *Social Problems* 33, no. 5: 374–90.

Turner, Ralph, and Lewis Killian. 1957. *Collective Behavior.* Englewood Cliffs, N.J.: Prentice-Hall.

Useem, Bert, and Mayer N. Zald. 1982. "From Pressure Group to Social Movement: Organizational Dilemmas of the Effort to Promote Nuclear Power," *Social Problems* 30 (December): 144–56.

Walsh, Edward J. 1981. "Resource Mobilization and Citizen Protest in Communities Around Three Mile Island." *Social Problems* 29, no. 1 (October): 1–21.

Zald, Mayer N., and Roberta Ash. 1966. "Social Movement Organizations: Growth, Decay and Change." *Social Forces* 44, no. 3 (March): 327–41.

7

AIDS, Anger, and Activism: ACT UP As a Social Movement Organization

Abigail Halcli

The AIDS activist movement is one of the most visible social movements to emerge since the 1980s. Arising initially out of the gay and lesbian community, AIDS activism has generated a diverse array of social movement organizations whose structures, goals, strategies, and tactics vary widely. The organizations that have emerged in response to AIDS range from those that are bureaucratic and centralized to others that are informally structured and activist driven. Those involved in the movement share the same broad goal of ending the AIDS epidemic but they differ considerably in their views on how to achieve this.

The organizational forms and goals adopted by movement organizations shape their ability to mobilize resources, participants, and supporters, to affect policy-making, and to maintain the organization over time (Freeman 1975, this volume; Gamson 1975; Piven and Cloward 1977; Staggenborg 1989). In this chapter I explore some of the consequences of choices about structures and strategies for social movement organizations (SMOs) through a discussion of the AIDS activist group ACT UP (the AIDS Coalition To Unleash Power) during its origins and peak period of mobilization, roughly 1987 through 1991. This research is based on interviews and participant observation in ACT UP chapters in Columbus, Ohio, and New York City.

ACT UP's organizational philosophy, strategies, and tactics differed in important ways from other SMOs that emerged in response to the AIDS epidemic. Many, such as the national network of AIDS Task Forces, have formal organizational structures and emphasize conventional programs to educate the public about this health crisis and provide services to the affected communities. The founders of ACT UP were firmly committed to creating a nonbureaucratic and participatory SMO. Members often engaged in unconventional actions in order to challenge cultural perceptions of AIDS and the stigmatization of people with AIDS (PWAs) and to provide a positive identity for the activists. At the same time, ACT UP wanted to have dialogues with medical institutions and influence policymaking at the highest levels. The effort to find a workable balance between this mix of sometimes seemingly contradictory goals and tactics created tensions within ACT UP chapters throughout the United States. ACT UP, therefore, serves as an instructive case for understanding some of the ways in which SMOs address a variety of organizational dilemmas.

Approaches to Understanding Social Movement Organizations

A number of typologies have been developed to make sense of the variety of goals, structures, strategies, and tactics exhibited by SMOs. A common distinction is whether an SMO's goals are primarily instrumental or expressive (Curtis and Zurcher 1974). Instrumental SMOs are thought to have external goals and to provide their members with purposive incentives based on attaining these goals. Expressive SMOs, on the other hand, are presumed to provide participants with solidary incentives derived from the act of taking part in the organization. This distinction between instrumental and expressive movements is broadly reflected in the differences between the two predominant theories of social movements—resource mobilization and new social movement theories.

Because they assume "there is no fundamental difference between movement behavior and institutionalized behavior" (Morris and Herring 1986, 157), resource mobilization theorists have adopted an instrumental framework for analyzing the formal elements of SMOs. This approach focuses on how movement organizations are affected by the availability of resources, the effectiveness of organizational structures, and the constraints and opportunities provided by their larger environment (Jenkins 1983). It assumes that instrumental goals are the central purpose of SMOs while solidary goals, including the satisfaction of the social and psychological needs of participants, are secondary. Resource mobilization theorists contend that SMOs that adopt bureaucratized and centralized structures will have a greater likelihood of success (Gamson 1975). This theory has been criticized for overlooking the informal and noninstitutional or even anti-institutional dimensions of social movement activity. It does not adequately address the cultural, expressive, and identity-building elements central to many social movement organizations.

New social movement theory provides an alternative model for analyzing social movements, focusing primarily on their cultural and identity-building elements, including the significance of politicized identities. Though there has been debate over what is really "new" about contemporary movements (Dalton and Kuechler 1990, Scott 1990, Calhoun 1993, D'Anieri et al. 1990), it is generally agreed that their use of unconventional and direct action forms and their anti-institutional orientation distinguish social movements from conventional forms of political participation (Klandermans and Tarrow 1988, Touraine 1981, Offe 1985). Critics of new social movement theory contend that this approach does not adequately explain the formalized dimensions of movement organizations or their internal structures. New social movement theorists have also been criticized for overstating the cultural aspects of new movements while underestimating the linkages between movements and more institutionally oriented political behavior.[1]

It's clear that the conceptual distinction between organizations that are either formal and instrumental or informal and expressive oversimplifies the mode of operation of many SMOs. In organizations such as ACT UP, the instrumental and expressive elements cannot be separated in its goal structure. Though it was most widely known for its unconventional tactics that challenged the cultural perceptions of AIDS and people with AIDS, ACT UP members were also involved in activities that, rather than being primarily expressive, had clear instrumental goals and political targets. In the following sections I explore the coexistence of instrumental and expressive dimensions within ACT UP while highlighting the tensions that resulted from the existence of diverse goals and constituencies within a single social movement organization.

Origins of the AIDS Movement: The Mobilization of the Gay and Lesbian Community

Most organizations that developed in response to AIDS trace their roots to the gay community. Though the fact that AIDS had a devastating impact on this population is very significant, it does not adequately explain why AIDS activism and its organizations first developed in the gay community rather than among other affected groups, such as intravenous drug users, Haitians, and hemophiliacs. Nor does it explain the diversity of organizational types, goals, and actions that characterized this movement. To explain why this community was the first to mobilize around this issue, it is necessary to highlight some of its distinctive characteristics, which contributed to its mobilization potential.

With its emphasis on the emergent phase of movements and the way in which organizations mobilize resources and participants, resource mobilization theory provides a valuable framework for explaining why the gay and lesbian community had a higher potential for mobilization than other affected groups. Research has indicated that indigenous organizations and preexisting networks play an important role in mobilizing people into social movements (Freeman, 1975, this volume). In his study of the origins of the civil rights movement, Morris (1984) focuses on the role played by indigenous black institutions, particularly black churches, in the rise of this movement. He asserts that the internal organization of the black community and the resources and leadership this provided were the critical factors that enabled the civil rights movement to gain momentum and endure widespread repression. Studies of social movements have shown that groups with distinctive and exclusive identities, as well as dense interpersonal networks, are more readily mobilized. In his study of the United Farm Workers Union, Jenkins (1983) found that seasonal farm workers had a greater potential for mobilization into the union than permanent workers or migrants because they lived together in residential communities and were not dependent on labor contractors for housing or transportation. As a result, the seasonal workers developed cohesive interpersonal networks that facilitated communication and the formation of common definitions of grievances. Similar factors contributed to the early mobilization of the gay community in response to the AIDS epidemic. The existence of large gay populations in cities such as New York and San Francisco promoted the development of social networks and common cultural ties among community members (D'Emilio 1983). In addition, certain segments of the community had been organized politically since the late 1960s into a gay and lesbian movement.

Initially, AIDS groups drew almost exclusively upon the organizations and networks of this movement, with such groups as the National Gay and Lesbian Task Force and the Gay Rights Lobby providing experienced activists and contacts (Altman 1987). A large portion of the funding for AIDS organizations came directly from gay and lesbian individuals and groups (Kramer 1989). Finally, as a predominately white, educated, and middle-class community, gay men and lesbians were in a more favorable position to mobilize and articulate their demands than other affected groups (Altman 1988). The presence of these features facilitated the mobilization of the gay and lesbian community when it first experienced the impact of AIDS by providing it with the necessary resources to develop social movement organizations.

Since the mid-1980s, the AIDS epidemic has given rise to a diverse social movement with many organizational forms. Some resemble the professional social movement organizations identified by McCarthy and Zald

(1977) in that they are bureaucratic and centralized with a full-time, paid leadership cadre that operates the organization on behalf of the "beneficiary constituents." These organizations tend to focus on raising funds from "conscience constituents" so they can provide services for people with AIDS and operate educational programs designed to alter individual "high-risk" behaviors and therefore stem the spread of HIV. ACT UP, on the other hand, emerged as a reaction to what the founders perceived as the government's mismanagement of the AIDS epidemic and the inadequacy of the response mounted by more service-oriented groups. With an explicit commitment to the use of direct action tactics, ACT UP's founders wanted to apply pressure to the political and medical institutions charged with managing this health crisis while also drawing public attention to a wide variety of AIDS-related issues.

The Development of ACT UP

Our continued existence as gay men upon the face of the earth is at stake. Unless we fight for our lives, we shall die. In all the history of homosexuality we have never before been so close to death and extinction. (Kramer 1989, 127)

While giving a speech at the Gay and Lesbian Community Center in New York City in March 1987, Larry Kramer, a well-known playwright and gay activist, recited the above passage from an article he had written for the gay newspaper *The New York Native*. The article was entitled "1,112 And Counting," in reference to the number of people who had died from AIDS at the time of its printing in 1983. Four years later, as Kramer addressed an audience of 250 men and women, the official AIDS death count had risen to 32,000, of whom 10,000 were residents of New York City. As Kramer indicated, nearly every member of New York City's gay community had in some way been touched by this deadly illness. Kramer continued his speech by criticizing the Gay Men's Health Crisis (GMHC), which he had cofounded in September 1981. GMHC was devoted to raising funds for AIDS research and educating the gay community about this health crisis. Kramer complained that GMHC had become a wealthy and bureaucratic organization that was primarily involved in providing services for PWAs. He asserted that this approach would only manage the AIDS epidemic but not stop it. Kramer also contended that the government and medical response to AIDS was shockingly inadequate. AIDS research, he argued, was being held up by bureaucratic delays and insufficient funding as well as the insensitivity of government officials and doctors to what was widely perceived as a "gay issue." In order to influence the organizations charged with managing the AIDS crisis, Kramer believed that more radical political action, including "protests, pickets, and arrests" (Kramer 1989, 136), was necessary, and he concluded his speech by encouraging his audience to join him in starting a new organization devoted to such direct action tactics. Evidently, Kramer managed to tap into feelings of anger and indignation within the gay community because two days later over 300 people turned out for a meeting to form ACT UP.

Organizational Membership and Structure

ACT UP grew very quickly; by 1991 there were 113 chapters worldwide (table 7.1). Because the founders were committed to a decentralized organizational structure, all ACT UP chapters remained independent of one another, though they maintained close ties and often coordinated their efforts for demonstrations, conferences, and the sharing of information pertaining to AIDS-related issues. ACT UP chapters did not keep an official membership list, and anyone who was interested in attending meetings and participating in demonstrations was welcomed by the group. Each chapter elected an office coordinator who was responsible for managing the day-to-day business of the organization and the weekly general membership meetings. Like all ACT UP members, the office coordinator served as an unpaid volunteer.

Though ACT UP explicitly rejected the notion of having "official" leadership positions, most chapters had a leadership cadre that played a central role in making decisions concerning finances and organizational strategies; it also represented ACT UP in meetings with medical representatives and policy makers. Because of its informal structure and encouragement of open discussion and debate, ACT UP's weekly meetings were often very long and heated affairs. Group decisions were made either by consensus or majority rule, depending on the size and preference of the membership. In their efforts to maintain a nonbureaucratic structure ACT UP members chose not to write a constitution, but rather developed a "working document" that described the purposes of the different committees, election procedures, funding, and methods for organizing protests and direct action. It also outlined individual rights during interactions with the police and the FBI (ACT UP/Columbus 1990b). ACT UP chapters had a "workspace" rather than an office in an attempt, as one member reported, "to not be so professional."

Though commonly perceived as a gay and lesbian organization, ACT UP explicitly defined itself as a diverse and inclusive AIDS activist group (ACT UP/Columbus 1990a). Nonetheless, like other AIDS organizations,

TABLE 7.1
National and International ACT UP Chapters (1991)

Adelaide	Hawaii	Perth
Albany	Houston	Philadelphia
Albany Youth Chapter	Ithaca	Phoenix
Alexandria	Jackson	Pittsburgh
Amsterdam	Jacksonville	Portland
Anchorage	Kansas City	Provincetown
Atlanta	Lancaster	Puerto Rico
Austin	Lawrence	Redwood Region (CA)
Baltimore	Leeds	Research Triangle Park
Barcelona	Little Rock	(NC)
Belgium	London	Rhode Island
Berlin	Long Beach	Rochester
Boise	Long Island	Sacramento
Boston	Los Angeles	St. Louis
Brighton	Madison	San Diego
Brisbane	Maine	San Francisco
Canberra	Manchester	Santa Barbara
Central Illinois	Melbourne	Santa Fe
Central Jersey	Mendocino	Seattle
Central Valley (CA)	Miami	Shreveport
Chicago	Milwaukee	Sonoma Co. (CA)
Cincinnati	Minnesota	South Jersey
Columbia (Portland, OR)	Monroe	Stockholm
Columbus	Montreal	Sydney
Contra Costa Co. (CA)	Moscow	Syracuse
Dallas	Nevada	Tallahassee
Delaware	New Hampshire	Tennessee
Denver	New Haven	Tokyo
Detroit	New Jersey	Tulsa
District of Columbia	New Orleans	Vancouver
East Bay (CA)	North Carolina	Vermont
Edinburgh	North Coast (CA)	Victoria B.C.
Fort Lauderdale	Oberlin	Warsaw
Gainesville	Oklahoma	Westchester
Glasgow	Oklahoma City	Western MA
Golden Gate	Olympia	Western NY State
Harrisburg	Orange County	Wichita State Univ.
Hartford	Paris	Windy City

Sources: ACT UP/New York and ACT UP/San Francisco.

ACT UP recruited a substantial number of its participants from the gay
and lesbian community. While ACT UP's membership consisted primarily of gay white men, an increasing number of women and people of color
also became involved as larger numbers of these groups were affected by
AIDS. By 1991, some members estimated that about one-third of ACT
UP's participants were women. Most members were in their twenties and
thirties and were drawn from a variety of fields including the arts, social
services, medical professions, and business. It was widely perceived by
ACT UP members that the organization was greatly enriched by the diverse skills, knowledge, and resources provided by its membership.

Though many ACT UP participants were HIV infected, certainly not
everyone in the organization had the virus. Many participants were
drawn to AIDS activism because they had friends or family members who
were HIV infected or had died from AIDS. When explaining their
involvement in ACT UP, it was quite typical to hear members say, "I got
tired of seeing my friends die," and they therefore felt a strong desire to
get involved with other people who were committed to fighting the
spread of AIDS. Many members who were activists in the gay and lesbian
movement said they became involved in AIDS activism because they saw
it as the central issue on the gay and lesbian political agenda.

Goals, Strategies, and Tactics

As their statement of purpose declared, the primary goal of ACT UP was
to obtain treatment for people with HIV infection, or as one organizational slogan proclaimed, "get drugs into bodies." Connected with this
goal was the idea of fighting "expertism" (ACT UP/Columbus 1990a).
Government agencies, doctors, and pharmaceutical companies are generally considered to be the experts in managing a health crisis, and they also
control the organizations and resources utilized to address them. ACT UP
members contended that such expertism allowed credentialed individuals to make decisions affecting the survival of people with AIDS while
rendering the affected communities powerless. ACT UP was therefore
committed to gaining access to and disseminating the latest information
on AIDS research while negotiating a role for PWAs in the political and
medical decision-making processes. At the same time, ACT UP members
were concerned with challenging societal perceptions of AIDS and PWAs.

In order to accomplish these goals, ACT UP members utilized a variety
of direct action tactics. As one member indicated:

> ACT UP's tactics are researching issues, telling the truth, asking people to do
> the right thing. And if they don't do it when we ask politely, which we al-

ways do at first, then we start asking more loudly and more insistently. But we never hurt anybody.

Committed in principle to nonviolence, ACT UP's tactics included demonstrations, civil disobedience, and boycotts. Often they targeted the government agencies and medical institutions that had the primary responsibility for managing the AIDS epidemic. Because it controls the licensing of new drugs in the United States, the Food and Drug Administration (FDA) was a constant target of ACT UP. On several occasions, group members used civil disobedience and protests to try to force the FDA to speed its lengthy research procedures and the release of promising new drugs. In their first demonstration, which occurred a few weeks after the group was formed, over 250 activists stopped traffic for hours on Wall Street to protest the drug approval process. An effigy of Dr. Frank Young, then commissioner of the FDA, was also hanged during the demonstration. Several weeks later, when Young announced the establishment of a speedier drug approval process, CBS's Dan Rather credited ACT UP's pressure tactics for this success (Crimp and Rolston 1990).

In addition, private pharmaceutical companies that research or manufacture drugs for AIDS patients were also targeted through boycotts and demonstrations. Burroughs Wellcome, the manufacturer of the AIDS drug AZT, was targeted by ACT UP because of the high cost of this drug. In one of ACT UP's most celebrated actions, an affinity group (a small group of members who participate as units in acts of civil disobedience but whose actions are not necessarily sanctioned by ACT UP) calling themselves the "Power Tools" managed to stop trading on the floor of the New York Stock Exchange in September 1989. The activists chained themselves to a balcony, blew foghorns, and unfurled a banner proclaiming "SELL WELLCOME," thus encouraging people to sell their stocks in a corporation that was perceived as contributing to the suffering of PWAs. Within an hour, over 1,500 demonstrators showed up to protest the high price of AZT. A few weeks later, when Burroughs Wellcome lowered the price of AZT from $8,000 to $6,400 a year, ACT UP's pressure tactics were once again credited (*Newsweek* 1990).

A considerable amount of ACT UP's activities were centered on challenging the moralization that has accompanied the AIDS crisis. ACT UP attacked the numerous and primarily negative cultural perceptions of both AIDS and homosexuality. At the same time, this organization was involved in trying to forge a positive identity for homosexuals and for people with AIDS (Gamson 1989). This focus on changing cultural attitudes and identity-building was evident in their art work as illustrated by a well-known ACT UP poster that appeared on city buses in San Francisco and New York City. This poster portrayed three stylish interracial couples kissing. Though it was modeled after a United Colors of Benneton fashion advertisement, ACT UP's version was different in that it depicted heterosexual, gay, and lesbian couples. The caption read "Kissing doesn't kill. Greed and indifference do." This poster clearly attacked a commonly held belief about the transmission of the HIV virus as well as stereotypes about gays and lesbians. In addition, it shifted the blame for this health crisis from "deviant" sexual practices to the inadequacy of the social response.

Street theater was another cultural and expressive tactic for which ACT UP was well known. Performed in conjunction with demonstrations, this tactic included staging "die-ins" where participants "died" while others drew chalk outlines around their bodies. They also incorporated coffins, fake blood, and "red tape" into their demonstrations. By using street theater as a tactic, ACT UP members attempted to illustrate the effects of the AIDS crisis in dramatic and shocking ways.

ACT UP's activities during the Gulf War also demonstrate its use of shock tactics and civil disobedience to dramatically publicize AIDS issues. Chanting "Act Up, Fight Back, Fight AIDS, Not Iraq," ACT UP affinity groups disrupted the CBS "Evening News" and the PBS "MacNeil-Lehrer NewsHour." Before being arrested at CBS, one protester managed to jump on camera while anchor Dan Rather directed a break to a commercial, and another activist at PBS tried to chain himself to newscaster Robert MacNeil (*Columbus Dispatch* 1991a). By coming into the living rooms of households throughout the United States, ACT UP hoped to shock people into an awareness of the use of tax dollars to fund a war instead of health care. The following day, ACT UP protesters in New York marched through the city and clogged traffic at Grand Central Terminal during the evening rush hour, once again to publicize their outrage at military spending. Chanting "Money For AIDS, Not For War," activists emptied racks of train schedules and tossed them in the air. They also spilled fake blood and strung red tape across the platforms while chanting "We're Dying Of Red Tape" (*Columbus Dispatch* 1991b).

While attacking the popular perception of AIDS as "the gay disease," ACT UP still flaunted "gayness" as a shock tactic. Picketers chanted, "we're here, we're queer, and we're not going shopping!" When the Washington police wore bright yellow gloves while arresting sixty-four protesters, thus fueling the public's fear of contracting AIDS through casual contact, demonstrators chanted, "Your Gloves Don't Match Your Shoes! You'll See It On The News!" (Crimp and Rolston 1990). ACT UP prominently displayed symbols of the gay community, such as the pink triangle. Once required by German Nazis to be worn by homosexuals, gays and lesbians appropriated it to emphasize their history of oppression. ACT UP used the pink triangle to symbolize its connection to the gay and lesbian movement, but inverted it in order to resignify and claim it as their own (Gamson 1989; Crimp and Rolston 1990).

Tactics like these brought notoriety. The media portrayed ACT UP as "radical," "militant," and even as "the gay community's shock troops in the war against AIDS" (*Newsweek* 1990). This characterization was generally shared by its members, though some did question it. As one member indicated:

> I think [the radical reputation] has a lot more to do with our perceived sexual orientation than it does with what we are actually doing. Or maybe our perceived infection. Somehow we are seen as terribly violent and dangerous. And it may just have to do with the fact that we challenge certain conventions that other people don't.

ACT UP's "Stop the Church" demonstration in New York City stirred up a great deal of controversy in the media and in the gay and lesbian community. In order to protest Cardinal O'Conner's policies against safer sex education, activists staged a die-in at St. Patrick's Cathedral during Sunday Mass, in which some protesters tossed condoms in the air and chained themselves to pews. Not surprisingly, the media response to this action was overwhelmingly negative, but some gays and lesbians also felt the demonstrators had gone too far by disrupting a church service. Participants in the demonstration responded to their critics by asserting the great urgency of their claims and the nonviolent nature of their protest. One participant said: "because we went inside the cathedral, we denied Catholic parishioners their freedom of religion. Their rights became the focus; our life-and-death issues were secondary" (Crimp and Rolston 1990, 138). Another observed, "The mere act of my lying silently in the aisle . . . was regarded the most violent, dangerous act. I laid down on the floor! Silently! What could be more simple and nonthreatening than that?"

Street actions such as these played a significant role in the group's ideology. Many joined because they believed that maneuvering through the established political channels was too slow and that shock tactics were not only morally justifiable but absolutely essential. As ACT UP founder Larry Kramer stated, "you don't get anything by being nice, good little boys and girls" (Kramer 1989, 290). Another member said: "We do a lot of really nasty things, but it gets stuff done. I don't see how you could stop at anything if someone you love is dying and that can be changed and you feel that not enough is being done." ACT UP also sees its action as benefiting other groups. One said: "What [ACT UP] is doing is crucial, because yelling and screaming makes it an issue. Everything we have done, even the most controversial things, have gotten us more press, more attention, and more members. [Other AIDS organizations] can be that much more radical because we are stretching the limits within which they are conservative. I think that is one of the functions that ACT UP serves."

Direct action provided a unifying focus for many ACT UP members. However, ACT UP chapters were also involved in more institutionally oriented activities. Like a conventional interest group, ACT UP wanted to influence AIDS funding and legislation. Therefore, some members testified before state legislatures and attained appointments to research advisory boards and government committees. One member was nominated by Physicians for Life to sit on a congressional committee devoted to women and AIDS as a result of the amicable dialogue her chapter established with this organization. On a national level, ACT UP members held positions on the advisory boards of the AIDS Clinical Trials Group and pharmaceutical companies. Activities such as these illustrate how both expressive and instrumental goals coexisted within ACT UP. As we will see in the following section, efforts to find a workable balance between these different goals were at times the source of tensions within the organization.

Diverse Constituencies and Organizational Tensions

In combining diverse goals, strategies, and tactics, ACT UP appealed to two broad groups with differing opinions on the scope of ACT UP's goals. One group, particularly the members of ACT UP's Treatment and Data Committee (T&D), wanted to focus on AIDS as a medical condition and getting treatment for people with HIV. They concentrated on negotiating with government officials, researchers, and pharmaceutical corporations in order to affect decisions about AIDS research and drug trials. The other group believed that since the government and medical response to AIDS was shaped by homophobia, race, sex, and class, these issues must be tackled as well. They encouraged members to become involved in policy issues such as national health care, housing, needle exchange, and immigration laws.

These different approaches were evident during a heated debate at an ACT UP/New York general membership meeting in 1991. The Women's Action Committee had proposed a six-month moratorium in negotiations with the National Institute for Allergy and Infectious Diseases (NIAID) to protest AIDS Clinical Trial Group 076 (ACTG 076), which studied the effectiveness of AZT in preventing perinatal transmission of the HIV virus. This committee claimed that ACTG 076 was scientifically and ethically unsound for pregnant women and that these individuals had not made an informed consent about participation because NIAID withheld vital information about the study (ACT UP/New York 1991). Other ACT UP members complained that a moratorium would be a counterproductive tactic. A T&D committee member insisted that NIAID would be "thrilled" not to talk with ACT UP because "nobody in government cares about AIDS anymore!" Like many of the other T&D committee members, he urged ACT UP to keep up negotiations.

Such debates highlighted the divisions within ACT UP. Some members felt that the treatment focus promoted by the T&D committee marginalized other AIDS-related issues that were of particular importance to women, racial and ethnic minorities, and people with low incomes. The fact that T&D members tended to be white, male, and from professional backgrounds served to reinforce this perception. The access enjoyed by some T&D members to researchers and policy makers promoted a view that they were a privileged group at times out of touch with the urgent issues faced by less privileged members. A female member noted that "[T&D members] meet with high-level people all the time. How many women and Latinos meet with these people and have their phone numbers in their books?" T&D members were sensitive to these criticisms, though some countered that such internal debates served as a distraction from the fight against AIDS. As one T&D committee member said, "This is not about who is more radical; it's about results." He felt the T&D committee should be encouraged, not criticized.

ACT UP chapters across the United States experienced similar conflicts, and not all were able to resolve them. By 1991 this division split chapters in Seattle, San Francisco, Portland, and Chicago. Usually a few members would leave the larger group to form a new organization devoted to treatment issues while the original chapter maintained a broader focus. However, many members believed that ACT UP could and should accommodate diverse approaches. A New York ACT UP participant stated, "we've always done our best work with people on the inside and outside." Other members maintained that such ideological and tactical disagreements were inevitable. ACT UP, asserted one participant, "tends to attract strong personalities." An informant seemed to share this opinion: "It's a movement of people who know a lot and are angry because they know a lot. It's all very human and complicated and depends on individual personalities and communication and everything else. I don't think it works perfectly at all."

Other members did not view the existence of divisions within the organization as an obstacle, but as a potential source of organizational strength. While recognizing that many chapters were "going through identity crises," an activist in the New York chapter believed that the resulting tensions could in fact promote innovation and commitment among the membership. Activists expressed the hope that ACT UP would be able to maintain itself as long as members continued to view these central divisions as a healthy and positive aspect of the organization while accepting that certain constituencies would focus on different issues.

Conclusion

The late 1990s have witnessed a demobilization of ACT UP. By 1998 just eight chapters remained (table 7.2), compared to 113 in 1991. ACT UP members recognized that the organization no longer had a grassroots base and that they could not depend on large numbers coming to meetings simply because ACT UP was the "in place to be" within the gay and lesbian movement (Wolfe 1997). Activist "burnout" was another factor. In addition to organizational tensions, less hostile public and institutional attitudes toward PWAs and the proliferation of AIDS service organizations may have played a part in movement decline.

But by then ACT UP had made its mark. Its art work, demonstrations, and street theater had altered cultural perceptions of AIDS and homosexuality. Both its direct action and more conventional participation had made the institutions involved in managing AIDS more responsive to PWAs. ACT UP pushed them to lower the price of AZT, develop an AZT serum for children, and establish the concept of "parallel track" drug testing. It also forced insurance companies to maintain coverage for HIV-infected clients. Finally, ACT UP provided important benefits for its members. Activism gave many people touched by AIDS an outlet for their anger and a place to share experiences, while forging a positive identity for PWAs.

Thus ACT UP's blend of instrumental and expressive goals and tactics need not be perceived as a weakness, but rather as a rich source of innovation and diversity within a single SMO. ACT UP's success during its peak period of mobilization illustrates how distinct constituencies can join forces to work for social change when unified by a strongly shared goal. ACT UP members prided themselves on the fact that they were on the cutting edge of AIDS research, while their creative use of strategies and

TABLE 7.2
National and International ACT UP Chapters (1998)

New York	Atlanta
Golden Gate	Westchester (NY)
Los Angeles	Rhode Island
Philadelphia	Paris

Source: ACT UP/New York.

tactics shaped voluntary political action well beyond the AIDS activist movement. Ultimately, internal conflicts and personal clashes did lead to schism within some chapters, though as Gerlach points out (chapter 5 in this book), splinter groups do not necessarily signal organizational demise. On the contrary, they can significantly contribute to movement growth by spreading ideas and influence. By using multiple means, ACT UP not only improved medical treatment for PWAs, but challenged the moralization that has accompanied the AIDS crisis.

Notes

1. Scott (1990) asserts that many of the issues defined as cultural by new social movement theorists have political and ideological dimensions as well and should not be separated from conventional issues of political participation.

References

ACT UP/Columbus. 1990a. Membership Packet.
———. 1990b. Working Document.
ACT UP/New York. 1991. "ACTG 076 Is Bad Science and Is Unethical." Informational flyer.
Altman, Dennis. 1987. *AIDS in the Mind of America.* Garden City, N.Y.: Anchor Books.
———. 1988. "Legitimation through Disaster: AIDS and the Gay Movement." In *AIDS: The Burdens of History*, ed. Elizabeth Fee and Daniel M. Fox. Berkeley: University of California Press, 301–15.
Brandt, Allan M. 1988. "AIDS: From Social History to Social Policy." In *AIDS: The Burdens of History*, ed. Elizabeth Fee and Daniel M. Fox. Berkeley: University of California Press, 147–71.
Calhoun, Craig. 1993. " 'New Social Movements' of the Early Nineteenth Century." *Social Science History* 17, no. 3: 385–427.
Columbus Dispatch. 1991a. "Protesters disrupt news broadcasts" (23 January), B2.
———. 1991b. "AIDS activists arrested at protests in New York" (24 January), B6.
Crimp, Douglas, and Adam Rolston. 1990. *AIDS Demo Graphics.* Seattle: Bay Press.
Curtis, Russell L., and Louis A. Zurcher Jr. 1974. "Social Movements: An Analytical Exploration of Organizational Forms." *Social Problems* 21, no. 3: 356–70.
Dalton, Russell J., and Manfred Kuechler. 1990. *Challenging the Political Order.* New York: Oxford University Press.
D'Anieri, Paul, Claire Ernst, and Elizabeth Kier. 1990. "New Social Movements in Historical Perspective." *Comparative Politics* 22 (July): 445–58.
D'Emilio, John. 1983. *Sexual Politics, Sexual Communities: The Making of a Homosexual Minority in the United States, 1940–1970.* Chicago: University of Chicago Press.

Freeman, Jo. 1975. *The Politics of Women's Liberation.* New York: Longman.

———. 1979. "Resource Mobilization and Strategy: A Model for Analyzing Social Movement Organization Action." In *The Dynamics of Social Movements,* ed. Mayer N. Zald and John D. McCarthy. Cambridge, Mass.: Winthrop, 168–89.

———. 1983. "A Model for Analyzing the Strategic Options of Social Movement Organizations." In *Social Movements of the Sixties and Seventies.* New York: Longman, 193–210.

Gamson, Josh. 1989. "Silence, Death, and the Invisible Enemy: AIDS Activism and Social Movement Newness." *Social Problems* 36, no. 4: 351–67.

Gamson, William. 1975. *The Strategy of Social Protest.* Homewood, Ill.: Dorsey.

Gerlach, Luther P., and Virginia H. Hine. 1970. *People, Power, Change: Movements of Social Transformation.* Indianapolis: Bobbs-Merrill.

Klandermans, Bert, and Sidney Tarrow. 1988. "Mobilization into Social Movements: Synthesizing European and American Approaches." *International Social Movement Research* 1: 1–38.

Kramer, Larry. 1989. *Reports from the Holocaust: The Making of an AIDS Activist.* New York: St. Martin's Press.

Jenkins, J. Craig. 1983. "Resource Mobilization Theory and the Study of Social Movements." *Annual Review of Sociology* 9: 527–53.

McCarthy, John D., and Mayer N. Zald. 1977. "Resource Mobilization and Social Movements: A Partial Theory." *American Journal of Sociology* 82, no. 6: 1212–41.

Morris, Aldon. 1984. *The Origins of the Civil Rights Movement.* New York: Free Press.

Morris, Aldon, and Cedric Herring. 1986. "Theory and Research In Social Movements: A Critical Review." *Annual Review of Political Science* 2: 137–98.

Newsweek. 1990. "The Future of Gay America." (12 March): 20–25.

Offe, Claus. 1985. "New Social Movements: Challenging the Boundaries of Institutional Politics." *Social Research* 52, no. 4: 817–68.

Piven, Frances Fox, and Richard A. Cloward. 1977. *Poor People's Movements: Why They Succeed, How They Fail.* New York: Vintage Books.

Scott, Alan. 1990. *Ideology and the New Social Movements.* London: Unwin Hyman.

Staggenborg, Suzanne. 1989. "Stability and Innovation in the Women's Movement: A Comparison of Two Movement Organizations." *Social Problems* 36, no 1: 75–92.

Touraine, Alain. 1981. *The Voice and the Eye: An Analysis of Social Movements.* Translated by Alan Duff. London: Cambridge University Press.

Wolfe, Maxine. 1997. "After Ten Years." Plenary session talk at Conference on AIDS Activism, March 22. Hunter College, New York.

Zald, Mayer N., and John D. McCarthy. 1987. "Social Movement Industries: Competition and Conflict Among SMOs." In *Social Movements in an Organizational Society.* New Brunswick, N.J.: Transaction, 161–80.

Part Three

Consciousness

Part Three Introduction

Scholars have long recognized that changes in consciousness occur as part of the process of social movement emergence. How do these changes in meaning systems effect collective action? The concept of "collective identity" has been central to research on this question. Participants develop such an identity as they share experiences, concerns, and interpretations of grievances that warrant collective action. The study of consciousness brings in the cultural factors that resource mobilization left out.

John Green analyzes the change in collective identity that facilitated the transformation of (theologically) conservative evangelical activists into evangelical (political) conservatives. He argues that collective identity can play three different roles in social movements: it can be a source, a concomitant, and/or a result of movement activity. For the Christian Right, it was all three.

Verta Taylor and Nancy Whittier ask how informal networks within a lesbian feminist community change members into political actors. Linking identity and grievance construction, they present a framework for analyzing the process through which collective identity is constructed in social movements.

David Bromley and Diana Cutchin analyze the narratives constructed to mobilize anticult and anti-Satanist countermovements. They ask how countersubversive ideologies are fashioned when there are few facts to back them up. This question is answered with an illustration of how movement participants construct order and disorder to organize and interpret their social worlds through narratives. Systems of meaning constructed by movement participants, be they narratives or collective identity, orient an individual toward collective action.

8

The Spirit Willing: Collective Identity and the Development of the Christian Right

John C. Green

From its advent in the late 1970s to its prominence in the 1990s, the Christian Right has perplexed political observers and scholars alike. Simply put, this social movement among religious traditionalists seems out of place in a modern, secular polity. Scholars have helped account for this incongruity by noting that religion can provide the motives, means, and methods for political action (Green, Guth, and Wilcox 1998). This chapter explores one aspect of this phenomenon, the role of collective identities in the origin, development, and impact of the Christian Right.

The Christian Right originated in four groups of sectarian evangelical Protestants, who animated a first wave of movement activity, but whose longstanding antagonisms contributed to its decline. The development of new collective identities allowed for a second and more successful wave of Christian Right activity, but these identities had limitations as well. Among the chief impacts of the first two waves of the movement was the increased identification of activists with the Republican Party. This trend may presage a third wave of movement activism, which, if successful, could end the Christian Right as a social movement but leave it as a major power in the Republican Party. In sum, the movement helped transform theologically conservative evangelical activists into evangelical political conservatives, and is leading them to identify with the "right" political party.

Collective Identity and Social Movements

The concept of collective identity is useful in the study of social movements because it introduces crucial cultural factors and links them to non-cultural aspects of movements (Mueller 1992). At an individual level, collective identity is the cognitive encapsulation of group values (Taylor and Whittier 1992, this volume), group attachments (Friedman and McAdam 1992), and orientations toward group action (Melucci 1989). Such identity is central to the grievances that motivate social movements, but is also relevant to the mobilization of resources for the movement activity, as well as exploitation of opportunities by movement activists (Gamson 1992, 55). Of course, collective identities also exist apart from social movements, in routine aspects of social and political life, such as affiliation with religious communities and political parties (Koch 1995).

Collective identity can play three different roles in social movements: it can be a source, a concomitant, and/or a result of movement activity (Johnston, Larana, and Gusfield 1994; Friedman and McAdam 1992). First, collective identities can help generate a social movement. Movements frequently begin by tapping the preexisting collective identities of aggrieved groups. Sometimes such identities are nonpolitical, but they can also come from involvement with previous social movements. Second, collective identities can develop within a movement itself. Such new or modified identities can arise from common experiences within or intense pressures from outside the movement. Movement identities can help sustain movement activity beyond its initial mobilization. Third, collective identity can be the end product of a movement, either in the form of novel identities or the adoption of established identities beyond the movement itself. Such public identities can change the relationship of movement activists to the broader society. In each case, the group values, attachments, and action orientations encapsulated in collective identity help define— and redefine—the movement's sense of grievances, resources, and opportunities.

To some scholars, premovement identities are critical (Morris 1984), while others stress the creation of movement identities (Cohen 1985), and still others are most impressed with the adoption of public identities by movement activists (McAdam 1994, 48–54). And while some writers see no necessary relationship among these types of collective identity (Klandermans 1992), others see a causal sequence (Friedman and McAdam 1992). Indeed, it is the ability of movements to transform the prepolitical collective identities of "outsiders" into the public collective identities of "insiders" that fascinates many students of politics (Scott 1990). Social movements often play this role in the highly decentralized American party system, turning group identifiers first into movement identifiers and finally into party identifiers (Salisbury 1989). The Christian Right illustrates all three roles for collective identity as well as the transformative relationship among them.

Evangelical Identities and the Christian Right

The collective identities of sectarian evangelical Protestants were crucial to the origins of the Christian Right in the late 1970s and early 1980s. In this sense, the movement closely resembles the origins of "new social movements" on the left, such as feminism and environmentalism, where collective identities are regarded as important factors (Oldfield 1996b). In fact, the most important differences between the "new" liberal movements and the "new" Christian Right come from their cultural content: the former sought to challenge "traditional" values, while the latter sought to maintain them. Indeed, the success of the liberal movements in the 1960s and 1970s helped galvanize sectarian evangelical Protestants to engage in movement politics.

Evangelicals are the largest group of American Protestants, accounting for about 25 percent of the adult population (cf. Kellstedt et al. 1996). They are characterized by highly orthodox Protestant beliefs as well as numerous sects that seek to maintain particular versions of these beliefs. Evangelicals emphasize the salvation of individual souls, which requires individual acceptance of Jesus Christ as one's "Lord and Savior" (a "personal conversion") and religious organizations dedicated to seeking converts ("evangelizing"). From a religious perspective, evangelicals seek nothing less than a radical transformation of the individual believer, an expectation captured in the language of rebirth, or to be "born again."

On the second count, this intense individualism fosters enormous variation in religious expression. One result is the formation of church institutions to regulate religious expression and accommodate it to the broader society. Another result is the formation of sects, religious communities that seek to maintain a particular version of this religious expression against the "worldly" accommodations of churches.[1] Personal conversion within the context of a sect creates strong and distinctive collective identities. Indeed, the sense of a radical transformation by individual converts sets them apart from the broader society and often from other sects as well.

Two pairs of sectarian groups have been especially prominent among evangelicalism in the twentieth century. The best-known pair are fundamentalists and neo-evangelicals. Fundamentalism began in the early twentieth century as a reaction against the "worldly" accommodation of the major Protestant churches. It is named after *The Fundamentals*, a series of pamphlets detailing essential beliefs. Fundamentalists are known for their strict orthodoxy and strict separation from other "apostate" Christians and "nonbelievers." A group of "moderates" broke away in the late 1940s and took the name "neo-evangelical" (which is often shortened to "evangelical," causing confusion with the evangelical Protestant tradition, which includes neo-evangelicals and fundamentalists as well as other groups). Neo-evangelicals are less orthodox and separatist than fundamentalists, putting more emphasis on cooperation with outsiders.

The other pair of sectarian groups are Pentecostals and charismatics, both of which stress the direct experience of the Holy Spirit, such as speaking in tongues and faith healing. Pentecostalism originated at about the same time as fundamentalism in a series of ecstatic revivals also in reaction to the "worldly" tendencies of major Protestant churches (the name comes from Pentecost in the New Testament). Pentecostals are less orthodox and separatist than fundamentalists, but distinctive enough to generate a break-away of sorts in the 1950s, the charismatics (named for the Greek work for "gifts"). Charismatics practiced the gifts of the spirit in Christian churches that did not accept them. Consequently, charismatics are even less orthodox and separatist than Pentecostals.

The Politics of Moralism

The religious identities of these sectarian groups structured the sense of grievances, resources, and opportunities for the first wave of the Christian Right.[2] The movement was motivated by a strong sense of moral decay in American society (Jorstad 1981, Green et al. 1996). Fundamentalists, neo-evangelicals, Pentecostals, and charismatics were deeply offended by the social changes of the 1960s and 1970s. These sectarian groups were outraged by the increased permissiveness of heterosexuals, the openness of gays and lesbians, the legalization of abortion and pornography, and challenges to the nuclear family. They were also upset by a decreased respect for religious institutions and restrictions on religious expression in public life. The resulting sense of being an unpopular minority in an increasingly hostile society prompted a culturally defensive reaction.

This reaction occurred in a context propitious to movement activity. By the late 1970s, these sectarian groups had developed a dense web of religious organizations, including mega-churches, schools, charities, missions, and publishing and broadcasting outlets (Jorstad 1990). These institutions were quite successful in maintaining and recruiting adherents in an increasingly secular culture. At the same time, evangelicals as a whole enjoyed significant gains in socioeconomic status, many entering the middle class and moving to large urban areas. Thus, their moral grievances arose within resource-rich communities.

A series of political opportunities then led these sectarian groups to undertake political action. By the late 1970s, a few of their leaders had become involved in conservative politics (Bruce 1988). Some were mobilized by President Jimmy Carter, a self-identified born-again Christian, and then felt betrayed by the culturally "liberal" policies of his administration. Others were aroused to protest social issues, such as the legalization of abortion, or to oppose government regulation of their religious schools and broadcasting. Still others were recruited by secular conservative operatives seeking votes for conservative candidates. Once engaged in politics, these leaders tapped sectarian identities to mobilize activists.

What sectarian evangelicals had lacked was a consistent view of appropriate political action (Lienesch 1993, 172–94). These groups had for many years given priority to religious pursuits, and responded to social disorder in a private fashion, with evangelism and benevolent societies. Many found strong theological warrant to avoid politics, particularly liberal programs that sought to reform the social structure. Pentecostals were especially characterized by an apolitical stance. There were, however, some usable notions of appropriate politics available to some of these groups. First, religious conflicts had produced a tradition of resisting authority, an idea that could be easily translated into politics. Fundamentalists had, in fact, made such a transition when they participated in the anticommunist crusades of the 1950s and 1960s. Second, general notions of "Christian citizenship" required support of an orderly society where religious people could prosper, a view that was particularly common among neo-evangelicals and charismatics. Taken together, these ideas suggested that religious people ought to resist misguided authorities in defense of an appropriate social order.

The initial leaders of the Christian Right offered a new political vision that was at once consistent with these existing political orientations and an innovation (Neuhaus and Cromartie 1987). They proclaimed the existence of a "moral majority" in American society that was being ignored by governmental authorities. This vision had an ecumenical character, an unusual stance for sectarian groups, extending beyond evangelicalism to conservative mainline Protestants, traditionalist Roman Catholics, and even Orthodox Jews—a broad "religious right." Thus, sectarian evangelicals were not just isolated bastions of the true faith, fighting to defend their culture, but potentially part of a larger moral consensus. They needed to engage in politics to arouse this slumbering moral consensus to action.

A number of movement organizations appeared in short order, each drawing on special religious constituencies (Green 1996). The best-known group was the Moral Majority, led by televangelist Jerry Falwell, who mobilized fundamentalists linked to his ministries. The Religious Round-table organized fundamentalist and neo-evangelical ministers, while the National Christian Action Council focused especially on neo-evangelicals involved in religious schools and broadcasting. Christian Voice recruited neo-evangelicals and Pentecostals engaged in social issue protests, and Pat Robertson founded the Freedom Council among charismatics and Pentecostals drawn from his television ministry. Because of their previous political experience, fundamentalists were especially prominent.

This exploitation of sectarian identities gave the Christian Right a long reach but a weak grasp (cf. Jorstad 1990, Bruce 1988). On the first count, the movement was able to recruit and deploy thousands of activists in a wide variety of tasks, ranging from working in campaigns to lobbying the government. The Christian Right's electoral activities attracted the most attention, partly because they were novel and partly because they were effective. The movement was quite active in the 1980 elections in support of conservative candidates, including Ronald Reagan and a number of senators and members of Congress. A more coordinated effort occurred in 1984 under the aegis of the American Coalition for Traditional Values, which focused on the reelection of Reagan. In 1988, one of movement's leaders, Pat Robertson, made a determined effort to secure the Republican presidential nomination, and although he received only a handful of delegates, the momentum of his primary campaign kept the movement active in the general election. During this heady decade, Christian Rightists became a fixture in congressional politics as well (Moen 1989).

But on the second count, the Christian Right fell far short of its own goals and the expectations of outside observers (Wilcox 1996). For one thing, the movement never fully mobilized its own activist corps, let alone its mass constituency. Indeed, the vision of a "religious right" was initially an illusion: there was no "moral majority" awaiting to be aroused. In fact, the religious differences between fundamentalists, neo-evangelicals, Pentecostals, and charismatics presented a serious obstacle, making cooperation within the movement extremely difficult and recruitment of supporters from outside evangelicalism nigh impossible. And despite their secular political pretensions, Christian Right organizations were largely extensions of sectarian religious institutions, and perhaps because of this connection, all failed to develop strong grassroots units. Furthermore, sectarian evangelicals were often ineffective in routine politics. One problem was their ignorance of the political process and uncompromising "purist" style, which provoked a storm of opposition from across the political spectrum. For all these reasons, Ronald Reagan and other conservative officeholders expended little effort on the movement's moral agenda in the 1980s, and few tangible results were obtained.

Thus, the sectarian evangelical identities that were crucial to the initial mobilization of the Christian Right also proved to be a serious limitation. By 1989, all of the most prominent movement organizations were disbanded or inactive, and most observers believed the Christian Right was in rapid decline. No doubt this conclusion reflected some wishful thinking by the movement's many enemies. Nonetheless, more objective analysts noted that the movement had pushed its initial supporters as far as possible (Wilcox 1996).

The Second Coming of the Christian Right

Hardly had the first wave of the Christian Right subsided, however, than the movement experienced a dramatic "second coming" (Rozell and Wilcox 1996), in which the development of new movement identities played a critical role. In retrospect, the most significant aspect of the "politics of moralism" was the intense discussion it provoked among sectarian evangelicals. One group of activists withdrew from politics altogether, frustrated with the political process. Many of these people rededicated themselves to evangelical religious institutions, which continued to prosper during the period (Jorstad 1993). Another group responded by becoming more contentious, arguing that the defense of traditional values required extreme measures. Operation Rescue and the blockades of abortion clinics it inspired are the best example of this tendency (Wills 1989). Ironically, these withdrawals and departures helped make a third group ascendant, activists whose response was greater pragmatism (Cromartie 1993).

The original vision of a broad "religious right" had taken hold among this latter group of activists, producing some important changes in how they thought about themselves, and allowing them to recruit new, likeminded people. First, their religious identities became less insular, expanding to include an appreciation of one another and traditionalists from other religious backgrounds (Wilcox, Rozell, and Gunn 1997). Neo-evangelicals and charismatics adapted most quickly, becoming more numerous within the movement; fundamentalists did not adapt as well and became less common; Pentecostals fell somewhere in between.

Second, these activists developed new movement identities separate from their sectarian identifications (Reed 1996). One popular identity was the "pro-family movement," which captured the most popular part of the Christian Right's moral agenda. Another popular identity was "Christian conservative," which redefined the activists as a special part of the political right. These new identities appeared to arise in equal measure from the internal life of the movement and the intense opposition it had encountered, and they produced a new understanding of the movement's grievances, resources, and opportunities.

A refinement of grievances was a crucial part of these new identities (Moen 1992). The Christian Right's moralism was refocused from general moral decay to specific antagonisms. For example, general opposition to sexual permissiveness and homosexuality were replaced by demands for specific restrictions on abortion and gay rights. Similarly, cultural defensiveness was redefined in terms of "rights"—the rights of the unborn, the rights of parents, and the rights of religious people. The range of issues also expanded to include economic, foreign policy, and social welfare concerns. Christian Rightists had always been fairly conservative on these issues, but now they tried to link them systematically to their moral concerns. This new agenda was aimed more at persuasion than at an expression of grievances.

The 1980s had taught these pragmatists a great deal about practical politics, which they were ready to employ. Perhaps the most important lesson was about how to use religious resources:

> it was religious people, rather than religious institutions, that were the key to success. Such people needed to be marshaled in frankly political organizations, separate from the distractions and liabilities of religious pursuits. Evangelical churches and other religious organizations were places to recruit and mobilize followers, but were not themselves organizational building blocks. Now movement organizations were to be built by grassroots recruitment. (Moen 1992)

These new movement identities included new political orientations as well (Lienesch 1993, 247–60). Whereas the original Christian Rightists felt like an unpopular minority, movement activists now *knew* they were one, located in a nation composed of many such minorities, where there was only limited consensus on moral questions. The only way "pro-family" activists could defend their culture and contribute to an acceptable social order was to be intimately involved in the political process. Thus, "Christian conservatives" had to become skillful participants in a broader conservative coalition that included not just a "religious right," but also a broader political right. Central to this understanding was an appreciation of party politics as a critical avenue for movement activity.

These new movement identities were closely associated with the emergence of a second generation of Christian Right organizations, some newly founded and others redirected (Green 1996). These groups were largely separate from religious institutions, had broader membership, and specialized in different activities. The best known was the Christian Coalition, founded by Pat Robertson, but directed by Executive Director

Ralph Reed, a quintessential movement pragmatist. The Christian Coalition recruited heavily from across the evangelical spectrum, consciously seeking to include other religious traditionalists, especially Roman Catholic and black Protestants. The coalition focused on grassroots mobilization of voters. Another major group was Focus on the Family and the related Family Research Councils, which worked mostly on policy development and lobbying at the national and state levels. Smaller groups included Concerned Women for America, an evangelical women's group, and the American Family Association, representing critics of television and the entertainment industry.

By most measures, this second wave of the Christian Right was more successful than the first (Rozell and Wilcox 1995, 1997). For one thing, its organizations were much more sophisticated and had strong grassroots units. The movement was able to field a larger and more cohesive activist corps that used better tactics to reach voters. It was also a better ally, working with other conservative groups and within the Republican Party. These efforts paid off at the ballot box: the Christian Right played a small but crucial role in the GOP victories in 1994, when the party gained control of both Houses of Congress for the first time in forty years, and in 1996, when it retained control for the first time in over sixty years (Green 1995, 1997). Similar successes occurred at the state and local levels, especially in the South and Midwest. These electoral gains plus astute lobbying by the movement organizations yielded some tangible gains in Congress, such as the passage of a ban on some late-term abortions (vetoed by Clinton) and the enactment into law of a $500 per child tax credit.

The most noticed of these gains occurred within the Republican Party itself (Green, Guth, and Wilcox 1998). Movement activists increased their numbers at the GOP national conventions in 1992 and 1996, and experienced parallel increases at the state and local levels. For instance, by 1994, the Christian Right had obtained "dominant" influence in eighteen GOP state committees and "substantial" influence in another thirteen. While this presence usually fell short of outright "control" of party organizations, it gave the movement clout in intraparty battles. Christian Rightists contributed to the election of conservatives as national and state party chairs, the maintenance of strong pro-life language in the national and state party platforms, and the defeat of pro-choice candidates in caucuses and primaries. Indeed the movement effectively exercised a veto over GOP nominations in many states, including those crucial to the presidency.

However, there were still real limits to the Christian Right's influence (Oldfield 1996a). The new movement organizations were difficult to maintain and the recruitment of supporters beyond evangelicalism proved elusive. Electoral victories were mixed with defeats. Despite the victories in congressional and state elections, the Republicans lost both presidential elections in the 1990s. Although the role of the Christian Right in these defeats is often overstated (Green et al. 1994), there is no question the movement was often a divisive force (Wilcox 1994). Sectarian antagonisms were now replaced by ideological conflicts, with moderate and business-oriented Republicans frequently opposing the movement's agenda. Close association with the GOP was problematic in other ways as well, attracting legal scrutiny from the Federal Election Commission and raising questions about the movement's ultimate goals. On top of these problems, religious and secular liberals began extensive countermobilization (Green 1997).

So, as with the first wave of the Christian Right, collective identities were both a source of strength and a limitation. The development of "pro-family" activists and "Christian conservatives" helped the movement overcome internal religious divisions, but still set it apart from potential political allies. On the one hand, movement pragmatists achieved success in organization, at the ballot box, and in the halls of Congress. But on the other hand, they had a more limited message, tied their fortunes to candidates not of their own choosing, and faced more determined ideological foes. By the late 1990s, the second wave of the movement began to slow down, having pushed its supporters toward their natural limits (Wilcox 1996).

Evangelical Republicans?

Among the most important impacts of the first two waves of the Christian Right was the forging of a strong relationship between sectarian evangelical activists and the Republican Party (Guth et al. 1996a, 1996b). A large part of this shift has been the adoption and intensification of a public collective identity as partisan Republicans. This new identity may well presage a third wave of Christian Right activism as the movement struggles to secure power within the party. If it succeeds, sectarian evangelical activists may have the same kind of influence in the GOP as labor union, feminist, and African American activists have in the Democratic Party. But such success might also result in the end of the Christian Right as a social movement.

This increased Republican identification came by stages. Some sectarian evangelicals had always been Republicans, such as fundamentalists and neo-evangelicals in the North. Others were historically Democrats, especially fundamentalists and Pentecostals in the South and the West. But prior to 1980, partisanship was not central to the identity of these groups. It slowly became so during the first two waves of the movement, and may help redefine yet again its grievances, resources, and opportunities (Green et al. 1997).

During the first wave of the Christian Right, sectarian evangelicals supported conservative candidates, most of whom happened to be Republicans, although many movement leaders, such as Jerry Falwell, initially wanted to support conservative Democrats as well. Once engaged with GOP candidates and facing unremitting hostility from the Democrats, many movement activists began to develop new or firmer Republican attachments. Pat Robertson followed this trajectory, leaving the Democratic Party of his father, U.S. Senator Willis Robertson, to join the party of Ronald Reagan, who himself had moved from the Democrats to the GOP two decades earlier (Hertzke 1993).

During the second wave, movement activists chose to work with the GOP as a matter of strategy: it was the best avenue for pro-family activists and Christian conservatives to gain political power (Green 1996). They made some pretense of being "non-" or "bi-partisan" in their activities, but increasingly turned their backs on the Democrats, a trend aided by the election of President Bill Clinton, a "liberal" evangelical Protestant. The successes and failures of this partisan strategy produced even closer ties to the GOP, and the movement began to attract activists based as much on partisanship as on religion. For example, Ralph Reed was a Republican before his conversion experience. Eventually he became executive director of the Christian Coalition (Reed 1996).

By the late 1990s, the newest recruits in the movement activist corps were Republicans by conviction, and their partisanship was central to their collective identity. Former congressman Randy Tate, who replaced Ralph Reed as executive director of the Christian Coalition in 1997, is a good example of this trend. To these activists, the Republican message of limited government is central to the religious and political aspirations of sectarian evangelicals. Ironically, part of this understanding is a recognition of the limits of government enforcement of morality. Many of these activists believe that "traditional values" cannot be enacted into policy unless there is greater public support. Such support must be built first in private life by means of intensive evangelism, and second through vigorous political action, of which the GOP is an indispensable vehicle.

There is both pressure for and resistance to this integration of the movement into the party (Green 1997). On the one hand, many movement activists chafe at the limited impact the first two waves of activism had on national politics, and want to deploy their resources to exploit the opportunities in routine politics. There is considerable talk, for instance, of capturing formal offices in the Republican party organization at the local, state, and national levels. And it is widely believed that the movement must unify behind a single Republican candidate in the presidential elections in 2000 and beyond. Indeed, some of the movement's most talented activists have become campaign consultants, fund-raisers, and candidates, all critical posts from which to influence the direction of contemporary party politics.

On the other hand, these efforts have produced considerable opposition among sectarian evangelicals (Penning and Smidt 1996). The most vocal critics are on the "left," such as the Road to Renewal, a caucus of "progressive" evangelicals concerned with opposing the Christian Right, and especially the linkages between movement evangelicalism and the conservative economic agenda of the GOP. There are also critics on the "right," such as the Christian Action Network, who fear that a close association with the party will further dilute the movement's social issue agenda. Critical voices are heard in the "center" as well, where the National Association of Evangelicals and other evangelical institutions worry about the excessive entanglements of evangelicalism with secular politicians. Of course, partisanship is a broad and malleable collective identity that can potentially accommodate all these groups, perhaps as "liberal," "conservative," and "moderate" Republicans. However, such amorphous identities are unlikely to sustain movement politics for very long.

Whatever the future of the Christian Right, the concept of collective identity enriches our understanding of it. Sectarian identities were critical to its origins, new movement identities were crucial to its development, and Republican identification was its major impact to date. This case illustrates the transformative power of social movements, politicizing "outsider" identities and integrating them into mainstream ones. If nothing else, this understanding helps explain why religious fervor is still potent in a modern, secular polity: religion can generate strong, collective identities that can serve as the basis for political action.

Notes

1. Technically speaking, these sectarian groups are religious movements, challenges to religious institutions in much the same way social movements challenge political institutions. But to avoid confusion, the text refers to the religious kind as sectarian groups.

2. Social scientists have measured religious and political identities among evangelical activists and voters since the early 1980s (Wilcox, Jelen, and Leege 1993). Unfortunately, these measures have not been employed consistently over time, so it is difficult to be precise about impact and development of the relevant identities. This chapter is based on a careful assessment of these studies, and also on hundreds of interviews with Christian Right activists over the past two decades. Unless another source is cited, the conclusions in this chapter derive from these interviews.

References

Bruce, Steve. 1988. *The Rise and Fall of the Christian Right.* Oxford: Clarendon Press.

Cohen, Jean L. 1985. "Strategy or Identity: New Theoretical Paradigms and Contemporary Social Movements." *Social Research* 52, no. 4 (winter): 663–716.

Cromartie, Michael. 1993. *No Longer Exiles.* Washington, D.C.: Ethics and Public Policy Center.

Friedman, Debra, and Doug McAdam. 1992. "Collective Identity and Activism: Networks, Choices, and the Life of Social Movements." In *Frontiers in Social Movement Theory,* ed. Aldon D. Morris and Carol M. Mueller. New Haven: Yale University Press, 156–73.

Gamson, William A. 1992. "The Social Psychology of Collective Action." In *Frontiers in Social Movement Theory,* ed. Aldon D. Morris and Carol M. Mueller. New Haven: Yale University Press, 53–76.

Green, John C. 1997. "The Christian Right in the 1996 Elections: An Overview." In *God at the Grassroots 1996: The Christian Right in the 1996 Elections,* ed. Mark J. Rozell and Clyde Wilcox. Lanham, Md.: Rowman & Littlefield, 1–14.

———. 1996. *Understanding the Christian Right.* New York: American Jewish Committee.

———. 1995. "The Christian Right in the 1994 Elections: An Overview." In *God at the Grassroots: The Christian Right in the 1994 Elections,* ed. Mark J. Rozell and Clyde Wilcox. Lanham, Md.: Rowman & Littlefield, 1–18.

Green, John C., James L. Guth, Lyman A. Kellstedt, and Corwin E. Smidt. 1997. "Bringing in the Sheaves: The Christian Right and White Protestants 1976–1996." In *Sojourners in the Wilderness: The Christian Right in Comparative Perspective,* ed. Corwin E. Smidt and James M. Penning. Lanham, Md.: Rowman & Littlefield, 75–82.

Green, John C., James L. Guth, Lyman A. Kellstedt, and Corwin E. Smidt. 1994. "Murphy Brown Revisited: The Social Issues in the 1992 Election." In *Disciples and Democracy,* ed. Michael Cromartie. Grand Rapids, Mich.: Eerdmans, 43–78.

Green, John C., James L. Guth, Corwin E. Smidt, and Lyman A. Kellstedt. 1996. *Religion and the Culture Wars.* Lanham, Md.: Rowman & Littlefield.

Green, John C., James L. Guth, and Clyde Wilcox. 1998. "Less than Conquerors: The Christian Right in State Republican Parties." In *Social Movements and American Political Institutions,* ed. Anne Costain and Andrew McFarland. Lanham, Md.: Rowman & Littlefield, 117–35.

Guth, James L., John C. Green, Lyman A. Kellstedt, and Corwin E. Smidt. 1996a. "Fresh Troops and Hardened Veterans: Religious Activists and Party Realignment in the 1990s." In *Do Elections Matter?,* ed. Benjamin Ginsberg and Alan Stone, 3rd ed. Armonk, N.Y.: Sharpe, 205–32.

———. 1996b. "Onward Christian Soldiers: Religious Activist Groups in American Politics." In *Religion and the Culture Wars,* ed. John C. Green et al. Lanham, Md.: Rowman & Littlefield, 62–85.

Hertzke, Allen D. 1993. *Echoes of Discontent.* Washington, D.C.: CQ Press.

Johnston, Hank, Enrique Larana, and Joseph Gusfield. 1994. "Identities, Grievances, and New Social Movements." In *New Social Movements: From Ideology to*

Identity, ed. Enrique Larana, Hank Johnston, and Joseph R. Gusfield. Philadelphia: Temple University Press, 3–35.

Jorstad, Erling. 1981. *The Politics of Moralism.* Minneapolis: Augsburg.

———. 1990. *Holding Fast/Pressing On.* New York: Praeger Press.

———. 1993. *Popular Religion in America.* Westport, Conn.: Greenwood Press.

Kellstedt, Lyman A., John C. Green, Corwin E. Smidt, and James L. Guth. 1996. "The Puzzle of Evangelical Protestantism." In *Religion and the Culture Wars,* ed. John C. Green, James L. Guth, Corwin E. Smidt, and Lyman A. Kellstedt. Lanham, Md.: Rowman & Littlefield, 240–66.

Klandermans, Bert. 1992. "The Social Construction of Protest and Multiorganizational Fields." In *Frontiers in Social Movement Theory,* ed. Aldon D. Morris and Carol M. Mueller. New Haven: Yale University Press, 77–103.

Koch, Jeffrey W. 1995. *Social Reference Groups and Political Life.* Lanham, Md.: University Press of America.

Lienesch, Michael. 1993. *Redeeming America.* Chapel Hill: University of North Carolina Press.

McAdam, Doug. 1994. "Culture and Social Movements." In *New Social Movements: From Ideology to Identity,* ed. Enrique Larana, Hank Johnston, and Joseph R. Gusfield. Philadelphia: Temple University Press, 36–57.

Melucci, Alberto. 1989. *Nomads of the Present: Social Movements and Individual Needs in Contemporary Society.* Philadelphia: Temple University Press.

Moen, Matthew. 1989. *The Christian Right in Congress.* Tuscaloosa: University of Alabama Press.

———. 1992. *The Transformation of the Christian Right.* Tuscaloosa: University of Alabama Press.

Morris, Aldon D. 1984. *The Origins of the Civil Rights Movement.* New York: Free Press.

Neuhaus, Richard John, and Michael Cromartie, eds. 1987. *Piety and Politics.* Washington, D.C.: Ethics and Public Policy Center.

Oldfield, Duane M. 1996a. *The Right and the Righteous: The Christian Right Confronts the Republican Party.* Lanham, Md.: Rowman & Littlefield.

———. 1996b. "Something Is Happening, But They Don't Know What Is: New Social Movement Theory from the Perspective of the Christian Right." Delivered at the annual meeting of the American Political Science Association, San Francisco.

Penning, James M., and Corwin E. Smidt. 1996. "What Coalition?" *Christian Century* (January 15): 37–38.

Reed, Ralph. 1996. *Active Faith.* New York: Free Press.

Rozell, Mark J., and Clyde Wilcox, eds. 1995. *God at the Grassroots: The Christian Right in the 1994 Elections.* Lanham, Md.: Rowman & Littlefield.

———. 1996. *Second Coming.* Baltimore: Johns Hopkins Press.

———. 1997. *God at the Grassroots 1996: The Christian Right in the 1996 Elections.* Lanham, Md.: Rowman & Littlefield.

Salisbury, Robert H. 1989. "Political Movements in American Politics: An Essay on Concept and Analysis." *National Journal of Political Science* 1: 15–30.

Scott, Alan. 1990. *Ideology and the New Social Movements.* London: Unwin Hyman.

Taylor, Verta, and Nancy E. Whittier. 1992. "Collective Identity in Social Movement Communities: Lesbian Feminist Mobilization." In *Frontiers in Social Movement Theory*, ed. Aldon D. Morris and Carol M. Mueller. New Haven: Yale University Press, 104–30.

Wilcox, Clyde. 1994. "Premillenialists at the Millennium." *Sociology of Religion* 55, no. 3 (Fall): 243–62.

———. 1996. *The Dilemma of the Christian Right*. Boulder: Westview Press.

Wilcox, Clyde, Ted G. Jelen, and David C. Leege. 1993. "Religious Group Identification: Toward a Cognitive Theory of Religious Mobilization." In *Rediscovering the Religious Factor in American Politics*, ed. David C. Leege and Lyman A. Kellstedt. Armonk, N.Y.: Sharpe, 72–99.

Wilcox, Clyde, Mark J. Rozell, and Ronald Gunn. 1997. "Religious Coalitions in the New Christian Right." *Social Science Quarterly* 77, no. 3 (September): 543–58.

Wills, Gary. 1989. "Evangels of Abortion." *New York Review of Books* 36, no. 10 (June 15): 15–21.

9

Collective Identity in Social Movement Communities: Lesbian Feminist Mobilization

Verta Taylor and Nancy E. Whittier

Understanding the relationship between group consciousness and collective action has been a major focus of social science research (Morris 1990). The resource mobilization and political process perspectives, in contrast to earlier microlevel analyses, have shifted attention to the macrolevel, deemphasizing group grievances and focusing instead on the external political processes and internal organizational dynamics that influence the rise and course of movements (Rule and Tilly 1972; Oberschall 1973; McCarthy and Zald 1973, 1977; Gamson 1975; Jenkins and Perrow 1977; Schwartz 1976; Tilly 1978; McAdam 1982; Jenkins 1983; Morris 1984). But the resource mobilization and political process theories cannot explain how structural inequality gets translated into subjectively experienced discontent (Fireman and Gamson 1979; Ferree and Miller 1985; Snow et al. 1986; Klandermans 1984; Klandermans and Tarrow 1988; Ferree 1992). In a recent review of the field, McAdam, McCarthy, and Zald (1988) respond by offering the concept of the micromobilization context to characterize the link between the macrolevel and microlevel processes that generate collective action. Drawing from a wide range of research documenting the importance of preexisting group ties for movement formation, they view informal networks held together by strong bonds as the "basic building blocks" of social movements. Still missing, however, is an understanding of the way these networks transform their members into political actors.

European analyses of recent social movements, loosely grouped under the rubric "new social movement theory," suggest that a key concept that allows us to understand this process is collective identity (Pizzorno 1978; Boggs 1986; Cohen 1985; Melucci 1985, 1989; Touraine 1985; Epstein 1990). Collective identity is the shared definition of a group that derives from members' common interests, experiences, and solidarity. For new social movement theorists, political organizing around a common identity is what distinguishes recent social movements in Europe and the United States from the more class-based movements of the past (Kauffman 1990). It is our view, based on existing scholarship (Friedman and McAdam 1992, Fantasia 1988, Mueller 1990, Rupp and Taylor 1987, Taylor and Rupp 1993, Whittier 1991), that identity construction processes are crucial to grievance interpretation in all forms of collective action, not just in the so-called new movements. Despite the centrality of collective identity to new social movement theory, no one has dissected the way that constituencies involved in defending their rights develop politicized group identities.

In this chapter, we present a framework for analyzing the construction of collective identity in social movements. The framework is grounded in exploratory research on the contemporary lesbian feminist movement in the United States. Drawing from Gerson and Peiss's (1985) model for analyzing gender relations, we offer a conceptual bridge linking theoretical approaches in the symbolic interactionist tradition with existing theory in social movements. Our aim is to provide a definition of collective identity that is broad enough to encompass mobilizations ranging from those based on race, gender, ethnicity, and sexuality to constituencies organized around more focused visions.

After discussing the data sources, we trace the evolution of lesbian feminism in the early 1970s out of the radical branch of the modern women's movement and analyze lesbian feminism as a social movement community. Substantively, our aim is to demonstrate that lesbian feminist communities sustain a collective identity that encourages women to engage in a wide range of social and political actions that challenge the dominant system. Theoretically, we use this case to present an analytical definition of the concept of collective identity. Finally, we conclude by arguing that the existence of lesbian feminist communities challenges the popular perception that feminists have withdrawn from the battle and the scholarly view that organizing around identity directs attention away from challenges to institutionalized power structures (Epstein 1990).

We have used two main sources of data: published primary materials and interviews with participants in lesbian feminist communities. The written sources include books, periodicals, and narratives by community members (Johnston 1973, Koedt et al. 1973, Daly 1978, Baetz 1980, Cruik-shank 1980, Stanley and Wolfe 1980, Moraga and Anzaldua 1981, Beck 1980, Smith 1983, Daly and Caputi 1987, Frye 1983, Grahn 1984, Johnson 1987) and newsletters, position papers, and other documents from lesbian feminist organizations. We have also incorporated secondary data from histories of the women's movement and ethnographies of lesbian communities (Hole and Levine 1971, Barnhart 1975, Ponse 1978, Lewis 1979, Wolf 1979, Krieger 1983, Davis and Kennedy 1986, Lockard 1986, Lord unpublished, Echols 1989).

In addition, we have conducted twenty-one interviews with lesbian feminists who served as informants about their communities, which included Boston, Provincetown, and the rural Berkshire region of Massachusetts; Portland, Maine; Washington, D.C.; New York City; Key West and St. Petersburg, Florida; Columbus, Yellow Springs, Cleveland, and Cincinnati, Ohio; Minneapolis; Chicago; Denver; Atlanta; and Charlotte, North Carolina. The informants range in age from twenty-one to sixty-eight; sixteen are white, four are black, and one is Hispanic; the majority are from middle-class backgrounds. They are employed as professionals or semiprofessionals, small business owners, students, and blue-collar workers. Interviewees were recruited through snowballing procedures and announcements and notices posted at lesbian events. The in-depth interviews were open-ended and semistructured, lasting from one to three hours, and were tape-recorded and transcribed. The analysis also draws on our experiences as members of the larger community.

Since this work focuses primarily on lesbian feminist activism in the midwestern and eastern regions of the United States, we regard our conclusions as exploratory and generalizable primarily to this sector of the larger lesbian community. It is important to keep in mind that not all lesbians are associated with the communities described here.

The Lesbian Feminist Social Movement Community

Analyzing the historical evolution of organizational forms in the American women's movement, Buechler (1990) proposes the concept of a social movement community to expand our understanding of the variety of forms of collective action. Buechler's concept underscores the importance to mobilization of informational networks, decentralized structures, and alternative institutions. But, like most work in the resource mobilization tradition, it overlooks the values and symbolic understandings created by discontented groups in the course of struggling to achieve change (Lofland 1979, 1985).

Here it is useful to turn to recent literature on lesbian communities that emphasizes the cultural components of lesbian activism, specifically the development of counterinstitutions, shared norms, values, and symbolic, forms of resistance (Wolf 1979, Krieger 1983, Lockard 1986, Davis and Kennedy 1986, Phelan 1989, Esterberg 1990). From this perspective, we expand on Buechler's model by defining a social movement community as a network of individuals and groups loosely linked through an institutional base, multiple goals and actions, and a collective identity that affirms members' common interests in opposition to dominant groups.

We describe lesbian feminism as a social movement community that operates at the national level through connections among local communities in the decentralized, segmented, and reticulate structure described by Gerlach and Hine (1970). Like other new social movements, the lesbian feminist movement does not mobilize through formal social movement organizations. Rather, structurally the movement is composed of what Melucci (1989) terms "submerged networks" propelled by constantly shifting forms of resistance that include alternative symbolic systems as well as new forms of political struggle and participation (Emberley and Landry 1989). Although participants use different labels to describe the movement, we are interested here in the segment of the contemporary women's movement characterized as "cultural feminism" (Ferree and Hess 1985, Echols 1989) or "lesbian feminism" (Adam 1987, Phelan 1989). We prefer "lesbian feminism" for three reasons. It is the label most often used in movement writings, although participants also refer to the "women's community," "feminist community," and "lesbian community." Second, it locates the origins of this community in the contemporary women's movement. Finally, the term makes explicit the vital role of lesbians in the women's movement. The term "cultural feminism" erases the participation of lesbians and obscures the fact that a great deal of the current criticism leveled at cultural feminism is, in reality, directed at lesbian feminism.

Scholars have depicted the women's movement that blossomed in the 1960s and 1970s as having two segments, a women's rights or liberal branch and a women's liberation or radical branch (Freeman 1975). The liberal branch consisted primarily of national-level, hierarchically organized, formal organizations like the National Organization for Women (NOW) that used institutionalized legal tactics to pursue equal rights (Gelb and Palley 1982). The radical branch emerged in the late 1960s out of the civil rights and New Left movements and formed a decentralized network of primarily local, autonomous groups lacking formal organization and using flamboyant and disruptive tactics to pursue fundamental transformation of patriarchal structures and values (Hole and Levine 1971, Evans 1979). It is impossible to comprehend contemporary lesbian feminism without locating it in the radical feminist tradition.

Ideologically and strategically, radical feminism opposed liberalism, pursued social transformation through the creation of alternative nonhierarchical institutions and forms of organization intended to prefigure a utopian feminist society, held gender oppression to be primary and the model of all other forms of oppression, and emphasized women's commonality as a sex-class through consciousness-raising. Although it coalesced around common issues such as rape, battering, and abortion, radical feminism was never monolithic (Jaggar and Struhl 1978, Ferree and Hess 1985). By the mid-1970s, radical feminism confronted an increasingly conservative and inhospitable social climate and was fraught with conflict over differences of sexuality, race, and class (Taylor 1989a). Recent scholarship argues that the most important disputes focused on the question of lesbianism (Echols 1989, Ryan 1989).

Conflict between lesbian and heterosexual feminists originated in the early 1970s. Although women who love other women have always been among those who participated in the feminist struggle, it was not until the emergence of the gay liberation movement that lesbians demanded recognition and support from the women's movement. Instead they encountered overt hostility in both the liberal and radical branches. The founder of NOW, Betty Friedan, for example, dismissed lesbianism as the "lavender herring" of the movement. Since charges of lesbianism have often been used to discredit women who challenge traditional roles (Rupp 1989, Schneider 1986), feminists sought to avoid public admission that there were, in fact, lesbians in their ranks.

Echols (1989) traces the beginning of lesbian feminism to 1971 with the founding of the Furies in Washington, D.C. This was the first separate lesbian feminist group, and others formed shortly thereafter in New York, Boston, Chicago, San Francisco, and other urban localities around the country. The Furies is significant because it included women such as Charlotte Bunch, Rita Mae Brown, and Colletta Reid who, along with Ti-Grace Atkinson, ex-president of the New York chapter of NOW and founder of the Feminists, articulated the position that would lay the foundation for lesbian feminism (Hole and Levine 1971, Atkinson 1974, Bunch 1986). They advocated lesbian separatism and recast lesbianism as a political strategy that was the logical outcome of feminism, the quintessential expression of the "personal as political." As a result, heterosexual feminists found themselves increasingly on the defensive.

If early radical feminism was driven by the belief that women are more alike than different, then the fissures that beset radical feminism in the mid-1970s were about clarifying the differences—on the basis of race, class, and ethnicity as well as sexual identity—among the "group called women" (Cassell 1977). Recent scholarship argues that such conflict ultimately led to the demise of radical feminism and the rise of what its critics have called "cultural feminism," leaving liberal feminism in control of the women's movement (Echols 1989, Ryan 1989).

We agree with the dominant view that disputes over sexuality, class, and race contributed to the decline of the radical feminist branch of the movement. We do not, however, agree that radical feminism was replaced by a cultural haven for women who have withdrawn from the battle (Snitow, Stansell, and Thompson 1983, Vance 1984, Echols 1989). Rather, we hold that radical feminism gave way to a new cycle of feminist activism sustained by lesbian feminist communities. These communities socialize members into a collective oppositional consciousness that channels women into a variety of actions geared toward personal, social, and political change.

Although no research has been undertaken to document the extent of lesbian communities across the nation, existing work has focused on a number of different localities (e.g., Barnhart's [1975] ethnography of Portland, Wolf's [1979] study of San Francisco, Krieger's [1983] ethnography of midwestern community, Lockard's [1986] description of a southwestern community). White (1980) describes the major trend-setting centers of the gay and lesbian movement as Boston, Washington, San Francisco, and New York. Although our analysis is exploratory and based on only seventeen communities, our data suggest that developments in the major cities are reflected throughout the United States in urban areas as well as in smaller communities with major colleges and universities.

Collective Identity: Boundaries, Consciousness, and Negotiation

The study of identity in sociology has been approached at the individual and systemic levels as well as in both structural and more dynamic social constructionist terms (Weigert et al. 1986). New social movement theorists, in particular Pizzorno (1978), Boggs (1986), Melucci (1985, 1989), Offe (1985), and Touraine (1985), take the politics of personal transformation as one of their central theoretical problematics, which is why these approaches are sometimes referred to as "identity-oriented paradigms" (Cohen 1985). Sometimes labeled postmodernist, new social movement perspectives are social constructionist paradigms (Epstein 1990). From this standpoint, collective political actors do not exist de facto by virtue of individuals sharing a common structural location; they are created in the course of social movement activity. To understand any politicized identity community, it is necessary to analyze the social and political struggle that created the identity.

In some ways, the most apparent feature of the new movements has been a vision of power as operating at different levels so that collective self-transformation is itself a major strategy of political change. Reviewing work in the new social movement tradition suggests three elements of collective identity. First, individuals see themselves as part of a group when some shared characteristic becomes salient and is defined as important. For Touraine (1985) and Melucci (1989), this sense of "we" is evidence of all increasingly fragmented and pluralistic social reality that is, in part, a result of the new movements. A crucial characteristic of the movements of the seventies and eighties has been the advocacy of new group understandings, self-conceptions, ways of thinking, and cultural categories. In Touraine's model, it is all awareness of how the group's interests conflict with the interests of its adversaries, the adoption of a critical picture of the culture as a whole, and the recognition of the broad stakes of the conflict that differentiate contemporary movements from classical ones. Thus, the second component of collective identity is what Cohen (1985) terms "consciousness." Consistent with the vision of the movements themselves, Melucci defines a movement's "cognitive frameworks" broadly to include not only political consciousness and relational networks but its "goals, means, and environment of action" (1989, 35). Finally, for new social movement theorists, the concept of collective identity implies direct opposition to the dominant order. Melucci holds that social movements build "submerged networks" of political culture that are interwoven with everyday life and provide new expressions of identity that challenge dominant representations (1989, 35). In essence, as Pizzorno (1978) suggests, the purposeful and expressive disclosure to others of one's subjective feelings, desires, and experiences—or social identity—for the purpose of gaining recognition and influence is collective action.

Our framework draws from feminist theoretical approaches in the symbolic interactionist tradition (Gerson and Peiss 1985, Margolis 1985, West and Zimmerman 1987, Chafetz 1988). These formulations differ from structural and other social psychological approaches that tend to reify gender as a role category or trait of individuals. Instead, they view gender hierarchy as constantly created through displays and interactions governed by gender-normative behavior that comes to be perceived as natural and normal. Gerson and Peiss (1985) offer a model for understanding how gender inequality is reproduced and maintained through social interaction. Although they recognize the social change potential of the model, they do not address this aspect systematically.

Building on their work, we propose three factors as analytical tools for understanding the construction of collective identity in social movements. The concept of *boundaries* refers to the social, psychological, and physical structures that establish differences between a challenging group and dominant groups. *Consciousness* consists of the interpretive frameworks that emerge out of a challenging group's struggle to define and realize its interests. *Negotiation* encompasses the symbols and everyday actions subordinate groups use to resist and restructure existing systems of domination.

Boundaries

Boundaries mark the social territories of group relations by highlighting differences between activists and the web of others in the contested social world. Of course, it is usually the dominant group that erects social, political, economic, and cultural boundaries to accentuate the differences between itself and minority populations. Paradoxically, however, for groups organizing to pursue collective ends, the process of asserting "who we are" often involves a kind of reverse affirmation of the characteristics attributed to it by the larger society. Boundary markers are, therefore, central to the formation of collective identity because they promote a heightened awareness of a group's commonalities and frame interaction between members of the in-group and the out-group.

For any subordinate group, the construction of positive identity requires both a withdrawal from the values and structures of the dominant, oppressive society and the creation of new self-affirming values and structures. Newer approaches to the study of ethnic mobilization define ethnicity not in essentialist terms but in relation to socially and politically constructed boundaries that differentiate ethnic populations (Barth 1969, Olzak 1983). This is a useful way of understanding the commonalities that develop among members of any socially recognized group or category organized around a shared characteristic. It underscores the extent to which differentiation and devaluation is a fundamental process in all hierarchical systems and has two advantages over other approaches (Reskin 1988).

First, the concept of boundaries avoids the reification of ascriptive and other differentiating characteristics that are the basis for dominance systems (Reskin 1988). Second, it transcends the assumption of group sameness implied by single-factor stratification systems because it allows us to analyze the impact of multiple systems of domination based on race, sex, class, ethnicity, age, sexuality, and other factors (Morris 1990). These distinct hierarchies not only produce differentiation within subordinate groups but affect the permeability of boundaries between the subordinate and dominant groups (Collins 1989, Morris 1990, Zinn 1990).

Boundary markers can vary from geographical, racial, and religious characteristics to more symbolically constructed differences such as social institutions and cultural systems. Our analysis focuses on two types of boundary strategies adopted by lesbian feminists as a means of countering male domination: the creation of separate institutions and the development of a distinct women's culture guided by "female" values.

Alternative institutions were originally conceived by radical feminists both as islands of resistance against patriarchy and as a means to gain power by improving women's lives and enhancing their resources (Taylor 1989a, Echols 1989). Beginning in the early 1970s, radical feminists established separate health centers, rape crisis centers, battered women's shelters, bookstores, publishing and record companies, newspapers, credit unions, and poetry and writing groups. Through the 1980s, feminist institutions proliferated to include recovery groups, business guilds, martial arts groups, restaurants, AIDS projects, spirituality groups, artists' colonies, and groups for women of color, Jewish feminists, disabled women, lesbian mothers, and older women. Some lesbian feminist groups were not entirely autonomous but functioned as separate units or caucuses in existing organizations, such as women's centers and women's studies programs in universities.

As the mass women's movement receded in the 1980s, the liberal branch abandoned protest and unruly tactics in favor of actions geared toward gaining access in the political arena (Rupp and Taylor 1986, Mueller 1987, Echols 1989). An elaborate network of feminist counterinstitutions remained, however, and increasingly were driven by the commitment of lesbian feminists. This is not to say that they were the sole preserve of lesbians. Rather, it is our view that what is described generally as "women's culture" to emphasize its availability to all women has become a predominantly lesbian feminist culture.

A number of national events link local lesbian feminist communities, including the annual five-day Michigan Womyn's Music Festival attended by four thousand to ten thousand women, the National Women's Writers' Conference, and the National Women's Studies Association Conference. In addition, local and regional events and conferences on the arts, literature, and, in the academic professions, feminist issues proliferated through the 1980s. National newspapers such as *off our backs*, national magazines such as *Outlook*, publishing companies such as Naiad, Persephone, and Kitchen Table: Women of Color Press, and a variety of journals and newsletters continue to publicize feminist ideas and activities. In short, throughout the 1980s, as neoconservatism was winning political and intellectual victories, lesbian feminists struggled to build a world apart from male domination.

The second boundary that is central to lesbian feminist identity is the creation of a symbolic system that affirms the culture's idealization of the female and, as a challenge to the misogyny of the dominant society, vilifies the male. Perhaps the strongest thread running through the tapestry of lesbian feminist culture is the belief that women's nature and modes of

relating differ fundamentally from men's. For those who hold this position, the set of traits generally perceived as female are egalitarianism, col-
lectivism, an ethic of care, a respect for knowledge derived from experience, pacifism, and cooperation. In contrast, male characteristics are
thought to include an emphasis on hierarchy, oppressive individualism,
an ethic of individual rights, abstraction, violence, and competition.
These gender boundaries are confirmed by a formal body of feminist
scholarship (see, e.g., Rich 1976, 1980; Chodorow 1978; Gilligan 1982;
Rubin 1984; Collins 1989) as well as in popular writings (see, e.g., Walker
1974; Daly 1978, 1984; Cavin 1985; Dworkin 1981; Johnson 1987). Johnson,
for example, characterizes the differences between women and men as
based on the contrast between "masculine life-hating values" and "wom-
en's life-loving culture" (1987, 226).

Our interviews suggest that the belief that there are fundamental differences between women and men is widely held by individual activists.
One lesbian feminist explains that "we've been acculturated into two cultures, the male culture and the female culture. And luckily we've been
able to preserve the ways of nurturing by being in this alternative culture."

Because women's standards are deemed superior, it is not surprising
that men, including older male children, are often excluded from community events and business establishments. At the Michigan Womyn's Music
Festival, for example, male children over the age of three are not permitted in the festival area, but must stay at a separate camp. Reversing the
common cultural practice of referring to adult women as "girls," it is not
unusual for lesbian feminists to refer to men, including gay men, as
"boys."

Maintaining an oppositional identity depends upon creating a world
apart from the dominant society. The boundaries that are drawn around
a group are not entirely a matter of choice. The process of reshaping one's
collective world, however, involves the investiture of meaning that goes
beyond the objective conditions out of which a group is created. Seen in
this way, it is easy to understand how identity politics promotes a kind
of cultural endogamy that, paradoxically, erects boundaries within the
challenging group, dividing it on the basis of race, class, age, religion, ethnicity, and other factors. When asked to define the lesbian feminist community, one participant highlights this process by stating that "if there is
such a thing as a lesboworld, then there are just as many diversities of
communities in that world as there are in the heteroworld."

Consciousness

Boundaries locate persons as members of a group, but it is group consciousness that imparts larger significance to a collectivity. We use the

concept of consciousness to refer to the interpretive frameworks that emerge from a group's struggle to define and realize members' common interests in opposition to the dominant order. Although sociologists have focused primarily on class consciousness, Morris (1990) argues that the term *political consciousness* is more useful because it emphasizes that all systems of human domination create opposing interests capable of generating oppositional consciousness. Whatever the term, the important point is that collective actors must attribute their discontent to structural, cultural, or systemic causes rather than to personal failings or individual deviance (Ferree and Miller 1985, Touraine 1985).

Our notion of consciousness builds on the idea of cognitive liberation (McAdam 1982), frames (Snow et al. 1986), cognitive frameworks (Melucci 1989), and collective consciousness (Mueller 1987). We see the development of consciousness as an ongoing process in which groups reevaluate themselves, their subjective experiences, their opportunities, and their shared interests. Consciousness is imparted through a formal body of writings, speeches, and documents. More important, when a movement is successful at creating a collective identity, its interpretive orientations are interwoven with the fabric of everyday life. Consciousness not only provides socially and politically marginalized groups with an understanding of their structural position but establishes new expectations regarding treatment appropriate to their category. Of course, groups can mobilize around a collective consciousness that supports the status quo. Thus, it is only when a group develops an account that challenges dominant understandings that we can use the term *oppositional consciousness* (Morris 1990).

Contemporary lesbian feminist consciousness is not monolithic. But its mainspring is the view that heterosexuality is an institution of patriarchal control and that lesbian relationships are a means of subverting domination. The relationship between feminism and lesbianism is well summarized by the classic slogan "feminism is the theory and lesbianism is the practice," mentioned by a number of our informants. Arguing that sexism and heterosexism are inextricably intertwined, lesbian feminists in the early 1970s characterized lesbianism as "the rage of all women condensed to the point of explosion" (Radicalesbians 1973, 240) and held that women who choose lesbianism are the vanguard of the women's movement (Birkby et al. 1973; Myron and Bunch 1975; Daly 1978, 1984; Frye 1983; Hoagland 1988). The classic rationale for this position, frequently reprinted in newsletters and other lesbian publications, is Ti-Grace Atkinson's analogy: "Can you imagine a Frenchman, serving in the French army from 9 A.M. to 5 P.M., then trotting 'home' to Germany for supper overnight?" (1974, 11).

Despite the common thread running through lesbian feminist consciousness that sexual relationships between women are to be understood in reference to the political structure of male supremacy and male domination, there are two distinct strands of thought about lesbian identity. One position holds that lesbianism is not an essential or biological characteristic but is socially constructed. In a recent analysis of the history of lesbian political consciousness, Phelan (1989) argues that lesbian feminist consciousness emerged and has been driven by a rejection of the liberal view that sexuality is a private or individual matter. A classic exposition of the social constructionist position can be found in Rich's "Compulsory Heterosexuality and Lesbian Existence" (1980), which defines lesbian identity not as sexual but as political. Rich introduces the concept of the "lesbian continuum" to include all women who are woman-identified and who resist patriarchy. By locating lesbianism squarely within the new scholarship on the female world, Rich, like other social constructionists, suggests that sexuality is a matter of choice.

If it is not sexual experience but an emotional and political orientation toward women that defines one as lesbian, then, as the song by Alix Dobkin puts it, "any woman can be a lesbian." Lesbian feminist communities in fact contain women who are oriented toward women emotionally and politically but not sexually. These women are sometimes referred to as "political dykes" or "heterodykes" (Clausen 1990, Smeller unpublished), and community members think of them as women who "haven't come out yet." Some women who have had both male and female lovers resist being labeled bisexual and cling to a lesbian identity. For example, well-known singer and songwriter Holly Near explains: "I am too closely linked to the political perspective of lesbian feminism. . . . it is part of my world view, part of my passion for women and central in my objection to male domination" (1990). The significance of lesbian identity for feminist activists is well summarized by the name of a feminist support group at a major university, Lesbians Who Just Happen to Be Dating Politically Correct Men.

The second strand of lesbian feminist thought aims to bring sex back into the definition of lesbianism (Treblecot 1979, Califia 1982, Ferguson 1982, Zita 1982, Hollibaugh and Moraga 1983, Rubin 1984, Nestle 1987, Penelope 1990). Criticizing the asexuality of lesbian feminism, Echols suggests that, in contemporary women's communities, "women's sexuality is assumed to be more spiritual than sexual, and considerably less central to their lives than is sexuality to men's" (1984, 60). Putting it more bluntly, sadomasochism advocate Pat Califia characterizes contemporary lesbian feminism as "anti-sex," using the term "vanilla feminism" to dismiss what she charges is a traditionally feminine passive attitude toward sex (1980). These "pro-sex" or "sex radical" writers tend to view sexuality less as a matter of choice and more as an essential characteristic. So, too, do some lesbian separatists, who have little else in common with the sex radicals. Arguing against social constructionism, Penelope (1990) places lesbianism squarely in the sexual arena. She points to the historical presence of women who loved other women sexually and emotionally prior to the nineteenth-century invention of the term lesbian and emphasizes that currently there are a variety of ways that women come to call themselves lesbian. In our interviews with lesbian activists, it was not uncommon for women who embraced essentialist notions to engage in biographical reconstruction, reinterpreting all of their prelesbian experiences as evidence of lesbian sexuality.

The emphasis on sexuality calls attention to the unknown numbers of women engaged in same-sex behavior who do not designate themselves lesbian and the enclaves of women who identify as lesbian but have not adopted lesbian feminist ideology and practice. These include lesbians who organize their social lives around gay bars (Nestle 1987), women who remain in the closet, pretending to be heterosexual but having sexual relationships with other women, and women who marry men and have relationships with women on the side. Describing the variousness of the contemporary lesbian experience and the multiple ways women come to call themselves lesbian, one of our interviewees discussed "pc [politically correct] dykes," "heterodykes," "maybelline dykes," "earth crunchy lesbians," "bar dykes," "phys ed dykes," "professional dykes," and "fluffy dykes."

For a large number of women, locating lesbianism in the feminist arena precludes forming meaningful political alliances with gay men. In part, this is because issues of sexual freedom that many feminists have viewed as exploiting women, including pornography, sexual contact between the young and old, and consensual sadomasochism, have been central to the predominantly male gay liberation movement (Adam 1987). Adam, however, suggests that, despite some conflicting interests, the latter part of the 1980s saw growing coalitions between lesbian feminists and gay liberationists surrounding the issue of AIDS. Our data confirm this hypothesis.

Yet it is perhaps not coincidental that at a time when lesbian feminist communities serve increasingly as mobilization contexts for the larger lesbian and gay movement, lesbian activists describe a resurgence of lesbian separatism. Calls for more "women only space" pervaded gay and lesbian newsletters by the end of the 1980s (Japenga 1990).

Thus, our analysis suggests that an important element of lesbian feminist consciousness is the reevaluation of lesbianism as feminism. A number of recent studies, though admittedly based on small samples, confirm that the majority of women who openly embrace a lesbian identity interpret lesbianism within the framework of radical feminist ideology (Kitzinger 1987, Devor 1989, Phelan 1989). Removing lesbian behavior from the deviant clinical realm and placing it in the somewhat more acceptable feminist arena establishes lesbian identity as distinct from gay identity. Yet an increasingly vocal segment of lesbian feminists endorses a more essentialist, or what Epstein (1987) terms "modified social constructionist," explanation of lesbianism. They have undoubtedly been influenced by the identity politics of the liberal branch of the gay liberation movement that has, in recent years, advocated that sexuality is less a matter of choice and more a matter of biology and early socialization.

Highlighting the significance of a dominated group's own explanation of its position for political action, Kitzinger (1987) uses the term *identity accounts* to distinguish the range of group understandings that emerge among oppressed groups to make sense of themselves and their situation. Our findings confirm that these self-understandings not only influence mobilization possibilities and directions but determine the types of individual and collective actions that groups pursue to challenge dominant arrangements. In the next section, we examine lesbian feminist practice, emphasizing that it is comprehensible only because it presupposes the existence of a theory of lesbian identity.

Negotiation

Viewing collective identity as the result of repeatedly activated shared definitions, as new social movement theorists do, makes it difficult to distinguish between "doing" and "being," or between social movement organizations and their strategies. Although recent social movement analyses tend to emphasize primarily the political and structural aims of challenging groups, personal transformation and expressive action have been central to most movements (Morris 1984, Fantasia 1988, McNall 1988). The insistence that the construction and expression of a collective vision is politics, or the politicization of the self and daily life, is nevertheless the core of what is "new" about the new social movements (Breines 1982, Melucci 1988, Kauffman 1990). Thus, we propose a framework that recognizes that identity can be a fundamental focus of political work.

Margolis (1985) suggests the concept of negotiation, drawn from the symbolic interactionist tradition, as a way of analyzing the process by which social movements work to change symbolic meanings. Most interactions between dominant and opposing groups reinforce established definitions. Individuals differentiated on the basis of characteristics are continuously responded to in ways that perpetuate their disadvantaged status (Reskin 1988). West and Zimmerman (1987) use the term *identificatory displays* to emphasize, for example, that gender inequality is embedded and reproduced in even the most routine interactions. Similar analyses might be undertaken with regard to class, ethnicity, sexuality, and other sources of stratification. From a social movement standpoint, the concept of negotiations points to the myriad of ways that activists work to resist negative social definitions and demand that others value and treat oppositional groups differently (Goffman 1959).

The analysis of social movement negotiations forces us to recognize that, if not sociologically, then in reality, "doing" and "being" overlap (West and Zimmerman 1987). Yet we need a way to distinguish analytically between the politics of the public sphere, or world transformation directed primarily at the traditional political arena of the state, and the politics of identity, or self-transformation aimed primarily at the individual. We think that the concept of negotiations calls attention to forms of political activism embedded in everyday life that are distinct from those generally analyzed as tactics and strategies in the literature on social movements.

Building on Margolis's (1985) work on gender identity, we suggest two types of negotiation central to the construction of politicized collective identities. First, groups negotiate new ways of thinking and acting in *private* settings with other members of the collectivity, as well as in *public* settings before a larger audience. Second, identity negotiations can be *explicit*, involving open and direct attempts to free the group from dominant representations, or *implicit*, consisting of what Margolis terms a "condensed symbol or display" that undermines the status quo (1985, 340). In this section, we identify actions that lesbian feminist communities engage in to renegotiate the meaning of "woman." Opposition to male domination and the societal devaluation of women is directed both at the rules of daily life and at the institutions that perpetuate them.

In many respects, the phrase "the personal is political," coined by radical feminist Carol Hanisch and elaborated in Kate Millett's *Sexual Politics* (1970), is the hallmark of radical feminism (Echols 1989). Influenced by the civil rights and New Left movements, feminists began in the late 1960s to form consciousness-raising groups designed to reinterpret personal experiences in political terms. Analyzing virtually every aspect of individual and social experience as male-dominated, the groups encouraged participants to challenge prevailing representations of women in every sphere of life as a means of transforming the institutions that produced and disseminated them (Cassell 1977). The politicization of everyday life extended beyond the black power and feminist movements into other movements of the 1960s. In contemporary lesbian feminist communities the valorization of personal experience continues to have a profound impact.

Community members see lesbianism as a strategy for feminist social change that represents what one respondent describes as "an attempt . . . to stop doing what you were taught—hating women." Other women speak of the importance of learning to "value women," becoming "woman-centered," and "giving women energy." Being woman-centered is viewed as challenging conventional expectations that women orient themselves psychologically and socially toward men, compete with other women for male attention, and devalue other women. To make a more complete break with patriarchal identities and ways of life, some women exchange their male-given surnames for woman-centered ones, such as "Sarachild" or "Blackwomyn." Loving and valuing women becomes a means to resist a culture that hates and belittles women. Invoking Alice Walker's (1974) concept of "womanist," one black woman that we interviewed explained, "My lesbianism has nothing to do with men. It's not about not choosing men, but about choosing women."

At the group level, lesbian feminists structure organizations collectively (Rothschild-Whitt 1979) and attempt to eliminate hierarchy, make decisions by consensus, and form coalitions only with groups that are not, as one activist said, "giving energy to the patriarchy." Demands for societal change seek to replace existing organizational forms and values with ones similar to those implemented in the community (Breines 1982). A worker at a women's festival illustrated the importance of community structure as a model for social change by commenting to women as they left the festival, "You've seen the way the real world can be, and now it's up to you to go out there and change it."

Because a traditionally feminine appearance, demeanor, self-concept, and style of personal relations are thought to be among the mainsprings of women's oppression, lesbian feminist communities have adopted different standards of gender behavior. For example, one of the visions of feminism has been to reconstitute the experience of victimization. Thus, women who have been battered or raped or have experienced incest and other forms of abuse are termed "survivors" to redefine their experiences as resistance to male violence. New recruits to the community are resocialized through participating in a variety of organizations—women's twelve-step programs, battered women's shelters, martial arts groups, incest survivors' groups—that provide not only self-help but also a means for women to renegotiate a lesbian feminist identity. The very name of one such organization in New York City, Identity House, is illustrative. Lesbian mothers organize support groups called "momazonians" or "dykes with tykes" to emphasize that motherhood is a crucial locus of contestation. "Take Back the Night" marches against violence, pro-choice demonstrations, participation in spontaneous protests, and feminist music, theater, and dramatic presentations are other examples of public arenas for negotiating new standards of gender behavior.

Essential to contemporary lesbian feminist identity is a distinction between the lesbian who is a staunch feminist activist and the lesbian who is not of the vanguard. Thus, commitment to the politics of direct action distinguishes members of the lesbian feminist community from the larger population of lesbians. One participant illustrates the importance of this distinction, stating that women "who say that they are lesbians and maybe have sexual relationships with women, but don't have the feminist politics" compose a category who "could have been in the community, but they've opted out." Women even choose partners based on political commitment, noting that "sleeping with a woman who is not a feminist just doesn't work for me; there's too much political conflict." The tendency to choose life partners and form other close personal relationships based on shared political assumptions is not, however, unique to lesbian feminism but has been reported in relation to other movements as well (Rupp and Taylor 1986, McAdam 1988). In short, negotiating new gender definitions is central to lesbian feminist collective identity.

Challenging further the notion of femininity as frailty, passivity, and preoccupation with reigning standards of beauty, many women wear clothing that enables freedom of movement, adopt short or simple haircuts, walk with firm self-assured strides, and choose not to shave their legs or wear heavy makeup. Devor (1989) terms this mode of self-presentation "gender blending," arguing that it represents an explicit rejection of the norms of femininity and, by extension, of women's subjugation. By reversing reigning cultural standards of femininity, beauty, and respectability, lesbian feminists strike a blow against female objectification. How central this is to lesbian feminist identity is illustrated by a lesbian support group at a major university with the name Women in Comfortable Shoes.

Because appearance and demeanor are also implicit means of expressing one's opposition, community members' presentation of self is subject to close scrutiny or, to use the vernacular of the activists themselves, is monitored by the "pc police." Women who dress in stereotypically "feminine" ways are often criticized and admit to feeling "politically incorrect." As one respondent commented, "I've always had a lot of guilt feelings about, why don't I just buckle down and put on some bluejeans, and clip my hair short, and not wear makeup, and go aggressively through the world." Some of our interviewees report a return to gendered fashion in contemporary lesbian communities. Women who identify as sex radicals, in particular, have adopted styles of dress traditionally associated with the "sex trade," or prostitution, such as miniskirts, low-cut tops, and fishnet stockings, sometimes combined with more traditionally masculine styles in what is known as a "gender fuck" style of dressing. Suggesting that "the most profound and potentially the most radical politics come directly out of our own identity" (Combahee River Collective 1982), African American feminists criticize the tendency of many white lesbian feminists to dictate a politics based on hegemonic cultural standards. Some women who are identifiably butch and dress in studded leather clothing and punk and neon haircuts offer class-based motivations for their demeanor, and African American, Asian American, and Latina lesbians embrace different cultural styles. In short, the changes in appearance and behavior women undergo as they come out cannot be fully understood as individually chosen but are often the ultimatum of identity communities (Krieger 1982).

We have presented three dimensions for analyzing collective identity in social movements: the concepts of boundaries, consciousness, and negotiation. Although we have treated each as if it were independent, in reality the three interact. Using these factors to analyze lesbian feminist identity suggests three elements that shape the social construction of lesbian feminism. First, lesbian feminist communities draw boundaries that affirm femaleness and separate them from a larger world perceived as hostile. Second, to undermine the dominant view of lesbianism as perversion, lesbian feminists offer identity accounts that politicize sexuality. Finally, by defining lesbians as the vanguard of the women's movement, lesbian feminists valorize personal experience, which, paradoxically, further reifies the boundaries between lesbians and nonlesbians and creates the impression that the differences between women and men and between lesbian and heterosexual feminists are essential.

Conclusion

In this chapter, we argue that lesbian feminist consciousness is rooted in a social movement community with ties to but distinguishable from both the gay liberation and the liberal feminist movements. In effect, we are suggesting that with the absorption of the liberal feminist agenda into the liberal mainstream, the legacy of radical feminism continues in the lesbian feminist community. It is difficult to imagine an argument that would be more controversial in feminist circles, for it confirms the premise that, at least in the contemporary context, lesbianism and feminism are intertwined. This leads to the question posed in a recent speech by feminist philosopher Marilyn Frye (1990), "Do you have to be a lesbian to be a feminist?" It is our view that lesbian communities are a type of social movement abeyance structure that absorbs highly committed feminists whose radical politics have grown increasingly marginal since the mass women's movement has receded (Taylor and Whittier 1992). However insulated, they function to sustain the feminist challenge in a less receptive political climate (Taylor 1989b). Our findings are controversial in another respect. By calling attention to the centrality of feminism for lesbian activism, our study paints a picture of the tenuousness of the coalition between gay men and lesbians in the larger gay and lesbian movement.

Drawing from new data and recent scholarship on lesbian communities, we use this case to illustrate the significance of collective identity for mobilization and to present a framework for analyzing identity processes in social movements. Adapting Gerson and Peiss's (1985) framework, we identify as factors that contribute to the formation of collective identity: (1) the creation of boundaries that insulate and differentiate a category of persons from the dominant society; (2) the development of consciousness that presumes the existence of socially constituted criteria that account for a group's structural position; and (3) the valorization of a group's "essential differences" through the politicization of everyday life.

The concept of collective identity is associated primarily with the social movements of the 1970s and 1980s because of their distinctive cultural appearance. It is our hypothesis, however, that collective identity is a significant variable in all social movements, even among the so-called traditional nineteenth-century movements. Thus, we frame our approach broadly to apply to oppositional identities based on class, race, ethnicity, gender, sexuality, and other persistent social cleavages. Certainly any theory derived from a single case is open to criticism. But recent research in the resource mobilization tradition points to the impact that changes in consciousness have on mobilization (Klein 1984, Downey 1986, Mueller 1987, McAdam 1988).

There is a growing realization among scholars of social movements that the theoretical pendulum between classical and contemporary approaches to social movements has swung too far. Social psychological factors that were central to collective behavior theory (Blumer 1946, Smelser 1962, Killian 1964, Turner and Killian 1972) have become the theoretical blind spots of resource mobilization theory. Ignoring the grievances or injustices that mobilize protest movements has, as Klandermans (1986) suggests, stripped social movements of their political significance. In contrast to the structural and organizational emphases of resource mobilization theory, new social movement theory attends to the social psychological and cultural discontent that propels movements. But it provides little understanding of how the injustices that are at the heart of most movements are translated into the everyday lives of collective actors. Our analysis suggests that the study of collective identity, because it highlights the role of meaning and ideology in the mobilization and maintenance of collective action, is an important key to understanding this process.

References

Adam, Barry D. 1987. *The Rise of a Gay and Lesbian Movement*. Boston: Twayne.
Atkinson, Ti-Grace. 1974. *Amazon Odyssey*. New York: Link Books.

Baetz, Ruth. 1980. *Lesbian Crossroads.* New York: Morrow.

Barnhart, Elizabeth. 1975. "Friends and Lovers in a Lesbian Counterculture Community." In *Old Family, New Family,* ed. N. Glazer-Malbin. New York: Van Nostrand, 90–115.

Barth, F. 1969. "Introduction." In *Ethnic Groups and Boundaries,* ed. F. Barth. Boston: Little, Brown, 1–38.

Beck, E. T. 1980. *Nice Jewish Girls: A Lesbian Anthology.* Watertown, Mass.: Persephone.

Birkby, Phyllis, Bertha Harris, Jill Johnston, Esther Newton, and Jane O'Wyatt. 1973. *Amazon Expedition: A Lesbian Feminist Anthology.* New York: Times Change Press.

Blumer, Herbert. 1946. "Collective Behavior." In *New Outline of the Principles of Sociology,* ed. A. M. Lee. New York: Barnes and Noble, 170–222.

Boggs, Carl. 1986. *Social Movements and Political Power.* Philadelphia: Temple University Press.

Breines, Wini. 1982. *Community and Organization in the New Left, 1962–68.* New York: Praeger.

Buechler, Steven M. 1990. *Women's Movements in the United States.* New Brunswick: Rutgers University Press.

Bunch, Charlotte. 1986. "Not for Lesbians Only." In *Feminist Frontiers II,* ed. Laurel Richardson and Verta Taylor. New York: Random House, 452–54.

Califia, Pat. 1980. "Feminism vs. Sex: A New Conservative Wave." *Advocate* (February 21).

———. 1982. "Public Sex." *Advocate* (September 30).

Cassell, Joan. 1977. *A Group Called Women: Sisterhood and Symbolism in the Feminist Movement.* New York: McKay.

Cavin, Susan. 1985. *Lesbian Origins.* San Francisco: Ism Press.

Chafetz, Janet Saltzman. 1988. *Feminist Sociology.* Itaska, Ill.: Peacock.

Chodorow, Nancy. 1978. *The Reproduction of Mothering: Psychoanalysis and the Sociology of Gender.* Berkeley: University of California Press.

Clausen, Jan. 1990. "My Interesting Condition." *Outlook* 2: 11–21.

Cohen, Jean L. 1985. "Strategy or Identity: New Theoretical Paradigms and Contemporary Social Movements." *Social Research* 52: 663–716.

Collins, Patricia Hill. 1989. "The Social Construction of Black Feminist Thought." *Signs* 14, no. 4: 745–73.

Combahee River Collective. 1982. "A Black Feminist Statement." In *But Some of Us Are Brave: Black Women's Studies,* ed. Gloria T. Hull, Patricia Bell Scott, and Barbara Smith. Old Westbury, N.Y.: Feminist Press, 13–22.

Cruikshank, Margaret. 1980. *The Lesbian Path.* Monterey, Calif.: Angel Press.

Daly, Mary. 1978. *Gyn/Ecology: The Metaethics of Radical Feminism.* Boston: Beacon Press.

———. 1984. *Pure Lust: Elemental Feminist Philosophy.* Boston: Beacon Press.

Daly, Mary, and Jane Caputi. 1987. *Websters' First New Intergalactic Wickedary of the English Language.* Boston: Beacon Press.

Davis, Madeleine, and Elizabeth Laprovsky Kennedy. 1986. "Oral History and the Study of Sexuality in the Lesbian Community." *Feminist Studies* 12: 6–26.

Devor, Holly. 1989. *Gender Blending*. Bloomington: Indiana University Press.

Downey, Gary L. 1986. "Ideology and the Clamshell Identity: Organizational Dilemmas in the Anti-Nuclear Power Movement." *Social Problems* 33: 357–73.

Dworkin, Andrea. 1981. *Pornography and Silence: Culture's Revenge against Nature.* New York: Harper and Row.

Echols, Alice. 1984. "The Taming of the Id: Feminist Sexual Politics, 1968–83." In *Pleasure and Danger: Exploring Female Sexuality*, ed. Carole S. Vance. Boston: Routledge and Kegan Paul, 50–72.

———. 1989. *Daring to Be Bad: Radical Feminism in America, 1967–1975*. Minneapolis: University of Minnesota Press.

Emberley, Julia, and Donna Landry. 1989. "Coverage of Greenham and Greenham as 'Coverage.' " *Feminist Studies* 15: 485–98.

Epstein, Barbara. 1990. "Rethinking Social Movement Theory." *Socialist Review* 20: 35–66.

Epstein, Steven. 1987. "Gay Politics, Ethnic Identity: The Limits of Social Constructionism." *Socialist Review* 17: 9–54.

Esterberg, Kristin Gay. 1990. "Salience and Solidarity: Identity, Correctness, and Conformity in a Lesbian Community." Paper presented at the annual meeting of the American Sociological Association, August 11–15, Washington, D.C.

Evans, Sarah. 1979. *Personal Politics.* New York: Vintage.

Fantasia, Rick. 1988. *Cultures of Solidarity.* Berkeley: University of California Press.

Ferguson, Ann. 1982. "Patriarchy, Sexual Identity, and the Sexual Revolution." In *Feminist Theory: A Critique of Ideology*, ed. Nannerl O. Keohane, Michelle Z. Rosaldo, and Barbara L. Gelpi. Chicago: University of Chicago Press, 147–61.

Ferree, Myra Marx. 1992. "The Political Context of Rationality: Rational Choice Theory and Resource Mobilization." In *Frontiers in Social Movement Theory*, ed. Aldon D. Morris and Carol McClurg Mueller. New Haven: Yale University Press, 29–52.

Ferree, Myra Marx, and Beth B. Hess. 1985. *Controversy and Coalition: The New Feminist Movement.* Boston: Twayne.

Ferree, Myra Marx, and Frederick D. Miller. 1985. "Mobilization and Meaning: Some Social-Psychological Contributions to the Resource Mobilization Perspective on Social Movements." *Sociological Inquiry* 55: 38–61.

Fireman, Bruce, and William Gamson. 1979. "Utilitarian Logic in the Resource Mobilization Perspective." In *The Dynamics of Social Movements*, ed. Mayer N. Zald and John D. McCarthy. Cambridge, Mass.: Winthrop, 8–44.

Freeman, Jo. 1975. *The Politics of Women's Liberation.* New York: McKay.

Friedman, Debra, and Doug McAdam. 1992. "Collective Identity and Activism: Networks, Choices, and the Life of a Social Movement." In *Frontiers in Social Movement Theory*, ed. Aldon Morris and Carol Mueller. New Haven: Yale University Press, 156–73.

Frye, Marilyn. 1983. *The Politics of Reality: Essays in Feminist Theory.* Trumansburg, N.Y.: Crossing Press.

———. 1990. "Do You Have to Be a Lesbian to Be a Feminist?" *Off Our Backs* 20: 21–23.

Gamson, William A. 1975. *The Strategy of Social Protest.* Homewood, Ill.: Dorsey Press.

Gelb, Joyce, and Marian Lief Palley. 1982. *Women and Public Policy.* Princeton: Princeton University Press.

Gerlach, Luther P., and Virginia H. Hine. 1970. *People, Power, Change: Movements of Social Transformation.* Indianapolis: Bobbs-Merrill.

Gerson, Judith M., and Kathy Peiss. 1985. "Boundaries, Negotiation, Consciousness: Reconceptualizing Gender Relations." *Social Problems* 32: 317–31.

Gilligan, Carol. 1982. *In a Different Voice.* Cambridge: Harvard University Press.

Goffman, Erving. 1959. *The Presentation of Self in Everyday Life.* Englewood Cliffs, N.J.: Prentice-Hall.

Grahn, Judy. 1984. *Another Mother Tongue: Gay Words, Gay Worlds.* Boston: Beacon Press.

Hoagland, Sarah Lucia. 1988. *Lesbian Ethics: Toward New Value.* Palo Alto, Calif.: Institute of Lesbian Studies.

Hole, Judith, and Ellen Levine. 1971. *Rebirth of Feminism.* New York: Quadrangle.

Hollibaugh, Amber, and Cherrie Moraga. 1983. "What We're Rollin' Around in Bed With: Sexual Silences in Feminism." In *Powers of Desire,* ed. Ann Snitow, Christine Stansell, and Sharon Thompson. New York: Monthly Review Press, 394–405.

Jaggar, Alison M., and Paula Rothenberg Struhl. 1978. *Feminist Frameworks.* New York: McGraw-Hill.

Japenga, Ann. 1990. "The Separatist Revival." *Outlook* 2: 78–83.

Jenkins, J. Craig. 1983. "Resource Mobilization Theory and the Study of Social Movements." *Annual Review of Sociology* 9: 527–53.

Jenkins, J. Craig, and Charles Perrow. 1977. "Insurgency of the Powerless: Farm Workers Movement (1946–72)." *American Sociological Review* 42: 249–68.

Johnson, Sonia. 1987. *Going Out of Our Minds: The Metaphysics of Liberation.* Freedom, Calif.: Crossing Press.

Johnston, Jill. 1973. *Lesbian Nation:* The *Feminist Solution.* New York: Simon and Schuster.

Kauffman, L. A. 1990. "The Anti-Politics of Identity." *Socialist Review* 20: 67–80.

Killian, Lewis M. 1964. "Social Movements." In *Handbook of Modern Sociology,* ed. R. E. L. Faris. Chicago: Rand McNally, 426–55.

Kitzinger, Celia. 1987. *The Social Construction of Lesbianism.* London: Sage.

Klandermans, Bert. 1984. "Mobilization and Participation: Social-Psychological Expansions of Resource Mobilization Theory." *American Sociological Review* 49: 583–600.

———. 1986. "New Social Movements and Resource Mobilization: The European and American Approach." *Journal of Mass Emergencies and Disasters* 4: 13–37.

Klandermans, Bert, and Sidney Tarrow. 1988. "Mobilization into Social Movements: Synthesizing European and American Approaches." In *From Structure to Action: Comparing Movement Participation across Cultures.* International Social Movement Research, vol. 1, ed. Bert Klandermans, Hanspeter Kriesi, and Sidney Tarrow. Greenwich, Conn.: JAI Press, 1–38.

Klein, Ethel. 1984. *Gender Politics.* Cambridge: Harvard University Press.

Koedt, Anne, Ellen Levine, and Anita Rapone. 1973. *Radical Feminism.* New York: Quadrangle.

Krieger, Susan. 1982. "Lesbian Identity and Community: Recent Social Science Literature." *Signs* 8: 91–108.

———. 1983. *The Mirror Dance: Identity in a Women's Community.* Philadelphia: Temple University Press.

Lewis, Sasha Gregory. 1979. *Sunday's Women.* Boston: Beacon Press.

Lockard, Denyse. 1986. "The Lesbian Community: An Anthropological Approach." In *The Many Faces of Homosexuality,* ed. Evelyn Blackwood. New York: Harrington Park Press, 83–95.

Lofland, John. 1979. "White-Hot Mobilization: Strategies of a Millenarian Movement." In *Dynamics of Social Movements,* ed. Mayer N. Zald and John D. McCarthy. Cambridge, Mass.: Winthrop, 157–66.

———. 1985. "Social Movement Culture." In *Protest,* ed. John Lofland. New Brunswick, N.J.: Transaction, 219–39.

Lord, Eleanor. Unpublished. "Lesbian Lives and the Lesbian Community in Berkshire County." Mimeograph.

Margolis, Diane Rothbard. 1985. "Redefining the Situation: Negotiations on the Meaning of Woman." *Social Problems* 32: 332–47.

McAdam, Doug. 1982. *Political Process and the Development of Black Insurgency, 1930–70.* Chicago: University of Chicago Press.

———. 1988. *Freedom Summer.* New York: Oxford University Press.

McAdam, Doug, John D. McCarthy, and Mayer N. Zald. 1988. "Social Movements." In *Handbook of Sociology,* ed. Neil Smelser. Newbury Park, Calif.: Sage, 695–737.

McCarthy, John D., and Mayer N. Zald. 1973. *The Trend of Social Movements in America.* Morristown, N.J.: General Learning Press.

———. 1977. "Resource Mobilization and Social Movements: A Partial Theory." *American Journal of Sociology* 82: 1212–41.

McNall, Scott G. 1988. *The Road to Rebellion: Class Formation and Populism, 1865–1900.* Chicago: University of Chicago Press.

Melucci, Alberto. 1985. "'The Symbolic Challenge of Contemporary Movements." *Social Research* 52: 781–816.

———. 1988. "Getting Involved: Identity and Mobilization in Social Movements." In *From Structure to Action: Comparing Movement Participation across Cultures.* International Social Movement Research, vol. 1, ed. Bert Klandermans, Hanspeter Kriesi, and Sidney Tarrow. Greenwich, Conn.: JAI Press, 329–48.

———. 1989. *Nomads of the Present: Social Movements and Individual Needs in Contemporary Society.* Philadelphia: Temple University Press.

Millett, Kate. 1970. *Sexual Politics.* New York: Ballantine.

Moraga, Cherrie, and Gloria Anzaldua. 1981. *This Bridge Called My Back: Writings by Radical Women of Color.* Watertown, Mass.: Persephone.

Morris, Aldon D. 1984. *The Origin of the Civil Rights Movement.* New York: Free Press.

———. 1990. "Consciousness and Collective Action: Towards a Sociology of Consciousness and Domination." Paper presented at the annual meeting of the American Sociological Association, August 9–13, San Francisco.

Mueller, Carol McClurg. 1987. "Collective Consciousness, Identity Transformation, and the Rise of Women in Public Office in the United States." In *The Women's Movement of the United States and Western Europe*, ed. M. F. Katzenstein and C. M. Mueller. Philadelphia: Temple University Press, 89–108.

———. 1990. "Collective Identities and the Mobilization of Women: The American Case, 1960–1970." Paper presented at the colloquium on New Social Movements and the End of Ideology, July 16–20, Universidad Internacional Menendez Pelayo.

Myron, Nancy, and Charlotte Bunch. 1975. *Lesbianism and the Women's Movement.* Baltimore: Diana Press.

Near, Holly. 1990. *Fire in the Rain, Singer in the Storm.* New York: Morrow.

Nestle, Joan. 1987. *A Restricted Country.* Ithaca: Firebrand Books.

Oberschall, Anthony. 1973. *Social Conflict and Social Movements.* Englewood Cliffs, N.J.: Prentice-Hall.

Offe, Claus. 1985. "New Social Movements: Challenging the Boundaries of Institutional Politics." *Social Research* 52: 817–68.

Olzak, Susan. 1983. "Contemporary Ethnic Mobilization." *Annual Review of Sociology* 9: 355–71.

Penelope, Julia. 1990. "A Case of Mistaken Identity." *Women's Review of Books* 8: 11–12.

Phelan, Shane. 1989. *Identity Politics: Lesbian Feminism and the Limits of Community.* Philadelphia: Temple University Press.

Pizzorno, Alessandro. 1978. "Political Science and Collective Identity in Industrial Conflict." In *The Resurgence of Class Conflict in Europe Since 1968*, ed. C. Crouch and A. Pizzorno. New York: Holmes and Meier, 277–98.

Ponse, Barbara. 1978. *Identities in the Lesbian World: The Social Construction of Self.* Westport, Conn.: Greenwood Press.

Radicalesbians. 1973. "The Woman Identified Woman." In *Radical Feminism*, ed. Anne Koedt, Ellen Levine, and Anita Rapone. New York: Quadrangle, 240–45.

Reskin, Barbara. 1988. "Bringing the Men Back In: Sex Differentiation and the Devaluation of Women's Work." *Gender and Society* 2: 58–81.

Rich, Adrienne. 1976. *Of Woman Born.* New York: Norton.

———. 1980. "Compulsory Heterosexuality and Lesbian Existence." *Signs* 5: 631–60.

Rothschild-Whitt, Joyce. 1979. "The Collectivist Organization: An Alternative to Rational-Bureaucratic Models." *American Sociological Review* 44: 509–27.

Rubin, Gayle. 1984. "Thinking Sex: Notes for a Radical Theory of the Politics of Sexuality." In *Pleasure and Danger*, ed. Carol S. Vance. Boston: Routledge and Kegan Paul, 267–319.

Rule, James, and Charles Tilly. 1972. "1830 and the Unnatural History of Revolution." *Journal of Social Issues* 28: 49–76.

Rupp, Leila J. 1989. "Feminism and the Sexual Revolution in the Early Twentieth Century: The Case of Doris Stevens." *Feminist Studies* 51: 289–309.

Rupp, Leila J., and Verta Taylor. 1986. "The Women's Movement since 1960: Structure, Strategies, and New Directions. In *American Choices: Social Dilemma and Public Policy since 1960*, ed. Robert H. Bremner, Richard Hopkins, and Gary W. Reichard. Columbus: Ohio State University Press, 75–104.

Rupp, Leila J., and Verta Taylor. 1987. *Survival in the Doldrums: The American Women's Rights Movement, 1945 to the 1960s*. New York: Oxford University Press.
Ryan, Barbara. 1989. "Ideological Purity and Feminism: The U.S. Women's Movement from 1966 to 1975." *Gender and Society* 3: 239–57.
Schneider, Beth. 1986. "I Am Not a Feminist But . . ." Paper presented at the annual meeting of the American Sociological Association, New York, September 2.
Schwartz, Michael. 1976. *Radical Protest and Social Structure: The Southern Farmers' Alliance and the One-Crop Tenancy System*. New York: Academic Press.
Smeller, Michelle M. Unpublished. "From Dyke to Doll: The Processual Formation of Sexual Identity," Ohio State University.
Smelser, Neil. 1962. *Theory of Collective Behavior*. New York: Free Press.
Smith, Barbara. 1983. *Home Girls: A Black Feminist Anthology*. New York: Kitchen Table Women of Color Press.
Snitow, Ann, Christine Stansell, and Sharon Thompson. 1983. *Powers of Desire: The Politics of Sexuality*. New York: Monthly Review Press.
Snow, David A., E. Burke Rochford Jr., Steven K. Worden, and Robert D. Benford. 1986. "Frame Alignment Processes, Micromobilization, and Movement Participation. *American Sociological Review* 51: 464–81.
Stanley, Julia Penelope, and Susan J. Wolfe. 1980. *The Coming Out Stories*. Watertown, Mass.: Persephone.
Taylor, Verta. 1989a. "The Future of Feminism." In *Feminist Frontiers*, ed. Laurel Richardson and Verta Taylor. New York: Random House, 434–51.
———. 1989b. "Social Movement Continuity: The Women's Movement in Abeyance." *American Sociological Review* 54: 761–75.
Taylor, Verta, and Leila J. Rupp. 1993. "Women's Culture and Lesbian Feminist Activism: A Reconsideration of Cultural Feminism." *Signs: Journal of Women in Culture and Society* 1: 32–61.
Taylor, Verta, and Nancy Whittier. 1992. "'The New Feminist Movement." In *Feminist Frontiers: Rethinking Sex, Gender, and Society*, ed. Laurel Richardson and Verta Taylor. New York: McGraw-Hill.
Tilly, Charles. 1978. *From Mobilization to Revolution*. Reading, Mass.: Addison-Wesley.
Touraine, Alain. 1985. "An Introduction to the Study of Social Movements." *Social Research* 52: 749–87.
Treblecot, Joyce. 1979. "Conceiving Women: Notes on the Logic of Feminism." *Sinister Wisdom* 11: 3–50.
Turner, Ralph H., and Lewis M. Killian. 1972. *Collective Behavior*, 2d ed. Englewood Cliffs, N.J.: Prentice-Hall.
Vance, Carole S. 1984. *Pleasure and Danger*. Boston: Routledge and Kegan Paul.
Walker, Alice. 1974. *In Search of Our Mothers' Gardens*. New York: Harcourt Brace Jovanovich.
Weigert, Andrew J., J. Smith Teitge, and Dennis W. Teitge. 1986. *Society and Identity*. New York: Cambridge University Press.
West, Candace, and Don H. Zimmerman. 1987. "Doing Gender." *Gender and Society* 1: 125–51.

White, Edmund. 1980. *States of Desire*. New York: Dutton.

Whittier, Nancy. 1991. "Feminists in the Post-Feminist Age: Collective Identity and the Persistence of the Women's Movement." Ph.D. diss., Ohio State University.

Wolf, Deborah Goleman. 1979. *The Lesbian Community*. Berkeley: University of California Press.

Zinn, Maxine Baca. 1990. "Family, Feminism, and Race in America." *Gender and Society* 4: 68–82.

Zita, Jacquelyn. 1982. "Historical Amnesia and the Lesbian Continuum." In *Feminist Theory: A Critique of Ideology*, ed. Nannerl O. Keohane, Michelle Z. Rosaldo, and Barbara L. Gelpi. Chicago: University of Chicago Press, 161–76.

The Social Construction of Subversive Evil: The Contemporary Anticult and Anti-Satanism Movements

David G. Bromley and Diana Gay Cutchin

Recent decades have been punctuated by two major cases of subversion fears, initially by groups labeled "religious cults" (Bromley and Shupe 1981) and subsequently by "Satanic cults" (Richardson, Best, and Bromley 1991). During the 1970s subversion fears centered on a cohort of new religious movements that emerged beginning in the late 1960s. A series of high-profile, violent incidents involving groups such as the Peoples Temple and Branch Davidians in the United States, Temple Solaire in Canada and Europe, and Aum Shinrikyo in Japan continued to fuel public disquiet over alternative religious groups through the 1980s and 1990s. As these fears of subversion by religious cults were beginning to wane somewhat, a new subversion episode riveted public attention on Satanic cults. During the 1980s subversion fears erupted over a putative underground cult of practicing Satanists believed to be responsible for coordinating a variety of nefarious activities, the most shocking of which was alleged ritual abuse and sacrifice of large numbers of infants. For two decades a succession of incidents—ranging from the grisly multiple murders in Matamoros, Mexico, to highly publicized cases of teenage suicide linked to the Dungeons and Dragons fantasy game, to the charges of ritual abuse at the McMartin Preschool in California—has raised the specter of Satanic subversion. In each of these subversion episodes a countersubversion movement mobilized rapidly to identify and resist various groups within American society alleged to be the source of subversive activity.

The objective of this chapter is an analysis of these two countersubversion movement ideologies as *social dramas*.[1] Countersubversion ideologies postulate the existence of a subversive conspiracy directed at undermining a fundamental source of order within a society and attribute to the subversives transcendent (i.e., extraordinary or supernatural) power of some kind.[2] By definition subversives are dedicated to destructive principles and practices. They specifically undermine normal, natural individual and group functioning. Countersubversion movements thus conceive of themselves as engaged in an epic confrontation between forces of good and evil. In this chapter we interpret countersubversion ideologies as a form of drama, a narrative portrayal of the struggle of good against evil.

A useful point of departure in sociologically interpreting these radical belief systems is the virtual axiom in social science theory that the reality we inhabit as human beings is constructed on both cultural and social dimensions (Berger and Luckmann 1966). Sociological understandings of how humans create an ordered existence traditionally have tended to accentuate the social dimension of human organization, but recent scholarship has begun to reassert the co-equal importance of the cultural dimension. This new balance is gaining a prominent place in research in the area of social movements. The earlier emphasis on the organizational dimension of social movements, which led to a conception of belief systems as epiphenomenal, is now being counterbalanced by serious treatment of ideas through which social movement participants create systems of meaning that orient their individual and collective action. Snow and Benford (1992, 136), two major architects of this perspective, describe the change in the following way: "We do not view social movements merely as carriers of extant ideas and meanings that stand in isomorphic relationship to structural arrangements and/or unanticipated events. Rather, we see movement organizations and actors as actively engaged in the production and maintenance of meaning for constituents, antagonists, and bystanders or observers." From this perspective the social and cultural elements of human organization are interrelated, but neither can be reduced to the other.

It follows from the assertion that the reality that humans inhabit is socially constructed that the order (or disorder) we experience is partially of our own making. One of the most important ways in which we construct order and disorder culturally is through the production of narratives of various kinds through which we organize and interpret social reality to ourselves. To create social reality through the production of narratives, of course, means that we quite literally become actors in our own stories. When social order is imperiled, therefore, humans become involved in real-life dramas of our own making (Turner 1982). Social movements offer a particularly apt context for developing this perspective since movements constitute organized challenges to the prevailing social order. That is, extant and proposed visions of the social order are in conflict. Social movements are organizational actors in the dramas of human experience that form in response to crises of order in specific social locations.

Countersubversion movements create an extraordinarily high order of drama indeed. The postulation of an organized conspiracy to undermine the very foundation of the social order by a group that possesses extraordinary powers constitutes one of the most powerful ways in which humans create a sense of impending chaos. The question to be addressed here is *how* such ideologies are fashioned, how it is that we symbolize such ultimate evil. Let us create context for this analysis by briefly describing the two subversion episodes.

The Religious Cult Subversion Episode

Beginning about 1970, intense opposition mobilized to a cohort of new religious movements such as the Unification Church, Hare Krishnas, and The Family (at the time named the Children of God), which were initially labeled "religious cults." Founded on the assertion that they in fact are pseudoreligions, "cults" were denounced for using "brainwashing" or "coercive mind control" to secure and control members. Anticultists assert that the gurus who lead religious cults are driven by a thirst for political and economic power as evidenced by empire-building and a dictatorial leadership style. Individual followers were seen as vulnerable young adults. Anticultists claimed the "cults" successfully evaded legal controls by cloaking their organization and activity with the mantle of religion and by operating through a variety of apparently legitimate "front groups." As a result, the number, size, power, and wealth of these monolithic, ruthless, authoritarian groups have increased dramatically, making them a grave threat to the social order.

Organized countermovement opposition to new religious movements coalesced soon after the first of these groups began recruiting young adults (Bromley and Shupe 1993, Shupe and Bromley 1980). There are several wings of the anticult movement; the secular wing, which is the focus of attention here, was formed and has largely been energized by family members of converts.[3] The historical moment when new religious movements were most successful in attracting adherents was one of transition and tension for families and young adults. In recognition of the increasing importance of education for career success, parents began organizing family life around preparation for higher education opportunities. This necessitated granting autonomy to young adults while at the same time maintaining parental direction during this extended socialization process. For their part, young adults found themselves caught between adolescence and adulthood; this tension was dramatically elevated by the sociopolitical conflicts of the 1960s and 1970s that yielded a range of protest and countercultural activity centered in the young adult population. The effect of conversions to new religious movements was to construct a niche that neutralized the control systems of both family and educational systems. Further, these movements not only rejected the dominant forms of social relations, they *sacralized their antithesis* by supplanting family relationships and secular careers with collectivist relationships and spiritual careers. Families of converts, initially mystified at the rebellion of their offspring, soon began to interpret these radical departures as a conspiracy by cultic groups to subvert the free will of their offspring. The families that organized the anticult movement subsequently were joined by mainline churches, opposing what they regard as doctrinal heresy; a minority group within the mental health community, for whom counseling exiting members of these movements became a practitioner specialty; and some governmental agencies, over practices deemed inappropriate to a religious organization.

The most novel feature of the anticult campaign is the practice of "deprogramming." Assuming that adherents are brainwashed, the anticult movement developed a procedure designed to reverse the effects of cultic mind control through "deprogramming." In its initial form, deprogramming involved abduction and physical restraint of new religious movement members until they agreed to renounce their religious affiliations (Bromley 1988). A network of entrepreneurial deprogrammers emerged who offered their services to families, based on assertions that they possessed special knowledge of techniques for reversing brainwashing effects. An increase in the number of deprogrammings and growing resistance to them resulted in anticult-sponsored legislative initiatives in numerous states to legalize deprogramming under mental health codes.

Although none of these initiatives ultimately was successful, the anticult movement has achieved a moderate measure of success. For a time the countermovement was able to abduct and deprogram converts to new religious movements with relative impunity, and subsequently developed voluntary "exit counseling" procedures have served as the functional equivalent in persuading members to renounce their former affiliations (Bromley 1988). Anticult organizations have prompted legislative hearings and investigations at which their grievances could be voiced. They swung public opinion toward some form of legal controls over the organization and operation of unconventional religious movements. And they added "religious cult" and "brainwashing" to the popular vernacular (Bromley and Breschel 1992). Nonetheless, the anticult movement has been unable to secure an institutional forum or access to established institutions through which it could invoke social sanctions against its targets. Thus it remains marginal in its stability and influence.

The anticult movement has confronted resistance from several sources, including organizations representing mainstream mental health professionals, which contest the data and methods upon which anticult claims rest; the judicial system, which demands empirical verification for legal claims made against the movements; civil libertarian organizations, which fear a limitation of religious liberties will result from distinguishing between acceptable and nonacceptable religious groups; and social scientists engaged in research on the new movements, whose research findings fail to confirm key countermovement allegations. These critics have continued to challenge the assumption of recruitment through brainwashing upon which the concept of "cult," and ultimately the entire anticult agenda, is based. Consider the following:

- Critics point out that it is hard to build a compelling case for subversive mind control on the basis of Korean POW data since only 25 of the approximately 3,500 servicemen held by the communists actually refused repatriation, despite being under the total control of their captors for months or even years.
- There is no plausible explanation for how such a diverse array of groups from different parts of the world and with no connection to one another—the Hare Krishnas from India, the Unificationists from Korea, The Family in the United States—all discovered and implemented this psycho-technology at precisely the same moment.
- For a process as potent as brainwashing is purported to be, the results are abysmal. The public recruitment campaigns by these groups produce a conversion success rate that is extremely low, probably considerably lower than conventional churches that proselytize, such as the Mormons and Jehovah's Witnesses. Further, these groups seem equally unsuccessful in retaining converts; in fact, many groups suffer defection rates of 50 to 100 percent per year (Barker 1984).
- Not only do these movements fail to recruit or retain members successfully, numerous accounts indicate that ongoing members are hardly passive and compliant. In fact, many of these groups manifest a pervasive pattern of factionalism, schism, and conflict.
- Virtually every account of the groups that triggered the cult controversy indicates that they grew very rapidly through the 1970s by recruiting young adults but then began to decline just as rapidly, despite intensive recruitment campaigns, once the counterculture period of the 1960s ran its course. If coercive mind control is the se-

cret to their success, on the basis of trial and error alone these groups should become more rather than less proficient with practice.

The Satanic Cult Subversion Episode

During the 1980s subversion fears centered on a putative underground cult of practicing Satanists organized into a vast international, secret network of tightly organized, hierarchically structured "Satanic cults." There is an eerie parallel between depictions of religious cults and Satanic cults in that the central characteristic of the latter cults too is their knowledge and application of a sophisticated combination of drugging, terrorism, and brainwashing techniques as a means of enslaving the young children whom they target. According to their opponents, Satanists seek primarily enhancement of personal pleasure and power through exploitation of children. Victims are forced to perform as sexual partners for the pleasure of adult Satanists or as actors in pornographic films that finance cult activity, and Satanists ritualistically sacrifice children in the belief that victims' life energy can thereby be appropriated. In addition to child sacrifice, Satanists are believed to be responsible for coordinating a variety of other sinister activities, including worship of Satan, luring youth into Satanic cults through dissemination of occult material in fantasy games and subliminal messages implanted in heavy metal rock music, precipitating criminal homicides, and carrying out widespread desecration of graves and mutilation of animals. Anticultists claim that Satanic cults also seek political power and religious status in order to shield their organizations and activity from legal prosecution. They have already infiltrated some institutions, most notably preschools and daycare centers, that provide them with unrestricted access to children. The startling rise in the number of individuals claiming to be "ritual abuse survivors" is presented as dramatic evidence of the rapidly growing power and danger posed by Satanic cults.

The anti-Satanism movement is made up of several loosely connected strands; the focus of attention here is that component of the movement comprised of families with young children whose parents came to believe they were being victimized by organized groups of Satanists located in various types of child care facilities.[4] The historical moment when the anti-Satanism movement emerged was one during which American families experienced an acute sense of loss of control over the welfare of their own children. Among the perceived sources of corrupting or exploitive influence were strangers (abduction, rape, murder), media (violence, sexuality, and antisocial messages in music, television, and film), and peer groups (promotion of sexual activity and drug use). The most immediate source of tension that led to the rise of Satanism fears was competing demands of family and economy, which translated directly into a loss of family control over early childhood socialization (Bromley 1991). Briefly, recent decades have witnessed a decline in income and increasing debt, longer workweeks and less leisure time, and dramatically escalating costs for housing and education. One of the most important outcomes in the middle class has been a sharp increase in the number of women entering the labor force, particularly mothers with young children. As a result, these families have been forced to rely on expensive, unregulated daycare facilities. Given the meteoric rise in sexual abuse allegations and the conviction among certain elements of the mental health professions that many childhood and adult emotional problems are attributable to early childhood abuse, it is not surprising that the emotional tumult surrounding the transfer of child care to strangers was accompanied by suspicion and reservation. The demonization of daycare is grounded in a fear that children might be treated as human commodities by daycare centers organized as businesses rather than as sacred trusts by daycare centers organized as surrogate families.

What energized the anti-Satanism movement was a coalition between families and a network of entrepreneurial therapists who developed a novel mental health practice, "recovered memory therapy." As Davis (1996, 17) summarizes the assumptions underlying this therapy: "The experience of abuse is overwhelming, and so in order to survive, victims must build an internal defense structure to protect themselves. In some cases, victims block all memory of the abuse out of consciousness." It becomes the objective of this form of therapy to recover the deeply buried memories of abuse and to guide the client to linking present emotional distress with prior abuse. In the case of the anti-Satanism movement, during the therapy process, therapists offer Satanic ritual abuse as the central theme of the therapy narrative. The process of validating that narrative involves a variety of recovery techniques, which often involve altered states of consciousness, and a support network comprised of therapist, family, and other ritual abuse survivors. The recovered memories of ritual abuse are then proffered as the primary evidence of the existence and operation of the Satanic cult network.

Like the anticult movement, the anti-Satanism movement has had considerable social impact. During local rumor-panics large numbers of families have withdrawn their children from school; for a time law enforcement officials conducted extensive and costly investigations in an effort to locate Satanic ritual sites and the remains of ritual sacrifice victims; there has been a plethora of daycare center investigations across the nation based on the fear that these facilities had been infiltrated by Satanists; a number of states have created task forces to investigate the possibility of Satanic cult activity within their borders; a few states have revised criminal statutes to incorporate penalties for ritualistic crimes; in some criminal trials defendants have been sentenced to extraordinarily long prison terms, usually on the testimony of adult "ritual abuse survivors" or of very young children; and media representatives have given extensive coverage to extreme and bizarre stories of ritual abuse, which has convinced a substantial proportion of the population of the existence of a menacing Satanic cult network.

As in the case of the religious cult subversion episode, resistance rather soon began to mount from a variety of social locations: family members accused of participating in Satanic groups banded together to combat allegations made against them; police agencies began resisting what became interminable investigations that yielded no meaningful physical evidence; jurists have expressed reservations about accepting uncorroborated testimony of young children whose accounts appear to have been influenced by examining therapists; mental health professional associations have resisted theories of recovered memory that would open the door to countless claims and that are impossible to verify (Davis 1996); and legislative bodies have demurred from initiating legislation targeting groups and defining offense categories for which confirming evidence is meager at best. In this instance, it is the very existence of the putative Satanic cult network and its ritual sacrifice victims that has been challenged.

Critics have noted that research on Satanic churches yields no evidence that sexual abuse, child molestation, and human sacrifice are elements of their theologies or rituals (Bromley and Ainsley 1995); research on subliminal messages finds neither evidence of Satanic messages in recorded music nor significant influence on behavior from subliminal messages generally (Thorne and Himelstein 1984, Vokey and Read 1985); rumor-panics over impending abduction of children by Satanists across the country have yielded no actual cases but rather are interpreted as instances of collective behavior deriving from long-standing urban legends with a child endangerment motif (Brunvand 1981, Victor 1990); virtually every investigation of animal mutilation cases has concluded that unexplained large-animal deaths are the product of roadkills, hunting, trapping, disease, or poisoning (Cade 1977, Stewart 1977); and in the several dozen homicide cases attributed to Satanism, investigators have concluded that perpetrators have confessed to Satanic involvement in the hope of diminishing legal responsibility for their acts or to seek publicity by adding a Satanic gloss to their crimes.

Critics have challenged not only countermovement interpretations of the various events and activities that would attribute them to a Satanic conspiracy but also evidence put forth to demonstrate the existence of a Satanic cult network.

- No organizational records of any kind (e.g., correspondence, membership lists, phone logs, travel records, bank accounts, meeting places, ritual implements, pornographic films) have ever been recovered from a network that must be large, complex, and international in scope and must have engaged in nefarious activities for an extended period of time. Nor is there any evidence of a theology or set of rituals that forms the basis for the current practice of Satanism or of any historical tradition from which Satanic beliefs and practices might have been drawn.
- Claims that lack of hard evidence proving the existence of the Satanic cult network is due to its phenomenally efficient, infallible organization are belied by the parade of ritual abuse survivors who freely recount their stories to the media.
- The extensiveness of the Satanic cult network and the estimated number of Satanic cult victims is so large as to preclude any possibility that they could be concealed. Indeed, even by conservative countermovement estimates ritual sacrifice victims would equal the total number of war-related deaths from World War II, Korea, and Vietnam combined. Yet despite intensive investigation, there has not been a single discovery of a victim whose death can be linked to a Satanic ritual (Lanning 1989).
- Finally, while there is virtually no evidence of either the existence of an international Satanic cult network or ritual sacrifice victims, there are numerous instances of refutation of Satanic cult claims. For example, there have been a number of instances in which "ritual abuse survivors" have specified the location of ritual sacrifices, but official investigations have not uncovered any evidence (Lyons 1988, 143–45); important autobiographical details of survivors' lives have been disconfirmed (Passantino et al. 1989, American Library Association 1990); and there is convincing evidence that therapists rather than clients introduce Satanism into the jointly constructed therapeutic narratives (Mulhern 1991).

Anticultism and Anti-Satanism: Points of Continuity

The preceding synopses of two contemporary subversion episodes rehearses the precipitating tensions and countermovement responses for two cases in which groups in some social locations clearly have understood themselves to be locked in an epic struggle with conspiratorial forces of evil. There are some obvious similarities between the two. Both involve fears of child endangerment. In both, alliances between family members and individuals claiming mental health professional status are key. Both see the undermining of individual autonomy as the main threat. The two countermovements are also alike in that neither has achieved an institutional base or an institutional alliance that confers legitimacy and authorization to invoke social control. Yet both countermovements have achieved influence. For a time at least, public opinion was swayed, public officials were engaged, victimization was validated, and subversives were identified and prosecuted. In each case there was, then, a shared sense that organized subversive groups might well be afoot and endangering the social order before resistance to the subversive conspiracy proposal carried the day. One significant question these two episodes raise, therefore, is *how* such an intense sense of evil is created.

Encountering Subversion

In the normal course of events humans culturally narrate their own action and become actors in their own narratives. In a subversion episode the socioculturally constructed order is experienced as disintegrating. The resulting sense of disorder is constructed as a dramatic encounter between the forces of good and subversive evil. The question posed here is how that sense of dramatic confrontation is so powerfully created in countersubversion narratives. The proposed answer is that the stage upon which human action takes place and the cast of actors scripted into the action both expand. At least in the most extreme subversion episodes, those caught up in the drama perceive that what they believed to be a single world is actually two worlds. The "Other" is a subversive order that has suddenly intersected their own world, and it is the clash of these two mutually opposed orders that organizes and energizes the drama. We shall argue that six elements are integral to constructing subversive evil in countersubversion narratives.

The first four elements of the countersubversion narrative construct the staging and plot of the drama. They describe the history, location, power, and purpose of subversives. First, subversive evil has a *transcendent temporality*; that is, it possesses its own historical existence and course, about which little is known, and therefore it appears and recurs unpredictably in times and places of its own choosing. The apparent stability and order of the everyday world can therefore be unexpectedly disrupted by subversive forces, and the present is transformed into a moment of high drama. Second, subversive evil is given *transcendent spatiality*; that is, it is located in a separate domain. Subversives are defined as aliens who exist outside of conventional society in concealed, secret locations where their sinister activity is shielded from public view. They infiltrate conventional society from these remote sites. This separation of the conventional and subversive worlds makes for dramatic encounters across the boundary points and within the conventional domain as clusters of subversives are discovered. Third, subversive evil involves *transcendent power*; that is, exotic, potent power capable of corrupting and undermining individuals' normal, natural essence. A highpoint of the drama occurs when subversives unleash their overwhelming power on unwitting victims, rendering them thralls to subversive purpose. Fourth, subversive organization typically is symbolized as the *inversion of legitimate organization*; it is described as complex, conspiratorial, and dedicated to nefarious purpose. These categorical distinctions become the basis for the dramatic battle between the forces of good and evil. Fifth, the countersubversion narrative provides an *identification of the key actors* in the drama, in this case the most important are innocent victims, evil perpetrators, and heroic defenders. It is through these three roles that the dramatic encounters are enacted. Finally, the narrative is directed toward *audience mobilization*; that is, third parties who may be drawn into the drama as allies of countermovement activists. Audience mobilization is effected through heightening apprehension about subversives as a large, rapidly growing force that is on the verge of taking over one or more sectors of the social order, is extremely dangerous, and is impervious to normal social control mechanisms.

Transcendent Temporality: Historical Roots of Contemporary Evil

Historical continuity is created primarily through linking cultic brainwashing to communist thought reform programs in China and the former Soviet Union during the Korean War era. The parent of a young woman who joined the Unification Church draws precisely that connection in explaining her daughter's conversion: "We think the brainwashing is very similar to what happened to our prisoners of war in Korea. It's a system of mind control the Orientals know very well, but we know very little about" (Shupe and Bromley 1981a, 179). Two behavioral scientists connected with the anticult movement identify "first and second generations of interest." The latter is a more potent attack on individuals as it targets the core as opposed to the periphery of the self. They aver that first generation programs simply attack "one's political and social views," while second generation programs of the type employed by religious cults "appear to directly attack the core sense of being—the central self-image, the very sense of realness and existence of the self" (Ofshe and Singer 1986, 18).

Similarly, contemporary Satanism is represented as the most recent in a long series of incursions by Satanic forces that extend over countless human generations and even societal histories. These eruptions of Satanism appear in diverse forms in different historical eras, and sometimes

their true source is not correctly identified by contemporaries of the period. In a close parallel to the linking of religious cult practices to communist brainwashing, contemporary Satanists' brainwashing and drugging
of victims are traced in some accounts to medical experiments conducted
by Nazi physicians. The doctors who developed these techniques (and a
mysterious, infamous Dr. Green, in particular) are alleged to be Satanists
who brought their destructive knowledge with them when they fled Germany and settled in the United States.[5] Again, the current outbreak is particularly pernicious. One "cult crime specialist" places contemporary Satanism in historical context while distinguishing the unique and virulent
current outbreak in daycare centers (*Geraldo* 1987):

> Well, cults have always existed throughout history, but it's only been recently
> that they've really become very active in this country. 1982 is a period or
> cycle for them that's known—every twenty-eight years is the "feast of the
> beast" and it last occurred in 1982. And it gives them a whole new game
> plan on what they're doing. Well, part of what [*sic*] *their game plan was to
> infiltrate preschool centers and such and to bring others into their service.*

Transcendent Spatiality: The Cultic Realm

Anticult accounts often stress the remote, secretive, impenetrable sites
that cults occupy. Ted Patrick, a founder of the anticult movement and
the originator of deprogramming, provides an account of a rural Children
of God commune to which he gained entrance (Patrick with Dulack 1976,
62).

> The colony was way up in the mountains, some twenty-four miles back on a
> dirt road five miles off the main highway. There was nothing else on the road
> except the colony, which consisted of three buildings—old farm buildings—
> surrounded by a seven-foot-high fence with a locked gate. . . . The grounds
> were patrolled by three vicious German shepherds. And one of the buildings
> was topped by a watchtower so that no one could come up that road without
> being detected at least five minutes before he reached the gate.

He depicts himself as on the verge of becoming a virtual prisoner, using
the term "escape" in reference to making plans to leave the commune.

Renderings of Satanic cults emphasize their underground, secret, hidden nature in locations such as cemeteries, isolated wooded sites, or even
the criminal "underworld." In a recent California court case, for example,
two daughters and the granddaughter of a seventy-six-year-old woman
testified that the woman forced them to engage in a variety of perverted
sexual acts, infanticide, and even cannibalism. One of the daughters asserted that the rituals in which she was forced to take part were con-

ducted in secret caves that probably are located in the surrounding San Bernadino mountains (*Los Angeles Times* 1991). In *Cults That Kill,* law enforcement official Larry Kahaner describes how he discovered an entire underworld Satanic domain in the course of investigating surface-level manifestations of Satanism.

> I found a hidden society, much larger and more disquieting than the world of Satanism alone, a place few people know exists. . . . It is the underworld of "occult crime." . . . The crimes are frightening: . . . ritual sacrifices at wooded sites where black-robed cultists mutilate animals on alters; other homicides where the corpses are found drained of blood with symbols such as a pentagram or inverted cross carved into their chests; . . . Satanic rituals and human sacrifices involving children—fantastic stories told by hundreds of children in scores of preschools throughout the United States, all of them relating similar horrors. (1988, vii)

Transcendent Power: Imposition of Subversive Control

At the height of the religious cult subversion episode, brainwashing was regarded as so highly coercive that even a perfunctory encounter with cultists might result in loss of free will. A variety of apostates from new religious movements testify to being subjected to such techniques. By one such account (Edwards 1979, 60): "She took my hand and looked me straight in the eyes. As her wide eyes gazed into mine, I felt myself rapidly losing control, being drawn to her by a strange and frightening force. I had never felt such mysterious power radiate from a human being before." In a more sophisticated formulation, Flo Conway and Jim Siegelman (1979, 134–35) argue that cultic mind control results in "snapping," a novel phenomenon that goes beyond intense physical experiences and psychological stresses by incorporating what they call a "different kind of information." Individuals subjected to this process may surrender and relinquish control over their own wills. "And more than anything else it is this act of capitulation that sets off the explosion we call snapping. . . . In that moment, something quite remarkable may happen. With that flick of a switch, that change of heart and mind, an individual's personality may come apart." The result, anticult proponents contend, is that cult members remain in a dissociated state, which results in mental disorder and prevents individuals from being able to express their individual autonomy. As one anticult movement–affiliated therapist commented after evaluating a young woman who joined the Hare Krishna, "It's my opinion that she was not at that point freely using her own will and volition, but being influenced and manipulated and made to comply with the wishes of the various Krishna organization representatives" (Bromley 1989, 276). Parents of members of religious cults report that they begin to suspect cultic brainwashing when they observe such changes in personality. In one such account, for example, "His parents noticed with alarm that he was becoming pale, withdrawn, nervous and acting almost as if he were in a trance. . . . He was becoming a walking zombie and nothing at all like the son we had known" (Shupe and Bromley, 1981c, 256).

According to the Satanic cult countersubversion ideology, brainwashing is practiced upon very young children, who are extremely vulnerable and who may be under the control of Satanists for years at a time. This combination of high vulnerability and prolonged exposure creates an enormous capacity for control. "The process of ritual abuse takes place over an extended period of time, often for years. The process includes a variety of exercises and ceremonies, each with an intended purpose, and which collectively attack all levels of the child's normal orientation" (Massachusetts State Police 1989, 3–4).

Therapists who treat individuals designated as "ritual abuse survivors" have attempted to discover the nature of the brainwashing techniques employed by Satanists based on the material elicited from clients during the therapy process. One therapist (Snowden, n.d.), who has compiled a list of these techniques, asserts that Satanists induce dissociation to fragment the personality, shatter emotional spontaneity, disrupt the developmental process, and destroy all memory of the brainwashing process. She describes the brainwashing process, which is often combined with drugging, as "sophisticated hypnosis which involves the associative pairing of induced pain/terror & the cult message & the trigger cue(s) . . . planted in the unconscious. . . . They are later utilized by the cult to control the survivor without his or her conscious awareness." One individual claiming to be a survivor describes her experiences in terms that closely parallel religious cult brainwashing claims (Smith and Pazder 1980, 102):

> I had no idea how long the struggle went on. In Victor's windowless basement, time had no meaning. It could have been a day, a week, a month . . . I just couldn't tell. I do know that as each hour passed, each minute became more agonizing. I was forced to endure sleep and food deprivation. Certainly I was familiar with torture, but not this type. There were no rituals. . . . This was the kind of breaking process I had heard that prisoners of war went through in concentration camps.

She remembers that her capacity to resist was finally broken when she was confined in a barrel with the lid closed and the parts of a sacrificed baby were dropped on top of her. She recalls, "It was over. I was broken. Brainwashed" (Smith and Pazder 1980, 104).

Organization and Activity: An Inverted Order

Anticult portrayals of religious cults seek to demonstrate their pseudoreligious character by contrasting their attributes with those of legitimate churches and arguing that these deviant characteristics are consciously planned and carefully developed. New religious movements are thus depicted as little more than economic scams or schemes for amassing political power. Singer and West (1980, 3295) attribute a "lack of sincerity" to cults and assert that "Many cults demonstrate extreme interest in financial or political aggrandizement, rather than the spiritual development of the faithful." Such qualities distinguish cults from more legitimate religious groups, which proceed from "theological or moral motives, rather than avarice, personal convenience, or a desire for power." One former member of the Unification Church is more pointed, asserting that "it is just one big money-making scheme and they brainwash you into thinking you're doing God's work. It's the greatest rip-off of them all" (*Knickerbocker News* 1976). An anticult-sponsored bill in a state legislature distinguishes the logic of cult and legitimate church organization in exactly these terms (Bromley and Shupe 1986, 175):

> A person is guilty of promoting a pseudo-religious cult when he knowingly organizes or maintains an organization which other persons are induced to join or participate in through the use of mind control methods, hypnosis, brainwashing techniques or other systematic forms of indoctrination and in which the members or participants of such organization engage in soliciting funds primarily for the benefit of such organization or its leaders and are not permitted to travel or communicate with anyone outside such organization unless another member or participant of such organization is present.

Anti-Satanism movement descriptions of Satanic cult activity dwell even more heavily on the complex structure of Satanic organization, in large measure because the movement relies on such description to demonstrate this network actually exists at all. Four distinct levels of organization typically are identified in the ideology (Hicks 1990, 283). At the lowest level are *Dabblers,* young people who experiment with Satanic materials such as heavy metal rock music and fantasy games like Dungeons and Dragons. The second level consists of *Self-styled Satanists,* criminals who create or borrow Satanic themes as a rationale for their antisocial acts. A third level involves *Organized Satanists,* members of public, Satanic churches such as the Church of Satan and Temple of Set. At the highest level are the *Traditional Satanists,* individuals organized into a secret cult network engaged in child abuse and sacrifice. In congressional testimony on ritual child abuse, Kee McFarlane, who interviewed children at the McMartin Preschool, drew a graphic picture of a large, powerful, well-financed, underground organization: "I believe we're dealing with an organized operation of child predators designed to prevent detection. The preschool, in such a case, serves as a ruse for a larger, unthinkable network of crimes against children. If such an operation involves child pornography or selling of children, as is frequently alleged, it may have greater financial, legal and community resources at its disposal than those attempting to expose it" (Bromley 1991, 53). This network of Satanists allegedly finances its activities by using children in daycare centers and preschools as subjects in pornographic films.

Actors and Motives

In the religious cult drama the role of evil agents is filled by the leaders of the religious movements or their inner circle of subordinates, the innocent victim role by lower-ranking movement members, and the heroic defender role by family members and their deprogrammer/therapist allies. Consistent with the logic of religious cults as organized conspiracies to gain wealth and power, the leaders of these groups naturally are depicted as religious charlatans for whom the movements are simply a resource base to be exploited for their own financial and political aggrandizement. One mental health professional allied with the countermovement, writing from the perspective of her work with former members of various new religious movements, summarizes her sense of this exploitation as follows: "After talking with over 700 ex and current cult members, none have told me that they set out to find a guru or a messiah who would set them up in prostitution, flower-selling, cocaine-dealing, gun-smuggling, child abuse, or living off garbage" (Bromley 1989, 274). Deprogrammer Ted Patrick reaches the same conclusion about Sun Myung Moon and the Unification Church (Patrick with Dulack 1976, 11): "Moon's got nothing to do with religion! . . . Moon's a crook, plain and simple. They're all crooks."

By contrast with the villainous gurus, converts are portrayed as innocent and vulnerable victims. As one anticult movement activist puts it, "These were merely naive, friendly, trusting, altruistic people hoping to make friends and to help make a better world" (Bromley 1989, 274). One way that converts' innocence is exemplified is through descriptions of converts as simply pursuing normal, everyday activity when they are set upon by predatory cult recruiters who exploit their naiveté or trusting natures. A convert to the Unification Church, for example, described himself as a new student at the University of California at Berkeley who was just out strolling around campus a few days before classes were to start when he was lured to an isolated church-run conversion camp through a deceptive poster advertising what was called the "Ideal City Project" (Kemperman 1981, 32). Another way that victimization is conveyed is through the physical and psychological damage that victims exhibit. Anticult ideology enumerates a series of these characteristics: truncated vocabulary; monotonic, inflection-free voice level; fixed, permanent smile; glassy eyes and dilated pupils; facial skin rash (due to dietary deficiencies); gaunt facial appearance and hollow eyes; hyperactivity; extreme nervousness; and hunched frame (Shupe and Bromley 1981c, 255).

Parents and the deprogrammer/therapist allies play the role of heroic defenders who take on the subversive cultists to rescue innocent victims, often at considerable risk to themselves. As the mother of a convert to Hare Krishna asserted while in the process of trying to extricate her son from the group (Bromley 1989, 262): "I think you should know that we are not trying to get Ed back into the fold; we are just trying to get him back to sanity. He's not thinking for himself. We are trying to get him the proper attention he needs." Deprogrammer Ted Patrick likewise disavows any personal interest in the anticult campaign, insisting that "I never planned to be a deprogrammer. It's not a job I applied for. . . . It's not a job I want to continue to do. . . . But until now . . . no one else has been willing to step forward and rectify a dangerous situation in this country. . . . Until someone does, I feel I have no choice except to continue in my work" (Patrick with Dulack 1976, 28). He later goes on to state that he recognizes that the price might be very high: "Possible threats to my family, maybe real violence" (1976, 57).

In the Satanic cult drama the three major roles strikingly parallel those of the religious cult narrative. The Satanic leaders are the diabolic architects of the ritual abuse conspiracy, infants and young children are the immediate victims, and a coalition of family members/therapists/police officers are the heroic defenders. It follows from the portrayal of Satanic cults that high-ranking Satanists and their henchmen are guilty of the basest motives, ritualized degradation and destruction of children for their personal pleasure and power. Their primary motive is self-empowerment through appropriation of blood, which contains the "life force" (Kahaner 1988, 140–41).

> If you have it, you have power. That's why they drink it in their rituals and pour it over themselves. . . . So is sacrificing people. When you sacrifice someone, for the instant just before they die, they supposedly emit their life energy. That power, Satanists believe, can be harnessed for their use.

The alleged victims of Satanic ritual abuse are even more vulnerable than targets of religious cults as they are likely to recount experiences that go back to early childhood. These innocent children are entrusted to various types of child care facilities that turn out to be controlled by Satanists. One of the most publicized cases involved the McMartin Preschool in Manhattan Beach, California. Very respected within the community, the school had a long list of children who were awaiting admission. One mother whose son was enrolled in the school described it as "the most desirable preschool in the area" that boasted "a proven track record with a list of satisfied parents" (*Los Angeles Magazine* 1989, 128). The community was therefore stunned when accusations of Satanic ritual abuse surfaced at this facility. Like the anticult movement, the anti-Satanism movement identifies a number of bizarre behaviors by innocent young children that become telltale indicators of ritual abuse even though the children often are too young to inform adults about the horrors they are experiencing. These behaviors include, for example, preoccupation with urine and feces; aggressive play that has a marked sadistic quality; mutilation themes predominating in play behavior; fear of ghosts and monsters; fear of "bad people" taking the child away, breaking into the house, killing the child or the parents, burning the house down; and preoccupation with the devil, magic, potions, supernatural power, and crucifixions (Hicks 1991, 245–46).

Both family members and their allies report that efforts to extricate children from Satanists' control meet with determined resistance and threats. Therapists are particularly likely targets as they uncover the evidence of Satanic subversion. They report that both they and their clients are placed under surveillance, have their phones tapped, and are threatened with violence. One therapist recalls that his client brought him a human penis that he attested had been sent to him by the cult as a warning to discontinue therapy (*Seattle Times* 1989). Another therapist who works with ritually abused children and also reports harassment finally concluded that "It's something I don't want to be identified as knowing that much about. I think anybody who works in this area ought to carry a badge and wear a gun. And not have a family" (*Chicago Tribune* 1985).

Audience Mobilization

Religious cults are depicted as constituting an unprecedented menace that has swept across the nation. Since they exist in virtually every locale, there is no longer any safe haven: "Never before have religious cults been so geographically widespread. They are in every area of the United States, in every major city and on college campuses throughout the nation" (Rudin and Rudin 1980, 16). The growth in the number and geographical spread of religious cults is reflected in what is presented as a virtual explosion of cult membership. Countermovement activists assert that the number of cultic groups of which the public is largely unaware is staggering. Former Unificationist Steve Kemperman estimates that "In the United States alone, cults number between 2,500 and 5,000" (1981, 176). Countermovement estimates of the membership of specific groups, such as the Unification Church and Hare Krishna, have been as high as several hundred thousand each (Appel 1981, 12–13). Total cult membership is projected in the millions. For example, "a cult expert, who counsels former cult members," estimates that "there are 2 to 3 million people in these groups" (Rudin and Rudin 1980, 15–16).

Not only are these groups and their memberships multitudinous, but each is characterized as literally a ticking time bomb of extremism that may erupt into violence at any moment. During the 1980s, for example, the image of the conflagration at Jonestown was liberally invoked as if each group were poised on the brink of murderous or suicidal action, or both: "The threat of the cults is tremendous. . . . The possibility of another Ghana [*sic*] is present in every cult that exists" (Shupe, Bromley, and Breschel 1989, 16). Likewise, in a congressional briefing an anticult movement spokesperson sought to convey the threat of cultic extremism by comparing religious cults to the Nazi youth movement:

> Senator Dole, the last time I ever witnessed a movement that was totally monolithic, that was replete with fanatical followers prepared to do anything, that hated everyone outside and fostered suspicions of parents—the last time I saw this was the Nazi youth movement, and I tell you, I'm scared. (Shupe and Bromley 1981b, 249)

If religious cultism finds parallels in Communism and Nazism, countersubversion activists argue that American society is completely unprepared for this potent subversive force. Conway and Siegelman (1979, 37) argue that contemporary cult mind control techniques are unique. They aver that "Our culture has never witnessed transformation of precisely this kind before, although there have been many similar examples throughout the history of religion." Because we have not previously encountered such virulent evil, we are virtually defenseless against these new subversion tactics. Write Conway and Siegleman (1979, 59): "The cult experience and its accompanying state of mind defies all legal precedents. It has also taken the mental-health profession by surprise. The conceptual models and diagnostic tools of psychiatry and psychology have proved inadequate to explain or treat the condition."

Anti-Satanism activists likewise offer estimates of Satanic cult membership that are astonishing. They acknowledge that true membership size is extremely elusive in this case since the cult has been successful in concealing all direct, physical evidence of its existence. The size of the Satanist network is therefore inferred from signs of its activity and from reports of ritual abuse survivors who manage to escape its clutches. One way that national membership is calculated is through projections from local incidents. There are many reports to the effect that

> In virtually every state in the nation, authorities are investigating some form of Satanic activity. In 22 municipalities in Los Angeles County alone, detec-

tives and social workers are enmeshed in investigations of child-porn rings with ritualistic overtones. Cult murders are being reported at a fantastic rate. (Norris and Potter 1986, 48)

Missing children constitute another source of estimating cult size and activity. If, as some activists claim, most of these children are Satanic ritual victims, then 50,000–60,000 ritual sacrifice victims annually becomes plausible. These estimates of large numbers of Satanic incidents and ritual victims, of course, suggest a vast network of practicing Satanists.

While episodic outbreaks of violence become publicly visible, the Satanic cult conspiracy creates the specter of a relentless organizational machine that literally has consumed millions of innocent children through its history. It is not surprising, therefore, that countermovement activists share psychiatrist Roland Summit's view that the ritual abuse of children is "the most serious threat to children and to society that we must face in our lifetime" (Victor 1993, 104).

Countermovement activists also profess relative helplessness in the face of this unprecedented menace. As one law enforcement officer commented about the capacity of police agencies to combat Satanists, "When confronted with those criminals who are led or controlled by supernatural evil beings, philosophies or motivations, traditional police tools are not effective" (Hicks 1991, 55). There are a variety of reasons why public officials feel powerless. For example, ritual abuse survivors contend that they are so brainwashed that control over them can be reestablished through "trigger cues" that are implanted in their minds (Hicks 1991, 164). And Satanists are not above using violence to defend themselves if less radical methods fail. For example, one ritual abuse survivor recounts an instance of two undercover police officers who attempted to infiltrate the cult with which she was involved; the result was that "one ended up joining and the other was murdered" (Hicks 1991, 173).

Creating Subversive Evil

Because we as humans socially construct the social world that we inhabit, we create both order and disorder; indeed, the creation of disorder flows directly out of the human project to create order. In times and locations where there is acute, pervasive tension, individuals and groups construct explanations and means of redress for the disorder they experience. One way to symbolize a profound sense of disorder is to attribute it to the work of an organized group that is actively and willfully conspiring to subvert the social order. In constructing such a narrative those involved produce a real-life drama, in which they become actors, depicting a struggle between the forces of good and subversive evil. We have argued that one way that groups create the compelling sense of good-evil confrontation in these two subversion episodes is through narratives that expand the stage upon which human action takes place. This is accomplished, we argue, by creating transcendent temporality, spatiality, and power; depicting subversives as embodying the inversion of institutionalized or sacralized values; identifying the key roles in the dramatic confrontation; and seeking to mobilize the audience as participants in the drama by heightening apprehension about the prospects for a subversive victory. The religious and Satanic cult episodes are instructive because, although countermovement claims have largely been rejected, each mobilized a social control apparatus and produced a pervasive sense of fear for a time. In fact, it is because the plausibility of the claims made by these two countermovements has begun to recede that the backstage culture work by countermovement activists is becoming clearer. Entrancing drama is always more fully appreciated at the conclusion of the performance.

Notes

1. Countersubversion movements may be most appropriately categorized as countermovements. In many instances the appearance of social movements is soon followed by the formation of countermovements, that is, movements mobilized to oppose other social movements (Zald and Useem 1987; see also Mottl 1980). While there is a wealth of research on a diverse array of social movements, there is much less systematic theorizing or empirical investigation of countermovements. This is a significant lacuna in social science research since the struggle over issues ranging from smoking in public places to abortion to capital punishment has been carried on by a set of movements and countermovements that are symbiotically related.

2. In the Western historical tradition the social construction of religion usually has involved the creation of a transcendent realm—that is, one operating on the basis of "structural principles or relations of a level lying above or outside the level of structure taken as the point of reference"—which is the domain of the sacred (Turner 1977, 69).

3. For a description of the various elements of the anticult movement, see Shupe and Bromley 1980.

4. For a discussion of the oppositional coalition constituting what is here termed the anti-Satanism movement, see Richardson, Best, and Bromley 1991.

5. Personal communication with Robert Hicks.

References

American Library Association. 1990. "Satanism Book Withdrawn." *Newsletter on Intellectual Freedom* 39: 81.

Appel, Willa. 1981. *Cults in America: Programmed for Paradise.* New York: Holt, Rinehart and Winston.

Barker, Eileen. 1984. *The Making of a Moonie: Brainwashing or Choice?* Oxford: Blackwell.

Berger, Peter, and Thomas Luckmann. 1966. *The Social Construction of Reality.* Garden City, N.Y.: Doubleday.

Bromley, David G. 1988. "Deprogramming as a Mode of Exit from New Religious Movements: The Case of the Unificationist Movement." In *Falling from the Faith: Causes and Consequences of Religious Apostasy,* ed. David G. Bromley. Newbury Park, Calif.: Sage, 185–204.

———. 1989. "ISKCON and the Anti-Cult Movement." In *Krishna Consciousness in the West,* ed. David G. Bromley and Larry D. Shinn. Lewisburg, Pa.: Bucknell University Press, 255–92.

———. 1991. "Satanism: The New Cult Scare." In *The Satanism Scare,* ed. James T. Richardson, Joel Best, and David G. Bromley. Hawthorne, N.Y.: Aldine de Gruyter, 49–72.

Bromley, David G., and Susan Ainsley. 1995. "Satanism and Satanic Churches: The Contemporary Incarnations." In *America's Alternative Religions,* ed. Timothy Miller. Albany: State University of New York Press, 401–9.

Bromley, David G., and Edward F. Breschel. 1992. "General Population and Institutional Elite Perceptions of Cults: Evidence from National Survey Data." *Behavioral Sciences and the Law* 10: 39–52. Special Issue on "Cults and the Law."

Bromley, David G., and Anson Shupe. 1981. *Strange Gods: The Great American Cult Scare.* Boston: Beacon Press.

———. 1986. "Cults, Crusaders and the Constitution." In *Laws of Our Fathers: Popular Culture and the U.S. Constitution,* ed. Ray Browne and Glenn Browne. Bowling Green, Ky.: Bowling Green State University Popular Press, 167–86.

———. 1993. "New Religions and Countermovements." In *Handbook on Cults and Sects in America,* eds David G. Bromley and Jeffrey K. Hadden. Greenwich, Conn.: Association for the Sociology of Religion, Society for the Scientific Study of Religion, and JAI Press, 177–98.

Brunvand, Jan Harold. 1981. *The Vanishing Hitchhiker: American Urban Legends and Their Meanings.* New York: Norton.

Cade, Leland. 1977. "Cattle Mutilations—Are They for Real?" *Montana Farmer-Stockman* 3 (March).

Chicago Tribune. 1985. "Satanism Haunts Tales of Child Sex Abuse" (29 July).

Conway, Flo, and Jim Siegelman. 1979. *Snapping: America's Epidemic of Sudden Personality Change.* Philadelphia: Lippincott.

Davis, Joseph. 1996. "Resisting Status Challenges from Below: The False Memory Countermovement Response to Adult Survivor Therapy." Unpublished paper, Department of Sociology, University of Virginia.

Edwards, Christopher. 1979. *Crazy for God.* Englewood Cliffs, N.J.: Prentice-Hall.

Geraldo. 1987. "Satanic Cults and Children" (19 November).

Hicks, Robert. 1990. "Police Pursuit of Satanic Crime." *Skeptical Inquirer* 14, no. 3 (Spring): 276–86.

———. 1991. *In Pursuit of Satan: The Police and the Occult.* Buffalo: Prometheus Books.

Kahaner, Larry. 1988. *Cults That Kill: Probing the Underworld of Occult Crime.* New York: Warner Books.

Kemperman, Steve. 1981. *Lord of the Second Advent.* Ventura, Calif.: Regal Books.

Knickerbocker News (Albany, N.Y.). 1976. "He Was Walking Zombie" (16 May).

Lanning, Kenneth. 1989. "Satanic, Occult, Ritualistic Crime: A Law Enforcement Perspective." *The Police Chief* 56 (October): 62–83.

Los Angeles Magazine. 1989. "A Case of Dominoes" (October), 128.

Los Angeles Times. 1991. "Forced to Kill Her Baby, Woman Says" (21 March).

Lyons, Arthur. 1988. *Satan Wants You.* New York: Mysterious Press.

Massachusetts State Police. 1989. *Roll Call Newsletter* (January), 3–4.

Mottl, Tahi. 1980. "The Analysis of Countermovements." *Social Problems* 27, no. 3 (June): 620–35.

Mulhern, Sherrill. 1991. "Satanism and Psychotherapy: A Rumor in Search of an Inquisition." In *The Satanism Scare,* ed. James Richardson, Joel Best, and David Bromley. Hawthorne, N.Y.: Aldine de Gruyter, 145–74.

Norris, Joel, and Jerry Allen Potter. 1986. "The Devil Made Me Do It." *Penthouse* (January): 48.

Ofshe, Richard, and Margaret Singer. 1986. "Attacks on Peripheral versus Central Elements of Self and the Impact of Thought Reforming Techniques." *Cultic Studies Journal* 3, no. 1 (Spring/Summer): 3–24.

Passantino, Gretchen, et al. 1989. "Satan's Sideshow." *Cornerstone Magazine* 18, no. 90: 24–28.

Patrick, Ted, with Tom Dulack. 1976. *Let Our Children Go!* New York: Ballantine Books.

Richardson, James, Joel Best, and David Bromley, eds. 1991. *The Satanism Scare.* Hawthorne, N.Y.: Aldine de Gruyter.

Rudin, A. James, and Rudin, Marcia. 1980. *Prison or Paradise? The New Religious Cults.* Philadelphia: Fortress Press.

Seattle Times. 1989. "Searching for Evidence" (20 February), A12–A13.

Shupe, Anson, and David G. Bromley. 1980. *The New Vigilantes: Anti-Cultists, De-programmers and the New Religions.* Beverly Hills, Calif.: Sage.

———. 1981a. "Apostates and Atrocity Stories: Some Parameters in the Dynamics of Deprogramming." In *The Social Impact of New Religious Movements,* ed. Bryan Wilson. New York: Rose of Sharon Press, 179–215.

———. 1981b. *The New Vigilantes: Deprogrammers, Anti-Cultists and the New Religions.* Beverly Hills, Calif.: Sage.

———. 1981c. "Witches, Moonies, and Accusations of Evil." In *In Gods We Trust: New Patterns of Religious Pluralism in America,* ed. Thomas Robbins and Dick Anthony. New Brunswick, N.J.: Transaction, 247–62.

Shupe, Anson, David Bromley, and Edward Breschel. 1989. "The Legacy of Jonestown and the Development of the Anti-Cult Movement." In *Jonestown: A Ten Year Retrospective,* ed. Rebecca Moore and Fielding McGehee. Lewiston, N.Y.: Edwin Mellen Press, 153–78.

Singer, Margaret Thaler, and Louis J. West. 1980. "Cults, Quacks, and Nonprofessional Psychotherapies." In *Comprehensive Textbook of Psychiatry/III,* ed. Harold Kaplan, Alfred Freedman, and Benjamin Sadock. Baltimore: Williams and Wilkins, 3295–3358.

Smith, Michelle, and Lawrence Pazder. 1980. *Michelle Remembers*. New York: Congdon and Lattes.

Snow, David, and Robert Benford. 1992. "Master Frames and Cycles of Protest." In *Frontiers of Social Movement Theory*, ed. Aldon Morris and Carol Mueller. New Haven: Yale University Press, 133–55.

Snowden, Kathy K. n.d. "Satanic Cult Ritual Abuse." Unpublished manuscript.

Stewart, James. 1977. "Cattle Mutilations: An Episode of Collective Delusion." *The Zetetic* 1 (Spring/Summer): 55–66.

Thorne, Stephen, and Philip H. Himelstein. 1984. "Perception of Satanic Messages in Rock-And-Roll Recordings." *Journal of Psychology* 116, no. 2: 245–48.

Turner, Terence. 1977. "Transformation, Hierarchy and Transcendence: A Reformulation of Van Gennep's Model of the Structure of Rites de Passage." In *Secular Ritual*, ed. Sally Moore and Barbara Myerhoff. Assen, Netherlands: Van Gorcum, 53–70.

Turner, Victor. 1982. "Social Dramas and Stories about Them." In *The Human Seriousness of Play*. New York: Performing Arts Journal Publications, 61–88.

Victor, Jeffrey. 1990. "Satanic Cult Rumors as Contemporary Legend." *Western Folklore* 49 (January): 51–81.

———. 1993. *Satanic Panic: The Creation of a Contemporary Legend*. Chicago: Open Court.

Vokey, John, and J. Don Read. 1985. "Subliminal Messages: Between the Devil and the Media." *American Psychologist* 40, no. 11: 1231–39.

Zald, Mayer, and Bert Useem. 1987. "Movement and Countermovement Interaction: Mobilization, Tactics, and State Involvement." In *Social Movements in an Organizational Society*, ed. Mayer Zald and John McCarthy. New Brunswick, N.J.: Transaction, 247–74.

Part Four

Strategy and Tactics

Part Four Introduction

Probably the single most dominant concern of both movement participants and scholars is that of strategy. What works and what doesn't? Jo Freeman argues that movement organizations are not free to choose any strategy. The factors that affect strategic choices are the nature of available resources, constraints on the use of those resources, the type of social movement organization, and expectations about potential targets.

Victoria Johnson focuses in on a specific tactic: the use of blockades of abortion clinics by Operation Rescue. She analyzes five factors—accessible resources, state facilitation, public relations, tactical effectiveness, and tactical interaction—to explain the emergence of blockades and subsequent changes.

David Meyer analyzes a specific tactic: civil disobedience. Drawing upon the civil rights and peace movements, he argues that this tactic serves different purposes at different points in a protest cycle. Initially it garners attention and helps with mobilization. At the peak of a cycle it provides tactical diversity. Subsequently it can help hold a movement together.

Craig Jenkins compares three separate attempts to organize farmworkers in California. He concludes that failure occurred because of structural obstacles to the mobilization of farmworkers, systematic political repression, and major strategic errors. Only when the United Farm Workers used collective solidarity as its mobilization strategy, and the larger labor movement provided crucial financial resources, did the movement achieve at least partial success.

11

A Model for Analyzing the Strategic Options of Social Movement Organizations

Jo Freeman

Strategic decisions about how a movement will act are not always made by a leader, or even by a small committee of experts, because most movements are not subject to hierarchical control. Often, major strategic decisions flow from circumstances or are made and executed by an otherwise insignificant group of protesters whose success is then emulated by others. For example, the 1960 sit-in at a North Carolina lunch counter was planned by a few college students, not the leaders of the major civil rights organizations. While these leaders were quick to see its uses, the idea of sitting-in spread largely through the media and informal communications networks of students. On the other hand, the decision in 1955 to boycott public buses in Montgomery, Alabama, was made by the black community leaders of that city and organized through the churches. This chapter presents a model within which strategic considerations, both planned and spontaneous, leader-directed and grassroots, can be analyzed. It highlights the resources available to a social movement organization at a given time, the limitations on the use of these resources, and how the resources can potentially be deployed.

My model of strategic decision-making (Fig. 11.1) by social movement

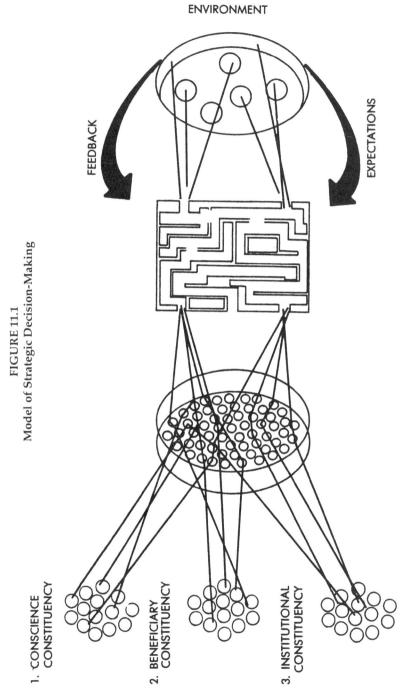

FIGURE 11.1
Model of Strategic Decision-Making

organizations has four major elements and numerous components. The elements are: mobilizable resources, constraints on these resources, social movement organization (SMO) structure and internal environment, and expectations about potential targets. Although the model is applicable to SMOs generally, I will illustrate points with examples drawn primarily from the women's liberation movement and the civil rights movement.

Mobilizable Resources

The resources available to organizers are either tangible or intangible. Tangible resources include money, space, and a means of publicizing the movement's existence and ideas. These resources are interchangeable, but only up to a point. Money can buy space, but not always vice versa. On the other hand, money can be used to publicize the movement, most of the time, and publicizing the movement can be used to raise money. It is a mistake to judge the affluence of the movement by its monetary contributions. A primary reason many new movements emerge out of older ones is not only that older movements provide co-optable communications networks but that they also provide some very valuable resources that would be at best expensive, and at worst unattainable, without the older movements. Both branches of the women's movement relied on space donated by others during their early days. The younger branch used a room and mimeograph temporarily contributed by the Institute for Policy Studies (IPS), a radical think tank in Washington, D.C., to organize its first national conference in 1968. The National Organization for Women (NOW) initially was organized out of the Extension Division of the University of Wisconsin and then out of the office of the United Auto Workers (UAW) Women's Committee in Detroit. When this was lost in 1967, due to the UAW's dismay at NOW's support for the Equal Rights Amendment, NOW was forced to divert precious funds to renting an office in Washington, D.C., which it had trouble staffing.

The younger branch had something more important than space—access to the network of underground newspapers and numerous New Left conferences held every year. Had this branch of the movement emerged five years earlier (or later), when such resources were minimal, it would have had a much harder time growing. The value of this particular resource for publicizing the new movement among potential adherents was so great that it is practically impossible to translate it into monetary terms. NOW did not have access to such a resource, and although it had more money than the younger branch, it did not have the enormous amount of money that would have been necessary to achieve the equivalent amount of press coverage. It took NOW years longer to achieve the numbers of the younger branch. Thus, movements that seem to be poor, that draw from seriously deprived constituencies, may in fact be rich in some less obvious, but still tangible, resources.

People are the primary intangible resource of a movement, and movements rely on them heavily. In fact, a major difference between a social movement and an organized interest group is the particular mix of resources each relies on. Interest groups tend to rely on tangible resources, especially money, some of which are used to hire professional staff to translate the rest of the resources into political pressure. Social movements are low on tangible resources, and the flow of money is erratic, but they are strong on people resources. Such resources are harder to convert into political pressure, let alone social change, in part because they are not very liquid, but for many activities they are more valuable. The civil rights movement recruited many young people to spend summers in the South registering blacks to vote. This was dangerous. Even had enough money been available, it is doubtful that this resource could have been bought. It is also questionable whether it would have been as effective. Parents of the summer volunteers raised money for their projects and focused press attention on their activities. Money and press attention wouldn't have come to a paid professional staff.

Not all people can make the same contribution to a movement. They provide at least three categories of resources. The first I call "specialized" resources. Their essential characteristic is that they are possessed by only a few participants—and only a few really need to possess them, for the point of diminishing returns is reached very quickly. These resources include expertise of various sorts, access to networks through which other resources can be mobilized, access to decision makers relevant to the movement, and status, whether within the movement's constituencies or within the polity the movement is trying to influence.

The other two categories are unspecialized in that any participant could contribute them if so inclined. These are time, primarily to perform necessary labor and/or sit through meetings, and commitment. Commitment is not dedication. Commitment is the willingness to take risks or entertain inconvenience. Whenever a deprived group triumphs over a more privileged one without major outside interference, it is because their constituencies have compensated with a great deal of time and commitment.

Since a movement relies so heavily on people resources, most activities involve their deployment. If a lot of time is demanded to attend meetings, there may be a lot less time available to do work. If the standard of commitment leads to acts that result in arrests, movement resources may be quickly diverted to fighting legal battles. Groups that have little access to specialized resources through their own constituencies must frequently spend other resources developing conscience constituencies to supply their specialized needs. Even this can backfire. The southern civil rights movement effectively mobilized young white students to supply specialized resources, especially northern public attention. But within two years the movement decided that their value had been expended and that their presence interfered with local people developing organizing skills.

Table 11.1 compares the resources available to the younger and older branches of the women's movement in the early 1970s. We next have to ask where they come from, and what are the costs of mobilizing them.

There are three major sources of mobilizable resources: the beneficiary constituency, any conscience constituencies, and nonconstituency institutions. According to McCarthy and Zald, the beneficiary constituency consists of political beneficiaries of the movement who also supply it with resources, and the conscience constituency are those sympathizers who provide resources but are not themselves beneficiaries.[1] Institutional resources are those that are available independent of the movement's existence, which can potentially be co-opted by it. For example, if a law exists prohibiting discrimination, the power of the state to enforce this law can theoretically be co-opted to help a movement eradicate discrimination.

TABLE 11.1
Resources Mobilized by the Early Feminist Movement

Resources	Younger Branch	Older Branch
Tangible		
Money	little	some
Space	people's homes; IPS	various offices
Publicity	underground papers; New Left conferences	women; lists; limited access to establishment papers
Specialized		
Expertise	community organizing; pamphleteering	public relations; lobbying
Access to networks	"radical community"; students	committees on status of women; professional groups
Access to decision makers	none	some in government; media and unions
Status in polity	none	little
Status in group	only in the "movement"	little
Unspecialized		
Time	a great deal	little
Commitment	a great deal	some

Before Title VII of the 1964 Civil Rights Act was passed, making racial discrimination in employment illegal, the civil rights movement occasionally used sit-ins to force employers to hire more blacks. Afterward, the movement encouraged individuals to file complaints with the relevant government agency and helped many to go to court to compel employers to end discrimination. By co-opting the institutional resource of the court, through the passage of Title VII, the civil rights movement acquired legitimacy for its fight against employment discrimination and was able to have an impact on far more employers and far more jobs.

Strategy

The primary distinction between a conscience constituency and a co-opted institution is that one has a *right* to the resources of the latter; access is institutionalized. The most obvious source of co-optable institutional resources is the government, but it is not the only source. When the YWCA made the ending of racism its "one imperative," it was in effect saying that the black movement had a *right* to the Y's resources for that end.

Regardless of the origin or kind of resource, resources are not just there for the asking. They have to be mobilized, and this in turn takes resources, which a particular SMO may not always have in abundance. Before passage of Title VII, the major resource the civil rights movement used to attack employment discrimination was large numbers of individuals sufficiently committed to risk arrest in a sit-in. This resource was most frequently supplied by the Congress of Racial Equality (CORE), whose history of nonviolent action had attracted to it large numbers of individuals, black and white, who were willing to engage in these tactics. After 1964, the major resource the civil rights movement needed was lawyers to argue cases in court. CORE had few of these, and its role in ending employment discrimination dissolved. Fortunately, the civil rights movement had another organization, the National Association for the Advancement of Colored People (NAACP), which was well endowed with lawyers who could provide this now necessary resource.

Sometimes not having the resources necessary to take advantage of a particular opportunity can be disabling. The women's liberation movement did not use court action as readily as the civil rights movement did—even though Title VII also proscribed sex discrimination—because it did not have organized legal resources. Yet it could not use the sit-in against employment discrimination because the mere existence of a legal channel undermined the legitimacy of such a disruptive tactic. Fortunately the independent development of a "Title VII bar," made up of lawyers who specialized in these type of cases, has provided that resource, even though it is not under movement control. Similarly, the American Civil Liberties Union (ACLU) Women's Rights Project, under a Ford Foundation grant, eventually provided much of the legal planning and talent for the women's movement that the NAACP Legal Defense and Education Fund provided for the black movement. To a certain extent one could say the women's movement co-opted the resources of the ACLU.

A major factor affecting the costs of mobilizing resources is their density. Since campuses attract young people in large numbers, an SMO seeking to reach them can efficiently do so by going to the campus. Women are rather dispersed, however, so even with a mailing list of potential supporters, greater amounts of time and money must be spent to mobilize women for a particular activity than to mobilize students. Without such a list, the costs escalate.

Aggrieved groups that are atomized and scattered throughout the population require enormous resources to be reached, let alone mobilized. Those that are concentrated can be mobilized much more easily, which is one reason why students are so readily available to so many movements. Groups that are scattered can be concentrated by being drawn together as part of the mobilization process of another movement or some other agency. For example, the Community Action Programs set up under the "war on poverty" became fertile grounds for welfare rights movement organizers. Without the government, the movement might not have been able to develop.

The reason many different movements tend to appear during the same historical period is not because different groups just happen to discover their grievances at the same time, or even because the example of one group alerts others to opportunities to alleviate their own grievances. Rather, it happens because the resources one movement generates can be used for cognate movements. Skills gained in one movement are readily transferable to another. One movement's conscience constituency can become the next movement's beneficiary constituency. The civil rights movement contributed significantly to the emergence of many other movements for just this reason.

Constraints

It is easy to think of resources as abstract entities that, like money, can be used for almost anything if enough are available. Unfortunately, movement resources are not liquid. Instead, all resources—even money—have constraints on their uses. These constraints differ, depending on the source, but their existence acts as a kind of filter between resources and

SMOs. These filters are so important that they can totally redirect the resources of a movement, much as a prism does a beam of light. And it is these filtered resources that an SMO has to work with, not the raw product.

The two branches of the women's movement drew upon similar if not identical resources, in comparable if not identical amounts, from people with closely matched class and educational backgrounds. Yet one branch formed numerous national associations, many of which opened Washington offices to lobby the government. The other branch organized numerous small groups whose primary tasks were education, personal conversion, and service projects. The younger branch of the movement *could* have formed a national organization at its 1968 conference, yet it didn't even make plans for an annual conference. It *could* have used the IPS office in Washington as a base from which to put pressure on the government, but it never even discussed such a possibility. It *could* have organized mass demonstrations, like NOW did in 1970, but took to WITCH (Women's International Terrorist Conspiracy from Hell) hexes instead. Such divergence of energies cannot be explained unless one looks at the constraints, conscious and unconscious, on the resources available for action.

I have identified five different categories of constraints, and more could be found. These are: values, past experiences, a constituency's reference group, expectations, and relations with target groups. The first and the last in the list have been identified by others,[2] while the middle three have either been overlooked or referred to only vaguely.

Since these terms don't really require definitions, their filtering function can best be explored by applying them to the two branches of the women's liberation movement. Both the age difference and the political networks from which the two branches emerged provided their members with different values, experiences, reference groups, expectations, and relations with target groups. These differences strongly influenced the kind of SMOs created, and the SMO structure in turn joined with these filters in a synergistic effect that molded the strategic possibilities.

Early participants in the younger branch came largely from the radical community, and their values reflected that community's interpretation of basic American concerns.[3] The radical movement's concepts of participatory democracy, equality, liberty, and community emphasized that everyone should participate in the decisions that affected her life, and that everyone's contribution was equally valid.[4] These values led easily to the idea that hierarchy is bad because it gives some people power over others and does not allow everyone's talents to develop. The belief was that all people should be able to share, criticize, and learn from one another's ideas—equally. Any structure or any leader who might influence this equal sharing was automatically bad.[5] The logical conclusion to be drawn from this train of thought—that all structure and all leadership are intrinsically wrong—was not initially articulated. But the potential was clearly there, and it did not take long for the idea of leaderless, structureless groups to emerge and eventually dominate this branch of the movement.

The adherence to these values was premised on the assumption that all women were equally capable of making decisions, carrying out actions, performing tasks, and forming policy.[6] This assumption could be made because the women involved had little experience in democratic organizations other than those of the New Left where they saw dominance for its own sake, competition for positions in the leadership hierarchy, and "male ego tripping" rule the day.[7] They had felt similar domination and control for its own sake in the social structures—primarily school and family—of which they had been part. The idea that there was some relationship between authority and responsibility, between organization and equal participation, and between leadership and self-government was not within their realm of experience.

The founders and early activists of NOW had gained their political experience in party politics, various bureaucracies, and the civil rights and labor movements. They felt structure in organizations was a help, not a hindrance; they were highly task oriented, found parliamentary procedure a convenience, were trained in public relations, and did not feel it necessary to live out egalitarian ideals in their own organization. Getting equality was more important than living it.

NOW's concept of a well-run organization was not one in which everyone participated, but one in which everyone contributed to the tasks of the movement. The concept of democracy was not one in which everyone had a say in all decisions, but one in which any who wanted to could have a say. Equality meant equal respect, not equal influence. Leadership was good, not bad.

The more immediate experiences of the early participants in the two branches also had an effect on their initial choice of tactics. Both had experience with mass demonstrations, and both had experience with the press. But radical women shared with radical men a certain jadedness about the value of mass demonstrations. They certainly hadn't ended the Vietnam War, and they appeared to absorb enormous amounts of time and energy to proclaim messages that fell on deaf ears. Instead, what was needed were actions that would catch people's attention by challenging old ideas and raising new ones. The women in the younger branch did this creatively with WITCH hexes, zap actions, and a "freedom trash can" at the 1968 Miss America contest into which "instruments of female oppression" were tossed. Ironically, while women used these tactics to catch the eye of the public and press, they didn't want to talk to reporters. In fact, they were afraid of them, and since they had access to the underground press, they didn't feel an acute need to appear in the establishment press. They had participated in so many demonstrations that were reported inaccurately that they did not feel their words would be reported the way they wanted them to be.

NOW women would have felt much too inhibited to engage in WITCH hexes (they thought they were silly) but felt no inhibitions about the press. Many were PR professionals and knew how to present their case, as well as not to expect too much. They were also willing to demonstrate, even though many knew the days of mass action were probably over. The first contemporary feminist picket line was organized by NOW in December 1967 to protest the Equal Employment Opportunity Commission's (EEOC) inaction on rewriting their want-ad guidelines.[8] NOW members had learned the uses of pickets and parades from the civil rights and union activities in which most had engaged. They did not give them up even when some of their "more respectable" members left in disgust to form the Women's Equity Action League (WEAL).

These direct-action tactics, and NOW's other activities, were not just to catch the public eye but to pressure the government. They were part of an overall campaign that also used letter writing, court suits, and meetings with government officials. Many early NOW members had engaged in lobbying for other groups, and it seemed perfectly logical to continue the same types of activities for a new movement. Besides, the initial impetus for NOW's formation had come from the EEOC's reluctance to enforce the provision in Title VII prohibiting sex discrimination, so pressuring for equal enforcement had to be a priority.

Another major difference between the women of the younger and older branches was their "reference groups." A reference group is not always a group; it is a standard against which people compare themselves in order to judge their behavior and attitudes.[9] This well-established concept from social psychology is not one that has been used to analyze social movements, but it has a great deal of explanatory power. When I first watched and read about Weatherman's "Days of Rage" and other low-key terrorist tactics, I found myself puzzled by what seemed to be a totally unrealistic assessment of potential support from the American public. Only after I had extensively read literature by and about the group[10] did they begin to make sense. I discovered that many of them had spent the preceding years visiting international revolutionaries outside the United States, largely Cubans and North Vietnamese, or had talked to those who had. These revolutionaries in effect became their reference group. From them they acquired the idea that the true revolutionary is one who is not afraid to strike a blow in "the belly of the monster" (i.e., the United States), even if the blow was suicidal. I suspect that Weatherman tactics were calculated not to gain support, or even attention, from the American public but to gain a sense of having met revolutionary standards.

The standards new feminists wanted to meet were very different for the two branches. Women in the younger branch first and foremost considered themselves *radical* women. While women of both branches wanted to "start a mass movement of women to put an end to the barriers of segregation and discrimination based on sex,"[11] younger-branch women felt this could be done only through "radical action and radical thinking." The desire to be radical virtually precluded any activities that resembled lobbying. The greatest fear of radicals in the late sixties was that they would be "co-opted" by the system into helping improve it through reform rather than destroy it through revolution. The idea that they could instead co-opt institutional resources to their own aims was totally alien.

> Our role was not to be . . . a large "membership organization." What we were talking about being was . . . a "zap" action, political agitation and education group something like what the Student Non-Violent Coordinating Committee (S.N.C.C.) had been. We would be the first to dare to say and do the undareable, what women really felt and wanted.[12]

This kind of thinking meant actions that "blew people's minds" were okay, but picketing the EEOC to change its guidelines was not.

The movement's most prevalent activity and organization, the consciousness-raising rap group, also grew from this radical orientation. The women who developed this tactic felt "the first job now was to raise awareness and understanding, our own and others—awareness that would prompt people to organize and to act on a mass scale."

> Consciousness-raising—studying the whole gamut of women's lives, starting with the full reality of one's own—would also be a way of keeping the movement radical by preventing it from getting sidetracked into single issue reforms and single issue organizing. It would be a way of carrying theory about women further than it had ever been carried before, as the groundwork for achieving a radical solution for women as yet attained nowhere.[13]

While C-R, as it came to be called, started with one group, it quickly spread throughout the movement. First, many groups of women who met to discuss women's oppression and plan their strategy on how to change it found themselves talking more and more about their personal experiences. This was an activity for which they had ample resources. For those who had strong ties with the New Left, this was not an acceptable endeavor because it wasn't "political." When the women of New York presented consciousness raising as a form of radical action at the 1968 conference, it gave them a rationalization for what they were doing anyway.

Second, there was extraordinary hostility and resistance by radical men to women's simply discussing their situation. Men dismissed the topics as petty and the process as therapy. Radical women took this resistance as a sign that they were on the right track.

> In the beginning we had set out to do our studying in order to take better action. We hadn't realized that just studying this subject and naming the problem and problems would be a radical action in itself, action so radical as to engender tremendous and persistent opposition. . . .[14]

Gerlach and Hine have emphasized the importance of opposition in maintaining movement cohesion.[15] The opposition of radical men to C-R not only created a high degree of group solidarity for the women engaged in it but strongly reinforced their belief that it was the way to be radical. As a result, C-R practically took over the younger branch of the movement as its sole raison d'être.

The women of NOW and the other national associations were not in the least concerned with being radical for the sake of being radical. Many felt that "equal rights" would take women only so far and that structural questions would have to be dealt with, but they did not feel it necessary to provide an analysis and program for dealing with these issues. What they did feel was necessary was to be *effective.* Effectiveness was the standard they had acquired from the professional and political associations of which they had been members. Since the best way to be effective is to make demands for small changes, and to concentrate one's resources on a few specific areas, this is what they did. The most vulnerable areas were those where women could demand the same rights that blacks had already won. The immediate targets thus became attaining changes that would give women legal parity with blacks. Both their immediate goals and their tactics were borrowed directly from the civil rights movement. Only as these goals and tactics were exhausted did the movement begin to move in new directions.

The expectations of the women in the two branches were governed by their past experiences and the expectations of those they associated with. For young women, the goal was revolution, and the expectation was that it would come soon. Their job was not only to help bring it about but to prepare a plan for women's role in the revolutionary society. Consciousness raising and study groups were two ways of doing this. As the Left became more and more disillusioned with the idea that revolution was around the corner, attaining it could no longer be the primary goal. By then, however, the rap group had become the primary unit of the women's movement, and women were aware that these groups functioned not only to help women analyze their lives but to "change their heads." Just as important, these changes could be seen and felt within a short time. "People changing" consequently became the primary function of rap groups.

Older-branch women expected to change institutions, not people. And they expected these changes to be slow and gradual. While younger women expected the revolution to come any month, those of the older branch debated whether the attaining of equal rights alone would take twenty years or a century. With a longer perspective, they could be content with smaller changes.

Analyzing the relations of feminists with their target groups is a little tricky, because first one has to decide what the targets were. For the women of NOW, WEAL, and similar organizations, the targets were concrete and identifiable. They were laws, institutions, discriminatory practices, and the people who could affect these things. In the younger branch, the first major debate was over just who the target was. Was it men or male-dominated institutions? Was it capitalism or patriarchy? Even when the women of a particular group knew which of these targets they wanted to attack, they were usually distant enough to raise some difficult strategic questions. For this reason, the usual targets became those much closer to home, the men in one's life and the women in one's group. And, contrary to what other sociologists have said,[16] the fact that feminists had generally close and intimate relations to both these targets did not keep them from using some very coercive tactics.

SMO Structure

There are two heuristic models of SMO structure in the literature. One is the centralized, hierarchical organization with a well-developed division of labor.[17] The other model is the decentralized, segmented, reticulate movement with no real center and at best a simple division of labor.[18] Strategically, the former seems to be better for attaining short-range goals involving institutional change in which organizational survival is not the dominant concern. The latter appears better for attaining personal changes in orientation and attitude through recruitment and conversion in which organizational survival is a dominant concern.

The centralized movement devotes minimal resources to group maintenance needs in order to focus them on goal attainment. However, this is somewhat reinforcing, for short-range goal attainment in turn becomes a means of maintaining group cohesion. The decentralized movement, on the other hand, is compelled to devote major resources to group maintenance. As long as it defines its major task as "people changing," this too is reinforcing because maintaining a strong sense of group solidarity is the means through which personal changes are accomplished. These simple, heuristic relationships work out fine as long as a movement group is conscious of the way in which its structure limits its strategic possibilities. A source of problems for many movements is the frequent attempt to pursue strategies for which their structures are inappropriate.

As Zald and Ash,[19] among others, have pointed out, the most viable movement is one that has several organizations that can play different roles and pursue different strategic possibilities. Thus the growth, development, and demise of a movement are not the same as the growth, development, and demise of the individual organizations within it. Most contemporary movements in this country have had complex structures and consequently fit both heuristic models. For example, the younger branch of the women's liberation movement was almost a paradigmatic example of the decentralized model, as it had no national organizations and consciously rejected hierarchy and a division of labor. The older branch had several national organizations that reticulated only slightly with one another. None fits the classic hierarchical model perfectly, but they are close enough for analytic purposes.

Neither branch of the movement deliberately created a structure specifically geared to accomplish its desired goals. Instead, the founders of both branches drew upon their previous political experience. Women of the older branch had been trained in and used the traditional forms of political action. They were familiar with national associations, and that is what they created. Women of the younger branch inherited the loose, flexible, person-oriented attitude of the youth and student movements, as well as these movements' disillusionment with traditional politics and traditional forms of political action. They strove for something new—and radical.

Once these different structures were created, they in turn molded the strategic possibilities—occasionally contrary to the professed desires of at least some of their members. Both branches made some efforts to change their structures, yet both remained essentially the same as they began. Organizational structure cannot be changed at will. What arises in response to one set of concerns in effect sets the agenda for what the movement can do next.

The younger branch was an excellent example of this molding effect because the original intention of its founders was not consciousness raising but radical action. C-R was supposed to be a means to an end, not the major task of the movement. Nonetheless, the loose, fluid, supportive C-R group was so successful that it became the model for all other groups. People resisted the idea that different movement tasks required different structures, or for that matter any structure. Instead, they elevated the operating principles of the small group to the status of feminist ideology, making it virtually impossible to adopt any other structure.

I have discussed the problems derived from "the tyranny of structure-lessness" elsewhere[20] and will not go into them here. Suffice it to say that the activities that could be developed by this branch of the movement were limited to those that could be performed by small homogeneous groups without major divisions of labor. These activities were primarily educational and/or service projects that could be set up on a local level. Consequently, the younger branch of the movement formed numerous women's centers, abortion counseling services, bookstores, liberation schools, daycare centers, film and tape production units, research projects, and rock-and-roll bands. The production of a feminist publication was one of the most feasible projects for a small group to handle, and hundreds were developed. But there was never any national coordination of these projects; many were repetitive or competitive; and they frequently became closed, encapsulated units whose primary purpose was to provide a raison d'être for their members to stay together.

The molding effect is less obvious with older-branch organizations because there was a greater congruence between strategic intentions and organizational structure, but it is there nonetheless. NOW and the National Women's Political Caucus (NWPC) provide an interesting study in contrasting problems. NOW was created to be a national lobbying organization, and initially that is what it was. From the beginning it required national dues to be paid by all members, whether they were members of chapters or not. Chapters in turn, apart from paying dues, were largely autonomous units. After congressional passage of the Equal Rights Amendment in 1972, it gradually became apparent that a mid-level structure of state organizations was necessary to press for ratification in the states. Neither individual chapters nor the national organization were capable of being effective on the state level. The creation of state organizations proved to be a difficult, time-consuming task. In unratified states they facilitated lobbying efforts. But in ratified states they generally undermined the autonomy of the local chapters by creating a new level of bureaucracy that made it difficult for chapters to act.

The NWPC was created in 1972 in order to try to elect more women to office. Modeled on the American political party, it created state organizations from the beginning but did not require national dues. This hampered its effectiveness on the national level, and it too went through a difficult period of trying to establish, and collect, national dues from recalcitrant chapters that preferred to concentrate their resources on state legislatures and local elections.

Another organization, WEAL, changed its strategy to fit its organization. Founded in 1968 in Ohio as a split-off from NOW, WEAL was intended to be a small, powerful organization for professional, executive, and influential women around the country. Over time, it discovered that a significant percentage of its membership was in Washington, D.C., and that its members there had some influence on Washington politicians. Therefore, it redefined its primary purpose to become a national lobbying organization whose primary resource was not numbers but expertise.

Expectations about Potential Targets

As an SMO searches for effective actions there are three factors it must consider about potential targets and the external environment. They are (1) the structure of available opportunities for action, (2) social-control measures that might be taken, and (3) the effect on bystander publics.

As Schattschneider has pointed out, "The function of institutions is to channel conflict; institutions do not treat all forms of conflict impartially, just as football rules do not treat all forms of violence with indiscriminate equality."[21] Nor do political institutions treat all demands from all groups impartially. Instead, institutions and the "rules of the game" operate as a filter to eliminate some and redirect others. Because SMOs are generally dissident groups, they frequently lack the resources to exploit the "usual" opportunities for action. Thus the success of such a movement is often determined by its ingenuity at finding less obvious leverage points from which to pressure its targets, creating new avenues for action, and/or effectively substituting resources it has in abundance for those it does not have.

Finding leverage points within the political system generally requires some intimate knowledge of its workings and thus is an alternative available only to those not totally alienated from the system. Ralph Nader's "Raiders" have been very effective at finding leverage points. Affirmative action in higher education became a public issue when a faculty woman sought a remedy for her failure to get a particular job for which she was qualified and found that none of the antidiscrimination laws covered her situation. Her discovery of Executive Order 11375, which required affirmative action for sex as well as race, reflected the fact that such leverage points can be found as much through luck as through knowledge.[22]

Creating new avenues is a far more common form of action for dissident movements, especially when they have minimal knowledge of or access to the political system. The civil rights and student movements very effectively attracted public attention to their causes through nonviolent demonstrations that prevented people from engaging in "business as usual" without so flagrantly violating norms of behavior that the demonstrators could be dismissed as pathological deviants. Unfortunately, such tactics are usually "creative" only when they are new; their effect wears off over time. Sometimes such tactics do become institutionalized, as did the strike and boycott, which were originally developed by the labor movement. But at other times they simply lose their impact. The arrest in 1977 of over one thousand people protesting at a nuclear plant at Seabrook, New Hampshire, made less of a public impression than the "freedom ride" buses of the fifties or the campus arrests of the sixties.

Resource substitution is a particularly common strategy for social movements that want to utilize institutional channels but do not possess the usual resources for their utilization. Groups that cannot command large voting blocks to elect favorable candidates can achieve equivalent access by supplying the time and commitment of their members as campaign workers. This has been successfully done by the gay rights movement to gain support from local politicians and other groups.

Not infrequently, the structure of available opportunities for action presents *no* feasible alternatives to some SMOs. This may be because a particular SMO constituency is too alienated or too ignorant to take advantage of what is available, as is the case with movements of the seriously deprived. It may also be because the particular resources of a movement do not fit the channels available for action, that the SMO's structure or values do not allow it to participate in those channels, or that the available channels are not capable of dealing with a movement's demands. In theory the younger branch of the women's liberation movement was just as capable as the older branch of mobilizing its supporters for lobbying activities, but the constraints on the uses of its people resources, as well as its small-group structure, made this opportunity for action unfeasible.

When there are no feasible opportunities, movements do not simply go away; instead, discontent takes forms other than political action. Many riots are now seen as a form of political activity. Withdrawal movements of varying kinds are common when dissident groups feel highly alienated. These withdrawal movements may be "apolitical" in the sense that their members identify their activities as spiritual or cultural. Yet many redefine their politics in "alternative" forms. When the New Left turned to "alternative institutions," it saw these as a new means of pursuing its politics, not a rejection of politics. As has happened with communes and some other leftist activities, however, it is not uncommon for what began as an alternative political institution to become an apolitical one. In this way some movements can be "cooled out" so that what began as a means of making public demands becomes a refuge for seeking personal solutions.

When a movement does appear to find successful avenues for action, it generally encounters social control measures of one sort or other. These may suppress a movement, but not always—direct opposition is a two-edged sword. As Gurr, as well as Gerlach and Hine,[23] have illustrated, some opposition is necessary to maintain movement viability. A solid opponent can do more to unify a group and heal its splits than any other factor. Many of the student sit-ins of the sixties would have never gotten off the ground if the university authorities hadn't brought in the police. But even if the enemy is not so blatant, it is the perceived and not the real opposition that is important. Movements that neither perceive nor experience opposition find it difficult to maintain the degree of commitment necessary for a viable, active organization. Often opposition will be blown up larger than life because to do so serves the needs of group cohesion.

Nevertheless, the relationship between opposition (real or perceived) and movement strength is not linear. Effective application of social control measures can kill a movement; so can completely ignoring it. Similarly, a perceived opposition of great strength can effectively destroy a movement by convincing people that their actions are futile. In the 1970s, leftist and feminist groups developed many infiltration and conspiracy theories to explain their internal problems. Their initial effect was to heighten commitment against a pernicious enemy. But these theories also created suspicion and undermined the mutual trust necessary for movement survival. An opposition that contributes to commitment in the short range can kill it in the long run.

The degree and success of opposition affect not only the movement but the relevant bystander publics. Bystander publics are not direct targets of a movement's actions, but they can affect the outcome of these actions. As a general rule, movements try to turn bystander publics into conscience constituencies that will supply the movement with additional resources and prevent them from becoming antagonists who will discourage targets from responding to movement demands.[24] Movements that cannot find leverage points are very dependent on the reactions of bystander publics, and it is not uncommon for demonstrations to be used, not to directly affect a particular target, but to gain sympathy and support from other parties. The southern civil rights movement used nonviolent demonstrations in expectation that an overtly violent social control response would attract third-party support. When it brought these same tactics to the North where the bystander publics were the targets, it largely failed.

The civil rights movement's failure to appreciate that tactics viable in one area wouldn't work in another is a common one. SMOs plan their actions on the basis of expectations about potential target and bystander public response. These expectations are initially derived from prior experiences, or those of cognate groups. Once actions are initiated, direct feedback becomes relevant. When an activity proves successful, it is generally repeated without analyzing the context that permitted that success.

For reasons already discussed, the younger branch of the women's liberation movement was not interested in ordinary pressure tactics aimed at political institutions. Even if it had been, none of its participants had the experience in this kind of action necessary to know how to do it. They did have experience with zap actions, and did several of these during the first years of the movement's existence. While the actions were approved by other movement participants, they did not receive favorable feedback from the public at which they were aimed. Usually they were ignored; and when not ignored, they were ridiculed. Had this been the only available outlet for their energies, zap actions might have continued.

In the meantime, consciousness raising was systemized and spread widely. Feedback from this process was immediate and favorable. Women recruited into C-R groups spoke frequently of the emotional release they got from the groups, and they kept coming back. C-R was sufficiently popular to become the prevalent activity. Its success altered the movement's immediate targets from the general public to that of the women in the C-R groups. Other younger-branch activities became the magnet by which to attract new recruits into C-R groups.

The older branch meanwhile maintained its basic, successful strategy of institutional pressure, though it expanded its repertoire beyond the initial one of lobbying. While some organizations within the older branch, such as NOW, added C-R activities, they did so as a membership service and not as a strategic device. This branch of the movement has been very attuned to the structure of available opportunities for action. It has paid much less attention to actual and potential social control measures and bystander publics. Nonetheless, it is still affected by both these factors; its leaders are merely unaware of how.

In conclusion, some flaws in the model presented should be pointed out. The most glaring one is that it is not a dynamic model. It does not explain changes over time in any of its components or in strategic outcomes. Rather, it enables one to look at an SMO at one point in time to determine the resources available for mobilization and the potential ways in which these resources can be deployed. In addition, the model ignores fortuitous circumstances that might benefit a particular movement's goals and the accidents of history that are often so crucial in a movement's success or failure. Fortuitous resources, as well as accidents, certainly have an effect on final outcome, but unless their availability can be reasonably predicted or controlled by an SMO, they play little part in strategic decision-making.

Notes

1. John D. McCarthy and Mayer N. Zald, "Toward a Resource Mobilization Theory of SMOs" (paper presented at the Southern Sociological Society, 12 April

1973), citing Michael Harrington, *Toward a Democratic Left: A Radical Program for a New Majority* (New York: Macmillan, 1968).

2. Ralph H. Turner, "Determinants of Social Movement Strategies," in *Human Nature and Collective Behavior*, ed. Tamotsu Shibutani (Englewood Cliffs, N.J.: Prentice-Hall, 1970), 151.

3. Daniel C. Kramer, *Participatory Democracy: Developing Ideals of the Political Left* (Cambridge, Mass.: Schenkman, 1972).

4. Linda Lewis and Sally Baideme, "The Women's Liberation Movement," in *New Left Thought: An Introduction*, ed. Lyman T. Sargent (Homewood, Ill.: Dorsey, 1972), 83.

5. Martha Shelly, "Subversion in the Women's Movement, What Is to Be Done," *off our backs* (8 November 1970), 7.

6. Lewis and Baideme, "The Women's Liberation Movement," 87.

7. Marge Piercy, "The Grand Coolie Damn," in *Sisterhood Is Powerful*, ed. Robin Morgan (New York: Random House, 1970). Robin Morgan, "Goodbye to All That," in *Voices from Women's Liberation*, ed. Leslie Tanner (New York: New American Library, 1970).

8. The EEOC had initially ruled that separate want-ad columns with racial labels were a violation of Title VII, but those with sex labels were not. NOW wanted the EEOC to "de-sexigate" the want-ads by ruling that all labels were illegal.

9. This term was first used in 1942 by H. H. Hyman, "The Psychology of Status," *Archives of Psychology*, no. 269 (1942), but the idea goes back much farther.

10. See especially the compilation *Weatherman*, ed. Harold Jacobs (San Francisco: Ramparts, 1971).

11. Kathie Sarachild, "Consciousness-Raising: A Radical Weapon," in *Feminist Revolution*, ed. Redstockings (New York: Redstockings, 1975), 131.

12. Sarachild, "Conscious-Raising," 132.

13. Sarachild, "Conscious-Raising," 132.

14. Sarachild, "Conscious-Raising," 132.

15. Luther P. Gerlach and Virginia H. Hine, *People, Power, Change: Movements of Social Transformation* (Indianapolis: Bobbs-Merrill, 1970), chap. 7.

16. Turner, "Determinants of Social Movement Strategy," 153.

17. William Gamson most explicitly discusses the strategic possibilities of this model in *The Strategy of Social Protest* (Homewood, Ill.: Dorsey, 1975), 197.

18. Luther P. Gerlach, chap. 5 in this book.

19. Mayer N. Zald and Roberta Ash, "Social Movement Organizations: Growth, Decay, and Change," *Social Forces* 44 (March 1966): 327–40.

20. Jo Freeman, *The Second Wave*, vol. 2, no. 1, 1972, 20. Reprinted in *Radical Feminism*, ed. Anne Koedt, Ellen Levine, and Anita Rapone (New York: Quadrangle, 1973), 285–99. Revised version in *Ms.* (July 1973), 76.

21. E. E. Schattschneider, *The Semi-Sovereign People* (New York: Holt, Rinehart and Winston, 1960), 72.

22. Jo Freeman, *Politics of Women's Liberation* (New York: Longman, 1975), 191–209.

23. Gerlach and Hine, *People, Power, Change*, chap. 8. Ted Robert Gurr, *Why Men Rebel* (Princeton: Princeton University Press, 1970).

24. Turner, "Determinants of Social Movement Strategy," 152. McCarthy and Zald, "Toward a Resource Mobilization."

12

The Strategic Determinants of a Countermovement: The Emergence and Impact of Operation Rescue Blockades

Victoria Johnson

To study the interaction among protest groups, we must first distinguish between social movements, countermovements, and conservative movements. Social movements are attempts to create or deter social change by networks of activists who usually employ extra-institutional tactics, although not exclusively. The majority of movement participants tend to operate outside of established institutions of power (Gamson 1990). Countermovements seek to undermine the changes achieved by social movements. I agree with Mottl that social movements "challenge groups higher up in the stratification hierarchy, while countermovements are oriented against changes from below" (1980, 621). Countermovements seek to protect their constituents' socioeconomic positions, which have been threatened by social movements seeking greater access to resources, status, and power for their constituencies. While both countermovements and conservative social movements act to conserve traditional privileges, they are distinct in that the latter do not organize in direct response to social movements. The militia movement is one example of a conservative movement rather than a countermovement. It primarily targets the federal government. Participation in conservative and countermovements is not mutually exclusive.

Social movements can achieve both "linear" and "fluid" social change (Gusfield 1981). Linear change occurs when movements make concrete economic or political gains. Fluid success involves more subtle cultural

---

changes in beliefs and values. For example, the civil rights movement led to the passage of the Civil Rights Act of 1964 and the movements for abortion law reform and the women's liberation movement led to the 1973 Supreme Court ruling that decriminalized most abortions. Fluid changes included greater public sensitivity to the problems of race and gender inequality, and the delegitimation of legal segregation.

By the 1970s, countermovements emerged to challenge the linear and fluid changes achieved by the social movements of the 1960s. While there have been insightful analyses of the strategic determinants of social movements (Turner 1970; Freeman 1983, this book; Turner and Killian 1987) and case studies of specific countermovements, there has been little research about countermovements as a distinctive form of collective action (Mottl 1980, Lo 1982, Zald and Useem 1987). Are the strategic determinants of social movement organizations (SMOs) and countermovement organizations (CMOs) the same? If not, what are the distinctions? In this chapter I look at the strategic determinants of a countermovement organization, Operation Rescue (OR), which spearheaded anti-abortion blockades in the 1980s. I analyze five strategic determinants that explain the emergence of OR blockades and changes in their strategy over time—accessible resources, state facilitation, public relations, tactical effectiveness, and tactical interaction.

This study will also identify two distinctions between social movements and countermovements. First, because countermovements are protecting established socioeconomic interests, they usually have access to resources that more readily facilitate their emergence (Mottl 1980, Lo 1982). Second, in order to mobilize support from the public, countermovements often draw upon the successful rhetorical appeals constructed by social movements, but redefine them to communicate opposing ideological goals. While social movements and countermovements share numerous characteristics, the distinctions between them are important for understanding the dynamics of social change. Their differing access to resources and opposing ideological goals shape the strategies of political and symbolic struggles. The outcomes of such struggles, in part, determine political policies and the cultural climate.

I begin by looking at the ascendancy of the religious right, the matrix out of which OR emerged. Then the five strategic determinants are examined, beginning with "tactical interaction" (McAdam 1983), or the ways that movements change their tactics or develop new ones in response to those of their opponents. Next I analyze the other four strategic determinants—accessible resources, state facilitation, public relations, and tactical effectiveness—to identify the strategic advantages gained through the creation of OR in the 1980s. Finally, I assess the impact of OR blockades in relation to both linear and fluid social change.

The Ascendancy of the Religious Right

Much has been written about the rise of the religious right (Leibman and Wuthnow 1983, Bruce 1988, Moen 1989, Lienesch 1993). I will limit my discussion to changes in the character of abortion protest from the early 1970s to the early 1980s, and to the religious right's creation of a resource base that facilitated the emergence of OR.

Early Abortion Protests

Small-scale protests occurred at abortion clinics soon after the *Roe v. Wade* ruling on January 22, 1973. Most of the demonstrations were organized by Catholics. Throughout the 1970s the anti-abortion rights movement was most closely connected to the Catholic church. Over half of the budget that funded the National Committee for a Human Life Amendment and the New York State Right to Life Committee came from donations solicited on Catholic church grounds (Lo 1982, 114; Jaffe 1981, 77, 81). Some of the participants were also opposed to nuclear arms and capital punishment as part of a "seamless garment" tradition that claims to value life both before and after birth. The early demonstrators were peaceful and, for the most part, noncoercive. But in the 1980s the movement became increasingly influenced by the religious right, whose leaders were mostly from neo-evangelical, fundamentalist, and Pentecostal churches. During the early to mid-1980s growing numbers of anti-abortion rights activists adopted more coercive rhetoric (Condit 1990) and tactics.

The Orchestration of a Countermovement

Elites were important to the emergence of the religious right, at least in its initial stages. At the end of the 1970s, a group of business and political professionals orchestrated the creation of several Protestant CMOs. Prominent among organizers were Paul Weyrich of the Committee for the Survival of a Free Congress and Richard Viguerie, director of direct mail operations for a number of conservative causes. The Survival of a Free Congress was organized in the early 1970s as an alternative to the American Conservative Union's political fund. By 1976 the new organization, along with conservative political action committees (PACs) coordinated by Viguerie, was raising more money than the Republican National Committee and its House and Senate committees combined (Davis 1986, 170). By the late 1970s, Weyrich and Viguerie saw a potential for an alliance between secular and religious conservatives and approached religious school lobbyist Robert Billings of the National Christian Action Coalition and Ed McAteer of the Christian Freedom Foundation with a plan. This group recruited several leading "televangelists," most notably Jerry Falwell, host of the "Old Time Gospel Hour," and Pat Robertson from the "700 Club" (Lienesch 1993). They laid the groundwork for a number of countermovement organizations, including the Moral Majority.

The Moral Majority was formed in 1979 and became one of the largest and most successful of the early CMOs. Appeals were made through Falwell's "Old Time Gospel Hour" TV ministry, which was broadcast on over 300 television stations, and through the pastors of local churches. In 1980 fundraising through the ministry brought in close to $1 million a week (Liebman 1983, 58). The Gospel Hour's 2.5 million mailing list was used to raise $2.2 million for the Moral Majority within its first fiscal year (Liebman 1983, 61). By the end of August 1981, the Moral Majority national office had spent over $6 million (Liebman 1983, 55).

The expansion of single issue direct mail campaigns, pioneered by Viguerie and directed toward secular and religious conservatives, created new interlocking constituencies among CMOs, conservative social movements, and interest groups. They ranged from the Americans for Effective Law Enforcement, the National Rifle Association, and numerous anti-busing organizations to Jerry Falwell's Moral Majority, Phyllis Schlafly's anti-ERA Eagle Forum, and Anita Bryant's anti-gay rights campaign. But the largest constituencies were the "Right-to Life" organizations (Davis 1986, 170).

By the early 1980s, the goals of the religious right included opposition to abortion, feminism, the Equal Rights Amendment, gay rights, domestic violence legislation, busing, "secular humanist" school books, the Supreme Court ruling against prayers in public schools, pornography, welfare spending, and reductions in military spending. Stopping abortion mobilized both religious and secular conservatives because it represented much more than the death of an embryo/fetus. Abortion also symbolized the emancipation of women, an avenue to sexual freedom, independence from marriage, and consequently, a threat to traditional gender and sexual relations (Petchesky 1990, 241).

The religious right succeeded in gaining positions within the Reagan administration. This included C. Everett Koop, who became Surgeon General, and Robert Billings, the former executive director of the Moral Majority, who became an official in the Department of Education. But by 1984, not much had actually changed to achieve the goals of the religious right. Viguerie expressed disappointment to the *Wall Street Journal* that conservatives had been allowed to work for the Republicans but they had not been allowed to "govern" (Bruce 1988, 135). This same year, other countermovement activists, impatient with ineffective electoral and lobbying strategies, were organizing to carry out actions that would get results.

The Emergence of Operation Rescue

When goals appear blocked, it is not uncommon for movements to generate a militant direct action wing.[1] In the mid-1980s grassroots CMOs formed to use direct action with local rather than elite leadership. In 1984 some groups held an "Action for Life" conference in Florida where Joseph Scheidler presented a workshop on "Effective Confrontation." As part of the training 200 participants went to the Women's Awareness Clinic in Fort Lauderdale and blocked all entrances.

In 1985 the "Action for Life II" conference was held in Wisconsin. Participants pledged to create a "year of pain and fear" for anyone performing or receiving an abortion. The conference marquee stated "Have a Blast," while some participants wore firecrackers as lapel pins to symbolize dynamite.[2] Participating organizations, including the Pro Life Action League and the Pro Life Direct Action League, named their nationally coordinated organization the Pro Life Action Network (PLAN). Its goal was to close down abortion clinics nationwide.

At PLAN's third annual conference in Missouri in 1986, participants decided to increase the blockades at women's clinics. Over time a plan to blockade clinics under the name of Operation Rescue was devised. The plan was finalized during a visit between Joseph Scheidler and Randall Terry in New York in 1987. OR was formed by a five-man national advisory committee, elected at the 1987 PLAN conference. The team included Randall Terry, who later became OR's leader, and Joseph Scheidler, called the "godfather" of OR due to his earlier use of direct-action tactics.[3]

OR's first blockade took place in November 1987 at a women's clinic in Cherry Hill, New Jersey. National media coverage came in the summer of 1988 when 1,200 people were arrested in OR's "siege on Atlanta" during the Democratic National Convention. According to OR and other sources, over 11,000 participants were arrested for blockading health clinics in 1988 (*Nuclear Resister* 1989). The following description is typical of early blockades. Many of the activists were recruited at a preblockade rally held at a local church the night before. Potential blockaders gathered in a church parking lot or other designated location before 6:00 A.M. OR leaders were the only ones who knew where the blockade would take place in order to elude pro-abortion rights activists seeking to warn the clinics. The police were informed earlier by OR that a blockade would take place to assure them that activists would be nonviolent. Just before leaving, participants were given directions to the location of the clinic. Once they arrived, the largest men surrounded the doors of the clinic. Other activists densely packed themselves around the front and back entrances and any windows, linking arms while either standing or sitting. The demonstrators prayed, sang religious hymns, and in some cases, songs from the civil rights movement. Inspirational speeches were also made. Participants were instructed not to talk to the public. "Sidewalk counselors" were appointed to speak to women trying to enter the clinic to talk them out of having abortions. Other OR leaders were designated as media spokespersons. When the police made arrests, blockaders "went limp" so the police would carry or drag them away. This increased the amount of time that the clinic was closed. Other OR tactics included picketing, "phone blockades"—tying up the phone lines so clients could not make appointments—and "exposure" tactics like distributing "wanted posters" of physicians who performed abortions.

For the most part, OR leadership comes from conservative neo-evangelical and fundamentalist denominations who believe in the literal interpretation of the Bible and want society to "return" to a "Christian America." If this were accomplished, Terry argues, we would see the end to numerous social problems (Terry 1988, 1990). According to police records, during the peak years for blockades, 1988–89, 60 to 70 percent of those arrested were men. Almost all of the leaders and up to 50 percent of the participants were in their late twenties to mid-thirties (Faludi 1989).[4]

Dynamics and Tactical Interaction

In its first year of intense blockading (1988), OR did succeed in catching clinics and women's rights organizations off guard. Some clinics capitulated by closing down on the days scheduled for blockades. In many cases, clinics and physicians' offices were inaccessible because of blockades, if just for a day or a few hours. But over time developments undermined OR's initial effectiveness and elicited changes in their tactics. This section describes the dynamics and the "tactical interaction" among OR and pro-abortion rights activists, the media, the police, courts, and the state from 1988 to 1995.

Clinic Defense

When events call for disruptive tactics, informal SMOs tend to play an instrumental role. Formalized organizations do at times engage in direct action, although they prefer more routine tactics (Staggenborg 1989). After the experience of the first blockades, the National Organization for Women (NOW), the National Abortion Rights Action League (NARAL), and Planned Parenthood (PP), as well as others, worked with clinic owners to organize for clinic defense. They recruited pro-abortion rights activists to "escort" women into clinics during blockades, encouraged the police to take swift action to remove demonstrators, and in some cases recorded who was present and any illegal actions for evidence to be used in court. On the morning that had been designated for a blockade, clinic defenders waited at the location of the preblockade rally and followed OR on their way to the clinic. Once the location was apparent, this information was communicated to other clinic defenders who then tried to get to the targeted clinic prior to OR in order to occupy space around the door so women could enter. Escorts and women seeking abortions were encouraged to ignore the blockaders and/or pickets. Some women wore head phones with music playing so they would not have to hear the OR sidewalk counselors.

This strategy, however, often left escorts and women seeking abortions outnumbered and on the defensive. In the early days, the idea of having large numbers of pro-abortion rights activists present to counter OR was objected to by many clinic owners and much of the leadership of organizations like NOW. Objections ranged from concern that women seeking abortions would be more intimidated by the larger crowd to the argument that medical facilities were not appropriate locations for political demonstrations.

Within the first year of blockading, radical grassroots SMOs dedicated to clinic defense also emerged. Unlike mainstream organizations, the radical activists went on the offensive. They were much more confrontational and theatrical in their approach to OR blockaders. On the East Coast, new SMOs included members of AIDS Coalition to Unleash Power (ACT UP) and Refuse and Resist. Members objected to OR attacks on abortion rights and gay rights, as parts of a larger "right-wing agenda." In the South, Refuse and Resist members organized the Coalition Opposing Operation Rescue (COOR) as a response to blockades in Atlanta in 1988. In northern California, the Bay Area Coalition Against Operation Rescue (BACAOR) was formed. To get women into clinics, activists arrived early at all clinics that were likely targets. They placed large wooden shields around the clinic door to keep blockaders from gaining space. When OR showed up and surrounded the clinic, BACAOR activists lifted women over blockaders into the space behind the shields, and through the clinic door. They also, on occasion, physically removed blockaders by lifting them out of their space and replacing them with pro-abortion rights activists. Such tactics have been effective in getting women into clinics and demoralizing blockaders. Needless to say, this created antagonistic relations with the police. Some BACAOR members have been arrested. Initially there was some tension between the radical clinic defense SMOs, clinic owners, and mainstream women's movement leaders. But as blockading and harassment increased over time, relations improved and coalitions developed.

The presence of organized clinic defenders, especially those who were more confrontational, had the effect of decreasing the numbers of "casual blockaders" who participated in the early stages when most clinics closed down because OR vastly outnumbered pro-abortion rights activists. When the interactions became more intense, and at times ugly, some blockaders (and pro-abortion rights activists) who were intimidated by the conflict ceased to come. But there was a consistent core of dedicated blockaders and new recruits coming in. The number of blockades and the resulting arrests peaked during OR's "surge" (Lofland and Johnson 1991) in 1988 and 1989. At least 11,732 people were arrested at 182 blockades in 1988, and 12,358 were arrested in roughly 201 blockades in 1989.[5] But by 1990, OR blockades declined to the point where BACAOR changed its name to the Bay Area Coalition for Our Reproductive Rights (BACORR).

Injunctions

Although Operation Rescue strategists surely recognized that blockades would result in legal costs, they may not have foreseen quite how much these would be. In 1988–89, injunctions were implemented in numerous states where OR had blockaded or threatened to blockade, including California, Georgia, Washington state, Pennsylvania, and New York. As a result of the New York blockades, NOW obtained an injunction against trespass at clinics. OR appealed, but in May 1990 the Supreme Court declined to review the lower court decision.[6] After OR ignored a trial court order prohibiting it from blockading in New York City, and refused to pay a $50,000 contempt fine, federal marshals seized its payroll accounts. By February 1990 these contempt fines had increased to $450,000 against Terry, Operation Rescue, Bi-State Operation Rescue Network, and eight other defendants. In early spring of 1990, Terry announced that the national office of Operation Rescue was closing for financial reasons. But later that year, OR's national headquarters was relocated to North Carolina and Keith Tucci took over as the national director. Terry continued to promote blockades through a North Carolina "Operation Rescue National" address. The implementation of injunctions did have the effect of limiting the number of blockades and participants. By 1990 only 1,363 were arrested at thirty-four blockades.[7]

The Media

OR publicized themselves as the "civil rights movement of the eighties." News programs around the country aired five-second media "bytes" showing participants singing freedom songs and "sitting-in." But, notably, not only did OR spokespeople claim that they were participating in classic nonviolence, the media parroted their claims. During the northern California blockades in the spring of 1989, one Sacramento TV station announced, "Like the civil rights movements of the sixties. . . ." Major magazine writers made similar comments. Garry Wills in *Time* described their tactics as "consciously drawn from the nonviolent techniques of Gandhi and King" (Wills 1989). In fact these comparisons became so prevalent that it prompted leaders from the civil rights movement to make a public statement disavowing OR's comparison (Planned Parenthood 1989).

But this media interpretation declined over time as pro-abortion rights counterprotests and organized clinic defenders gained momentum. The portrayal of blockaders as "peaceful demonstrators" changed when they were confronted with equally dedicated pro-abortion rights activists. As a result, some OR blockades began to resemble shouting and shoving matches. Pro-abortion rights activists had become so well organized by March 1989 that they matched the numbers of OR activists during a series of blockades in Los Angeles. As a result, Archbishop Roger Mahoney, an OR sympathizer, decided not to participate in the blockades. He explained that "When it becomes a real confrontation between two screaming groups, I wonder how effective it is" (Fleeman 1989).

By this point the media coverage of OR had changed. The shift can be highlighted through a comparison with the successful media strategies of the civil rights movement. Civil rights movement strategists used nonviolent civil disobedience to contrast with the violence of white racists in front of the media. The nonviolent responses of activists, when brutally attacked by the police and segregationists, made front-page coverage and the TV news. The images of nonviolent demonstrators being victimized aroused public sympathy and national and international support for their cause.

During OR blockades the media was predictably drawn to the conflict. But as counterprotests were organized, cameras recorded the increasing instances of anti-abortion rights and pro-abortion rights activists arguing, pushing, shoving, and grabbing each other at blockades. One form of conflict often recorded was the verbal and physical aggression by OR sidewalk counselors in their attempts to deter women from seeking abortions. News coverage began to portray OR as the victimizers. Associated Press coverage of the Wichita blockades in 1992 noted that it was one of the "most violent protests yet," and further stated that one OR participant had encouraged children to blockade by "lying down in front of cars." Such actions damaged the strategic potential of OR to be characterized as nonviolent victims of repression and to gain sympathy from the public.

Terry consistently complained about such "biased" coverage by the "liberal pro-abortion media." In 1992 he began communicating OR's message directly on a radio program called "Randall Terry Live." The national program was organized to "expand the use of Christian radio to expose, resist . . . and to confront the critical issues. . . ."[8] By 1994 it was broadcast on roughly thirty stations.

The Police and the Courts (Municipal and State)

Prior to blockading, OR leaders usually met with the police to persuade them to take their time while making arrests. In exchange they agreed not to resist arrest and to be nonviolent. Although the response varied in different cities, initially police action was slow. In New York in 1988, the police took two to four hours to clear blockaders from a clinic. Although many officers were present, they were described as "just standing around." After political pressure was put on the police and they became a party to the NOW injunction, demonstrators were cleared in less then one hour. During a blockade in Washington, D.C., in the fall of 1989, the police threatened pro-abortion rights activists (who were holding space in front of the clinic door) with arrests. When they dispersed, OR moved in and blockaded the clinic. The OR demonstrators were arrested after several hours of keeping the clinic closed. Blockaders were commonly charged with a misdemeanor for illegal trespass on private property and freed on their own recognizance. Many joined the blockades again the next day.

After repetitive blockading led to public pressure, the police became more effective. By 1988–89 a number of city councils in California, including Los Angeles, passed resolutions against Operation Rescue. The City Council of Davis, California, went so far as to pass a resolution declaring itself a "Pro-Choice City" in November 1989. This resolution, like the others, was intended to have a symbolic impact and to communicate to the police and district attorney that blockading should be taken seriously.

Over time the courts began to give stiffer sentences to repeat offenders, and increased fines for violations of injunctions. In a letter to Terry's supporters written on May 25, 1989, he complained that "Many police, judges, prison guards and D.A.s have moved from being neutral participants in this struggle to ardent, aggressive defenders of child-killers." As the blockaders were removed more quickly and with less sympathy, complaints of police brutality increased. OR arranged for a Department of Justice investigation into the use of nunchukas and pain compliance techniques. However, the Justice Department concluded that the matter should be closed and no further action was taken. OR was able to generate public sympathy from the press and public when pain compliance devices were used. Police were criticized for their handling of demonstrators in Atlanta in 1988, and in Los Angeles and Sacramento in 1989, when a demonstrator's arm was broken and a protester was maced. A number of journalists who sympathized with OR, including William Buckley and Nat Hentoff, publicized such events.

The State (Congress and the Supreme Court): 1992–1995

In 1992, the first president who unequivocally supported abortion rights, Bill Clinton, was elected. In 1993, a physician was murdered at an abortion clinic and another was shot but not killed. In 1994 a physician, a clinic escort, and two clinic personnel were also murdered. No OR leader was indicted for these crimes. But the media and the public associated anti-abortion rights activists with the escalating violence. With participation already in decline, the murders that occurred in 1993 and 1994 reduced OR's resource base as a number of conservative churches distanced themselves (Risen 1994).

The murders produced dissension within OR's leadership regarding the tactical use of violence (Cobb 1994).[9] In 1994, Keith Tucci resigned and was replaced by Reverend Flip Benham as OR's national director; the headquarters were relocated to Dallas, Texas. Benham strongly opposed dealing with any advocates of "justifiable homicide" within the anti-abortion rights movement.

The escalation of violence by anti-abortion rights activists secured the passage of the FACE (Freedom of Access to Clinic Entrances) Act in May 1994. After a decade of harassment, arsons, bombings, and finally murder at women's clinics, the act was passed by Congress and signed by President Clinton. The FACE Act made it a federal crime to engage in any activities that use force, the threat of force, or "physical obstruction" to injure, intimidate, or interfere with any person "obtaining or providing reproductive health services" or exercising their "First Amendment right of religious freedom at a place of religious worship," or to intentionally destroy the property of a facility that provides reproductive health services or a place of worship. For an offense of "exclusively nonviolent physical obstruction," an offender can be fined up to $10,000 and receive up to six months in jail, or both. For a subsequent offense, a blockader can be fined up to $25,000 with a length of imprisonment not to exceed eighteen months, or both. Aside from legal penalties, the FACE Act also allows for "civil remedies" in which individuals seeking or providing reproductive health services can sue offenders for "compensatory and punitive damages."[10]

On the same day that President Clinton signed the FACE Act into law, May 24, 1994, several religious right organizations, including the American Life League, sued the Justice Department, in an attempt to have the law invalidated (Marcus 1994). In 1995, the Supreme Court rejected a challenge to the new law. The justices, without comment, let stand rulings that declared that FACE did not infringe on freedom of expression or religion.[11]

The same year there were two important Supreme Court rulings unfavorable to OR. In *NOW v. Scheidler,* the Supreme Court unanimously ruled that those engaged in organized, illegal anti-abortion extortion or violence can be sued under the Racketeer-Influenced and Corrupt Organizations Act (RICO), which was originally fashioned as a weapon against organized crime. It applied to both Scheidler and OR, as well as other anti-abortion rights activists and organizations. Under RICO, defendants face triple damages and leaders of anti-abortion groups may be sued as co-conspirators whether or not they attend demonstrations. Plaintiffs may also seek federal injunctions against anti-abortion blockades.[12]

The Supreme Court declared in *Madsen v. Women's Health Center* that 36-foot "bubbles," or protest-free zones around clinic doors, were constitutional, but 300-foot zones were not. The ruling was in response to an injunction granted by a state court in Florida. The injunction was issued due to continuous harassment, where clinic personnel were subjected to stalking and threats of violence. It barred OR members from entering a protective 36-foot bubble around the clinic doors and approved a 300-foot zone that barred protesters from approaching, uninvited, anyone seeking to enter or leave the clinic.[13]

Due to the combination of injunctions, escalation of violence by anti-abortion rights activists, passage of the FACE Act, and Supreme Court rulings, there was a dramatic decrease in the number of blockades and arrests by 1995 (see table 12.1). As the number of blockaders decreased, OR changed their tactics. They turned to increased sidewalk counseling and picketing of abortion clinics, physician's offices, homes, churches, and clubs. These actions were designed to pressure doctors to quit providing abortion services. Scheidler summed up the strategy by stating, "If you can't get an abortion, you can have all of the laws in favor of it that you want" (Frolik 1993).

The numbers of reported incidents of picketing went up from 151 in 1988 and 72 in 1989 to 7,827 by 1997 (see table 12.1). In response to the picketing of physician's homes, a number of cities enacted new anti-residential picketing ordinances. OR has challenged some of the ordinances in court for being in conflict with the First Amendment.

Strategic Determinants

So far we have looked at the emergence of OR and how its tactics changed over time through tactical interaction, a strategic determinant. The following analyzes four others—accessible resources, state facilitation, pub-

TABLE 12.1
**Number of Blockades, Arrests, and Incidents of Picketing of
Abortion Providers, 1988–1997**

	1988	1989	1990	1991	1992	1993	1994	1995	1996	1997
Blockades	182	201	34	41	83	66	25	3	7	25
Arrests at										
Blockades*	11,732	12,358	1,363	3,885	2,580	1,236	217	34	65	29
Incidents of										
Picketing	151	72	45	292	2,896	2,279	1,407	90	3,932	7,827

Source: National Abortion Federation's Violence and Disruption Statistics, 1995 (1), 1436 U Street, Suite 103, Washington, DC 20009. (The statistics for 1996 and 1997 were provided by the National Abortion Federation in a phone conversation on July 9, 1998.)
*The total number of arrests does not refer to the total number of people arrested, as some blockaders are arrested multiple times.
Note: The increase in incidents for 1991 may partly be explained by improvements in the NAF's tracking system in mid-1991.

lic relations, and tactical effectiveness—in order to identify the potential strategic advantages of adopting a civil disobedience tactic in the 1980s. In other words, why did the religious right adopt the tactic of blockading in the first place?[14]

Accessible Resources

Due to their media and institutional connections, religious and secular conservatives were able to rapidly mobilize resources. Abortion galvanized activists willing to commit time, labor, and money to their cause across a wide spectrum of people. Operation Rescue's "siege on Atlanta" in 1988 increased donations, including a check from Jerry Falwell for $10,000. In 1989, OR's annual income was announced as $300,000, much of it raised through direct mail solicitation. By 1992, OR National's annual budget reached $400,000 (Risen 1994).

Co-optable communication networks (Freeman 1973, 1983, this book) accessible to OR included religious television and radio programming, as well as conservative Christian newspapers. In some cases, Operation Rescue rallies were advertised in the religion section of secular newspapers. Randall Terry appeared on Pat Robertson's "700 Club" to mobilize support for OR blockades. Congregations that had become politicized were willing to let OR hold rallies on their church grounds to recruit participants. Church and media networks generated money and participants for blockades.

But not all conservative Christian churches provided resources for OR blockades. Engaging in political activity like voting and attending a march were quite different from illegally blockading a clinic. OR's blockades in Atlanta in 1988 were openly criticized by a number of conservative church leaders. One was Reverend Charles Stanley, pastor of the First Baptist Church in Atlanta and a former president of the Southern Baptist Convention. He circulated a pamphlet disagreeing with OR's tactics titled "A Biblical Perspective on Civil Disobedience." The National Right To Life Committee's president, John Wilke, told the *Washington Post* that he had no comment on Operation Rescue and that "we do not become involved in anything outside the law" (Kurtz 1989). Their newsletter did not cover OR activities during its surge in 1988–89.

State Facilitation 1980–1992

The state can be an instrumental player in the facilitation or repression of social movements and countermovements. A favorable "political opportunity structure" creates the potential for movements to gain resources and concessions (McAdam 1982, 1983; Tarrow 1994; Jenkins and Klandermans 1995; Meyer and Staggenborg 1996; Kriesi et al. 1997). From 1980 through 1992, the Reagan and Bush administrations politically and symbolically supported the anti-abortion rights movement. Presidents Reagan and Bush appointed officials who opposed abortion rights to high-level positions in their administrations, the Supreme Court, and other judicial positions, where they worked to restrict the availability of abortions. They also promoted religious right goals through symbolic actions. In 1986 Reagan declared January 19 as National Sanctity of Life Day. Both presidents made supportive public statements to the annual March for Life in Washington, D.C., on the anniversary of *Roe v. Wade*. On July 1, 1992 President Bush reaffirmed his anti-abortion support on morning talk shows by stating, "I favor the right to life, I am not in favor of *Roe v. Wade* and I would like to see the decision go the other way."

In 1987 President Reagan directed his Surgeon General to prepare a report on the health effects of abortion. The presumption was that research would show damaging effects, which could be used to overturn *Roe v. Wade*. The report his office produced was not released because the expected results were not found.[15] In 1991 the Supreme Court finally heard argument on whether blockaders violated an 1871 Civil Rights Act that prohibited conspiracies to deprive any person of the equal protection of the law. The Department of Justice filed a friend of the court brief on behalf of OR, arguing that only state, not federal, law applied to such matters. Justice also entered cases then being argued in U.S. District Courts that had used the same act to issue injunctions against OR demonstrations in other cities.[16] The District and Circuit Courts upheld the use of federal injunctions until 1993 when the Supreme Court concluded that this act could not be used to stop blockades.[17]

Administration support promoted a social climate conducive to the repression of abortion rights and increased the legitimacy and aspirations of those attempting to undermine them. In the same sense that the liberal Kennedy and Johnson administrations made supportive gestures toward the civil rights movement, the rhetoric and actions of the Reagan and Bush administrations signaled similar support for anti-abortion rights protesters. However, it is important to note that both presidents disavowed illegal protest actions, especially after OR blockades gained notoriety in 1988.

Public Relations

By the mid-1980s anti-abortion rights CMOs had three public relations problems. First, their movement had become associated with violence. The number of clinic bombings increased from eight incidents in 1977 through 1983, to eighteen in 1984 alone. Incidents of arson increased from thirteen in 1977–83, to fourteen in 1984 and 1985.[18] In 1982 an Illinois physician who performed abortions was kidnapped and threatened. By 1984, violent threats were made against Supreme Court Justice Blackmun, author of the *Roe v. Wade* decision (Barron 1984). In 1986 Joan Andrews attempted to shut down a Florida clinic by destroying surgical equipment. The male activist who accompanied her injured the clinic administrator and a pro-abortion rights activist in the process.[19] Months later Scheidler led a crowd of 100 protesters to the home of the judge who sentenced Andrews. A confrontation broke out when officers began making arrests. Shortly thereafter the Pro Life Action Network held a miniconference to discuss concern over public perception of such actions. They agreed to set guidelines to "improve public perception of the activist anti-abortion movement, [and] improve media relations."[20] A tactic was needed that would disassociate the anti-abortion rights movement with violence.

The second problem was the public association of abortion protest with religious beliefs. The religious right had been accused of imposing their beliefs on others in relation to a number of issues. But this association was particularly strong in relation to Catholicism and abortion. The first protests against *Roe v. Wade* were organized by Catholics and the leadership of the "right-to-life" movement was heavily influenced by the Catholic church hierarchy. Scheidler (1985) used the term "the Catholic problem" to describe the public perception that opposing abortion was the concern of people with certain religious beliefs. He emphasized the importance of changing this impression.

The last public relations problem involved the cultural work that countermovements do to undermine the fluid changes created by social movements. Social movements try to change beliefs, values, practices, and/or economic and political policies. To be effective they draw upon cultural symbols that the society is familiar with, but reinterpret them in ways that challenge traditional understandings. The construction of these "new codes" (Melucci 1989) is constrained by the necessity that they will have a resonance with a larger public. If a new code is successful, social movements and countermovements may draw upon it. It is not uncommon for countermovements to adopt tactics and ideological elements of social movements (Mottl 1980). But when they do, the codes must be redefined to represent the values and goals of the countermovement. In other words, social movements draw upon traditional symbols to create new cultural codes that promote social change, whereas countermovements draw upon the new codes constructed by social movements but redefine them to represent traditional views.

The tactic of nonviolent civil disobedience had the potential to solve all three of these public relations problems. To understand how, we must take into account the pivotal role of the media in social movement success and failure. Gamson points out that the media has had an increasing effect on social movement strategy since 1945. More than ever before, activists must engage in "battles over meaning" where "images, catch phrases, and metaphors used by the media . . . are central in determining their fate" (Gamson 1990, 147). He concludes that this "enlarged media role appears to enhance high profile, nonviolent forms of collective action" (1990, 177). Another strategic advantage is the potential for activists who have been subjected to violence to gain sympathy and support from the public and other third parties (Sharp 1973).

By making public claims that OR was participating in classic nonviolent civil disobedience, religious right activists could use the media to portray themselves as nonviolent people and thereby change negative public attitudes.[21] OR flyers emphasized that participants should be "free from any actions or words that would appear violent or hateful to those watching the event on television or reading about it in the paper" (Operation Rescue 1988).

The perception that abortion protest is a religious issue could also be changed through the use of this tactic. Gandhi and King are famous for leading progressive human rights movements. OR adopted tactics and rhetoric associated with Gandhi and King and other progressive social movements, including women's liberation. Rather than merely "saving babies," OR now portrayed itself as protecting the human rights of a group being discriminated against—fetuses. While the standard "abortion is murder" signs were prominent at blockades, there were also signs demanding "Civil Rights for the Unborn" and "Equal Rights for Unborn Women." In their media communications, OR spokespeople presented themselves as the "civil rights movement of the 1980s." Although some human rights rhetoric was used by the anti-abortion rights movement in the early 1980s (Condit 1990), its emphasis within the context of OR sit-ins crystallized the symbolic association of fetuses with autonomous human beings whose civil rights were being violated—a concern well established within the secular sensibilities of the American public.

Adopting the rhetoric of progressive movements from the 1960s also solved the religious right's third problem. OR appropriated the new codes that had been constructed by the civil rights movement and employed by the women's liberation movement. Both movements sought an expansion of civil rights, liberties, and federal legislation prohibiting discrimination, political stances mostly opposed by the religious right. But the cultural work of OR succeeded in redefining the antidiscrimination and equal rights codes to communicate opposing goals—that the reproductive equality won by progressive movements should be ended.

Tactical Effectiveness

Anti-abortion rights CMOs engaged in a variety of tactics during the 1980s. Through electoral and lobbying activities they succeeded in obtaining enactment of parental consent laws and removal of state funding to pay for the abortions of indigent women. However, they failed to pass a "Human Life Amendment" in the early 1980s, which would have declared a fertilized ovum a human being.

These CMOs conducted massive educational campaigns, including the distribution of photographs of aborted fetuses (often from the second or third trimester of pregnancy) and videos such as *The Silent Scream*.[22] Other approaches involved the distribution of leaflets that claimed abortion had damaging psychological and physical effects. Crisis Pregnancy Centers were created to persuade women not to have abortions by offering support in the form of baby clothes, referrals, and in some cases, shelter for the duration of a woman's pregnancy. Also included as tactics, although publicly disavowed by movement leaders, were phone threats and stalking of physicians and clinic personnel, vandalism of property, and the bombing and burning of women's health clinics, all of which escalated during the mid-1980s.

None of these overturned *Roe v. Wade*. In a 1989 flyer written to mobilize participants for a "National Day of Rescue," Terry complained that "fifteen years of lobbying and political education have gotten us virtually nowhere." He called for a more militant tactic where "children will be saved from death; mothers from exploitation." Terry argued that this tactic could illustrate their cause in a way that other tactics could not: "as your community and the nation sees good, decent citizens sitting, kneeling, and praying around a death camp, risking arrest for these children, they will take seriously our claims that abortion is murder" (Operation Rescue 1989). Presumably, this tactic would be more effective in changing public attitudes and voting patterns, which could lead to the recriminalization of abortion.

The adoption of nonviolent civil disobedience was also effective in attracting publicity while deterring repression from authorities. Lessons from the antinuclear, environmental, and peace movements indicated that such tactics can be disruptive enough to gain media attention, yet are likely to elicit minimal physical repression from the police and minor fines in most cases. In a 1988 flyer, Terry assured future blockaders that "Rescuers are usually arrested, charged with a minor infraction . . . and released the same day."

The Impact of OR Blockades

In this final section I will assess the impact of OR blockades in relation to both linear and fluid social change. OR's linear goals were to use civil disobedience and other pressure tactics to make abortions less accessible in the short term, and to generate public support to end legal abortion over the long term. Clearly OR did not recriminalize abortion, but it did succeed in making abortions less accessible. It was more difficult, and sometimes impossible, for women to get into clinics during blockades. However, eventually defenders were able to get women in, police removed blockaders in time for clients to make their appointments, and injunctions and federal legislation limited the number of blockades and participants.

The most serious obstacle to accessible abortion has been the decline in the number of physicians and facilities. OR played a role in this, but it is difficult to estimate to what degree. Some physicians claim that their decision to not do abortions has been influenced by harassment at the clinics.[23] Hospitals have responded to the pressure of anti-abortion activists by closing or minimizing their abortion services. The number of hospitals where abortions are performed decreased by 18 percent from 1988 to 1992, and less than one-third of American hospitals with the facilities to perform abortions do so (Joffe 1995, 3). While urban areas generally have abortion providers, only 14 percent of the counties in the United States have facilities where women can receive safe, legal abortions, making access difficult or nonexistent for women in rural areas.

The blockades did not lead to the fluid social changes that they were designed for. Not only did the public's beliefs about keeping abortion legal not decline, but they were strengthened among certain segments of the population. Between 1975 and 1988, roughly 22 percent of the population supported a woman's right to legal abortion under "any circumstances." In April 1990, after two and a half years of OR blockades, 31 percent of the American public supported a woman's right to legal abortion under "any circumstances." The number of those unconditionally opposed to abortion also dropped in 1990, from roughly 19 percent in 1975–88 to 12 percent. This is the largest shift recorded on the abortion issue in the previous fifteen years by the Gallup polls (Gallup 1990). The shift in public opinion cannot entirely be explained as a reaction to blockades, due to insufficient information.[24] However, a poll taken by the *Wichita Eagle* during the 1991 blockades showed that 78.2 percent disapproved of OR's tactics, while another 70 percent would continue women's right to abortion. A 1991 Gallup poll found that of those who had heard of the OR blockades, 15 percent approved, 77 percent disapproved, and 8 percent had no opinion.

Polls alone do not mean protests have no impact. Not all fluid changes are captured by surveys. OR effectively kept the message of abortion as "murder" and a "civil rights" issue in the media for over four years, with periods of intense coverage. Sidel has noted the impact that anti-abortion rights activism has had on teenage women making reproductive decisions. Having heard a constant bombardment of negative messages about abortion, some have dismissed it as an option, although "they recognize that they are not ready—emotionally, economically, socially, or in any way—to care for a child" (Sidel 1996, 127). Identifying the concrete linear changes produced by movements is easier than gauging the subtle fluid changes that affect our most personal decisions. If OR's tactics have convinced some women that they have no reproductive choice, then fluid change has been as much of an obstacle to safe, legal abortion as not having access to physicians, abortion facilities, or clinics during blockades.

Conclusion

This chapter looked at the strategic determinants of the countermovement organization Operation Rescue. I analyzed five strategic determinants that help us to understand the emergence, dynamics, and consequences of Operation Rescue blockades—accessible resources, state facilitation (1980–1992), public relations, tactical effectiveness, and tactical interaction. Two distinctions between social movements and counter-movements were identified. The first is the closer affiliation of counter-movements with institutions of economic and political power, which more readily facilitates their emergence. The second characteristic in-volves the kind of cultural work done by countermovements as they at-tempt to redefine the definitions of social problems that have become ac-cepted within the dominant culture due to the success of social movements.

Finally I assessed the success and failure of OR blockades. While block-ading proved effective in its initial stages, over time its advantages were undermined. This change was due to pro-abortion rights clinic defense, injunctions, Supreme Court rulings, and the violence that occurred at clinics. These secured passage of the FACE Act, which increased penalties for interference with women seeking reproductive health care or physi-cians and staff who provide it. OR did succeed at keeping media attention focused on their message of fetal rights as a civil rights issue for several years. Their tactics also succeeded in intimidating some doctors and hos-pitals, thereby contributing to the reduction in the number of physicians and abortion facilities. But blockades failed to convert the public to sup-port the recriminalization of abortion. In fact, throughout the 1990s public support for legal abortion increased according to opinion polls.

Notes

1. Data on OR tactics are from the following sources: direct observation of OR blockades in northern California, video coverage of OR blockades from the media, pro-choice activists, and clinic owners; files from the California state office of the National Organization for Women, including injunctions, transcripts from court proceedings, and police reports; OR literature and extensive newspaper and mag-azine coverage; attendance at speeches given by Joe Scheidler and OR attorney Cyrus Zal; interviews with people who have interacted with OR leaders, includ-ing NOW president Patricia Ireland and journalist Susan Faludi; interviews with pro-choice activists who have encountered OR, including members of BACAOR, a direct action clinic defense organization; discussions with OR participants in the northern California area; and "escorting" experiences (helping women seeking abortions to enter clinics without interference) at health facilities picketed by OR members.

2. Excerpts from the First Amended Class Action Complaint at 4, *NOW v. Scheidler*, No. 86 Civ. 7888 (N.D. Il., filed Jan. 17, 1986).

3. Id. at 4–8.

4. This figure conforms to the arrest records I reviewed for the cities of Concord, Sunnyvale, and Fremont, California.

5. National Abortion Federation, table 2. *National Abortion Federation's Violence and Disruption Statistics: Incidents of Violence and Disruption Against Abortion Providers*, 1995, Washington, D.C. These statistics are based on incidents reported to the NAF; the actual number is likely higher.

6. *NOW New York State v. Terry*, 697 F. Supp. 1324 (SDNY 1988) and 704 F. Supp. 1247 (SDNY 1989) appeals consolidated and aff'd as modified, 886 F.2d 1339 (2d Cir. 1989), cert. denied, 495 U.S. 947 (1990).

7. National Abortion Federation, table 2.

8. These quotes are taken from an advertisement for Terry's radio show titled "The Voice of Resistance," P.O. Box 570, Windsor, NY 13865.

9. In September 1994, Tucci disagreed with some OR leaders about having public debates regarding the tactical use of violence. Jeff White, the former chief strategist of OR, disagreed with Tucci's position, emphasizing that it is important to promote free speech in the organization. As a result, White was removed from the leadership circle.

10. *Freedom of Access to Clinic Entrances Act of 1994*, P.L. No. 103–256, § 636, 108 Stat. 694 (May 26, 1994).

11. *American Life League v. Reno*, 516 U.S. 809, 116 S.Ct. 55, 133 L.Ed.2nd 19, 1995 U.S. Lexis 5337 (1995).

12. *National Organization for Women v. Scheidler*, 510 U.S. 249, 114 S.Ct. 798, 127 L.Ed.2d 99, 1994 U.S. Lexis 1143 (1994). In 1998 a Chicago jury unanimously decided in favor of NOW in the 12-year-old *NOW v. Scheidler* case. With this verdict, NOW won a permanent injunction against the defendant's blockades, "extortion and other use of force at clinics." The plaintiff clinics will petition for triple damages as allowed by the RICO Act cited above. ("NOW Declares Victory Over Anti-Abortion Thugs!" April 20, 1998; http://www.now.org./issues/abortion/scheidlr.html.)

13. *Madsen v. Women's Health Center, Inc.*, 626 So.2d 664 (Fla. 1994), *aff'd in part and rev'd in part*, 512 U.S. 753 (1994).

14. Much of the analysis of strategic determinants is speculative. I was not able to directly observe the decision-making process among OR leadership. Randall Terry did not answer my letter inquiring about OR strategy. I drew heavily upon documentary analysis for this section. The conclusions are derived from multiple sources.

15. Dr. Koop instead wrote a letter to President Reagan that stated that the data were inconclusive on the psychological and physical health effects of abortion. However, in 1989 the Human Resources and Intergovernmental Relations Subcommittee of the Committee on Government Operations held an investigative hearing to review the findings of the report. They concluded that there were discrepancies between Koop's letter and the Surgeon General's report. The research had indicated that "abortion is medically safer than pregnancy and childbirth, both in terms of mortality and morbidity." In his testimony, "The Surgeon General concluded that psychological problems from abortion are rare and not significant from a public health viewpoint . . . [and that] delays in obtaining an abor-

tion, for whatever reason, jeopardize the physical and mental health of the mother." U.S. House of Representatives (1989), 12, 14, 16.

16. The 1871 act is at 42 U.S.C. §1985(3). One such case was *Women's Health Care Services, P.A. v. Operation Rescue–National,* 773 F. Supp. 258 (D. Kans. 1991), rev'd, 24 F.3d 107 (10th Cir. 1994).

17. *Bray v. Alexandria Women's Health Clinic,* 506 U.S. 263, 113 S.Ct. 753, 122 L.Ed. 2d 34, 1993 U.S. Lexis 833 (1993), rev'g in part, aff'g in part, *National Organization for Women v. Operation Rescue,* 914 F.2d 582 (4th Cir. 1990), aff'g 726 F. Supp. 1483 (E.D. Va. 1989).

18. National Abortion Federation, table 2.

19. Excerpts from the First Amended Class Action Complaint at 5, *NOW v. Scheidler,* No. 86 Civ. 7888 (N.D. Il., filed Jan. 17, 1986).

20. Id. at 6–7.

21. I have argued elsewhere that OR was not practicing nonviolent civil disobedience in the tradition of Gandhi and King. See Johnson 1997.

22. The pro-life movement released *The Silent Scream* in January 1985 on the 12th anniversary of *Roe v. Wade.* The video showed abortion from "the victim's vantage point" by using ultrasound to illustrate the abortion of a 12-week fetus. The narrator, Dr. Bernard Nathanson, stated that the fetus at this level of development "has had brain waves for at least six weeks" and is a "fully formed, absolutely identifiable human being." The video was criticized for presenting inaccurate information by the scientific community, including Dr. Michael Bennett, chairman of the Neuroscience Department at Albert Einstein Medical School, Dr. Patricia Goldman-Rakic, professor of neuroscience at Yale Medical School, and Isaac Asimov, a Ph.D. in chemistry and author of *The Human Brain,* among others. See Jaworski (1989), "Thinking about the Silent Scream."

23. Joffe (1995) acknowledges the impact of groups like OR, but also identifies reasons endemic to the medical profession that contributed to this decrease of providers.

24. This shift was likely due to a confluence of developments of which blockades were but one factor. No doubt the Supreme Court decisions restricting access to abortion in *Webster v. Reproductive Health Services* (492 U.S. 490, 1989) and *Planned Parenthood of Southeastern Pennsylvania v. Casey* (505 U.S. 833, 1992) played a role. Increased pro-abortion rights activism and media coverage in the late 1980s may have contributed. There was also the threat that President Bush, if reelected in 1992, would have appointed enough Supreme Court justices to create a majority in favor of overturning *Roe v. Wade.*

References

Barron, James. 1984. "Violence Increases Against Abortion Clinics." *New York Times* (Nov. 5), B15.

Bruce, Steve. 1988. *The Rise and Fall of the Christian Right.* Oxford: Clarendon Press.

Cobb, Kim. 1994. "Tucci's Resignation Downplayed; Shake-Up Comes Amid Crisis at Operation Rescue." *Houston Chronicle* (Feb. 12), A14.

Condit, Celeste. 1990. *Decoding Abortion Rhetoric: Communicating Social Change.* Urbana: University of Illinois Press.

Davis, Mike. 1986. *Prisoners of the American Dream: Politics and the Economy in the History of the US Working Class.* London: Verso.

Faludi, Susan. 1989. "Randall Terry's Holy War." *San Jose Mercury News* (July 9) West 9.

Fleeman, Michael. 1989. "Abortion Protests Hit Rough Sledding." *Sacramento Bee* (March 25), A4.

Freeman, Jo. 1973. "The Origins of the Women's Liberation Movement." *American Journal of Sociology* 78, no. 4 (January 1973): 792–811.

———. 1983. "A Model for Analyzing the Strategic Options of Social Movement Organizations." In *Social Movements of the Sixties and Seventies,* ed. Jo Freeman. New York: Longman, 193–210.

Frolik, Joe. 1993. "'No Rescues,' Says Local Anti-Abortion Organizer." *Cleveland Plain Dealer* (July 4), B1.

Gallup, George. 1990. "Selected National Trends." *Gallup Polls.* Wilmington, Del.: Scholarly Resources, 45–46.

Gamson, William. 1990. *The Strategy of Social Protest.* Belmont, Calif.: Wadsworth.

Gusfield, Joseph R. 1981. "Social Movements and Social Change: Perspectives of Linearity and Fluidity." In *Research in Social Movements, Conflict and Change,* ed. Kriesberg et al., vol. 4. Greenwich, Conn.: JAI Press, 317–39.

Jaffe, F. 1981. *Abortion Politics: Private Morality and Public Policy.* New York: McGraw-Hill.

Jaworski, Patricia. 1989. "Thinking about the Silent Scream: An Audio Documentary. " In Edd Doerr and James W. Prescott, eds., *Abortion Rights and Fetal "Personhood."* Long Beach, Calif.: Centerline Press, 61-70.

Jenkins, J. Craig, and Bert Klandermans, eds. 1995. *The Politics of Social Protest: Comparative Perspectives on States and Social Movements.* Minneapolis: University of Minnesota Press.

Joffe, Carol. 1995. *Doctors of Conscience: The Struggle to Provide Abortion Before and After Roe v. Wade.* Boston: Beacon Press.

Johnson, Victoria. 1997. "Operation Rescue, Vocabularies of Motive and Tactical Action: A Study of Movement Framing in the Practice of Quasi-nonviolence." In *Research in Social Movements, Conflict and Change,* ed. Kriesberg et al., vol. 20. Greenwich, Conn.: JAI Press, 103–50.

Kriesi, Hanspeter, Ruud Koopmans, Jan Willem Duyvendak, and Marco G. Giugni. 1997. "New Social Movements and Political Opportunities in Western Europe." In *Social Movements: Readings on Their Emergence, Mobilization, and Dynamics,* ed. Doug McAdam and David A. Snow. Los Angeles: Roxbury, 52–65.

Kurtz, Howard. 1989. "Operation Rescue: Aggressively Antiabortion," *Washington Post* (March 6), A3.

Liebman, Robert C. 1983. "Mobilizing the Moral Majority." In *The New Christian Right,* ed. Robert Liebman and Robert Wuthnow. New York: Aldine, 49–73.

Liebman, Robert C., and Robert Wuthnow, eds. 1983. *The New Christian Right.* New York: Aldine.

Lienesch, Michael. 1993. *Redeeming America: Piety and Politics in the New Christian Right.* Chapel Hill: University of North Carolina Press.

Lo, Clarence. 1982. "Countermovements and Conservative Movements in the Contemporary U.S." *Annual Review of Sociology* 8: 107–34.

Lofland, John, and Victoria Johnson. 1991. "Citizen Surges: A Domain in Movement Studies and A Perspective on Peace Activism in the Eighties." In *Research in Social Movements, Conflicts and Change,* ed. Kriesberg et al., vol. 13. Greenwich, Conn.: JAI Press, 52–65.

Marcus, Ruth. 1994. "President Signs Clinic Access Law: Foes File Lawsuit." *Washington Post* (May 27), A10.

McAdam, Doug. 1982. *Political Process and the Development of Black Insurgency, 1930–1970.* Chicago: University of Chicago Press.

———. 1983. "Tactical Innovation and the Pace of Insurgency." *American Sociological Review* 48 (December): 735–54.

Melucci, Alberto. 1989. *Nomads of the Present: Social Movements and Individual Needs in Contemporary Society.* Philadelphia: Temple University Press.

Meyer, David S., and Suzanne Staggenborg. 1996. "Movements, Countermovements, and the Structure of Political Opportunity." *American Journal of Sociology* 101, no. 6 (May): 1628–69.

Moen, Mathew. 1989. *The Christian Right and Congress.* Tuscaloosa: University of Alabama Press.

Mottl, Tahi L. 1980. "The Analysis of Countermovements." *Social Problems* 27, no. 3 (June): 620–35.

National Abortion Federation. 1995. National Abortion Federation's Violence and Disruption Statistics; Incidents of Violence and Disruption Against Abortion Providers, 1436 U St., NW, Suite 103, Washington, DC 20009.

NOW. 1986. Excerpts from the First Amended Class Action Complaint, *NOW v. Scheidler,* No. 86 Civ. 7888 (N.D. Il., filed Jan. 17).

Nuclear Resister. 1989. Cohen-Joppa, Felice and Jack, eds. (15 February) no. 60: 2. P.O. Box 43383, Tucson, AZ 85733.

Operation Rescue. 1988. "National Day of Rescue" (flyer), San Francisco Bay Area, October 2.

———. 1989. "Join Us in Operation Rescue" (flyer), Binghamton, N.Y., April 30–May 7.

Petchesky, Rosalind Pollack. 1990. *Abortion and Woman's Choice: The State, Sexuality, and Reproductive Freedom.* Boston: Northeastern University Press.

Planned Parenthood. 1989. News Release (AP), Julian Bond, Dorothy Cotton, James Farmer, Jesse Jackson, Andrew Young, et al. Planned Parenthood Federation of America, Inc., January 23.

Risen, James. 1994. "Operation Rescue Strength Being Sapped by Violence." *Houston Chronicle* (August 12) A19, from an article in the *Los Angeles Times.*

Scheidler, Joseph M. 1985. *CLOSED: 99 Ways to Stop Abortion.* Westchester, Ill.: Crossway Books.

Sharp, Gene. 1973. *The Politics of Nonviolent Action.* Boston: Porter Sargent.

Sidel, Ruth. 1996. *Keeping Women and Children Last: America's War on the Poor.* New York: Penguin Books.

Staggenborg, Suzanne. 1989. "Stability and Innovation in the Women's Movement: A Comparison of Two Movement Organizations." *Social Problems* 36, no. 1 (February): 75–92.

Tarrow, Sidney. 1994. *Power in Movement: Social Movements, Collective Action and Politics*. Cambridge, England: Cambridge University Press.

Terry, Randall. 1988. *Operation Rescue*. Springdale, Pa.: Whitaker House.

———. 1990. *Accessory to Murder: The Enemies, Allies and Accomplices to the Death of our Culture*. Brentwood, Tenn.: Wolgemuth and Hyatt.

Turner, Ralph H. 1970. "Determinants of Social Movement Strategy." In *Human Nature and Collective Behavior*, ed. Tamotsu Shibutan. Englewood Cliffs, N.J.: Prentice-Hall, 145–64.

Turner, Ralph, and Louis Killian. 1987. *Collective Behavior*. Englewood Cliffs, N.J.: Prentice-Hall.

U.S. House of Representatives, Committee on Government Operations. 1989a. *The Federal Role in Determining the Medical and Psychological Impact of Abortion on Women, Tenth Report by the Committee on Government Operations Together with Dissenting and Additional Views*. 101st Congress, 1st Sess., December 11. Washington, D.C.: U.S. Government Printing Office.

———. 1989b. *Medical and Psychological Impact of Abortion: Hearing Before the Human Resources and Intergovernmental Relations Subcommittee of the Committee on Government Operations*. 101st Congress, 1st Sess., March 16. Washington, D.C.: U.S. Government Printing Office.

Wills, Garry. 1989. "Save the Babies: Operation Rescue: A Case Study in Galvanizing the Antiabortion Movement." *Time* (May 1), 26–28.

Zald, Mayer N., and Bert Useem. 1987. "Movement and Countermovement Interaction: Mobilization, Tactics, and State Involvement." In *Social Movements in an Organizational Society: Collected Essays*, ed. Mayer N. Zald and John D. McCarthy. New Brunswick, N.J.: Transaction.

13

Civil Disobedience and Protest Cycles

David S. Meyer

On Ash Wednesday in 1997, Philip Berrigan and five others broke into a shipyard in Maine to bear witness against war. The "Plowshares Six" boarded an Aegis-class destroyer, and using household hammers and bottles of their own blood, did as much symbolic and substantive damage as they could (Goldberg 1997a). Without regret or apology, they later justified their actions in court as righteous efforts by people of conscience to speak against war, injustice, and poverty. They employed a "necessity defense," invoking international law, the Nuremberg precedents, and the democratic process, to maintain that their efforts could ultimately make the world more peaceful. A federal judge sentenced the defendants to terms of up to twenty-seven months in prison for damage and trespass.

This was not the first time Philip Berrigan, formerly a Josephite priest, or his brother, Jesuit priest Daniel Berrigan, made this argument to a federal judge after an action. Like most, but assuredly not all, of the Berrigans' civil disobedience actions, this one was barely visible beyond the site and the courtroom. The Ash Wednesday protest drew little attention nationally, spurred no apparent spinoff or follow-up actions, and did not generate a visible public debate about the morality or wisdom of the Aegis, American foreign policy, or war more generally. The *New York Times* reported the trial in Maine only as an occasion for the writer to reflect on Berrigan and his civil disobedience as anachronistic (Goldberg 1997b).

It wasn't always this way. On occasion, the Berrigans' civil disobedience actions have played critical roles in social movements. Beginning

Copyright © 1999 by David S. Meyer. An early version of this paper was presented at the annual meeting of the American Political Science Association in Chicago, September 2, 1992, and at the NYU seminar on Protest, Power, and Politics, in October 1995.

with a dramatic attack on a draft induction center in Catonsville, Maryland, in 1968, the Berrigans have spent the past three decades trying to stop war, and serving periodic sentences in jail for their efforts. In that first attempt to interfere symbolically with the conduct of the Vietnam War, the Berrigans and seven other Catholic activists poured homemade napalm and vials of their own blood (a staple in many faith-based protests) on draft files. They used the ensuing trial as a chance to publicize the horrors of U.S. conduct of the war in Southeast Asia. The Catonsville Nine drew national attention from their action, their trial, and a play by Daniel Berrigan (1970) dramatizing the events, which prompted the public to pay attention to the growing anti-war movement, provoked debate on civil disobedience, and inspired many activists within the movement.

Why is an action that was once so powerful in the popular imagination now so mundane and marginal? The Berrigans haven't changed; their rhetoric and moral commitment have remained the same for thirty years—one reason that outside observers describe their efforts as anachronistic. Nor are their claims as irrelevant as the lack of public interest make them appear. They protest nuclear weapons, neglect of the poor, and high military spending—concerns still appropriate, if less visible, in the post–cold war era. What has changed, however, is the relationship of their actions to larger protest cycles. Although some people, like the Berrigans, are continually engaged in making particular claims, larger numbers get involved in causes only episodically. Protest movements have peaks of high mobilization followed by troughs when only the core of a movement remains active. The peaks of mobilization are most likely to produce political responses, including substantive and procedural reforms, co-optation, and repression. These responses shape and affect the process of demobilization.

In order to understand the effects of civil disobedience, we need to consider it in the context of a movement's stage of development. The practice of civil disobedience serves different purposes at different points in time. At the early stages of a protest cycle, it can provoke attention and subsequent mobilization; at the peak of a protest movement, civil disobedience can diversify the tactics a movement employs and give activists more choices; after the peak of mobilization, civil disobedience can serve to hold a movement together.

Civil disobedience (CD) is the open, public violation of a law or laws in the service of some moral or political goal. I make no distinction between breaking laws dissidents feel are inherently wrong, such as those requiring racial segregation, and breaking otherwise unobjectionable laws in the course of staging an action, such as those compelling individuals to pay income taxes or apply for parade permits. I do distinguish CD from actions by people who conceal their identities or operate secretly to avoid arrest, even when they claim a moral purpose. The *public transgression of laws for a political purpose* is the defining feature of CD. Excluded are such actions as privately filing a fraudulent tax return, anonymously bombing an abortion clinic, or vandalizing a store in the context of a riot.

The Emergence of Civil Disobedience As a Political Tactic

Although CD has a lengthy history, it was popularized in this country in the 1950s by the southern civil rights movement. Two events in particular have become legends. The first was when Rosa Parks refused to move to the back of a Montgomery, Alabama, bus in December 1955. This led to the formation of the Montgomery Improvement Association which organized a year-long boycott of public buses that ended when the Supreme Court ruled bus segregation to be unconstitutional (Sitkoff 1981, 41–58). The second began on February 1, 1960, when four freshmen at North Carolina Agriculture and Technical College sat down at the Woolworth's lunch counter in Greensboro and waited all day for service. Dozens more students joined them the following day, and those who couldn't find space at Woolworth's sat-in at other lunch counters restricted to whites. By the end of the week, city officials offered to negotiate a settlement and, on Saturday night, 1,600 students rallied to celebrate their victory (Sitkoff 1981, 69–96).

The sit-ins at lunch counters and public facilities in the South during the early 1960s were followed by Freedom Rides, organized by the Congress of Racial Equality (CORE), a civil rights organization from the North that traced its roots to the pacifist movement prior to World War II. In 1961 the U.S. Supreme Court ruled racial segregation in interstate travel terminals to be unconstitutional, extending a ruling made in 1947 that applied only to the vehicles themselves. To test the 1947 decision CORE had sponsored a Journey of Reconciliation of black and white travelers throughout the upper South, which had seen few arrests, little violence, and no publicity. Inspired by the publicity received by the sit-ins, CORE decided to test the latest Supreme Court ruling. In the spring it sent seven blacks and six whites on buses to Alabama. Among the volunteers were white pacifists, well schooled in civil disobedience from their earlier antinuclear campaigns. They were harassed and beaten at several bus stations in South Carolina and Georgia. The violence escalated in Alabama, and the Freedom Riders were flown out of the state under the protection of the U.S. Justice Department. They were front-page news throughout the world (Sitkoff 1981, 97–105).

These experiences taught civil rights organizers that nonviolent CD could be used to provoke police brutality and, thus, public sympathy. In his study of civil rights activism and the Voting Rights Act of 1965, Garrow (1978) emphasizes that CD was a means to broaden the scope of political conflict (Schattschneider 1960), engaging other people, inside and outside of government, in the struggle for civil rights. Martin Luther King, Garrow argues, deliberately sought out protest sites where local authorities would react violently. King counted on disciplined CD to contrast sharply with overreaction by local police. This would bring in outside support while straining relations between segregationists and their passive allies in government.

When Commissioner of Public Safety Bull Connor used firehoses and dogs on nonviolent marchers in Birmingham, Alabama, in 1963 and it was displayed on national television news, the federal government intervened to protect the marchers. In contrast, the Albany, Georgia, campaign, which ran from 1961 through 1962, drew little outside attention when Police Chief Laurie Pritchett repeatedly and quietly arrested the numerous protesters and prevented a violent response from the white community. Learning from these examples, King began the 1965 campaign for voting rights with daily demonstrations at Selma, Alabama. County Sheriff Jim Clark's initial responses were not harsh enough for major news coverage. After two months, King announced a march from Selma to Montgomery. Governor George Wallace issued an order proscribing the demonstration. When 500 singing protesters reached a bridge on the route to the Alabama state capitol, Sheriff Clark and the Alabama national guard attacked, beating the demonstrators and bystanders with night sticks and blinding them with tear gas as they ran. This mobilized the federal government and sympathetic publics in the North. In August, President Lyndon Johnson signed the 1965 Voting Rights Act (Sitkoff 1981, 187–94).

The tactical choice of civil disobedience was part of a larger political strategy, based on predicted responses of both local and national audiences. Disobedience escalated the conflict, polarizing supporters and opponents, while the violent response from local authorities generated the publicity and outside pressure for legislation.

Civil Disobedience throughout a Protest Cycle

On June 15, 1955, in response to New York City's first air raid drill in the nuclear age, Dorothy Day, A. J. Muste, and activists from the Catholic Workers, the War Resisters League, and the Fellowship of Reconciliation refused to enter a nuclear fallout shelter. In the face of a nuclear threat, they sat on park benches and waved placards denouncing war and nuclear weapons (DeBenedetti 1990, 24; Ellsberg 1983, 277–78). Arrested, tried, and chastised by a judge, they were sentenced to brief prison terms, but returned each year to recreate the protest, often with larger numbers.

Other actions followed. In 1958, Albert Bigelow, a former naval commander who had become a pacifist, sailed a ship into the Pacific nuclear testing site, inviting arrest. Inspired by his example, antinuclear activists over the next five years trespassed on the nuclear test site in Nevada and construction sites elsewhere, risking their own lives while violating the law. Although small, these actions dramatized opposition to the nuclear arms race and shined a public light on nuclear weaponry while more moderate allies used conventional political tactics such as lobbying, public education, and electoral politics (Meyer 1993, Katz 1986). Indeed, the peace movement of the day negotiated a formal alliance between advocates of civil disobedience, coordinated by the Committee for Non-Violent Action (CNVA), and adherents of more institutionally oriented tactics, represented by the Committee for a Sane Nuclear Policy (SANE). CD kept the concerns of the antinuclear movement in the news. The risks taken by respectable people like ministers, veterans, and homemakers highlighted their belief that the nuclear age was not a normal time.

In September 1980, when nuclear weapons were not on the national agenda, a group of Catholic activists, including the Berrigan brothers, attacked a General Electric plant in King of Prussia, Pennsylvania, to bear witness against U.S. militarism. The Plowshares Eight action drew surprisingly extensive, and often sympathetic, attention in both mainstream and movement media, serving to draw critical attention to U.S. nuclear weapons policies and inspire more activism (Meyer 1990, 198), supporting the then-fledgling "nuclear freeze" movement. Their trial and appeals spun out over years, offering activists the space to proffer new claims about nuclear weapons and national security. At its peak, the freeze would generate huge support in public opinion polls, mobilize demonstrations across the country, including one assembly of one million people in New York City in 1982. This June 12 demonstration was followed two days later by the arrests of more than 1,100 activists who blockaded the entrances to the embassies of the five declared nuclear nations.

As institutional political action grew in the following years, however, civil disobedience actions garnered less attention, not only from the mainstream, but also from movement organs. Dozens of Plowshares actions followed in the United States, along with a handful in other countries; each drew progressively less attention (Wilcox 1991), until the Ash Wednesday action described previously. At the peak of mobilization, more conservative forces in the movement actively disavowed the civil disobedience actions, trying to portray themselves as the true face of a more modest and moderate movement.

Civil Disobedience Spreads to New Groups

The success of CD in publicizing the causes of relatively powerless groups encouraged its spread to other social movements. Student movements used it throughout the 1960s, regularly occupying campus buildings first to promote free speech and then to protest the Vietnam War. Harsh responses from university administrators had much the same effect as Bull Connor's police dogs, bringing publicity and sympathy to student activists, and effectively encouraging further, and often more disruptive, action.

CD spread far beyond its originators. In the late 1970s community activists in Boston who had resisted busing to integrate the public schools, chained themselves to the doors of fire and police stations to protest harsh cuts in the state's budget and services mandated by referendum-driven tax reductions (Useem 1980). In the mid-1980s, anti-abortion activists appropriated not only the tactics, but also the moral language and symbols of the civil rights movement, to organize illegal and harassing demonstrations outside medical offices and health centers that performed abortions.

As CD became common, institutions modified their responses to minimize adverse publicity. After a massive nuclear freeze rally in New York City in 1982, participants who wanted to be arrested lined up to be tagged by police. They then sat down, were put on stretchers, and were carried to paddy wagons. Police learned that asking protesters to designate who among them wanted to be arrested avoided the political and fiscal costs of unnecessary arrests and incarcerations with the attendant disruption to the court system. By negotiating with activists, police routinely estimate the number of demonstrators and disobedients so they can reserve an appropriate number of buses and stretchers to carry those who will not cooperate (see McCarthy and McPhail 1998).

The fact that protesters, politicians, and police all know what to expect from the use of civil disobedience, effectively reduces the risks for all involved (Benford and Hunt 1992). It also reduces the benefits. Increased legitimacy and predictability removes the likelihood of violence and undermines the news value of a protest.

Managing Internal Conflict

Even without news value CD serves other functions. One of these is to manage internal conflict. For a brief time the anti-abortion movement used CD to deescalate tactically while mobilizing new activists and broadening its appeal.

Abortion opponents had high expectations that abortion would again become illegal after Ronald Reagan was elected president in 1980. But these were soon dashed by adverse rulings by the Supreme Court and the failure of Congress to pass laws as restrictive as opponents wanted. Feeling betrayed, a substantial portion of the anti-abortion movement began to emphasize extrainstitutional means of participation (Ginsburg 1989, 49; Meyer and Staggenborg 1996) such as prayer vigils, marches, pickets, and large demonstrations. Soon more dangerous, divisive, and disruptive tactics appeared, including abortion clinic bombings, arson, parcel bombs, and shots fired at the home of Supreme Court Justice Harry Blackmun, author of the 1973 decision legalizing most abortions. Debate over violence exacerbated existing rifts within the movement.

Operation Rescue emerged to heal splits in the fragmented anti-abortion movement, by offering aggressive opposition to abortion without the negative and polarizing effects of violence. The anti-abortion movement strategically adopted the tactics and symbols of the civil rights movement, including prayers, songs, and vigils, to portray its adherents as morally motivated individuals ready to suffer on behalf of their cause rather than as extremists prepared to inflict suffering on others. Its primary tactic was to sit-in around the doors of abortion clinics, forcing arrests. In Wichita, Kansas, in the summer of 1991, for example, Operation Rescue was able to generate more than 2,700 arrests. It also borrowed symbolism from the civil rights and other progressive movements, calling its CD campaign the "Summer of Mercy" to evoke the romantic appeal of the 1964 Mississippi "Freedom Summer," the 1967 "Vietnam Summer," the 1977 antinuclear "Survival Summer," and the 1984 "Peace and Justice Summer."

Operation Rescue's blockades promised a direct way to stop at least some abortions while burdening local clinics and police departments with continual and often expensive conflict. But it generated less public support and more institutional repression than had the CD engaged in by the civil rights and student movements. In 1994 Congress passed the FACE Act (Freedom of Access to Clinic Entrances), which essentially made federal felonies of acts that had been misdemeanors under state law. The resulting prosecutions in federal court and lengthy sentences discouraged all but the most dedicated from getting arrested. By 1996, OR protesters had significantly declined in numbers, and left abortion clinics when the police told them to go.

Although some individuals are willing to face the most dire consequences in order to press their claims, few will choose CD if they believe it may lead to harsh punishments. Repression of unsympathetic causes is one way for the state to limit dissent. Pro-abortion organizations have also successfully sued OR under the RICO (Racketeer-Influenced and Corrupt

Organizations) Act, and been awarded damages sufficient to bankrupt OR. As OR faded, however, site-based violence at clinics increased.

Creating Community Values

In her study of the movement against nuclear power in the 1970s, Dwyer (1983) argued that when CD campaigns became the focus of mobilization for nuclear power opponents a governance structure developed to support it. To stop the construction of nuclear power plants, activists organized occupations of construction sites. Their model was the occupation of the ground proposed to house a nuclear plant at Seabrook, New Hampshire, in 1976, which led to 600 arrests. The following year, 1,414 protesters were arrested at Seabrook and kept in national guard armories for more than two weeks. This energized the antinuclear movement and publicized its cause, at a high cost to the state of New Hampshire. In 1978, to avoid arrests, New Hampshire negotiated a truce with the antinuclear movement, allowing a legal demonstration of some 25,000 demonstrators on the construction site. This demonstration marked the zenith of the campaign against Seabrook, as activists split over the wisdom of cooperating with the government.

The Seabrook reactor was eventually built, but activists claimed other accomplishments from their civil disobedience campaign. At the antinuclear power movement's height, the civil disobedience efforts at construction sites organized thousands of people into "affinity groups" of ten to twenty people. These groups, run by direct democracy and consensus with rapidly rotating leadership, became the basis for organization, ethics, and politics. Epstein (1991) contends that the movement used this structure to build community through "prefigurative politics"—that is, creating directly the kind of society in which they wanted to live.

Although the activists in what Epstein terms the "non-violent direct action movement" certainly hope to influence government policy, this is a long-term and indirect objective. More immediately, they want a new culture and new ways to organize society. Groups like the Clamshell Alliance and the Livermore Action Group created a "community of protest."

Such utopianism, like the site-based campaigns, however, proved to be short lived, as the movement was unable to innovate new tactics to continue mobilizing people. Protest at operating and proposed nuclear power plants, which were direct and visible targets, became the dominant tactic. Decentralized democracy proved to be inimical to tactical innovation; the presence of large numbers of people equally committed to the cause paradoxically meant that there were few predominantly concerned with the organization's survival.

Civil Disobedience and Protest Cycles

Civil disobedience is often present before, throughout, and after the sweep of a cycle of protest, but the number of people participating and their relationship to a larger political campaign change over time. Groups without the power to win unambiguous victories by military force or within the political system, those likely to choose civil disobedience, derive their greatest influence by demonstrating their capacity for disruption, by challenging opponents in unexpected ways, and by creating uncertainty about what challengers might do in the future (Tarrow 1994).

The beginning of a civil disobedience campaign can bring new attention to a constituency or an issue otherwise neglected by conventional politics. Thus, the Montgomery bus boycott, the Greensboro sit-ins, and the Freedom Rides directed attention to the situation of blacks in the South and the cause of civil rights. CD attracted activists, mobilized sympathetic bystanders, forced local authorities to respond to the disruption, and compelled national political figures to act on civil rights.

This visibility is limited in time. As authorities respond to activists with effective combinations of negotiations and concessions, or even promised negotiations, more moderate activists will be less likely to support civil disobedience, thus making it easier for mainstream political actors to repress or ignore disobedients. The peace and antinuclear movements continued the use of CD, but they rose and fell and rose and fell with the outside interest they generated.

However, CD can serve other purposes. For the anti-abortion movement it gave the strongly committed a way to act when faced with disappointment that did not incur the social disapproval of violence. For the antinuclear power movement it created a community. The use of civil disobedience at less promising political times, even in the face of public neglect, may maintain the values and commitment of the core of activists, providing a bridge to the future.

Acknowledgments

Preliminary research for this chapter was conducted at the National Endowment for the Humanities Summer Seminar on the "Political Histories of Collective Action," led by Sidney Tarrow at Cornell University during the summer of 1992. Helpful comments on some of the ideas in this piece were made by Karen Beckwith, Mary Bernstein, Jo Freeman, Don Herzog, Wolf Heydebrand, Kelly Moore, Lane Newman, Teresa Godwin Phelps, Kim Lane Scheppele, Sidney Tarrow, Charles Tilly, and Gilda Zwerman.

References

Benford, Robert D., and Scott A. Hunt. 1992. "Dramaturgy and Social Movements: The Social Construction and Communication of Power." *Sociological Inquiry* 62 (Winter): 36–55.

Berrigan, Daniel. 1970. *The Trial of the Catonsville Nine.* Boston: Beacon.

DeBenedetti, Charles. 1990. *An American Ordeal: The Antiwar Movement of the Vietnam Era.* Syracuse: Syracuse University Press.

Dwyer, Lynn. 1983. "Structure and Strategy in the Antinuclear Movement." In *Social Movements of the Sixties and Seventies,* ed. Jo Freeman. New York: Longman, 148–61.

Ellsberg, Robert, ed. 1983. *By Little and By Little: Selected Writings of Dorothy Day.* New York: Knopf.

Epstein, Barbara. 1991. *Political Protest and Cultural Revolution.* Berkeley: University of California Press.

Garrow, David J. 1978. *Protest at Selma: Martin Luther King, Jr. and the Voting Rights Act of 1965.* New Haven: Yale University Press.

Ginsburg, Faye D. 1989. *Contested Lives: The Abortion Debate in an American Community.* Berkeley: University of California.

Goldberg, Carey. 1997a. "From Prison, Old Militant Struggles On." *New York Times* (Saturday, November 29), A1, A11.

———. 1997b. "How Political Theater Lost its Audience." *New York Times* (Sunday, September 21) "Week in Review," 6.

Katz, Milton S. 1986. *Ban the Bomb: A History of SANE, the Committee for a Sane Nuclear Policy, 1957–1985.* New York: Greenwood.

McCarthy, John D., and Clark McPhail. 1998. "The Institutionalization of Protest in the United States." In *The Social Movement Society: Contentious Politics for a New Century,* ed. David S. Meyer and Sidney Tarrow. Lanham, Md.: Rowman & Littlefield, 83–110.

Meyer, David S. 1990. *A Winter of Discontent: The Nuclear Freeze and American Politics.* New York: Praeger.

———. 1993. "Institutionalizing Dissent: The United States Structure of Political Opportunity and the End of the Nuclear Freeze Movement." *Sociological Forum* 8 (June): 157–79.

Meyer, David S., and Suzanne Staggenborg. 1996. "Movements, Countermovements, and the Structure of Political Opportunity." *American Journal of Sociology* 101, no. 6 (May): 1628–60.

Schattschneider, E. E. 1960. *The Semisovereign People.* New York: Holt, Rinehart, and Winston.

Sitkoff, Harvard. 1981. *The Struggle for Black Equality 1954–1980.* New York: Hill and Wang.

Tarrow, Sidney. 1994. *Power in Movement.* Cambridge: Cambridge University Press.

Useem, Bert. 1980. "Solidarity Model, Breakdown Model, and the Boston Antibusing Movement." *American Sociological Review* 45, no. 3 (June): 357–69.

Wilcox, Fred A. 1991. *Uncommon Martyrs: The Plowshares Movement and the Catholic Left.* Reading, Mass.: Addison-Wesley.

14

The Transformation of a Constituency into a Social Movement Revisited: Farmworker Organizing in California

J. Craig Jenkins

On the afternoon of July 29, 1970, Cesar Chavez and twenty-nine growers assembled at the headquarters of the United Farm Workers Union on the outskirts of Delano, California, to sign union contracts covering the majority of the farmworkers in the table grape industry. The optimistic rhetoric of the growers about the "common interests" of employers and workers hardly concealed the fact that a major transformation in the structure of economic and political power was in the making. For the first time in the long history of farmworker insurgency, a farmworker movement had finally brought sufficient power to bear against growers to force significant concessions. Though it took five more years of struggle to consolidate these gains, the United Farm Workers had clearly entered the first solid wedge in the seemingly impenetrable armor of California agribusiness.

Why did the United Farm Workers succeed where so many previous challenges had failed? To answer this question, this chapter compares the three farmworker challenges launched in California since World War II: the National Farm Labor Union (NFLU), active from the spring of 1947 through the winter of 1952; the Agricultural Workers Organizing Committee (AWOC), launched with the strong sponsorship of the AFL-CIO in the winter of 1959, but effectively collapsing by the winter of 1961; and the United Farm Workers Union (UFW), which began in the early 1960s as the National Farm Workers Association (NFWA), a community organization of Mexican farmworkers organized by Cesar Chavez. My comparison will show that farmworker movements have traditionally failed because of structural obstacles to the mobilization of farmworkers, systematic political repression, and, at least for the AWOC, major strategic errors. The crucial ingredients for the UFW's success were the mobilization strategy adopted by the union organizers and major changes in national politics that enabled the UFW to mobilize sufficient external resources to compensate for the powerlessness of farmworkers.

The Structural Powerlessness of Farmworkers

The structure of the farm labor market has made farmworkers economically deprived, socially fragmented, and subject to powerful social controls. The agricultural production cycle creates a division of labor and interest among a small nucleus of "permanent" workers, seasonal "locals" who supplement farm labor income with other part-time work, and migrant workers who move from harvest to harvest. Because of the depressed wage scales and the erratic and seasonal nature of the work, all are economically insecure and few possess the material resources to support a strike. Of the three groups, seasonal local workers possess the greatest potential for mobilization.

Migrant workers lack community ties, are the most vulnerable to grower coercion, and are frequently the victims of discrimination. There have been two major systems of migrant labor recruitment: the *bracero* program and the labor contracting system. Between 1942 and 1964 the *bracero* program administered the importation of over one million seasonal contract workers from Mexico. The growers used the program to collectively "fix" wages and to systematically repress dissidence. Until it was terminated in 1964, the program was used to break farmworker strikes and depress the entire wage structure (Galarza 1964, Craig 1971). The growers then turned to the labor contracting system, an arrangement developed in the late 1800s to recruit short-term immigrant workers from China and Japan. Because of language barriers, only the contractors could communicate with both growers and immigrant workers. Contractors assumed primary responsibility for recruitment, supervision, and payment, and for the provision of housing and transportation to the workers. Because contractors' income derives from a fee levied against farmworkers' wages and charges for support services, contractors are opposed to union controls over hiring. They also have an economic interest in recruiting workers who are so deprived that they cannot furnish their own transportation and housing, with illegal immigrants being the favored recruits.

The extreme dependence of these immigrant workers, coupled with their marginal occupational commitment as short-term workers, guarantees their willingness to break strikes.

Permanent workers, or "hands," are employed year-round on a single "ranch," building canals, leveling land, and doing chores. During the harvest they often assume supervisory positions as foremen and contractors. Despite their greater economic security and stronger ties to work and community, permanent workers are subject to the paternalistic control of growers. Growers offer them steady employment, better jobs and wages, cheap housing, emergency loans, small gifts, and a show of personal concern in exchange for personal loyalty. Simultaneously, because of their authority and relative privilege among farmworkers, permanent workers tend to be the informal or "natural" leaders of the community. They have therefore been used by the growers to co-opt dissidence by sounding workers for grievances, pressuring quiescence, mediating individual complaints, and, if these moves fail, recruiting a new crew. Because permanent workers constitute one-fourth or more of the work force, their support is invaluable for strikes.

The greatest potential for mobilization has been among local seasonal workers. They live in local residential communities, and because they have their own transportation and housing, are rarely dependent on labor contractors. They generally derive their income from nonfarm or multi-farm jobs, and so supporting a strike does not necessarily endanger their livelihood. These local workers, however, constitute less than half of the harvest labor force. An effective strike requires the solid support of other workers, especially migrants.

Farmworker mobilization is further hampered by ethnic rivalries among workers, which overlap with occupational distinctions. This ethnic division of labor is a product of the intense competition among successive immigrant groups that have entered the agricultural labor market and discrimination by growers. The sharpest conflicts have been between domestic or more settled workers and the more recent immigrants. Because of low aspirations and short-term commitments, immigrants are readily available to break strikes. Growers have also promoted conflict by recruiting new groups whenever any one group has become numerous enough to pose a strike threat, by playing on group loyalties, and by discouraging acculturation or the forging of ties between different groups. For example, in the 1920s Mexicans and Filipinos were the new, strikebreaking groups, but by the 1930s their strikes were broken by Anglo "dust bowlers," who promptly assumed the more desirable jobs (Stein 1973). Since the 1940s, the new supply of farm labor has come primarily from Mexico, first *braceros,* then "green card" immigrants who held temporary visas, and illegal aliens. Domestic workers—Anglo, Filipino, and

Mexican American—have found their strikes undercut by Mexican immigrants.

These structural features of the labor market illuminate three factors that affect mobilization: group cohesiveness, social controls possessed by opponents, and resources controlled by the group. Group cohesion provides a basis for communication, facilitates the formation of common definitions of grievances, and fosters commitments to collective interests over individual gain. Members of a group fragmented along ethnic and occupational lines are not inclined to view problems as collective ones. Individuals are inadequately aware of others' grievances and are inclined to compete for the benefits that already exist rather than cooperate for new benefits.

Opponents employ both authoritative and coercive controls to counter mobilization. Growers have developed personal ties with their contractors and permanent hands to ensure their loyalty and have relied on coercion, threatening illegals and *braceros* with deportation. When these controls have failed, violent attacks have been mounted, ranging from police harassment of pickets to vigilante raids and assassinations.

Resources, such as disposable free time and organizing spaces, the finances to sustain a strike, experience in organizing, and communication facilities are crucial to any social movement. The fewer resources a group has, the more powerless it is and the more it needs an infusion of outside resources to mount an effective challenge. Two resources are central: power resources, such as organized strikes that enable the movement to apply leverage against opponents; and organizing resources, such as experienced cadres and communicative ties and facilities that allow the pooling of resources. While farmworkers possess considerable potential power in the harvest because of the perishability of most crops, organizing resources are extremely scarce. Farmwork is the lowest-paid occupation in the United States, consistently below the federal poverty line (Dunbar and Kravitz 1976, 23). Few can afford to go on strike indefinitely. Workers with experience in political action are rare. After fourteen-hour days, few workers have the time to invest in organizing efforts.

Between the NFLU and the UFW challenges, the structure of the farm labor market changed, improving the chances of organizing. Between the late 1940s and the 1960s the proportion of farmworkers who were migrants declined from approximately one-third to around 20 percent, and that of permanent workers declined from around 40 percent to less than one-third. The *bracero* program came to an end in 1964, forcing growers to depend on the less controllable green card immigrants and illegals for strikebreakers. By the time that the UFW began organizing, local seasonal workers increased to over half of the labor force (California Farm Placement Services, 1946–1975). Because these workers were enmeshed in local neighborhoods and were less dependent than other workers on the growers, the UFW was able to mobilize a significant base of support.

These changes were also accompanied by a reduction in ethnic diversity. During the NFLU's challenge, approximately one-half of the workers were Anglos, most of whom were permanent hands and locals. The majority of the migrants were ethnic minorities—black Americans, Filipinos, Mexican immigrants, Portuguese, and West Indians. These workers readily broke the Anglo-supported NFLU strikes. By the late 1960s, the Anglo workers had largely moved out of agriculture. They composed less than one-quarter of the labor force and held permanent positions. Black Americans, once concentrated in cotton production, had largely abandoned the fields. Filipinos remained prominent among the migrants but had declined to less than one quarter of the migrant labor force. Filling these positions, the Mexican workers took over the majority of both migrant and local seasonal jobs. By the early 1970s, Mexican workers comprised almost two-thirds of the total labor force (Metzler and Sayin 1948, Metzler 1964). While a potential rivalry existed among the Mexican workers between older immigrants who had become locals or permanent hands and the more recent green card or illegal immigrants, this was partially muted by common nationality. Still, the increased cohesion of the labor force brought about by these changes was not so great that the UFW strikes would receive solid support.

The Politics of Containment: The National Farm Labor Union

The NFLU challenge was launched in the spring of 1947 under the sponsorship of the American Federation of Labor and with financial support from a foundation and several international unions. The president of the NFLU, H. L. Mitchell, had been the principal organizer of the Southern Tenant Farmers Union, a depression-era union of Arkansas and Missouri tenant farmers. Mitchell was the main contact with organized labor and the liberal political community. Key organizers were veterans of union drives of the 1930s: Henry ("Hank") Hasiwar, a former organizer of auto and hotel workers; Bill Becker, former labor director of the Socialist Party; and Ernesto Galarza, previously the key liaison between the AFL and Latin American union movements.

The NFLU's initial strategy was an orthodox industrial union approach: Organize a majority of the workers in the largest enterprise, offer the economic gains of a union contract as the major incentive, build a strike fund from member dues, and strike as soon as the employer was vulnerable. The first strike target was the 1,100-acre DiGiorgio ranch located near Arvin. Because of its size and mix of crops, over half of the

2,200 workers employed at the harvest peak were permanent hands or local workers. Two-thirds of these were Anglos who had secured their positions by breaking Mexican strikes during the 1930s. On October 1, 1947, the NFLU struck the DiGiorgio ranch with the Anglos providing the major base of support. The first day, over two-thirds of the workers marched out, but the picket line held firm for only a week. The DiGiorgio manager promptly called on the Mexican consul, who instructed the 130 *braceros* to return to work or face deportation. Though *braceros* were legally barred from employment in labor disputes, the *bracero* program officials ignored the union petitions. DiGiorgio also dispatched a squad of labor contractors who shortly returned with over 400 workers, mostly illegals from Mexico and Mexican workers from the Los Angeles barrios. Hampered by court injunctions barring mass picket lines and the use of sound equipment, the strikers turned back few of the strikebreakers. Within a month the plum harvest had been completed, and although DiGiorgio had suffered major crop losses, the ranch was operating with nearly a full staff.

The NFLU also lacked strike relief to support the strikers. The strike pool of $3,000 was immediately depleted. The California Federation and local unions initially provided generous strike relief, but by the winter their interest waned as it become clear that the picket lines were not holding. Contributions plummeted, leaving the union able to support only a handful of loyal members. With strike morale at an ebb, the strikers began to melt away. By the spring of 1948 the picket line had dropped to less than 100 workers, a symbolic effort to keep the union visible.

The NFLU then attempted to mount a boycott against DiGiorgio and to raise funds from the liberal community. But the DiGiorgio Corporation mounted an effective political counterattack, obtaining an injunction barring the boycott as illegal under the National Labor Relations Act, despite the exemption of agriculture from the act. By the time the injunction was overruled a year later, the union challenge was in disarray. DiGiorgio also convinced a prominent California senator to investigate the union's political affiliations. Although allegations of communist ties were unfounded, the "red smear" campaign weakened remaining liberal and labor support. Vigilantes then attacked, critically wounding the president of the DiGiorgio union local in a midnight raid. Shortly afterward, DiGiorgio filed a multimillion-dollar libel suit against the NFLU and its labor supporters, charging that a film produced by the Hollywood Film Council and shown at public rallies throughout the state had "misrepresented" the corporation's labor policies. The California Federation refused to fight the suit, agreeing behind the scenes to scuttle its support for the NFLU if DiGiorgio would drop the suit (Galarza 1970). By the fall of 1949 the NFLU was politically isolated, cut off from liberal and labor allies.

Over the next three years the NFLU mounted several strikes but failed to build a membership. The leaders shifted to a new strategy of "area strikes" that focused on wage demands and the withdrawal of *braceros*. Mobilization focused on the domestic migrants, offering the incentive of short-term economic gains. While the strikes secured wage increases, these were soon rescinded, and the strikes produced only a handful of loyal members. By the winter of 1951 Hasiwar and Galarza decided to embark on another course. Targeting the expanding *bracero* program that was displacing the domestic Mexican American migrants who wintered in the Imperial Valley, the organizers adopted a new strategy organizing around the defense of citizen priority in hiring. Their organizing campaign was initially successful. The Mexican workers responded en masse, and on May 12, 1952, the NFLU challenged the growers, demanding that they grant hiring priority to domestic workers or face a strike. Though the domestic workers were solidly organized, the growers controlled over 5,000 *braceros*. Protected by the local police, the growers transferred the *braceros* from field to field. Labor contractors imported additional crews of illegal or undocumented workers. The U.S. Department of Labor turned a deaf ear to the NFLU's petitions, rejecting the findings of the California Conciliation Service that a strike existed and authorizing the "drying out" or conversion of illegal aliens into *braceros*. By the end of the four-week harvest, the majority of the strikers had abandoned the picket lines and were desperately seeking jobs to replace their lost earnings. The following winter, the NFLU renewed the strike, but despite favorable court injunctions barring *bracero* employment, the union failed to clear the fields of *braceros* and illegals (Galarza 1977, Mitchell 1980).

The NFLU had been politically overwhelmed. Growers had imported *braceros* and illegals. Local courts had issued court injunctions, barring picket lines and boycotts. Local police had escorted strikebreakers, illegals and *braceros,* through the picket lines. In addition, the NFLU had failed to sustain participation, in part because of the social fragmentation of the farmworkers and in part because the initial strategy of recruitment had offered few incentives independent of union contracts. Only in the last rounds did the organizers begin to focus on solidarity and broader social issues, such as citizenship claims and political rights. Even then, the union confronted the problem of repression, an insoluble problem as long as insurgents lacked strong allies.

The Flawed Organizing Strategy: The Agricultural Workers Organizing Committee

If the NFLU had demonstrated that an effective challenge could not be mounted by a powerless group in the face of extensive political repression and weak outside support, then the Agricultural Workers Organizing Committee demonstrated that strategic considerations can play a decisive role in a failed insurgency. Over a four-year period, the AWOC received massive support from organized labor—over $1 million in direct financial aid and considerable political support—but failed to develop an effective organizing strategy. The principal problem was the decision to focus exclusively on migrant workers, especially the rapidly declining body of Anglo migrants. Even more than the NFLU, the AWOC failed to offer incentives for participation beyond union contracts. Despite extensive organizing resources, this challenge was even less successful than the NFLU in recruiting a membership. The only success was the accidental mobilization of several crews of Filipino migrants, who later became part of the United Farm Workers.

The AWOC was launched in the fall of 1959 by the AFL-CIO under the leadership of Norman Smith, a veteran United Auto Workers (UAW) organizer. With an annual budget of $250,000, the AWOC fielded a team of fifteen full-time organizers. Rejecting the advice of veteran farmworker organizers, Smith instructed the organizers to concentrate on the 4 A.M. "shape-ups" at which day haul crews of farmworkers, mostly Anglos, were recruited. These shape-ups counted for less than 5 percent of the harvest workers, however, and were attended largely by drifters, alcoholics, and workers seeking only a single day's wages. Despite the ample AFL-CIO support, the organizing campaign produced few results. Throughout 1960, crews of local workers organized a series of "job actions" in Stockton cherries, DiGiorgio again, and Corchoran tomatoes but failed to produce a stable membership. Without an organized base, wage gains were promptly rescinded.

The AWOC's major target was the *bracero* program. The California Federation of Labor had played a key role in the election of Governor Edmund Brown in 1958, and he promised to enforce federal statutes prohibiting *bracero* employment in strikes. Smith then teamed up with the United Packinghouse Workers, which had lost several contracts to *braceros*, to attack the program in the Imperial Valley where the labor force was almost entirely *bracero*. Their strategy was to organize the few domestic workers with the promise that a strike would force a withdrawal of the *braceros*. If, as the organizers expected, Governor Brown failed to follow up his commitment, their plan was to attack the *bracero* camps in hopes that the conflagration would compel the Mexican government to end the program. On February 2, 1960, a handful of local workers marched out. The California Conciliation Service certified the strikes and, predictably, *bracero* officials rejected union petitions for removal on the specious grounds that the Imperial Valley Farmers Association, not the individual growers, was the legal employer. The growers moved the *bracero*s from field to field under police protection, harvesting as normal. A local judge issued an injunction barring picketing, and the unions responded with a mass demonstration at two *bracero* camps, burning buildings and man-handling several *braceros*. The police promptly arrested the entire organizing staff of both unions. The AFL-CIO, informed that the AWOC leaders were in jail, promptly cut off its support and instructed Smith to turn over all union records. By the time that Governor Brown ordered removal of the *braceros*, the issue was mute (London and Anderson 1970).

The AWOC remained dormant for the next two years. In the winter of 1962, pressure from Walter Reuther and an impassioned speech by farmworker representatives convinced the AFL-CIO Executive Council to renew support. Unfortunately, the new organizers adopted the same strategy. The only new element was the decision to enlist the support of labor contractors to serve as the "grassroots" leadership that would collect dues from crew members and coordinate strike actions. While labor contractors favored higher wages, which would increase their commissions, they were determined to block union controls over hiring, which would eliminate them as labor brokers. Moreover, intense rivalries among contractors and their personal ties to growers consistently undermined cooperation among labor contractors. The tactic did, however, generate a more stable income of union dues and the illusion of successful mobilization. The labor contractors simply ordered crew members to pay the union dues or get off the bus.

The few strikes in which the new AWOC became involved were accidental and did not build a strong basis for sustained unionization. Several crews of Filipino migrants were organized, largely because of their strong ethnic ties and job pride as the most skilled field workers. This success, however, happened despite the fact that C. Al Green, the new AWOC director, had instructed organizers to ignore Filipinos and concentrate on the handful of Anglo contractors. Green's only success was in maintaining Governor Brown's cooperation in restricting *bracero* employment. This was limited, however, because Brown soon reneged on his reelection campaign pledge to oppose renewal of the *bracero* program and instead flew to Washington to lobby for an extension (London and Anderson 1970).

The AWOC, then, demonstrated that serious flaws in the organizing strategy could produce failure. Despite lavish sponsorship, the AWOC focused on the least promising segment of the workers, ignored ethnic cleavages, refused to offer incentives beyond narrow economic gains, and, at the end, attempted to build an organization of labor contractors rather than farmworkers.

The Problem of Mobilization

Before looking at the United Farm Workers challenge, we should consider why the economic benefits of a union contract were insufficient to mobilize and sustain farmworkers' participation in the strikes. One answer is given by Mancur Olson in his book *The Logic of Collective Action* (1969). Olson argues that individuals rationally pursuing their self-interest will not participate in collective action because they stand to gain whether or not they participate. All workers benefit from a "collective good" like a union contract, but only those who strike actually pay for this benefit. Consequently, the most rational course of action for any individual member of a group is to be a "free rider" on the efforts of others. Of course, if all individuals acted this rationally, there would be no collective action, and no one would benefit. Therefore, Olson argues, organizers of collective action must provide "selective incentives" to those, and only those, who pay the cost of the collective action.

This is not easy. Even strike funds are insufficient to compensate strikers for lost wages, let alone provide additional incentives for striking. One reason unions seek "union shops" is so that contributions of dues and participation are a prerequisite to the benefits of a union contract. It is also why unionizing groups on strike try to muscle "scabs" off their jobs. Such coercion is a selective disincentive to support the strike even if one does not actually join the union.

For most of their history, farmworkers were such a socially fragmented and economically deprived group that they could not afford to pay the certain short-range costs of a sustained strike for the uncertain possibility of long-range gains. It was only the infusion of massive resources from outside, to pay for organizers and provide a small strike fund, that made their sporadic challenges possible. Yet these resources were also uncertain, and, at least until the 1960s, inadequate.

By the 1960s, outside support for farmworker organizing became more available due to the increased willingness of organized labor to invest in organizing and the more liberal political climate that encouraged sympathy with the dismal economic condition of farmworkers. Yet AWOC's use of this outside support was not successful because it could not translate it into effective incentives for farmworkers' support. The available resources were for paid organizers and strike funds, and these were only sufficient for an occasional action, not the creation of a sustained challenge. It took an organizer, Cesar Chavez, with a background in community organizing and with external sponsorship from sources other than unions, to realize that different kinds of incentives were necessary, and to forge these incentives out of the farmworker community itself.

The incentives that Chavez emphasized were not material but social. By emphasizing collective solidarity and commitment to collective purpose, the UFW was able to link individual interests to those of the larger group and thus mobilize people for collective action. Social incentives are at the same time individual (i.e., experienced by single individuals) and collective (i.e., dependent upon experiences shared with other individuals). The rewards entailed by "social" incentives are either intrinsic to participation in collective actions or tightly tied to such actions. In a way not possible for material incentives, social incentives resolve the free rider problem by restoring the link between individual incentives and social movement goals.

Social incentives are best described by James Q. Wilson in *Political Organization* (1973) as solidary incentives (individual and collective) and purposive incentives. Solidary incentives rest on emotional commitments; their receipt, on the maintenance of valued relations. They can only be experienced collectively, either as the major aim or as a by-product. Individual solidary incentives, which Wilson refers to as "specific solidary incentives," such as special honors and recognition, are handed out to single individuals who contribute significantly to group endeavors. Such honors are an important incentive for movement activists and cadres who invest large amounts of time and energy in movement activities. Individual solidary incentives, though, possess the drawback of being inherently scarce. Only a limited amount of honor can be bestowed upon individuals before its value declines. Nor, as Wilson (1973) points out, are such incentives wholly controllable by movement leaders. Honors have a tendency to become fixed on specific individuals and are thus difficult to use to motivate new participants.

Consequently, movement organizations tend to emphasize collective solidary incentives. Raising the social prestige of the group as a whole and enjoying the sociability of collective actions become key in creating the loyalties or attachments that mobilize a constituency into a movement. Like individual solidary incentives, collective solidary incentives are intrinsically social, but they are even more tightly tied to collective action itself. One cannot have the experience of attending exciting demonstrations without actually participating. In effect, participation in collective action becomes its own reward.

Nevertheless, groups held together primarily by solidary incentives are not social movements but social clubs. Such groups tend to be relatively flexible about their goals because it is not the goals but the process that is important. Although some movements do degenerate into social clubs (e.g., the Townsend movement clubs in the 1950s; see Messinger 1955), an active movement has to infuse solidarity with commitment to a political purpose or moral vision. Thus the primary incentives are purposive: commitment to the goals of the movement for their own sake. Purposive incentives depend on a deep commitment to a high purpose—on an internalized moral code adhered to by the individual. The payoff is the satisfaction received from contributing to a worthwhile cause: a payoff that is available only by acting on one's beliefs. When organizers provide such opportunities, participation in collective action again becomes its own reward.

In sum, movements solve the free rider problem by generating solidary and purposive rewards for collective action. Social incentives tie individual and collective benefits together, or at least make them closely interdependent. Mobilization, then, is the process of creating collective consciousness and self-images dependent on membership in the movement organization and the cause it represents. In the process the boundary between individual and collective action becomes blurred. Individual benefits become intrinsic to collective goods.

The implications of this argument for farmworker mobilization can be spelled out by looking at the two poles of the mobilization process—the group or constituency with an interest in social change, and the movement organizers who are trying to galvanize this potential membership into action. The social characteristics of the group—its cohesion, cultural commitments, social ties to opponents of mobilization (including targets like growers)—determine its structural potential for mobilization. The organizers' recruitment program—their focus on certain subgroup segments and the incentives for participation that they develop—define the extent to which potential members are recruited.

Organizing is often done by "bloc recruitment" (Oberschall 1973, 117) through preexisting groups. Some is individual recruitment through one-on-one solicitation to create commitments to the movement. The building of group solidarity and commitment to movement goals are central to both. In bloc recruitment, "natural" loyalties to work and neighborhood, and ethnic and fraternal affiliations, are reinforced and transferred to the movement. The social infrastructure of such a movement resembles that of a loose network of informal groups with multiple leaders (Gerlach, chap. 5 in this book). This provides the advantages of a small-scale group in creating and sustaining participation and simultaneously allowing mass membership. Individual recruitment requires intensive effort and considerable one-to-one interaction. It is more typical of cadre recruitment and of small person-changing movements such as sects and communes.

Bloc recruitment is feasible only when cohesive small groups already exist, linked together by informal social ties. It also helps if the social controls of movement opponents are weak, thus allowing organizers to recruit freely. The organization of the farmworker community, however, lacks these conditions. The chaotic, seasonal character of farmwork coupled with intense competition for jobs, ethnic rivalries, and weak community ties undermines strong workplace and community solidarity. Growers typically have strong paternalistic ties to permanent workers and labor contractors, which discourages mobilization.

As we will see, the UFW was more successful at organizing because it focused on local workers who were more independent of grower controls and more likely to have strong community ties. It also put greater emphasis on social incentives and relied on bloc recruitment. However, even these advantages were not enough.

The Dual Strategy: The United Farm Workers

The United Farm Worker story properly begins in the early 1960s with a dramatic shift in the temper of national politics. In 1960 John Kennedy was elected President by a narrow margin provided by black voters. In 1962 Congress underwent a major reapportionment that significantly weakened the power of the conservative "farm bloc." The civil rights movement had already mounted a campaign of mass action to dismantle racist institutions and by 1963 was organizing southern blacks into a voter bloc. Sensing the need to mobilize blacks and other minorities around a national program of social reform, Kennedy began laying the plans for a "war on poverty" and national civil rights legislation. One of the prices for the Mexican American and labor vote was a promise to terminate the *bracero* program, a price that had been politically cheapened by congressional reapportionment, which strengthened urban liberals in Congress. In the wake of Lyndon Johnson's landslide victory in 1964, congressional liberals pushed through the Civil Rights Act, the War on Poverty legislation, and a vote bringing the *bracero* program to an end.

In the winter of 1962 Cesar Chavez resigned as director of the Community Service Organization, an organization of urban Mexican Americans initially sponsored by Saul Alinsky, and set out to organize Mexican farmworkers into a union. Rather than build a union directly, Chavez chose the indirect route of community organizing. Recruitment focused on Mexican grape workers, the majority of whom were local workers residing in small rural towns in the southern San Joaquin Valley. The program centered on individual benefits, such as a credit union, a consumer co-op, and welfare and citizenship counseling, and on community issues such as racism in the local schools and exorbitant rent hikes. In other words, mobilization initially centered on two incentives: selective material benefits that did not depend on signing union contracts with growers, and social incentives anchored in existing community solidarities (London and Anderson 1970, Levy 1975).

Drawing upon the contacts he had developed as a community organizer, Chavez secured the financial support of several small foundations and church groups. His main sponsor was the Migrant Ministry, a mission agency of the National Council of Churches that had decided that the unionization of farmworkers was the most effective avenue of "Christian service" to its farmworker clientele. In June 1964 the Migrant Ministry fully merged its California program with Chavez's National Farm Worker Association, providing the NFWA with the resources to field five full-time organizers. By the winter of 1965 the ranks of the NFWA had grown to over a thousand active members.

In the spring of 1965 several Filipino crews nominally organized by the AWOC called strikes in the grape harvest. On September 8, when the Filipinos struck the Delano grape harvest, the home base of the NFWA, the NFWA was faced with a difficult decision. Chavez had not planned to openly transform the NFWA into a union for several years, but the Filipino strike forced the timetable. NFWA members worked in the same fields as the Filipinos and had to join the strike or break it. Despite an enthusiastic strike vote at a rally on Mexican independence day, September 16, the joint NFWA-Filipino picket lines held for less than a week. Though the growers were inconvenienced by loss of the *braceros,* they used labor contractors to recruit crews of strikebreakers from across the border or from urban areas. Strikebreaking was still a pervasive problem.

As the strike collapsed, Chavez embarked on a speaking tour of universities, church gatherings, and union meetings to mobilize outside support. The response was overwhelming. Student organizations and churches held benefit rallies. Student civil rights activists journeyed to Delano, volunteering to become full-time organizers for the new union. Unions collected strike funds and organized car caravans to bring food and clothing to the strikers. At the San Francisco docks, members of the Longshoremens and Teamsters Unions refused to load "scab" grapes. In December, Walter Reuther, then president of the United Auto Workers, brought national attention to the strike by defying the Delano police and marching through the streets of Delano with the strikers. By pledging $5,000 monthly, to be split equally between the NFWA Mexican Americans and the AWOC Filipinos, Reuther pressured the AFL-CIO to reconsider its exclusive support for Al Green's faltering AWOC (London and Anderson 1970).

Despite this support, the NFWA lacked the membership to mount strikes the following spring. Amid this collapse, Chavez pressed for a new strategy. Protest in the past had been designed to elicit contributions of organizing resources. The new protests would instead focus on creating external leverage against the growers through consumer boycotts. This meant that farmworker strikes did not need solid support but that urban consumers would shun grapes and other targeted crops, thus forcing growers to sign contracts. The first step was to capture popular attention through the mass media. With Reuther's prodding, Senator Robert Kennedy brought the Senate Subcommittee on Migratory Labor to Delano for public hearings. On March 17, 1966, while the television crews were still in town, the NFWA embarked on a 230-mile protest march to Sacramento that remained on the evening news for twenty-five consecutive days. En route, NFWA marchers carried signs proclaiming a consumer boycott against Schenley Industries, a mammoth liquor corporation that owned a ranch in the strike zone.

Though the NFWA had organized boycott committees in December, the media coverage brought public attention to the boycott. Sympathetic Teamsters blocked Schenley's main warehouse in a "hot cargo" action, and the San Francisco Bartenders Union threatened to pull all Schenley liquors from their shelves. Since the grape ranch represented less than 1 percent of Schenley's operations, the corporation offered to sign the first union contract in the long history of farmworker insurgency.

The following day, the marchers repainted their signs: *Boycott DiGiorgio!* The DiGiorgio Corporation owned a small grape ranch in the strike zone, but its profits depended primarily on processed fruits and marketing. The corporation immediately offered to hold a union recognition election. Over the next six months the NFWA battled company harassment, a "company union" set up by DiGiorgio, and the Teamsters, who held contracts on the farm's truck drivers. Chavez went on a fast to mobilize followers and prevent violence. When it appeared that the NFWA and AWOC would split the farmworker vote, the AFL-CIO forced a merger on the AWOC, placing Chavez in charge of the United Farm Workers Organizing Committee (UFWOC). After DiGiorgio held a rigged election, the UFWOC and its allies pressured Governor Brown to appoint an arbitrator for a new election, which the UFWOC promptly won, thus cementing the union's second contract (London and Anderson 1970).

In the spring of 1967 the UFWOC launched a series of strikes of the table grape harvest. Despite fielding fifty organizers who launched several strikes, the strikes all failed. Although the union could pull its loyal supporters out of the fields, court injunctions prevented the pickets from keeping out strikebreakers and the growers recruited crews of migrant workers, many of whom were green carders and illegals. In the spring of 1967, again in desperation, Chavez decided to create a national boycott team that would mount a nationwide consumer boycott on grapes. More than sixty boycotters were sent to over fifteen cities to organize boycotts against the entire table grape industry.

The table grape boycott reflected a major shift in the cadre's strategic thinking. Although they had used boycotts before, the UFW leaders had assumed that organizing workers for strikes and union elections would be the key power lever. But the collapse of the table grape strikes convinced them that boycotts were the key to bringing the growers to the bargaining table (Levy 1975).

Between 1967 and the summer of 1970 the UFW mobilized a nationwide boycott of California table grapes through committees set up in almost every major city in the United States. Truck drivers, longshoremen, and grocery clerks furnished the backbone of the boycott, conducting "hot cargo" actions by refusing to handle "scab" grapes; students and clergy marched through grocery stores, harassing store managers, conducting "shop-ins," and closing off entrances; liberal politicians, including two presidential candidates (Senators Kennedy and McGovern), joined prominent celebrities in endorsing the boycott; liberal clerics sermonized their congregations on the boycott; universities and Catholic schools cut off standing orders to grocers that continued to handle "scab" grapes; and millions of consumers shunned grapes and the grocery chains that continued to handle them. By the summer of 1970 the grape growers faced a closed marketplace. While they could still recruit strikebreakers to harvest their crops, half of their 1969 crop remained in cold storage. By May, four of the largest growers in the Coachella and San Joaquin valleys finally offered to negotiate, one after a landslide election, which the UFW won 152–2. In late July, the Delano grape growers finally conceded defeat. By the end of August 1970, the UFW held contracts on 150 ranches, representing 20,000 jobs and over 10,000 members (Taylor 1975).

Nevertheless, the UFW's future was far from secure. The union was still vulnerable if the growers could break the boycott. The grape contracts had not even been signed before the growers counterattacked by signing "back door" contracts with the Teamsters Union. Teamster contracts were clearly preferable to the growers because, despite wage gains and fringe benefits, they left hiring and supervision in the hands of growers and labor contractors. The UFW contracts created hiring halls run by the union and barred arbitrary firings and pesticides, and created a local union steward system that protected worker rights. The new "sweetheart" contracts with the Teamsters threatened the UFW's most potent weapon—the boycott. Growers could now claim a union label, switching the public definition of the conflict from a moral cause to a jurisdictional dispute between rival unions. Teamster labels also discouraged other unions from supporting the UFW, which hurt the union financially as well as reducing "hot cargo" and other sympathy protests. The contracts were also a windfall for the Teamsters. Without investing in organizing, the Teamsters skimmed off the union dues and strengthened their hold over the packing sheds (Meister and Loftis 1977).

The lettuce workers, mostly Mexican migrants who had been the target of recruitment efforts over the past two years, were outraged by the "sweetheart" contracts and spontaneously formed strike committees, phoning the UFW for instructions. The workers refused to sign Teamster authorization cards, attacked the Teamster organizers, and carried out spontaneous "job actions." In support, the UFW organized a mass march on Salinas, and on August 24 called the largest agricultural strike since the 1930s. Over 6,000 workers from 150 farms marched out, creating turmoil throughout the Salinas and Santa Maria valleys. Teamster guards, imported to protect strikebreakers, physically attacked UFW pickets. For a week, the strikers closed the packing sheds and shipping terminals. But by the third week, the growers and their Teamster allies had regained the edge by importing strikebreakers. The less committed UFW members, concerned about their lost earnings, began slipping back into the fields. When a judge barred strike and boycott activity on the grounds that the growers were the innocent victims of a jurisdictional dispute, the UFW defied the injunction, called a national boycott, and filed countersuits. Two lettuce growers vulnerable to a boycott hastily signed contracts. But the rest of the growers, representing over 70 percent of California and Arizona head lettuce production, kept their Teamster contracts (Taylor 1975).

Over the next four years the UFW suffered a series of major setbacks. Off-and-on boycotts of head lettuce cut into grower profits but failed to produce contracts because of the disorganization and vulnerability of lettuce workers. Moreover, the political strength of the union's liberal and labor allies was declining, and their support for the boycott was on the wane. The Teamsters pressured other unions that had been key supporters, especially the Retail Clerks and the Butchers unions, to withdraw support. The boycott teams had to revert to organizing consumers, always the least effective method. Public support declined because of confusion about the Teamster contracts and because lettuce was a staple, not a luxury. The UFW added to this confusion by twice calling off the boycott when the Teamsters pledged to withdraw and then renewing the call when the Teamsters backed away.

Strikes and boycotts against nonunion wineries were also unsuccessful and further alienated labor supporters, especially the Distillery Workers and the Glassblowers unions. Then the Nixon administration, strengthened by the landslide reelection in 1972, "packed" the National Labor Relations Board and threatened an injunction against the boycott. Though the boycott was clearly legal, the UFW backed down, accepted a single contract with the Heublein winery, and called off the boycott in exchange for a withdrawal of the injunction threat.

At the same time that external support dropped off, the recruitment campaign stalled. Ethnic symbolism had proven an effective rallying point for Mexican migrants, but it deeply offended Filipino, Portuguese, and Anglo workers. In the midst of an escalating ethnic conflict, Larry Itliong, the main organizer of the AWOC Filipinos and vice president of the UFW, resigned in protest (Meister and Loftis 1977). Shortly afterward, the UFW lost its first representation election because of Filipino defections to the Teamsters. In addition, the union confronted an administrative crisis traceable in part to the boycotts. With the leadership and core of loyal members working on the boycott, the administration of the grape contracts had fallen to inexperienced and occasionally disloyal hands. In addition, a rift developed among Mexican workers between locals, who preferred an annual base for dues and benefits, and migrants, who preferred a monthly base. The leadership tried to ignore this issue and alienated many migrant workers.

The UFW's vulnerability became fully apparent in the loss of the Schenley contract in June 1972 when Schenley sold the ranch to Buttes Land & Oil. After extensive but fruitless negotiations, the UFW called a strike, which Buttes overrode with strikebreakers. This prompted the grape growers to open secret negotiations with the Teamsters, and by July 1973, seventy-eight grape growers had signed with the Teamsters. The UFW called mass strikes, but the growers dispatched labor contractors, and by claiming a jurisdiction dispute, secured sixty-three injunctions barring virtually every conceivable form of strike activity. In Coachella, the Teamsters shipped in 400 guards, who attacked UFW strikers. The UFW defied the injunctions, packing the jails for publicity and to secure a legal basis to contest the injunctions. But despite strong worker support, the strikers failed to halt the harvest because of the contractor-imported strikebreakers, many of whom were illegals. Amid escalating violence that claimed two lives, the UFW called off the strike and announced a boycott. By late August the UFW was a shrunken version of its former self, reduced to twelve contracts covering around 6,500 jobs and 12,000 members (Meister and Loftis 1977).

The extent to which political support had declined was graphically illustrated by the UFW's inability to rekindle the boycott. Despite greater organizational resources, the renewed grape boycott failed to force growers to renege on the Teamster contracts. The key element, again, was weak labor support. The Teamsters pressured former supporters to ignore the boycott teams. In addition, the AFL-CIO leadership despaired of the UFW's failure to mobilize solid picket lines, and pressured by several affiliates, refused to endorse the secondary boycott against Safeway stores and the consumer boycott against Gallo wines. Nor were the boycotters able to build, as they had in the late 1960s, off the political enthusiasms created by other movements. The anti-war, student, and civil rights movements that had supported the grape boycott had largely demobilized, and after McGovern's crushing defeat in the 1972 presidential election, liberal politicians were in retreat. Although the boycott still had some impact—sales of Gallo wines dropped 9 percent and Safeway suffered declining sales—the pressure was insufficient to force a settlement (Meister and Loftis 1977).

The UFW was far from defeated, however, as it had cultivated allies other than labor. In the 1968 California Democratic primary Chavez had forged a key political alliance with Robert Kennedy by mobilizing the urban Chicano and middle-class vote behind liberal Democrats. In 1972 the UFW used this alliance with the Democratic Party to defeat Proposition 22, a Farm Bureau initiative designed to outlaw harvest strikes and boycotts. In 1974 the UFW again mobilized key support behind Jerry Brown's successful campaign for governor of California. Simultaneously, the UFW intensified farmworker organizing, mounting a challenge to the Teamsters by conducting "wildcat" strikes against Teamster ranches and infiltrating the Teamster structure to encourage workers to demand full Teamster enforcement of their contracts. Softened by the continued boycott and strike pressure, by the spring of 1975 the growers were finally prepared to reach a settlement. With Governor Brown pressing for a settlement, the Democratic-controlled California legislature enacted the Agricultural Labor Relations Act, which created a system of regulated union recognition elections controlled by the Agricultural Labor Relations Board (or ALRB) and legal protections on union organizing while preserving the right to boycott if a grower refused to sign a contract after a union election (Meister and Loftis 1977).

The UFW's dual strategy of simultaneously organizing farmworkers by emphasizing solidarity and commitment to *la causa* and mobilizing external support through boycotts provided the basis for consolidating a position. Over the late 1970s and early 1980s, the UFW won the majority of the union elections that it contested, losing only where ethnic rivalries and grower patronage had generated Teamster support. By 1982, union membership peaked at around 60,000. The Teamsters withdrew from farmworker organizing and, except for a handful of dairy farms organized by an Anglo-worker-based Christian Farmworker Union, the UFW finally had the union organizing field to itself.

The 1980s, however, brought major setbacks to the UFW. The growers launched a major counterattack. They successfully sued the UFW for over $2 million in boycott and strike damages, and hired professional labor relations consultants to "union-proof" their fields. In 1982, newly elected Republican Governor George Deukmejian restructured the ALRB. He appointed new pro-grower members, fired attorneys and staff perceived to be pro-UFW, and severely cut the budget. At one point in the mid-1980s, the ALRB was completely shut down for over six months. As a result,

UFW victories in union recognition elections dropped precipitously and their success in converting election victories into contracts plummeted. In the first-round elections in 1976–77, the UFW won over 80 percent of over 400 elections, but after the ALRB reorganization they virtually gave up petitioning for elections. Growers found that they could ignore the vote, claim to bargain "in good faith," and rebuff strikes by sending labor contractors out to recruit new workers. Several growers tilled under their crops rather than negotiate and some with UFW contracts sold off their farms, effectively terminating the contracts. The existence of union-supervised elections also defanged the boycott, leaving labor allies and urban consumers to conclude that the ALRB had solved the problem and that continued boycotting was no longer necessary. By the mid-1980s, UFW membership had dropped from 60,000 in 1982 to less than 20,000 members (Mooney and Majka 1995, 191–198; Edid 1994).

Changes in the farmworker labor force, particularly large numbers of ethnically diverse immigrants, increased the obstacles to farmworker organizing. Mixtec Indians from southern Mexico who did not speak Spanish, Vietnamese, Laotian, and Cambodian refugees, and workers from strife-torn Nicaragua and Guatemala undermined farmworker solidarity. In 1986, Congress passed the Simpson-Rodino bill, which gave green cards to illegal immigrants who could demonstrate continuous residence. This set off a wave of green card applications, generating an industry devoted to creating fraudulent documents in order to regularize immigrants. Border enforcement increasingly targeted at controlling drug traffic made illegal immigration easier, which in turn led to an oversupply of farm labor. Growers renewed their use of labor contractors.

By the early 1990s over half of California farmworkers were estimated to be illegal immigrants. A significant percentage held green cards while residing during the off-season in Mexico or Central America. Labor contractors hired over two-thirds of all workers (Edid 1994, Martin 1996). Along with ethnic diversity, seasonality and migrancy also increased, reducing the number of settled "local" workers who had earlier formed the backbone of the UFW. This made strikes impossible and weakened union locals.

These trends undermined both prongs of the dual strategy, making it more difficult to mobilize farmworkers and to gain the support of sympathetic outsiders. They were reinforced by a third problem: the organizational crisis of the UFW itself. Beginning in the late 1970s, Cesar Chavez became increasingly isolated and less committed to grassroots organizing. The reasons are beyond our concern here but they partially stemmed from his being a charismatic leader who demanded total commitment to *la causa*. As a consequence he spurned independent advice. The absence of institutional controls over his authority made it possible for him to isolate and remove those who criticized or disagreed with him. Between 1978 and 1981, Chavez fired or drove off virtually the entire cadre that had organized the UFW. Most of the experienced organizers and one of the strongest union legal staffs in the country were replaced with inexperienced new volunteers. An underlying issue was the long-running dispute over staff salaries and perquisites. From the outset, Chavez had insisted that the staff accept a minimum weekly salary (initially $1 per week, later $5, and then $10 in the early 1980s) plus union-provided housing and food. With the early contracts, most of the staff expected the union to become more institutionalized, with regular salaries, more delegation of authority, and greater staff autonomy. Chavez, however, refused to change, arguing that farmworkers should control the local "ranch" committees and negotiate their own contracts while staff should remain unpaid volunteers. Some staff resigned; others challenged the decision or became embroiled in other organizational disputes. Chavez refused to delegate authority, firing those who criticized or challenged his decisions and centralizing control over a rapidly growing union with hundreds of contracts to be negotiated. In a notable case in 1982, he fired the elected ranch committee presidents in the Salinas Valley, who had defied him in the 1981 union convention, and dissolved functioning UFW locals. He also turned to psychological "thought control" techniques, using psychotherapy techniques developed by the founder of Synanon to create commitments to the union and stronger control over the staff. Some staff resisted these measures while others felt "burned out" and resigned.

In this setting, Chavez made a strategic decision to abandon grassroots organizing, renew the boycott, and use political campaigns to counter the power of the growers. The UFW invested heavily in electoral campaigns, giving Willie Brown, speaker of the California Assembly, $750,000 to allocate to Democratic candidates throughout the state. In place of the farmworker-led boycott committees, he created a direct mail shop to send flyers and appeal letters throughout the country to promote the boycott and raise donations. These, however, had little impact compared to the earlier grape and lettuce boycotts. In place of mass marches, rallies, and grassroots lobbying campaigns, the UFW now relied on election contributions, formal lobbying, and direct mail advertising. The existence of the ALRB also weakened public support, leading many to conclude that their contributions were no longer needed. By Chavez's death in 1993, the UFW had shrunk to less than 20,000 members and had not organized a strike or major protest action in almost a decade (Mooney and Majka 1995, 186–91; Ganz 1997).

In the mid-1990s, the UFW returned to grassroots organizing. The new president, Arturo Rodriguez, launched new organizing campaigns focused on the more settled workers in the Salinas and Ventura valleys as well as apple workers in Washington state. Its premium apples were a trade brand. Since there were no legal bars on boycotts and organizing strikes, this was an ideal target for the dual strategy. Union membership grew to over 26,000 and, in 1997, the AFL-CIO pledged $1 million to strengthen the organizing campaign. Instead of organizing single farms, the UFW used a variety of tactics, including door-to-door canvassing and formal meetings, to organize support. It also opened informal negotiations with supermarket companies, packing shed owners, and grower associations to prepare the way for a possible boycott.

This experience highlights the importance of a movement leadership with the imagination, cultural understanding, and social networks to sustain a dual strategy. In the early 1960s, the NFWA cadre used community organizing, nonviolent protest, and a cagey sense of tactics to challenge grower power. They simultaneously mobilized farmworkers and organized strongly supported boycotts that forced growers to negotiate contracts. The organizational crisis of the 1980s removed this leadership and blunted the challenge, leaving the UFW unable to respond effectively to major obstacles.

A Strategy for Success?

Does the UFW's dual strategy offer a model for successful insurgency among other groups? For at least fifteen years, the UFW was effective in circumstances that had stymied every other approach. The combination of grassroots organizing and outside support was crucial. The distinctive community organizing approach developed by Cesar Chavez focused on cohesive small groups, built on existing cultural commitments, and offered a set of incentives that emphasized solidarity and moral commitments. It created a solid farmworker base that enabled the UFW to survive the repression and union competition in the early 1970s and to exert sufficient political leverage to force the growers to accept collective bargaining. At the same time, the UFW's mobilization of external support from students, organized labor, and consumers was essential to force the growers to the bargaining table. But the dual strategy relied on a homogenous community of farmworkers, and sympathic outsiders. When these were no longer present, the UFW declined.

References

California Farm Placement Services, Department of Human Resources, 1946–1975, *Annual Report*. Sacramento: State of California.

California State Assembly, Committee on Agriculture. 1969. *The California Farm Labor Force: A Profile.* Sacramento: State of California.

Craig, Richard. 1971. *The Bracero Program.* Austin: University of Texas Press.

Dunbar, Anthony, and Linda Kravitz. 1976. *Hard Traveling: Migrant Farm Workers in America.* Cambridge, Mass.: Ballinger.

Edid, Maralyn. 1994. *Farm Labor Organizing.* Ithaca, N.Y.: Industrial and Labor Relations Press.

Galarza, Ernesto. 1964. *The Merchants of Labor.* Santa Barbara, Calif.: McNally and Loftin.

———. 1970. *Spiders in the House and Workers in the Field.* South Bend: University of Notre Dame Press.

———. 1977. *Farm Workers and Agribusiness in California, 1947–1960.* South Bend: University of Notre Dame Press.

Ganz, Marshall. 1997. "The Paradox of Powerlessness: Leadership, Organization and Strategy in the Unionization of California Agriculture, 1959–1977." Unpublished paper, Dept. of Sociology, Harvard University.

Levy, Jacques. 1975. *Cesar Chavez: An Autobiography of La Causa.* New York: Norton.

London, Joan, and Henry Anderson. 1970. *So Shall Ye Reap: The Story of Cesar Chavez and the Farm Workers' Movement.* New York: Crowell.

Martin, Philip L. 1996. *Promises to Keep: Collective Bargaining in California Agriculture.* Ames: Iowa State University Press.

Meister, Dick, and Anne Loftis. 1977. *A Long Time Coming: The Struggle to Unionize America's Farm Workers.* New York: Macmillan.

Messinger, Sheldon L. 1955. "Organizational Transformation: A Case Study in a Declining Social Movement." *American Sociological Review* 20:3–10.

Metzler, William. 1964. *The Farm Worker in a Changing Agriculture.* Giannini Foundation Report No. 277. Davis: University of California Press.

Metzler, William, and Afife Sayin. 1948. *The Agricultural Labor Force in the San Joaquin Valley, California, 1948.* Washington, D.C.: U.S. Department of Agriculture.

Mitchell, H. L. 1980. *Mean Things Happening in This Land.* New York: Allanheld Osmun.

Mooney, Patrick, and Theo Majka. 1995. *Farmers' and Farm Workers' Movements.* New York: Twayne.

Oberschall, Anthony. 1973. *Social Movements and Social Conflicts.* Englewood Cliffs, N.J.: Prentice-Hall.

Olson, Mancur. 1969. *The Logic of Collective Action.* Cambridge: Harvard University Press.

Stein, Walter J. 1973. *California and the Dust Bowl Migration.* Westport, Conn.: Greenwood Press.

Taylor, Ronald B. 1975. *Chavez and the Farm Workers.* Boston: Beacon Press.

Wilson, James Q. 1973. *Political Organizations.* New York: Basic Books.

Part Five

Decline

Part Five Introduction

Movements are inherently unstable. As an unpredictable combination of conflicting tendencies in an ever-changing environment, they inevitably decline. But the causes and consequences vary. Some decline because the grievances that stimulated them are resolved. Some are repressed. Some fall apart because their resources disappear, the cost of participation becomes too high, or internal bickering splits them into competing factions. A movement may have a major transformative effect on society, or it may pass as a ripple, leaving no lasting effects. It may leave new organizations or institutions in its wake to try a different approach to the problems it tackled, or it may withdraw and speak only to the converted. It may change its goals to maintain its existence or may change its existence in response to new goals. It may decline as a social movement while continuing to develop as a social club, an interest group, or something else. Decline may be inevitable, but the type of decline is not.

Frederick Miller identifies four patterns of decline: success, co-optation, repression, and failure. Success is a primary cause of movement decline. He finds that SDS leaders deliberately altered their goals to avoid achieving them. The more successful it was, the more SDS attracted attention from the authorities and participants who wished to change the goals of the student movement at large. It was finally split by two factions whose goals were so unrealistic that both sides could safely assume that only the most committed would join them.

Two chapters on the civil rights movement both illustrate how success led to decline and why social movement organizations are unstable. Doug McAdam shows how the southern civil rights movement's success in attracting attention, removing legal segregation, and reducing barriers to black voting in the South stimulated it to go further and demand a share of societal power in the North as well. This brought factionalism, a loss of financial resources, and government repression. Emily Stoper focuses on one organization, SNCC, to highlight how a movement organization created for one set of circumstances unsuccessfully tried to adapt itself to another.

Although the term "decline" implies failure, a conclusion that movements inevitably fail would be inaccurate. Many movements described in this book were highly successful. Their decline as movements illustrates instability, not failure. The fact that instability is inherent and decline inevitable should not discourage movement participation so much as it should encourage movement participants, insofar as possible, to delay decline and structure its direction. The realization that social movements are not only an intrinsic part of American soceity but usually temporary should make it possible to maximize their impact while they are at their most powerful.

15

The End of SDS and the Emergence of Weatherman: Demise through Success

Frederick D. Miller

In the 1970s and 1980s, scholars of social movements turned from studying the psychological underpinnings of individual social movement participation (Hoffer 1951, Feuer 1969, Gurr 1970) to studying the structure
of social movement organizations (Gerlach and Hine 1970), their place in
the political system (Tilly, Tilly, and Tilly 1975), and factors that influence
their success or failure (Zald and Ash 1966, McCarthy and Zald 1973,
Gamson 1975). This has entailed a shift from the perspective of agents of
social control whose interest is in controlling individual actors to that of
social movement leaders whose interest is in why movements succeed or
fail, with an emphasis on how to make them succeed (cf. Gamson 1968).
Movement participation had previously been studied in terms of personal
psychology, but what happens to movements is the study of organizations, hence it draws on organizational, political, and economic models.
The organizational theories that became dominant by the 1980s have been
loosely gathered under the title "resource mobilization theory" because
of the emphasis they place on the role of resources—money, expertise,
access to publicity, paucity of social control—in determining the course
of social movements.

This chapter examines factors that contribute to the decline of social
movements and the organizations that comprise them. Starting from the
perspective that movements are developed by mobilizing resources, it is
possible to define influences that make resources less available to organizations or make organizations lose interest in resources they might other-

wise seek. The operation of such factors is illustrated with two examples of organizational decline and failure: the splitting and collapse of Students for a Democratic Society (SDS) in 1969, and the foundering of Weatherman, the most notorious group to emerge from that split.

A Model of Movement Decline

Most social movements consist of a variety of social movement organizations that, with varying degrees of cooperation or competition, seek to mobilize people and press demands. The history of a movement and its organizations is broadly determined by three factors: events in the world that influence the availability of resources and the success of tactics; movement ideologies that influence tactical and structural choices; and movement organizational structure, which also influences tactics and ways of accessing and mobilizing resources. Since all three of these factors are related to one another, they cannot be studied independently. Both movement ideology and structure, which shape each other, are created by the members' adaptive responses to external forces. Once created, neither ideology nor structure is static; both influence strategic choices that organizations make and remain somewhat responsive to external events. Strategic choices made at any time influence the range of choices that an organization will have available later. The history of any movement organization is determined by an interaction between factors internal to the organization and factors in the outside world.

The decline of specific social movement organizations does not always herald the decline of an entire social movement. Individual organizations may come and go within a movement, the replacement of one by another signifying vital growth and change. The movement as a whole declines only when all social movement organizations decline, leaving no group to effectively embody the goals of the movement, or when there no longer is a potential constituency for organizations to mobilize. In either situation, the movement may cease to exist. Four separate broad features—repression, co-optation, success, and failure—can bring about such decline in movements or individual organizations.

Repression

Repression occurs when agents of social control use force to prevent movement organizations from functioning or prevent people from joining movement organizations. The variety of repressive tactics includes indicting activists on criminal charges, using infiltrators to spy on or disrupt groups, physically attacking members and offices, harassing members and potential recruits by threatening their access to jobs and schools, spreading false information about groups and people, and anything else that makes it more difficult for the movement to put its views before relevant audiences. Repressive actions may be defined as legitimate by the state, for example, when it passes laws banning political parties or suspending civil liberties in emergencies, but they are never legitimate from the perspective of the movement. For both the agent of social control and the movement, the most relevant judge of legitimacy is the population at large. In the late sixties, public opinion polls found that large majorities of Americans, who saw crime as the country's most serious problem, took lenient views of violent police tactics used to stop political groups and demonstrations. In such a climate the repression of dissidents can be carried out rather easily.

As Gerlach and Hine (1970) point out, a weak attempt at repression may actually help a social movement organization by increasing solidarity among members who share the burden of repression. Above a certain point, however, repression disrupts an organization: if leaders and members are killed or jailed, if its activities are disrupted, or if the resources required to keep it going are inadequate to meet the increased costs of maintaining the group. Repression can destroy an entire social movement in a similar fashion by raising the costs for potential recruits and supporters beyond what they are willing or able to pay. The issues and grievances the movement addresses may still exist, but movement activity may start again only when the repressive cost comes down.

Co-optation

Co-optation strategies are brought into play when individual movement leaders are offered rewards that advance them as individuals while ignoring the collective goals of the movement. Such rewards serve to identify the interests of those co-opted with those of the dominant society. People who are co-opted often argue that by joining the opposition they are doing what can best further the movement, but generally it is easier to control people once they are dependent on an organization than when they are leading independent opposition organizations. This form of co-optation only hurts movement organizations when it removes irreplaceable members. It is most likely to be effective with movements of powerless constituencies who have few skilled activists.

A different means by which movement organizations are co-opted was described by Michels (1962) in his classic work on European socialist parties. He propounded an "iron law of oligarchy" according to which movement organizations have inherent tendencies to bureaucratize, centralize authority, and withdraw from political activity, regardless of their prior success. Michels argues that leaders who hold office for long periods cannot avoid becoming more concerned with retaining their positions and perquisites than with pressing movement demands. Since being an organizational leader offers them more rewards—and often more money—than they could get from any other available occupation, they curtail radical activity in the interest of maintaining the organization and their position within it.

Success

While every movement should seek and be able to enjoy success or victory, success is actually a bit more complicated. Growing by attracting new constituents and winning on particular issues both pose problems for social movements. It is conceivable that a movement could set goals, accomplish them, and subside, with success obviating the need for the movement. This is rare, however, probably limited to instances where people organize solely to achieve one goal. For example, if residents of an area mobilize to prevent construction of a new airport, and win their demand, the movement may demobilize without regret. The woman's suffrage movement was one of the rare movements to do this. But few movements that comprise many organizations raise single demands that can be satisfied. They present multifaceted programs, and the accomplishment of some demands leads to the raising of others. Few movements see the satisfaction of all their demands. Instead, they make or are forced into compromises that only sometimes are advantageous to the movement.

In obtaining concessions from the dominant system, movement organizations often have to relinquish some portion of their claim to represent an independent radical opposition. This process of *absorption* brings social movement organizations into the structure of interests in the polity, converting them into interest groups. The successful group, taking on increased responsibility and resources, tends to be more rigid and bureaucratic than a social movement organization. Funds make it possible to replace volunteers with professional staff, and responsibility discourages the spontaneous and freewheeling qualities often associated with movement organizations. When the absorption of social movement organizations causes a large number of constituents to identify their interests with those of the dominant society, the movement ceases to exist as a movement. It no longer has a role as an opposition to the polity.

Problems identified with success can affect movement organizations well before demands are realized. An organization that attracts attention and members is undergoing a form of success. Certainly, voluntary political organizations want to grow. Yet growth can change or even harm an organization. Recruits may be less committed to the organization than older members, or may differ in their beliefs in ways that encourage factional splits. A small organization may find it difficult to establish roles for new members and thus may not be able to hold recruits, alienating potential constituents in the process. Finally, rapid growth may swamp available resources, limiting the amount that organizations can accomplish while they struggle to integrate members.

Besides drawing members, growth can attract organizations that seek to attach themselves to the movement. New movement organizations often start by seeking to share resources developed by older groups. For example, many ethnic minorities have organized themselves in emulation of black Americans, and such groups as the disabled seek to be identified as a form of minority in the hope of reaping collective benefits. The danger this poses for the initial movement is that new arrivals can become competitors for resources and members, draining the resources of the originally successful group.

Failure

Success is a desirable end that brings problems. Failure is simply undesirable. With hindsight, organizational failure can often be identified as due to strategic or structural errors. A combination of skill and luck is required for an organization to press its demands successfully. Organizations often adopt ineffective strategies or experience organizational problems. Failure at the organizational level takes two major forms: factionalism and encapsulation.

Factionalism arises from the inability of the organization's members to agree over the best direction to take. While a movement may contain many factions, and even gain intellectually from the tensions of debate, a single organization can be halted by disunity. Factional dispute can prevent policies from being set, or can cause resources needed to raise demands to be squandered in fights within or between organizations. To the extent that the movement and its members are struggling with each other, they cannot attend to external political matters.

Encapsulation occurs when a movement organization develops an ideology or structure that interferes with efforts to recruit members or raise demands. This can come about in several ways. Under the pressure of repression, a group may prevent infiltration by cutting off the access by which potential members may join. Alternatively, members may develop such strong cohesion among themselves that outsiders become unwelcome. In prolonged interaction, a group may develop an ideology that is internally coherent but virtually unintelligible to recruits and outsiders who do not share all of the members' assumptions. Such groups are not uncommon in movements; they constitute the fringe of organizations that appears strange to outsiders. An encapsulated organization may find it easy to maintain its dedicated core of members, whose identities are linked to the group and who may have few outside contacts, but such groups have little chance of growing or increasing their influence. Most strikingly, they may lose interest in such things, contenting themselves with maintaining their encapsulated existence.

Failures at the level of individual social movement organizations need not harm the social movement as a whole. Factionalism and encapsulation may clear away some social movement organizations and leave the field open for more creative and successful ones. But beyond a point, the failure of individual organizations can leave the movement without effective groups or can identify the movement as one that cannot realize constituents' goals. When this happens, the movement itself will decline. Persistent factionalism will squander resources and divert attention from recruitment and raising demands. Encapsulation will prevent a movement from speaking for any sizable constituency. There are particular moments at which recruits and resources are available to movements and the distribution of power is such that a movement can mobilize effectively. When movement organizations lose such chances through tactical blunders, they can seldom be recovered. With hindsight, one can often spot errors that led movements to decline, but for those engaged in politics these are often matters of trial and error.

In summary, four broad sources of movement decline—repression, cooptation, success, and failure—have been briefly identified. The decline of specific movement organizations and movements is usually caused by combinations of these factors. In the next section, we consider two linked case histories of organizational decline in order to illustrate some of these processes in action.

The End of SDS

Students for a Democratic Society (SDS) was the largest and most influential organization in the 1960s American New Left. Its history encompasses most aspects of New Left organization, ideology, and tactics. SDS grew out of white students' involvement in the southern integration and voting registration struggles of the early sixties. It played a central role in the movement for student power and freedom, as well as in the first years of the opposition to the Vietnam War and the military draft. In addition, SDS sponsored community organizing projects in the mid-sixties and served as a major base from which the women's movement sprang. When SDS collapsed in a factional struggle in 1969, the contending factions defined it as a revolutionary group dedicated to overthrowing the American government, certainly no longer interested in student issues. By then, SDS was regarded by government and law enforcement officials as a dangerous subversive group. This was hardly how it organized itself.

SDS was founded in 1960 to replace the Student League for Industrial Democracy, the youth branch of the League for Industrial Democracy (LID, a small, moderate left group that survived the McCarthy era by espousing anticommunism and moderate support for liberal reforms). LID and its student affiliate stressed education rather than political action. The tiny original SDS sponsored conferences on northern campuses to publicize the civil rights movement. In June 1962, SDS issued the Port Huron Statement, a position paper that accurately expressed many students' discontent with the conformity and conservatism of American life in the fifties. As an alternative, SDS proposed a more participatory and communal society, and called for an alliance of civil rights groups, pacifist and antinuclear weapons groups, students, liberal organizations, and liberal publications to push the Democratic Party in a progressive direction.

The Port Huron Statement was widely praised on campuses, but the organization grew slowly over the next several years. During that period, members started to question the liberal reformist approach of the Port Huron Statement because of the failure of the Kennedy and Johnson administrations to support civil rights and antipoverty efforts adequately and because of the escalation of the Vietnam War. At the same time, SDS was unsure of what sort of political action to emphasize. While its resources and strength lay in college campus chapters, from 1963 through 1965 the major national effort of SDS went into the Education Research Action Project, a series of marginally successful community organizing projects in poverty areas.

In April 1965, SDS organized the first Washington march against the war in Vietnam. The march was a surprising success, drawing more than fifteen thousand demonstrators, most of them students. This led to a surge in membership to over one hundred chapters. During the next two years, SDS made starts at leading antiwar and draft-resistance struggles, but declined regular involvement in the succession of umbrella mobilization committees that led most national antiwar protests. SDS leaders feared that opposition to the war was too narrow a focus from which to build a movement for general societal reform.

Nevertheless, the number of campus chapters continued to grow as local chapters led student power struggles, movements against university complicity with the war and draft, and other fights. Each major struggle brought more members to the organization; it is estimated that as many as one hundred thousand joined in 1969 alone. Yet, at the height of success, measured in terms of membership and publicity, both the national organization and many of the chapters appeared to tear themselves apart. In 1969, SDS collapsed into a variety of small factions, none of which proved capable of maintaining SDS as a potent force in national politics.

Our task here is to interpret this collapse. A detailed history of SDS cannot be offered in these few pages. Interested readers should consult Sale's (1973) thorough volume and the excellent analysis of the development of New Left ideology by Vickers (1975).

SDS Structure and Success

SDS claimed to have no ideology in its early days, but this claim of non-ideology was itself an ideological position. It stood for rejecting other current ideologies—both Communist Party Marxism, with its overtones of authoritarian Stalinism, and cold war liberal red baiting, with its overtones of repressive McCarthyism—but not for rejecting having any beliefs at all. SDS favored racial equality, integration, disarmament, and an end to poverty. More importantly, the New Leftists saw the exercise of centralized authority in any system as undemocratic. They wished to create "participatory democracy" by decentralizing authority and inviting all people to participate in collective decision-making.

The openness of this system allowed SDS to encompass a broad diversity of views and led to an organization that was always loosely structured. There was a National Office, which maintained membership lists, put out a newspaper, and tried to provide publications to chapters. National officers kept communications open between chapters, encouraged new chapters, and provided whatever advice and help they could. The National Office was always short of money, behind schedule on mailings and recordkeeping, and generally chaotic. This left the chapters free to pursue issues they chose with more or less militance. Annual national and regional meetings passed resolutions on broad strategy issues, but the local chapters retained control over implementation. Most chapters were on college campuses, though some existed in other organizations or high schools.

This loose participatory structure, which worked well to incorporate members when the organization was small, was a source of problems as the organization grew larger. Since decisions were made in open meetings where all people had voice and vote, people with staying power and vocal volume could exercise power, regardless of whether they had good ideas. People who could last through the inevitably lengthy group meetings were often the most influential. Furthermore, it allowed organized factions to dominate decision-making. Since only a portion of the total members generally involved themselves in decision-making, a block of disciplined people representing one view could carry disproportionate weight in the organization.

For a time these matters seemed unimportant. In the summer of 1968, SDS was at the height of its success. Campus activism had increased steadily, climaxing in the dramatic SDS strike that closed Columbia University over war-related research at the university and university plans to expand into the neighboring Harlem community. Yet this success contained all the seeds of the SDS downfall, for while it brought members, public interest, and even some victories, it put strains on SDS's structure and ideology that the organization could not bear.

By 1968, SDS's successes had evoked a two-pronged response from campus authorities and government officials. On the one hand, officials harassed members and potential recruits, making political activity more difficult. At the same time, some liberal politicians sought to incorporate moderate leftist positions into liberal Democratic Party politics. The simultaneous presence of both responses illustrates the diversity of authority in the United States. Both tactics had the same result: to lessen the impact of SDS.

Government and police harassment of SDS and other New Left groups in the late sixties and early seventies was very wide ranging. The CIA, the FBI, the Defense Department, and many local police departments kept files on left-wing activists. State laws were passed to cut off scholarships and loans to student activists. In some instances, draft boards took away draft deferments from students who participated in antiwar activities. Students were recruited to spy on campus radical activities. SDS activists were expelled from many schools, and on some campuses SDS was banned. Rumors abounded that university admissions officers were checking applicants' political views to screen out activists. Police agents joined SDS chapters, where they spied, disrupted activity, and at times tried to provoke groups to violent or foolish action. At the University of Texas, a state police undercover agent was elected president of the campus SDS chapter. University officials freely called police to quell demonstrations on campuses. Government officials and presidential candidates excoriated campus protest as the worst social problem in America and the major obstacle to peace in Vietnam.

The full extent of this repressive and disruptive activity has not yet been documented. It is clear that it raised the cost and danger of being active in SDS, driving out some members and scaring off potential recruits, as well as wreaking havoc with the open, communal tone that had once been the hallmark of SDS chapters. The participatory democratic style was particularly vulnerable to infiltration because any recruit could assume an active role. Given infiltration and spying, members no longer knew if recruits or even old friends could be trusted. As that happened, chapters were forced to operate less democratically, which made them less attractive to potential recruits drawn to the New Left's participatory style. Chapters and their leaders had to devote time to defending themselves from legal and illegal attacks; this diverted time from political organizing.

Many movement members have argued that government repression destroyed SDS (cf. Oglesby 1974). However, repression can only be held to be the sole cause of SDS's demise if one ignores the other problems that success created and that SDS failed to solve. There can be no doubt that repression made it harder to solve those problems, but repression was not the only problem SDS faced.

Some of the group's more appealing moderate positions began to enter the realm of accepted political debate. By the spring of 1967, liberal politicians were giving friendly speeches at antiwar rallies, defining moderate opposition as an acceptable part of the political spectrum. Student demands for curriculum changes and relaxed parietal rules, as well as for a voice in university governance, were accepted at many institutions. These successes posed the threat of absorbing a portion of SDS's position into the political mainstream. Many national and chapter leaders who feared that such success would lead to compromises on crucial issues avoided absorption by adopting more extreme left-wing positions. This process of moving leftward to avoid being caught in the mainstream involved the danger that leaders would become too extreme to successfully recruit potential supporters. Alienating one's base in that fashion can make it impossible to mobilize a social movement.

Liberals were not the only politicians attracted by SDS's success. Other left-wing organizations grew interested in SDS because they saw it as a place to recruit for their own groups. One such group that had a major impact on SDS was the Progressive Labor Party (PL) and its youth group, the Worker Student Alliance (WSA). PL was an old left organization, rigidly disciplined, autocratic, disdainful of the youth-oriented counterculture, and ideologically dedicated to organizing the working class. Where SDS had a chaotic structure and a loose ideology, PL offered tight discipline and absolutist ideology. PL members started joining SDS in 1966; by 1968, PL factions were battling the national SDS leadership for control of the organization. SDS's participatory democratic structure favored PL in this struggle. SDS felt bound not to exclude people of any political persuasion, and PL found it could control open meetings by sending organized groups willing to stay until they had a majority. PL-SDS wrangling split many chapters and turned several national and regional meetings into unproductive squabbles. While SDS leaders were struggling with the various organized interests their success had attracted, they were also attracting recruits. Every time SDS led a major struggle, membership rolls and the number of chapters swelled. The loose structure of many SDS chapters made it difficult to find roles for recruits. While they were free to have a voice, many were unsure of what to say or how things were to be done. Nor was it easy to figure out SDS chaos. Chapters often were based on the friendship of people who got around to doing chapter work in sporadic bursts. This difficulty of integrating recruits worked to PL's advantage. PL could offer recruits a place in a well-defined structure, increasing PL's strength within SDS chapters. As Andrew Kopkind, a leftist commentator, put it:

> P.L. overwhelms newly politicized students with its sophisticated Marxism-Leninism on the one hand, and its simple promises of workable work-in programs on the other. . . . With its simple strategy of instant revolution by the working class and its logical and disciplined structure, P.L. appeals to young people who are tired of the tentative experimentalism and undiscipline of SDS organizing. (Cited in Jacobs 1970, 17–18)

Other Currents in 1968–1969

While PL fought SDS for leadership, the SDS leadership at both chapter and national levels was further split by the growing demands of women to assume leadership positions. Though never officially barred from power, women had for the most part been shunted into secondary roles in SDS. Women often performed essential but boring office work or leafleting, while men made decisions and assumed the more glamorous public roles. As women demanded a greater share of authority, men were more often incredulous than sympathetic—perhaps because they were unwilling to see themselves as oppressors. This conflict further split SDS. Male leaders' occasional requests that women hold off their demands until PL had been confronted only exacerbated the issue.

The battle with PL also influenced SDS's ideology. In seeking to avoid absorption, SDS had turned to Marxist ideas. This led to battles with the PL version of Marxism. For many of the newer recruits these struggles seemed odd at best. Many recruits were drawn to SDS not by left-wing ideology but by their opposition to the war and the draft, which was based on a mixture of humanitarian beliefs, a desire to avoid going to Vietnam, and their attraction to the counterculture. The struggle over the correct line for revolutionary anti-imperialism created a gulf between movement leaders and people who were potentially mobilizable for an antiwar movement.

In two major instances, the Columbia strike and the spring 1969 Harvard strike, it appeared to SDS leaders that this gap was closed. The appearance was illusory. In both instances, police violence galvanized large portions of the student body to strike under the leadership of SDS chapters whose actions had provoked the police presence. But in both cases the new recruits were more committed to opposing police brutality than to supporting demands raised by SDS leaders. As a result, both strikes eventually hurt campus SDS chapters. Liberal reforms wooed away the bulk of this new support and left the SDS leaders angered with their constituents over the desertion. Since the issue that mobilized students was police brutality, campus administrators learned to avoid problems by getting court injunctions to stop demonstrations, rather than send in the police. SDS could not repeat the Columbia/Harvard tactics.

Where Weatherman Came From

The Weatherman faction emerged in SDS in 1968 as an answer to PL's growing aggressiveness and the widening gap between SDS and most leftist students. Regardless of its actual impact, Weatherman attracted enormous attention by calling for immediate revolution. The idea of an armed revolution in the United States may seem farfetched today, but in the late sixties it seemed close at hand. As the Weather Underground stated in *Prairie Fire*, a 1974 position paper:

> The year 1968 was a high point and a turning point. It is not surprising that the maturing of the movement took place at a time when the world was in flames. 500,000 U.S. troops were dealt a staggering blow by the Vietnamese popular forces during Tet. Armed struggle raged throughout Latin America and the Palestinian liberation forces emerged in the Mideast. Student movements in France and throughout the industrialized world were in full revolt, challenging their own governments and demonstrating open solidarity with the people of the world. The Chinese Cultural Revolution was unleashing a new dimension to class struggle. (8)

The success of the Vietnamese in stalemating American military power was seen as a demonstration that America was not invincible. Though Che Guevara had died in 1967 trying to foment revolution in Bolivia, his slogan that there should be "two, three, many Vietnams" seemed to be embodied in the emergence of such revolutionary groups as the Tupomaros in Uruguay, Frelimo in Mozambique, and Fatah in the Middle East. Student movements were also becoming increasingly militant. In France in May 1968 a coalition of students and workers brought the country to the brink of revolution. Strong left-wing student movements appeared in Germany and Japan, and substantial opposition to the Vietnam War was demonstrated in many other countries. In the United States, armed black militant groups, most notably the Black Panthers, were proclaiming revolution and affirming their ties to liberation movements in the Third

World. The murders of Martin Luther King Jr. and Robert Kennedy in 1968 seemed to symbolize America's unwillingness to heed those who urged moderate reforms. The brutal handling of antiwar demonstrators at the Democratic National Convention in Chicago, which a majority of Americans applauded in public opinion polls, and the subsequent election of Richard Nixon further demonstrated conservative intransigence in American politics. In September 1968 an International Conference of Revolutionary Youth was held at Columbia University. While its open sessions were often chaotic and divisive, the meeting did bring Americans into contact with radicals from many countries. As one looked across this international scene, it was not hard to believe that a worldwide revolutionary struggle against an increasingly reactionary America was in progress.

The SDS regional conferences during the 1968–69 academic year saw increasingly angry struggles between PL followers and supporters of the SDS National Office. The two sides argued over which social class would make the revolution and what tactics should be followed. PL hewed to the traditional Marxist view that the working class must make the revolution and that students should subordinate their struggles over the draft and campus rights to the task of building worker-student alliances. Furthermore, PL took two stands that infuriated many SDS members. PL attacked North Vietnam because it took aid from the (anti-Chinese) Soviet Union. PL also opposed the Black Panthers and other black nationalist groups because they organized on national rather than class lines, a contradiction of Marx's insistence that class struggle cuts across all national and ethnic interests.

A group of Columbia veterans and National Office workers prepared an anti-PL paper for the 1969 SDS National Convention, taking the paper's title "You Don't Need a Weatherman to Know Which Way the Wind Blows" from a Bob Dylan song. The "Weatherman" paper argued that Third World opposition to American imperialism was the most important movement in the world and that the black liberation movement in America was the crux of the struggle because it represented the Third World in America. The role of white radicals was to support this process, not lead it, since the black movement would triumph by itself if necessary. The white youth movement was to be built around the issues of black liberation and the worldwide struggle against imperialism, not around the counterculture. It should abandon organizing college students and instead should recruit working-class and dropout youths into small disciplined collectives that would form the basis of a revolutionary party.

While the ideology has obvious flaws, it did place SDS in a framework of world revolution. It avoided absorption into established politics by calling for the complete overthrow of established politics. It countered PL's tactic of organizing workers and students by emphasizing recruitment of disaffected blue-collar youths. It called for abandoning the problem-riddled participatory democratic system. While the problems with the Weatherman position will become clear enough, it did try to answer each of SDS's problems.

Schism

The struggle between PL and SDS reached its climax at the June 1969 National Convention in Chicago. The details of this meeting are adequately reported by Sale (1973). PL had brought enough supporters to hold a small majority at the convention, even though they were still a minority in SDS. Also in Chicago were the Weatherman paper faction and its supporters—who called themselves the Revolutionary Youth Movement (RYM)—and a smaller number of unaffiliated delegates. The rancorous and disorderly convention ended with RYM expelling PL from SDS, and PL claiming to be the true SDS. SDS was finished as a New Left organization.

From the shambles, PL pursued its worker-student efforts in SDS's name to little avail on most campuses. After some years, PL discarded the SDS name as useless. The RYM group set about maintaining its own SDS, organizing youth along the Weatherman paper's lines and planning an action for the fall in Chicago against the war and the trial of the Chicago Eight, prominent activists accused of fomenting riots at the 1968 Democratic convention. RYM soon split again, the Weatherman paper authors arguing for more militant action, while a separate faction calling itself RYM 2 called for more recruiting and organizing before taking militant action. RYM 2 soon petered out, while Weatherman continued in operation. We will follow the Weathermen because they were more successful than PL or RYM 2 at remaining in the public eye.

Weatherman: Structure and Tactics

Weatherman ideology emerged as a response to both PL and several problems and events in 1968. This ideology, and the need for security from repression, determined Weatherman's structure. Weatherman faced severe repression of its revolutionary activism and some continued PL harassment. In response, Weatherman organized small collectives of acquaintances who maintained extremely strict criteria for screening new members. Weatherman ideology demanded that each member break all ties with American culture and be ready to die for the revolution. Members were expected to relinquish all possessions, abandon all monogamous relationships, and limit contact with people outside Weatherman.

The Weather Machine (Weatherman fell out of favor as a name because of its gender connotation) had a three-part structure. At the top was the Weather Bureau, perhaps twenty-five people. They were a tightly knit group of old friends and movement veterans. There was little turnover in this group. It dictated national policies to the local level and sporadically published a national newspaper. As in SDS, local collectives had a good deal of autonomy in day-to-day matters, although bureau members would occasionally reorganize local collectives. The disruptive impact of such arbitrary leadership is described in Stern's (1975) memoir of Weatherman in Seattle.

The collectives were scattered around American cities. They had five to twenty-five members, with perhaps a total of five hundred people involved at any time. Most collectives saw moderate turnover, often spurred by groups expelling disruptive members. Each collective had three internal aims: deepening members' knowledge of and trust in each other; learning medical, legal, defense, and propaganda skills; and engaging in internal political education. In addition, each collective had the external goal of recruiting participants for the fall Chicago National Action. Weather ideology dictated that working-class white youth were so alienated (by the war and the lack of meaningful jobs) that the demonstration of the existence of a fighting movement that would act rather than talk would rally them to its side. Thus Weatherman leafleted and recruited at high schools and hamburger joints and staged violent actions to show their fighting preparedness, such as briefly seizing high school or college classrooms. The actions were provocative but not successful as organizing devices.

Every collective did attract some hangers-on, people who never became members but who did some work and would attend rallies. There was a lot of turnover among the hangers-on. Weather persons were intolerant of people not totally committed to their extremist politics. Weatherman's insistence on ideological purity greatly widened the gap between leaders and potential followers that had started in SDS.

This rigidity was symptomatic of a major problem in Weatherman structure: It made little provision for vertical mobility, either into or within the organization. Weatherman officially denied the need for any white movement within the revolution, yet most of its efforts during the summer of 1969 were directed toward recruiting members. Still its uncertainties about recruitment were obvious in the difficulties facing those who wished to join collectives. To join, one had to demonstrate sincerity and trustworthiness. That could be done only through participation in collective actions. Yet, since most actions required secrecy, only collective members could be included in them. Thus it was easier for recruits to form a new collective than to join an existing one, although that involved the very difficult task of recruiting a group of people. In practice, Weatherman was so tightly organized that it had no mechanism for growth.

It similarly was difficult for people to move from a collective to the Weather Bureau, as the Bureau was a cohesive group with little interest in training new leaders. Leadership at the collective level seemed to be awarded on the basis of familiar New Left criteria of volume and longevity at meetings, but these were augmented by new criteria of merit—bravery in action, radical attitudes, toughness. Other left-wing groups criticized the Weatherman for espousing "macho" virtues.

Weatherman in Action

Weatherman's history was brief. Members attracted attention because they carried part of the SDS mantle and because of their promotion of violence, but their accomplishments were small. Though Weatherman declared many of its militant actions to be successes because they demonstrated members' willingness to fight and because they increased collective cohesion, these actions drew few recruits and little praise. The Chicago National Action, renamed the Days of Rage, drew between 500 and 800 participants, instead of the 5,000 predicted by the Weather Bureau. Those hundreds proceeded to "trash" Chicago's Gold Coast and battle the Chicago police. Their courage attracted much attention among leftists but few recruits, and it resulted in 300 arrests, the posting of $750,000 in bail, and a conspiracy indictment against twelve Weatherman leaders. After Chicago, the Bureau grew disenchanted with attempts to recruit members and recognized it could no longer afford aboveground action. At a desultory War Council in Flint, Michigan, at the end of December, most remembered because Bernardine Dohrn of the Weather Bureau made a speech praising convicted murderer Charles Manson, the Bureau announced that the core of the organization was to go underground. There it carried out bombings of symbolic targets—including the national capital—when no people were present and printed occasional papers. Three Weatherpersons died in an accidental explosion while making bombs in Greenwich Village in March 1970. In 1975, Senate investigators estimated that forty Weathermen were still underground.

The lack of vertical mobility in Weatherman prevented organizational growth. This meant that at best the group could only maintain itself as a stable organization. Yet even that proved impossible, as the collective's membership dwindled under the dual pressures of external harassment and the rigors of collective life. While these rigors—much work, self-sacrifice, organizationally ordered sex with all of one's brothers and sisters, group LSD trips, lengthy and often brutal criticism sessions—served one useful function by making Weatherman very difficult for informers to infiltrate, they also made life in the organization difficult to sustain. Some sense of what this was like is conveyed in this description from Weatherman Shin'ya Ono.

> New people began to learn what discipline means when no one was allowed to stay out of these collective discussions and collective tasks. People who preferred to read were compelled to join. People who fell asleep were woken up. Smoking was prohibited. Seating was "arbitrarily" changed according to the demands set by political criteria. Politics in command. Everything for the revolution. People began to get some sense of what these well-known Maoist slogans meant. We slept six hours and resumed our struggle in the morning. . . . (Cited in Jacobs 1970, 253)

The emphasis on toughness, on treating people as political objects whose incorrect lines were to be smashed, took its toll on members. At the same time, indictments and court costs for Weatherman's illegal actions were building up. A major reason for going underground was to escape these indictments, a task at which the underground organization proved very successful.

By the fall of 1969, major rifts were developing between Weatherman and the rest of the Left. The worse things got for Weatherman, the more intransigent the group became in insisting that leftists who did not commit themselves to Weatherman were enemies of the movement. While many on the Left had admired Weatherman courage, there was less sympathy for the extremity of Weatherman's fascination with violence and the ineffectiveness of its tactics.

Weatherman's position rested on a prediction that the war in Vietnam would not stop with a Hanoi victory but would be only the first step in a rising crescendo of Third World assaults that would lead to America's downfall—an ironic echo of the "domino theory" that justified America's presence in Vietnam on the grounds that Vietnam was the first step in a chain that would end with the invasion of America. Weatherman's self-justification further rested on its ability to rally disaffected white youths to support a black revolution. However, the Black Panthers, Weatherman's proclaimed revolutionary vanguard, were increasingly placed on the defensive by government repression that climaxed in the murder of two Illinois Panther leaders by Chicago police in December 1969. Instead of leading the revolution, the Panthers were fighting for their lives, heading toward their own schism, and leaning on white radicals for help.

This package of ideology and strategy had been developed to counter the position of PL, as well as to describe the world. When it was disconfirmed, and Weatherman faced an increasing lack of sympathy from the rest of the Left and even the Panthers, plus a growing list of indictments and trials, Weatherman folded its aboveground operations. It never truly had established a constituency.

Explaining Organizational Decline

Somewhat different explanations have to be offered for the decline of SDS and Weatherman. Nevertheless, both instances illustrate how a variety of causes may converge in the downfall of any organization.

SDS suffered from each of the causes of movement organization decline outlined earlier in this chapter except co-optation, and co-optation was not used only because the demands of the student movement made few incentives for co-optation desirable to its leaders. Primarily, SDS's decline was set in motion by the organization's rapid and surprising success. Success brought the weight of new members, the assault by PL, the mixture of repression and absorption, and the resulting factionalism and tactical blunders. The irony is that success is precisely what a movement should seek, even though the price of immediate success sometimes is long-term failure. For SDS, the biggest problems brought by success were the threats of absorption and factionalism.

A number of SDS positions were absorbed by the political system. The McCarthy and Kennedy campaigns in 1968 showed the enthusiasm with which civil rights and antiwar stands could be channeled into mainstream politics, and though SDS was gone, most of the Port Huron Statement was incorporated by the liberal wing of the Democratic Party by 1972. Why, then, did SDS continue to radicalize rather than become an interest group? The answer may lie in the unique position of students as people whose lives are in transition. Most political groups have permanent interests to protect. For workers, the permanent recognition of their rights as workers, though restraining union militance, may be worth trading some immediate demands for. But students have only their demands; they have no permanent position to protect. Thus the compromises involved in absorption have little attraction for student leaders. The student movement sacrifices nothing by pressing demands with renewed vigor, even after winning some victories.

The position of students has two important corollaries. First, because students often demanded things for others—the Vietnamese, the poor, the minorities—rather than for themselves, there were few incentives with which to co-opt SDS leaders. They often were people who had chosen not to seek available positions of wealth and power. Second, the constituency of student organizations had to be renewed annually. While a few university towns became centers for superannuated student hangers-on, the annual turnover in students meant that veterans were lost to graduation, and new ranks had to be recruited from entering students. The problem that recruiting new members posed for the New Left as a whole will be considered below.

The factionalism to which SDS succumbed was the cost of a success encouraged by the participatory democratic structure. This structure works well in organizations that are small or in which consensus is high about everything except details. But when powerfully divisive issues arise, the participatory approach lacks means to limit the length or acrimony of debate or protect the organization from irrelevant or deliberately destructive intrusions. Since it assumes that a consensus can be achieved on every issue, it is ill equipped to hold an organization together when factions absolutely fail to agree. It is tempting for the losing faction to form its own group, where it can have its own consensus. In order to survive, SDS would have had to adjust its structure to its changing size. Given that one of SDS's founding principles was to decentralize and democratize authority, this may have been impossible. The new groups like Weatherman rejected democracy completely, and a traditional centralized democracy had no defenders.

The repression directed at SDS did not physically destroy chapters, but it did create a climate of fear and divisiveness. The open participatory structure was particularly ill suited to prevent or counter repressive responses. The structure made SDS easy to infiltrate or disrupt. Repression was a background against which the factionalism and inability of SDS to mobilize newer students played out the organization's collapse.

The problems that led to Weatherman's decline were more straightforward. Weatherman's narrow ideology, more a response to PL than a tested or pragmatic plan, greatly limited Weatherman's tactical choices. At a time when antiwar and student movement resources appeared to be cresting, Weatherman turned to organizing a new constituency—blue-collar youth—with whom they had little contact or experience. Yet even this organizing attempt was extremely tentative. Weatherman's structure made it difficult for anyone to join the organization. Weatherman had set itself up as an encapsulated group. The multifaceted nature of this encapsulation should be noted. Weatherman's positions made most people and New Left groups turn away from it at the same time that Weatherman was losing interest in organizing people, substituting an apocalyptic vision of an uncontrollable violent world revolution.

An encapsulated group can maintain itself. As its members cut their ties to other groups, their cohesion with one another may assume greater importance and keep the group together. Two factors worked against this in Weatherman. One was the intense pressure that the constantly politicized life placed on members, encouraging some people to quit. The other was the mounting weight of trials, fines, and indictments. This legal repression went largely unchallenged by outsiders because the government easily convinced most people that the threat posed by Weatherman—a group advocating violence and lawlessness—justified a strong response. This did not require a deliberate campaign of persuasion. Weatherman, despite its large pool of initially available resources, lasted less than one year.

Explaining Movement Decline

The decline of any particular movement organization need not signal the decline of the movement. Nevertheless, the decline of SDS in the late sixties was coterminous with the decline of the New Left and the student antiwar movement in general. What makes this surprising is that there still appeared to be a large constituency for the student movement in the late sixties; indeed, the protests following the invasion of Cambodia and the Kent State killings in May 1970 were the largest campus demonstrations ever. There also were several organizations, such as the Socialist Workers Party, that tried to mobilize such people. Decline in activism is all the more striking given the absence of an immediate parallel decline in radical beliefs. Gold, Christie, and Friedman (1976), studying the Columbia class of 1972, found little evidence that students' acceptance of New Left ideology had declined from 1968 to 1972, although activism had clearly dwindled.

Still, the movement declined. The reason was not that New Left organizations no longer existed, nor that they lacked constituents and resources, but that their collective ability to speak for their constituency had faded because of factionalism, absorption, and repression. The opportunities presented in the sixties had passed and could not be recovered.

The external climate became less hospitable for movements when Richard Nixon became president in 1969 and the climate and pace of repression began to pick up. Nixon claimed to be ending the war. While overtly and covertly widening the war on some fronts, he did withdraw American troops and first limited and then ended the draft. This served to lessen the war's impact as an organizing issue.

The internal climate was less hospitable as well. By 1969, any large demonstration or organization would draw factions whose attitudes were radicalized far beyond those of the mass of constituents. The radicals no longer wanted to build an antiwar movement but were pushing toward revolution. Weatherman was only one example of this. Such groups had a dampening effect on all efforts to mobilize a mass movement among more moderate students, both by attracting more intense repression and by bidding the cost of movement membership higher.

At the same time, the mass of potential constituents was being wooed by a series of concessions: the draft lottery, extension of the franchise to eighteen-year-olds, school breaks for electoral politics, promises of withdrawal from the war, loosening of marijuana laws—which the older leaders could write off as inadequate but which could satisfy less ideologically integrated constituents. As the cost of participation rose, especially after the killings at Kent State, it became harder to mobilize people to push for additional concessions. To the extent that such people sought personal satisfaction through social movement participation, newer movements for women's rights and environmental protection offered activism with less risk. All these trends were accompanied by a chorus of "the sixties accomplished nothing," led by politicians and academics who were glad to see the old activism fade, supported by radical activists who wrote off the gains of the sixties as woefully short of their goals, and joined by younger students who were unaware of what changes the sixties had wrought.

Conclusion

The history of SDS shows that social movements are difficult to maintain. If a movement fails, it fails; but even if it succeeds, it may fail. A few points can be emphasized from the SDS and Weatherman experiences.

1. Structures must be flexible. The organization that works well at one size or on one issue may not work well at others. The participatory structure of SDS was fine for a small, cohesive group, but it allowed factionalism to flourish as the group grew. Since the organization was dedicated to its decentralized, participatory structure, it was unable to make adjustments when necessary.
2. Organizations must plan for new members. If members are sought, a group should have routes for joining (which Weatherman did not) and roles and positions for people who join (which SDS often did not).
3. Gaps between the tactics and goals endorsed by leaders and those sought by members must be addressed. This is a long-standing issue in revolutionary theory—should the leaders articulate the members' views, or should the leaders take a vanguard position and pull the members forward? There is no simple answer to this, but when the leadership reaches so far into the vanguard that it can no longer

communicate with its constituency, something is wrong. This was a problem for Weatherman.

4. Movement organizations must identify and focus their energies on their primary enemies. When they put more resources into fighting each other than seeking collective goals, the movement has a serious problem. Structures that allow or encourage resources to be channeled into factionalism are flawed and should be replaced.

References

Feuer, L. S. 1969. *The Conflict of Generations.* New York: Basic Books.

Gamson, W. A. 1968. *Power and Discontent.* Homewood, Ill.: Dorsey Press.

———. 1975. *The Strategy of Social Protest.* Homewood, Ill.: Dorsey Press.

Gerlach, L. P., and V. H. Hine. 1970. *People, Power, Change: Movements of Social Transformation.* Indianapolis: Bobbs-Merrill.

Gold, A. R., R. Christie, and L. N. Friedman. 1976. *Fists and Flowers: A Social Psychological Interpretation of Student Protest.* New York: Academic Press.

Gurr, T. R. 1970. *Why Men Rebel.* Princeton: Princeton University Press.

Hoffer, E. 1951. *The True Believer.* New York: Harper & Row.

Jacobs, H. 1970. *Weatherman.* San Francisco: Ramparts.

McCarthy D., and M. N. Zald. 1973. *The Trend of Social Movements in America: Professionalization and Resource Mobilization.* Morristown, N.J.: General Learning Press.

Michels, R. 1962. *Political Parties.* New York: Free Press.

Oglesby, C. 1974. "SDS Death: Panthers, PL, Weatherpeople." *Boston Phoenix* (4 June).

Sale, K. 1973. *SDS.* New York: Random House.

Stern, S. 1975. *With the Weathermen.* Garden City, N.Y.: Doubleday.

Tilly, C., L. Tilly, and R. Tilly. 1975. *The Rebellious Century, 1830–1930.* Cambridge: Harvard University Press.

Vickers, G. R. 1975. *The Formation of the New Left.* Lexington, Mass.: Lexington Books.

Zald, M. N., and R. Ash. 1966. "Social Movement Organizations: Growth, Decay and Change." *Social Forces* 44 (March): 327–41.

16

The Decline of the Civil Rights Movement

Doug McAdam

The most significant insurgent challenge to arise in this country during the third wave of social movements was the black protest movement of the 1950s and 1960s. Its significance derives from two sets of consequences: It stimulated other movements of the period, such as women's liberation and the student movement, and it resulted in important changes affecting many blacks. Although it never affected the fundamental restructuring of American society sought by many insurgents, the civil rights movement nonetheless created new opportunities, overturned an anachronistic regional caste system, and sparked something of a politico-cultural renaissance within the black community. Like all insurgent challenges, the black movement nonetheless waned as the 1960s drew to a close. Why? What can existing perspectives on movement decline tell us about the fate of the black movement?

Existing Theories

There are three theoretical perspectives on movement decline: the classical model, resource mobilization, and the political process model. The classical model associates movement decline with three processes: oligarchization, conservatization, and institutionalization (Weber in Gerth and Mills 1946, 297–301; Messinger 1955, 3–10; Michels 1959). Oligarchization involves the emergence of an elite that comes to exercise dispro-

Copyright © 1983 by Doug McAdam. Originally published in *Social Movements of the Sixties and Seventies,* ed. Jo Freeman (New York: Longman, 1983).

portionate control over the movement organization. These "leaders" share an interest in the organization's survival as a prerequisite of maintaining their privileged position within the organization, *even* when this survival requires the subordination of the movement's original goals. Consequently, oligarchization leads to the displacement of original goals with more conservative ones. When the personal interests of the movement's elite are inextricably linked to the survival of the organization, they avoid mobilizing an opposition capable of damaging the organization. The result is a diminution in radicalism as the leaders seek to accommodate to the viewpoints of dominant groups in society.

Institutionalization involves the development of a hierarchical organization, an explicit division of labor, and established administrative procedures. While created to facilitate organizational functioning, these inevitably dampen member enthusiasm and creativity in favor of predictability and organizational stability. Thus institutionalization encourages movement organizations to shift resources from achieving their original goals to maintaining their current structure.

Resource mobilization proponents have not explicitly advanced a theory of movement decline; theirs is a more general model of movement dynamics from which some implicit assumptions regarding the decline of insurgency can be drawn.[1] This model postulates that the emergence and development of a social movement is primarily a function of the resources available to support insurgency (McCarthy and Zald 1973). Unfortunately, many groups in society simply lack the resources to generate a movement on their own (Oberschall 1973). In such cases, movements must depend on external "sponsors." If external resources trigger a movement in the first place, this model implies that a significant withdrawal of such support would precipitate its decline.

The emphasis of the classical and resource mobilization models is strikingly different. The former focuses on processes *internal* to the movement, while the latter suggests that the dissolution of insurgency is primarily due to the withdrawal of *external* support. I propose that undue emphasis on either internal or external processes misses the dynamic interplay between the two that shapes a movement throughout its history. This fundamental premise lies at the heart of a third model of social insurgency.

The political process model emphasizes three factors that are crucial to the ongoing development of a movement: the organizational strength of movement forces; the "structure of political opportunities" (Eisenger 1973) available to insurgents to any point in time; and the response of other groups to the challenge posed by the movement. A significant negative change in any one of these factors is expected to diminish the ability of insurgents to sustain collective protest.

This chapter assesses the analytic utility of each model as an explanation for the decline in black insurgency in the late 1960s through content coding of relevant story synopses contained in the *Annual Index* of the *New York Times*. This provides a rough measure of the pace of black insurgency between 1948 and 1970.[2] The results show a general rise in movement activity between 1955 and 1965 followed by a steady decline thereafter. The causes of that decline occupy the remainder of this chapter.[3]

The conservatization predicted by the classical model clearly did not occur. Instead, the movement grew progressively more radical as the decade wore on. It shifted its demands from the integration of blacks into various areas of life to a more fundamental restructuring of this country's dominant political and economic institutions. As Stokely Carmichael asserted, "Integration is irrelevant. Political and economic power is what black people have to have" (quoted in Killian 1975, 106). This shift was also accompanied by a fundamental change in tactics. From strict adherence to nonviolence during the civil rights phase of the movement, many insurgents had, by decade's end, come to openly espouse violent insurrection. Nor did *oligarchization* or *institutionalization* take place to any great extent. Faced with a growing dissensus over the substantive and tactical thrust that insurgency should take, direction over the movement became increasingly fragmented and decentralized as the sixties wore on.

The implicit linkage stressed by some resource mobilization theorists between external resource support and the pace of insurgency is also found wanting in the case of the black movement. As can be seen in figure 16.1, the decline in black insurgency in the latter half of the 1960s occurred in the face of continued high levels of external funding. In general, throughout the study period, outside support increases sharply *following*, rather than preceding, peaks in insurgent activity.

Instead, the decline of the black movement is best understood as a complex by-product of the three sets of factors noted earlier. Specifically, it was changes in (1) the internal strength of movement forces, (2) the external "structure of political opportunities," and (3) the response of other groups to the movement that helped trigger the decline in black insurgency between 1966 and 1970.

Shifting Organizational Strength, 1961–1970

In any conflict situation the strength of a particular group is determined as much by the deployment of its forces as by its absolute numbers. However, theorists have disagreed as to the optimum distribution of a movement's personnel. Following Gerlach and Hine (1970), some have empha-

FIGURE 16.1
Number of Movement-Initiated Events and Level of
External Financial Support, 1948–70

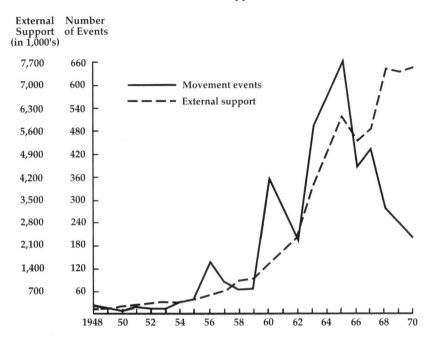

Source: For NAACP, Annual Reports for the National Association for the Advancement of Colored People, 1961–70; for CORE, Meier and Rudwick, 1973: 97, 149, 225, 335, 411, 420–30; for SCLC, Brink and Harris, 1963: 115; Clayton, 1964: 14; Lomax, 1962: 94; Muse, 1968: 276; for SNCC, Meier, 1971: 25; Zinn, 1965: 10. Data on Urban League was unavailable for inclusion in the chart. Where absolute dollar amounts were unavailable, knowledgeable estimates were substituted.

sized the advantages of a decentralized structure of local protest units. Other theorists have stressed the need for a more centralized structure, arguing that insurgents must be able to concentrate movement personnel and resources if they are ever to become an effective political force. Gamson's finding that movements with centralized organizational structures tend to be more successful than ones with decentralized structures has often been cited as evidence supporting this latter position (Gamson 1975).

My contention is that an optimum deployment of movement forces combines elements of both these structures. Strong organizations linked together by means of a reticulate structure would seem to preserve the functional benefits of the decentralized structure—resistance to repression, encouragement of innovation—without sacrificing the minimal concentrations of resources needed to sustain effective political action. In the black movement, something approaching this intermediate structure was achieved in the early sixties only to collapse by decade's end.

Organizational Proliferation

During the early 1960s four organizations jockeyed with one another for influence over the movement and the increased shares of publicity and money generated by protest activity. They were the National Association for the Advancement of Colored People (NAACP), the Southern Christian Leadership Conference (SCLC), the Congress of Racial Equality (CORE), and the Student Nonviolent Coordinating Committee (SNCC).[4] On the strength of Martin Luther King's extraordinary popular following and media appeal, SCLC was frequently able to preempt the stage, though none of these four groups succeeded in dominating the movement. Still, their attempts to do so lent much-needed vitality and diversity to the movement. Each organization carved out a unique program style and mode of operation that broadened the movement's recruiting and financial bases by offering a range of organizational alternatives from which potential members and benefactors could choose. As Clark (1970, 295) described it:

> The civil right groups vary in organizational efficiency as well as in philosophy, approach, and methods. The rank and file of liberal or religious whites might be more responsive to the seemingly nonthreatening, Christian approach of Martin Luther King, Jr. More tough-minded and pragmatic business and governmental leaders might find a greater point of control with the appeals and approaches of the NAACP and the Urban League. The more passionate Negroes and whites who seek immediate and concrete forms of justice will probably gravitate toward CORE and SNCC. . . . The variety of organizations and "leaders" among Negroes may be viewed as . . . the present strength of the movement rather than a symptom of weakness. Each organization influences the momentum and pace of the others. The inevitable interaction among them demands from each a level of effectiveness and relevance above the minimum possible for any single organization.

In addition to the positive effect that these organizations had on one another, their collective presence also confronted movement opponents with four sources of pressure. This considerably increased the difficulties and cost of defeating or containing the movement by not allowing opponents to concentrate resources for a concerted campaign of social control directed at any one group. After 1965, however, the dominance of the

"Big Four" within the movement waned considerably. Table 16.1 captures this trend.

In 1967 the four organizations initiated 74 percent of all events credited to formal movement organizations. By 1970 the proportion dropped to barely 32 percent. While only 15 percent of all events initiated by formal movement organizations in the 1961–65 period were attributed to groups other than the Big Four, the comparable proportion for the succeeding five years was 33 percent. Indeed, between 1968 and 1970 "other movement organizations" accounted for nearly half (47 percent) of all events initiated by formal movement groups. By the end of the sixties then, the structure of centralized national groups that had dominated the movement in the early 1960s had been replaced by a highly fluid, segmented structure of small, loosely connected local organizations.

At the root of this disintegration was the devaluation of integration as *the* fundamental goal of the movement. From 1955 through the mid-1960s black insurgency had focused almost exclusively on the issues of voter registration and desegregation of public facilities. During the late sixties this was replaced by a concern for many issues. Police brutality, institutional racism, international colonialism, the development of black pride, the establishment of black studies programs on college campuses, and many other issues came to be embraced by insurgents. Ironically, this substantive shift owed much to the early successes enjoyed by insurgents, who, in eradicating legal segregation, had come to realize the limited value of their victories. As Rustin expressed it, "What is the value of win-

TABLE 16.1
Distribution of All Events Initiated by
Formal Movement Organizations, 1961–70

Organization	1961–65		1966		1967		1968		1969		1970		1966–70	
	%	N	%	N	%	N	%	N	%	N	%	N	%	N
NAACP	24	(265)	21	(50)	27	(53)	16	(25)	16	(21)	21	(20)	21	(169)
CORE	22	(244)	4	(10)	18	(36)	7	(10)	6	(8)	2	(2)	8	(66)
SCLC (including M. L. King)	23	(257)	23	(56)	25	(49)	36	(55)	18	(24)	8	(8)	23	(192)
SNCC	6	(62)	9	(22)	4	(8)	1	(2)	0	(0)	1	(1)	4	(33)
Other movement organizations	15	(168)	23	(55)	17	(34)	33	(49)	56	(76)	59	(56)	33	(270)
Multiple movement organizations	10	(110)	20	(49)	8	(15)	7	(11)	4	(6)	8	(8)	11	(89)
Total	100	(1,107)	100	(242)	99	(195)	100	(152)	100	(135)	99	(95)	100	(819)

Source: Annual Index of the New York Times, 1961–70.

ning access to public accommodations for those who lack money to use them?" (1965, 28). However warranted this shift was, it nonetheless deprived the movement of the single dominant issue around which the diverse insurgent factions could be organized.

By the late sixties the substantive focus of the movement had clearly shifted from questions of caste to class. This change required a redefinition of the movement's opponents. Such traditional enemies as the southern sheriff, the hooded night rider, and the ax-wielding restaurant owner were replaced by the principal political and economic elites of the country as those ultimately responsible for the perpetuation of racism. This shift in targets also reflected the movement's growing hostility toward a federal establishment it felt had shown itself in the tough southern campaigns of the early 1960s to be a less than aggressive advocate of black rights.

This growing disaffection and its effect on the goals pursued by insurgents provides an excellent illustration of how the interaction between processes internal and external to a movement shapes the development of insurgency over time. The shift in goals discussed here owed as much to the actions (or lack thereof) of federal officials as it did to the organizational dynamics of insurgent groups. In turn, this substantive shift posed a far greater threat to existing political and economic interests in this country than had the earlier civil rights phase of the struggle. Thus, in response to this shift, both the federal government and other parties to the conflict modified their responses toward the movement in ways that were to contribute greatly to the decline of black insurgency.

The Rise of Intramovement Conflict

Even at the peak of black insurgency in the early 1960s, there existed considerable competition among the Big Four for the money and publicity needed to sustain their operations and position within the movement. At the same time the strong substantive and tactical consensus that prevailed during the early sixties prompted movement groups to set aside their rivalries to work together in numerous joint campaigns. However, after 1965 any semblance of cooperation was to crumble in the face of the growing ideological and tactical differences that increasingly split the movement (and often at times the organizations themselves) into two antagonistic factions.

Poised on the one hand were traditional integrationists including SCLC and NAACP who continued to eschew violence as unacceptable and/or ineffective. Aligned in increasing opposition to the integrationists was the so-called Black Power wing of the movement, with its rejection of integration as *the* fundamental goal of black insurgency and its approval of violence as an acceptable addition to the movement's tactical arsenal. The remaining two members of the Big Four—CORE and SNCC—were in varying degrees associated with this wing of the movement.

Relations between these two wings declined steadily after 1965 with charges of extremism, reverse racism, and "Uncle Tomism" regularly exchanged. Even within the factions there was considerable conflict. Relations between SCLC and the NAACP cooled noticeably following Martin Luther King's 1965 criticism of the Vietnam War. Two years later, two rival Black Power groups, US and the Black Panthers, staged a shootout in Los Angeles that stemmed, in part, from ideological differences over the direction the movement should take.

This basic division could also be found *within* specific movement organizations. Meier and Rudwick, for example, have documented the role such disputes played in the decline of CORE affiliate strength in the mid-to-late sixties. Representative of these disputes was one that split the Seattle chapter of CORE into a "conservative" faction and a dissident group called the Ad Hoc Committee. To quote at length from the authors' account of the dispute:

> Ad Hoc members were charged with circulating "divisive and derogatory allegations" that the chapter leaders had conspired to thwart direct action projects and had "foisted a compromising agreement on the membership." Ad Hoc people attacked the chapter's black chairman and vice-chairman as "too respectable" and too fearful of losing their jobs and homes by participating in militant tactics. . . . Defeated in its attempt to oust the chapter's established leadership in the next election and hoping to function independently as a ghetto-oriented organization, the Ad Hoc Committee withdrew, and soon after disintegrated. Meanwhile, amid the accusations and counter-accusations, a number of others left the Seattle Chapter, disgusted by the "lack of faith and trust we CORE people now have in each other." Thus the result of the conflict was to leave Seattle CORE seriously weakened. (Meier and Rudwick 1973, 311)

As recounted by Meier and Rudwick, the same fate befell other CORE affiliates. Indeed, the Seattle incident was symptomatic of a trend that was widespread throughout the movement. Once-effective insurgent organizations were rendered impotent by factional disputes that drained them of the unity, energy, and resolve needed to sustain protest activity. Thus the growing divisions within the movement not only reduced the possibility of cooperative action *between* movement groups but further diminished organizational strength by stimulating disputes *within* these groups.

The Evolving "Structure of Political Opportunities," 1961–1970

Simultaneous with organizational decline, several external processes were decreasing the political leverage exercised by blacks. These developments reversed a thirty-year trend that had created a political environment increasingly favorable to insurgent political action (McAdam 1982).

Mobilization of Political Reaction and the Devaluation of the Black Vote

Between 1910 and 1960 nearly five million southern blacks migrated northward. This exodus was politically significant for two reasons. First, as Brooks (1974, 17) has observed, "for blacks it was a move, almost literally, from no voting to voting." While the total black population of the United States increased by 92 percent between 1910 and 1960, the total number of blacks voting in presidential elections increased eightfold (Weiss 1970, Wilson 1966).

Second, the black vote became less dependably Democratic than it had been in the thirties. In the 1944 and 1948 elections, had blacks reversed the proportion of the votes they gave to the two major candidates, the Republican challenger, Thomas Dewey, would have defeated his Democratic opponents, Franklin Roosevelt and Harry Truman (Brooks 1974). In the 1952 and 1956 contests, the Republican candidate, Dwight Eisenhower, was able to reverse the trend. Republican gains were especially pronounced in 1956 with Eisenhower capturing an estimated 40 percent of the black vote (Lomax 1962). As a result both parties intensified their efforts to appeal to black voters. As Glantz (1970) commented before the 1960 election,

> Neither party can afford to ignore the numerical weight of the Negro vote. In the next campaign, the Democratic candidate will have the responsibility of reversing the changing image of the Democratic party, while the Republican candidate will have the responsibility of enlarging . . . the appeal of the Republican party. (261)

The 1960 election enhanced the political significance of the black vote, as for the third time in the previous five elections, black voters were widely credited with deciding the contest. Lawson's (1976) assessment is typical:

> An analysis of the returns demonstrated that Negro ballots were enough to give the Democratic contender a winning margin in New Jersey, Michigan, Illinois, Texas, and South Carolina, all states that had supported Eisenhower in 1956. Had the Republican-Democratic division in the black districts of

these states broken down in the same way as four years earlier, Richard Nixon would have become the thirty-fifth President. (256)

The 1960 election was to represent the high water mark of black electoral influence. In 1964 the conservative threat posed by the Goldwater campaign altered the context of insurgency to the point where black protest came at times to be redefined, even by allies, as a political liability. Pressure was brought on civil rights organizations to curtail protest activity during the crucial months of the presidential campaign, out of fear that protest would help Barry Goldwater. As Brooks (1974) tells it:

> white liberal money men were persuaded to threaten a cutoff in funds for civil rights activity as a means of containing the wilder enthusiasm of civil rights activists. The Democratic National Committee held back releasing funds allocated for voter registration drives among blacks to assure their use for registration and not hell-raising. The message was "cool it," and Roy Wilkins called civil rights leaders together to work out a "moratorium" on demonstrations. Wilkins, King, Young and Randolph signed a call, after three hours of debate on July 29, "to observe a broad curtailment, if not total moratorium, of all mass marches, mass picketing, and mass demonstrations until after election day." (237)

Although Lyndon Johnson won in a landslide vote, the off-year elections of 1966 began to show mass defections from the traditional Democratic electoral coalition that had swept John F. Kennedy and Johnson into office. Deflections were particularly heavy among the white urban ethnic groups of the industrial North. Now worried by northern riots and threatened by what they viewed as the black assault, via open housing demonstrations in their neighborhoods, these groups were unwilling to support a party that many had come to view as supportive of unacceptable black demands. In 1964 Lubell accurately forecast this trend:

> In the past, Democratic strategists have assumed that the civil rights issue helped hold together the "big city" vote. This may have been a valid political strategy as long as the civil rights cause appeared mainly a matter of improving the treatment of Negroes in the South.
>   But the new demands of Northern Negro militants have posed sharp conflicts with what many white voters see as their own rights. Agitation over civil rights . . . could alienate enough white voters to disrupt the Democratic majorities in the urban areas. (127–28)

In 1966 the black vote held generally firm, but the white ethnics abandoned in droves (Brink and Harris 1967). As a consequence of these defections, political strategists of both parties came to weigh the advantages of courting the black vote against the costs of antagonizing a large and ever-expanding segment of the white population.

In 1968 the Republicans sought to exploit this dilemma by devising a campaign strategy designed to play on the country's deepening racial cleavage and the post–New Deal association of blacks with the Democratic Party. By reminding voters of the latter, Republicans hoped to tap the growing undercurrent of racial antagonism engendered by the changing patterns of black insurgency in the mid-to-late 1960s. Consequently, a breakdown of the popular vote in 1968 along racial lines revealed that blacks retained their traditional loyalty to the Democratic party by casting 97 percent of their votes for Hubert Humphrey. By contrast, only 35 percent of the white electorate voted for the democratic presidential candidate (Converse et al. 1969, 1085).

The election did more than simply mirror the declining political fortunes of blacks; it contributed to the decline as well by electing someone with precious little political debt to blacks and considerable debt to their opponents. As Goldman (1970) reported, nothing in the substantive performance of the Nixon administration's first two years in power contradicted this expectation.

> Nixon . . . came to office with substantial political debts to the South—and, as his advisors were frank to say, none at all to the blacks. The most moderate Negro leaders found their lines of communication to the White House abruptly cut. Judicial conservatives were posted to vacancies on the Supreme Court. Pressure on the South to integrate its schools relented. . . . (23)

By 1970 the structure of political alignments in this country had changed considerably. Whereas the black vote had earlier constituted an electoral asset of considerable significance, the "white backlash" of the late 1960s served to render it a decided liability in many situations. The result was an overall diminution in the vulnerability of the political system to the demands of blacks and a consequent decline in the opportunities for successful insurgent activity.

The Declining Salience of the Racial Issue

Between 1961 and 1965, the salience of the "Negro question" reached such proportions that it came to be consistently identified in public opinion surveys as the most important problem confronting the country. In six of eleven polls between 1961 and 1965, "civil rights" was identified as the most important problem facing the country by more people than identified any other comparable issue. In three other polls it ranked second. Only twice did it rank as low as fourth.[5]

Over the same period, public support for many of the stated goals of the movement also increased steadily. Burstein (1978) has documented consistent gains in white support during the fifties and early sixties across a wide range of specific issue areas. That this support was grudging and/ or hypocritical in many cases, and no doubt erosive in the face of a more meaningful test of support (i.e., fund-raising, willingness to demonstrate), hardly diminishes its significance. This growing body of supportive opinion introduced a new set of political considerations into the calculations of other parties to the conflict, and in so doing helped define their response to the movement. Writing in the early 1960s, Wilson captured the nature of this dynamic. "The principal value of the white liberal . . . is to supply votes and the political pressures . . . that make it almost suicidal for an important Northern politician openly to court anti-Negro sentiment" (1965, 437). The mobilization of liberal support acted, then, to enhance the bargaining position of blacks by increasing the political consequences of opposing "acceptable" black demands.

From its peak in the 1963–65 period, the issue of civil rights declined in salience during the late sixties and early seventies. This decline is depicted in figure 16.2 which reports the proportion of survey respondents who identified "civil rights" and Vietnam as the "most important problem" facing America in a series of Gallup opinion polls between 1962 and 1971. The extent of this decline was such that by February 1971 only 7 percent of the people surveyed identified "race relations" as the country's most important problem, in contrast to the 52 percent who had done so six years earlier. As Goldman (1970) has sardonically observed, "Negroes did not precisely fall from grace at [this] juncture, but they did go out of fashion" (201).

One reason for the decline was the emergence of competing issues, notably Vietnam, that diverted attention from the racial conflict. As Killian (1975) has observed:

> In spite of the evidence of continued tension and growing polarization, the racial conflict that had seemed to threaten American society soon dropped from its preeminent position in public concern. Vietnam, ecology, inflation, the Arab-Israeli conflict, the energy crisis, and Watergate took their turns in preempting both the headlines of the newspapers and the interest of white Americans. (146)

Another reason was the diminished organizational strength of the movement. With the disintegration of the movement's organizational core, insurgents found it increasingly hard to mount the dramatic campaigns that had earlier caught public attention. Finally, declining public support for blacks reflected efforts by politicians to discredit the more

FIGURE 16.2
Proportion of General Public Identifying Civil Rights and Vietnam
as the "Most Important Problem Confronting the Country,"
March 1962 through February 1971

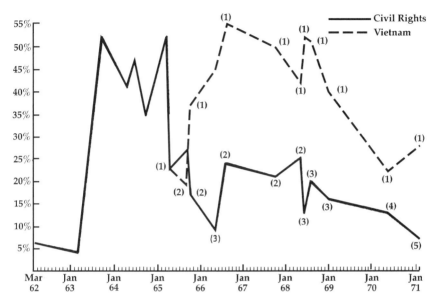

Source: Gallup, 1972: 1764, 1812, 1842, 1881, 1894, 1905, 1934, 1944, 1966. Parentheses refer to the rank of Vietnam among all the problems identified in the poll.

militant forms of black insurgency characteristic of the period. Thus, in the face of contradictory empirical evidence (cf. Fogelson 1971, Oberschall 1968), "responsible" public officials persisted in denouncing ghetto disorders as either insurrections instigated by subversive elements or exercises in rampant criminality.

The Shifting Response to Insurgency, 1961–1970

Black insurgency was further handicapped during the late 1960s by the shifting patterns of interaction between the movement and the three other major parties to the conflict: external support groups, white opposition, and the federal government. The growing threat posed by the shifting goals and tactics of insurgents served to mobilize increased opposition. The result was a less supportive balance of opposing and supporting forces confronting the movement and a consequent decline in insurgent activity.

External Support Groups

Figure 16.3 reports the estimated level of monetary support for Big Four movement organizations during each year from 1961 to 1970. The distinct patterns for various movement organizations show a decided shift in the response of external support groups to the movement beginning around mid-decade. The shift involved a tripartite funding pattern based on the relative "acceptability" of the goals and tactics embraced by various groups. In the face of the widespread legitimacy ascribed to movement goals in the early 1960s, all four principal movement groups benefited from a consistent rise in external monetary support until the mid-1960s. As movement goals and tactics began to shift around mid-decade, so too did the response of external "sponsors."

The first to experience the disaffection of liberal supporters were SNCC and CORE. After together commanding the largest share of external support between 1962 and 1965, their funding fell off rapidly after 1965. This

FIGURE 16.3
External Dollar Support for SCLC, NAACP, and CORE-SNCC, 1961–70

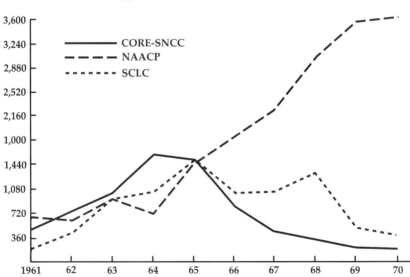

Sources: For number of movement initiated events, *Annual Index* of the *New York Times*; for financial data see Figure 16.1.

sharp drop was prompted by the ideological shift to Black Power advocated by both groups. To quote Brink and Harris, "the onset of black
power produced sharp birth pangs for its principal advocates . . . both
CORE and SNCC were reduced to serious financial straits as whites de-
serted in droves" (1967, 62).

Support for SCLC also declined, but for different reasons. When SCLC's
leader and chief fund-raiser, Martin Luther King, publicly criticized the
Vietnam War late in 1965, there was a significant loss of funds the following year. His assassination in 1968 did stimulate a brief resurgence in support, but this lasted only as long as the feelings of sympathy and guilt
generated by his death.

In marked contrast to the experience of SCLC, SNCC, and CORE, the
NAACP enjoyed a steep and steady rise in external funding during the
late 1960s. An examination of figure 16.3 shows that the NAACP's level
of external support remained virtually constant between 1961 and 1964,
while the dollar amounts received by both SCLC and SNCC-CORE increased steadily over the same period of time. After 1964, the patterns
were largely reversed. Together these patterns present an inescapable
conclusion: Over time, the NAACP came increasingly to be seen by external support groups as virtually the only "acceptable" funding alternative.[6] In response to the radicalization of SNCC and CORE and to King's
antiwar stance, many groups that had earlier contributed to one of these
three organizations shifted their support to the NAACP, reducing the
once formidable Big Four to a single strong movement organization by
the end of the decade.

White Opposition

White opposition to the movement was transformed during the decade
from a regionally based, organized force of counterinsurgents to a geographically dispersed mass of people recognizable only by their common
opposition to the movement. This broadened "white backlash" represented little more than a much publicized shift in public opinion rather
than the organized white resistance encountered by insurgents in the
South. Nonetheless, the change was to have important negative consequences for the movement.

This transformation was fueled by two trends. First, there was the rise
of Black Power as the substantive focus of insurgency. The movement's
critique of America had broadened to embody a holistic attack on the
complex patterns of institutional racism in which the interests of many
who had earlier "supported" the movement were implicated. Second, the
movement shifted from a southern to a national phenomenon. Confined
almost exclusively to the South during the early 1960s, the movement

posed little threat to residents of other regions of the country. With the advent of riots, open housing marches, and school busing, the comfortable illusion that the racial problem was a distinctly southern dilemma was shattered. When the movement threatened population segments earlier removed from the conflict, opposition ceased to be primarily a southern phenomenon.

The movement's shift northward also undermined the crucial conflict dynamic so evident in the earlier southern campaigns. One of the characteristics of southern supremacists was that they could be counted on to react in precisely the violent, disruptive fashion productive of media attention and federal intervention. The importance of this dynamic cannot be underestimated, for its recognition and conscious manipulation by insurgents helped produce the particularly high rates of black activism and significant victories characteristics of the years 1961 to 1965 (Garrow 1978, Hubbard 1968, McAdam 1982).

In effect, the shift northward deprived the movement of an enemy it had learned to exploit successfully. No such convenient foil was available to the movement outside the South. Clark (1970) has captured the amorphous quality of the opposition the movement came increasingly to confront during this period:

> What do you do in a situation in which you have the laws on your side, where whites smile and say that they are your friends, but where your white "friends" move to the suburbs leaving you confronted with segregation and inferior education in schools, ghetto housing, and a quiet and tacit discrimination in jobs? How can you demonstrate a philosophy of love in response to this? What is the appropriate form of protest? One can "sit-in" in the Board of Education building, and not a single child will come back from the suburbs or from the private and parochial schools. One can link arms with the Mayor of Boston and march on the Commons, but it will not affect the housing conditions of Negroes in Roxbury. (288)

In short, having developed effective tactics for one opponent, insurgents were unable to devise a suitable response for another.

Even if insurgents had been able to provoke in the North the same form of disruptive white opposition they had in the South, it is not likely that the federal government would have been as ready to intervene. The political repercussions had changed significantly. Killian (1975) wrote:

> The white people who are now resisting the movement are not the ancient foe, the southern whites. They are Jews, traditional liberal friends of blacks, now defending their middle-class suburban neighborhoods and their neighborhood schools. They are Americans of Irish, Italian, or Polish descent defending their labor unions, their neighborhood schools, and the imagined

integrity of their neighborhoods. . . . And there are, finally, the old American Protestants as well. (117)

The important characteristic of these groups is that they represented population segments vital to the political fortunes of both major parties. Consequently, the mobilization of broad-based white opposition to the movement in the late 1960s prompted a general devaluation of the political significance of blacks and, as noted earlier, a simultaneous tactical swing to the Right on the part of both major parties.

The Federal Government

After 1965, and especially 1967, the grudging support that had been forthcoming in earlier years gave way to an increasingly repressive federal response to the movement. To fully describe the extent of government repression against the movement would be beyond the scope of this chapter, but two broad categories of control activities can be identified. First were the countless instances of violence, intimidation, harassment, and surveillance directed at Black Power groups active during the late 1960s. Second were the efforts to control urban riots. In both cases it is difficult to distinguish between the efforts of federal, state, and local officials, for all three levels worked together in a loosely coordinated effort to counter the perceived threat posed by the Black Power wing of the movement.

Governmental efforts to damage specific movement organizations or leaders were certainly evident earlier than 1966–70 (Marx 1976). Nevertheless, the pace of such efforts increased markedly during the late 1960s. Perhaps the most celebrated Black Power group was the Black Panthers, founded in Oakland in October 1966. Typical of the treatment accorded any number of similar groups, the Panthers in the four years following their founding were subjected to a wide array of official control efforts ranging from infiltration to harassment through arrests for minor offenses to violent confrontations with law enforcement personnel.

Though unique in the extent of official attention they received, the Panthers were by no means the only group subjected to government-initiated control activities. Several other examples may help illustrate the pervasiveness of such efforts.

In Cleveland, three members of a black nationalists' group died in a 1968 shoot out with police triggered by an unsubstantiated report by an FBI informant that the group, the Black Nationalists of New Libya, were stockpiling weapons to carry out an assassination plot against moderate black leaders. (Masotti and Corsi 1969)

FBI officials planted a series of derogatory articles in papers during the SCLC-sponsored Poor Peoples Campaign in 1968 as a means of discrediting it. (Marx 1976, 5)

Police raided the Los Angeles office of SNCC on April 5, 1968, while chapter members were attending a memorial service for Martin Luther King. (Major 1971, 297)

In his study of a local black power group, Helmreich reports countless instances of official violence, harassment, and intimidation directed at the organization's leadership. In the most flagrant incident, two leaders were arrested on a charge of faulty brake lights, taken to the police station, and beaten severely. (Helmreich 1973, 120–21)

No fewer than 24 known black insurgent groups were subjected to tax surveillance as part of a larger effort to use the IRS to harass "extremist" groups of varying (though primarily leftist) political philosophy. (Senate Select Committee 1976, 3: 50–52)

These and other instances of repression served to diminish the pace of black insurgency in three ways. First, they increased the personal costs of movement participation significantly as members and potential recruits came to weigh their involvement against the very real threat of death, injury, or incarceration.

Second, instead of initiating new programs, Black Power groups were forced to devote increasing amounts of time and money to legal efforts aimed at preserving and defending the organization against external threats. Indeed, as Oberschall (1978) perceptively notes, the federal government's aggressive prosecution of movement activists in the late 1960s would appear to have been based, in part, on a desire to precipitate this kind of debilitating financial crisis. He writes: "The government's strategy appeared to be to tie down leaders in costly and time consuming legal battles which would impede their activities and put a tremendous drain on financial resources regardless of whether the government would be successful in court" (277–78).

Finally, it would be hard to overestimate the divisive internal effect that increased government surveillance had on insurgents. Fear of informers was itself sufficient in many cases to generate the climate of suspicion and distrust needed to precipitate serious internal problems. And where fear failed to produce the desired results, agents provocateurs could be counted on to stir up dissension. As one example, Gary Marx cites a 1970 memo in which "FBI agents were instructed to plant in the hands of Panthers phony documents (on FBI stationery) that would lead them to suspect one another of being police informers" (1974, 435). He concludes,

"Sociologists who have often observed the bickering and conflict among sectarian protest groups holding the same goals, and their ever-present problems of unity, must ask what role 'counterintelligence' activities may be playing" (436).

The net effect of increased governmental repression was to seriously weaken the capacity of the Black Power wing of the movement to sustain insurgency. As Killian observed in 1975, movement activity

> has subsided not because the racial crisis has passed but because white power has demonstrated that open black defiance is extremely dangerous and often suicidal. The ranks of the most dramatically defiant black leaders were decimated by imprisonment, emigration, and assassination. The best-known black nationalist organizations, such as the Black Panthers, the Republic of New Africa, the Revolutionary Action Movement, and the Student Nonviolent Coordinating Committee, have dwindled in strength. (155–56)

Intensified social control also marked the state's response to the escalation in rioting during the mid-to-late sixties. A sampling of these efforts conveys the trend of the times.

At the federal level, Congress attached antiriot provisions to the 1968 Civil Rights Act that provided harsh penalties for persons found guilty of crossing state lines or using interstate communication facilities to incite riots. This legislation provided the Justice Department with the legal basis to prosecute many black leaders in the late sixties. Furthermore, the Omnibus Crime Act of 1968 provided for a national training center to instruct local police in riot-control techniques and a program of fiscal aid to local law enforcement agencies seeking to bolster antiriot capabilities. The latter program provided 75 percent federal funding for local riot-control efforts. That there was no shortage of "takers" for the newly available funds is clear from statistics cited by Feagin and Hahn (1973).

Twenty states added antiriot sections to their penal codes between 1966 and 1969 (Feagin and Hahn 1973). Locally, ordinances were passed in many cities granting the mayor legal authority to declare martial law in the event of ghetto disorders. A more common response was simply to strengthen the riot-control capabilities of local law enforcement agencies. Webb (1969) reports that by 1969, 75 percent of the 1,267 cities providing information had instituted some form of police riot-control training. Additionally, there was a 45 percent increase in the number of cities reporting the development of riot-control plans and a 25 percent rise in those reporting that they had obtained or prepared their own riot-control manuals (Webb 1969).

The composite picture that emerges from these various sources is of a massive governmental control response designed to counter the escalation in ghetto rioting. That these combined efforts had a measurable effect on the actual handling of urban disorders is suggested by a comparison of data on the 1967 and April 1968 riots. Perhaps most importantly, the force levels used in containing the 1968 disorders were on the average 50 percent greater than those used the previous year (Lemberg Center for the Study of Violence 1968). Indeed, all major indices of official repression, save one, showed increases between 1967 and April 1968. The average number of injuries per disorder in 1968 was nearly 40 percent higher than in 1967. Even more spectacular was the nearly twofold increase in average number of arrests between the two years.

Not surprisingly, in the face of this massive control response, the intensity of racial disorders dropped precipitously in 1969 and 1970 (Feagin and Hahn 1973, Skolnick 1969). Confronted by governmental forces increasingly willing and able to suppress ghetto disorders, and painfully aware of the costs incurred in the earlier rioting, the pace of such actions declined sharply.

Conclusions

We can draw three conclusions from this study about the dynamics of movement decline. First, we should not assume an inevitable conservative trend as a social movement develops. In contradiction to the classical model, the black movement grew progressively more radical over time. In view of this and similar findings (Beach 1977), it would seem more profitable to specify which factors might dispose movements to develop in either direction.

Second, this study undermines any simplistic resource mobilization argument that equates the pace of insurgency with the absolute dollar amount of resources available to insurgents. This is not to suggest that resources are antithetical or irrelevant to the decline of insurgency. On the contrary, what is needed is a more sophisticated specification of the relationship between resources and insurgency based on a more interesting set of research questions. Are all resources of equal value? How do various sources of support differ in the constraints they place on a movement, and what effect does this have on the development of insurgency? What is the optimum distribution of resources within a movement?

Finally, in supporting a political process interpretation of black insurgency, this study should serve to remind us that the fate of any social movement is not simply a product of internal movement dynamics or external political processes but the interaction of the two. In the words of Gary Marx (1976):

Social movements are not autonomous forces hurling toward their destiny only in response to the oppression, intensity of commitment, and skill of activists. Nor are they epiphenomena completely at the mercy of groups in their external environment seeking to block or facilitate them. Movements represent a complex interplay of external and internal factors. (1)

Notes

1. Resource mobilization is little more than a label applied indiscriminately to a disparate group of theorists. So divergent are some perspectives to which the label has been applied that continued adherence to our present use of the term threatens to obscure important differences between distinct schools of thought. To remedy the confusion, Perrow (1979) has suggested a distinction between what he calls RM (resource mobilization) I and RM II. RM I refers to the works of Oberschall, Gamson, and Tilly, among others; RM II is represented by the work of McCarthy and Zald. I am solely concerned with the McCarthy/Zald version of resource mobilization here.

2. In the indexes for 1948–70 all story synopses under "Negroes-U.S.-General" and "Education U.S.-Racial Integration" were coded according to criteria drawn up prior to the start of research. The decision to code only these headings was based on a careful examination of the classification system and cross listings for several years in the *Index,* which convinced me that the overwhelming majority of events relevant to the movement were contained under these headings. That any number of other potentially relevant headings are in the *Index* is readily conceded, but the sheer volume of listings made it absolutely necessary to restrict coding in some fashion. For instance, in 1969 no less than 718 other *Index* headings were listed as relevant listings under the general category "Negroes-U.S.-General."

3. For the purposes of this analysis, movement-initiated activity is defined as any action, speech, or statement initiated by a black (or racially mixed) group or individual actively working to further racial equality in the United States.

4. Some have argued that the National Urban League should be included, but its influence was greater in social welfare and business circles than within the movement. Indeed, the organization's visibility within the "liberal establishment" of foundations, academia, and social welfare groups may help account for the prominent role ascribed to it by writers largely drawn from that same "establishment" (cf. Clark 1970). Few protest activities or movement campaigns involved the Urban League. The *Times* data attribute the following yearly event totals to the Urban League: 1955–1960, 26 (12%); 1961, 7 (6%); 1962, 13 (12%); 1963, 21 (8%); 1964, 25 (8%); 1965, 7 (2%); 1961–65, 73 (7%).

5. This analysis was based exclusively on comparable Gallup polls conducted between 1961 and 1965. Smith (1980) has assembled a richer data set consisting of all similar polls conducted by the major polling organizations between 1947 and 1976. His findings are consistent with those reported here. While he does not report the rank order of "civil rights" among all problems identified in each survey, the percentage of respondents listing that as the "most important" problem re-

mained high throughout the period. In ten of nineteen surveys, at least 20 percent of the respondents identified civil rights as the country's most important problem; in another three, the figure was between 10 and 20 percent.

6. The overwhelming conservative bias in external funding is well documented in a 1970 study of corporate America's financial contributions to urban affairs programs (Cohn 1970, 71, 73).

References

Beach, Stephen W. 1977. "Social Movement Radicalization: The Case of the People's Democracy in Northern Ireland." *Sociological Quarterly* 18, no. 3 (summer): 305–19.

Brink, William, and Louis Harris. 1963. *The Negro Revolution in America.* New York: Simon and Schuster.

———. 1967. *Black and White.* New York: Simon and Schuster.

Brooks, Thomas R. 1974. *Walls Come Tumbling Down: A History of the Civil Rights Movement, 1940–1970.* Englewood Cliffs, N.J.: Prentice-Hall.

Burstein, Paul. 1978. "Public Opinion, Demonstrations, Media Coverage, and the Passage of Anti-Discrimination Legislation." Unpublished ms., Yale University, Department of Sociology.

Clark, Kenneth B. 1970. "The Civil Rights Movement: Momentum and Organization." In *Roots of Rebellion: The Evolution of Black Politics and Protest Since World War II,* ed. Richard P. Young. New York: Harper & Row, 270–97.

Clayton, Edward, ed. 1964. *The SCLC Story.* Atlanta: Southern Christian Leadership Conference.

Cohn, Jules. 1970. "Is Business Meeting the Challenge of Urban Affairs?" *Fortune* 48 (March–April): 68–82.

Converse, Phillip E., Warren E. Miller, Jerrold G. Rusk, and Arthur C. Wolfe. 1969. "Continuity and Change in American Politics: Parties and Issues in the 1968 Election." *American Political Science Review* 63 (December): 1083–1105.

Downes, Bryan T. 1970. "A Critical Reexamination of Social and Political Characteristics of Riot Cities." *Social Science Quarterly* 51, no. 2: 349–60.

Eisinger, Peter K. 1973. "The Conditions of Protest Behavior in American Cities." *American Political Science Review* 67 (March): 11–28.

Feagin, Joe R., and Harlan Hahn. 1973. *Ghetto Revolts, the Politics of Violence in American Cities.* New York: Macmillan.

Fogelson, Robert M. 1971. *Violence as Protest.* Garden City, N.Y.: Doubleday.

Gallup, George H. 1972. *The Gallup Poll, Public Opinion 1935–1971,* vol. 3. New York: Random House.

Gamson, William A. 1975. *The Strategy of Social Protest.* Homewood, Ill.: Dorsey Press.

Garrow, David J. 1978. *Protest at Selma.* New Haven: Yale University Press.

Gerlach, Luther P., and Virginia H. Hine. 1970. *People, Power, Change: Movements of Social Transformation.* Indianapolis: Bobbs-Merrill.

Gerth, Hans H., and C. Wright Mills. *From Max Weber: Essays in Sociology.* New York: Oxford University Press.

Glantz, Oscar. 1970. "The Black Vote." In *The Segregation Era 1863–1954,* ed. Allen Weinstein and Frank Otto Gatell. New York: Oxford University Press, 248–61.

Goldman, Peter. 1970. *Report from Black America.* New York: Simon and Schuster.

Helmreich, William B. 1973. *The Black Crusaders: A Case Study of a Black Militant Organization.* New York: Harper & Row.

Hubbard, Howard. 1968. "Five Long Hot Summers and How They Grew." *Public Interest* 12 (Summer): 3–24.

Killian, Lewis M. 1975. *The Impossible Revolution, Phase II: Black Power and the American Dream.* New York: Random House.

Lawson, Steven F. 1976. *Black Ballots: Voting Rights in the South, 1944–1969.* New York: Columbia University Press.

Lemberg Center for the Study of Violence. 1968. "April Aftermath of the King Assassination." *Riot Data Review,* no. 2 (August), Brandeis University. Mimeographed.

Lomax, Louis E. 1962. *The Negro Revolt.* New York: Harper & Row.

Lubell, Samuel. 1964. *White and Black, Test of a Nation.* New York: Harper & Row.

Major, Reginald. 1971. *A Panther Is a Black Cat.* New York: Morrow.

Marx, Gary T. 1974. "Thoughts on a Neglected Category of Social Movement Participant: The Agent Provocateur and the Informant." *American Journal of Sociology* 80, no. 2: 402–42.

———. 1976. "External Efforts to Damage or Facilitate Social Movements: Some Patterns, Explanations, Outcomes, and Complications." Paper prepared for conference on the Dynamics of Social Movements: Resource Mobilization, Tactics and Social Control, Vanderbilt University, March.

Masotti, L., and J. Corsi. 1969. *Shootout in Cleveland.* Washington, D.C.: U.S. Government Printing Office.

McAdam, Doug. 1982. *Political Process and the Development of Black Insurgency, 1930–1970.* Chicago: University of Chicago Press.

McCarthy, John D., and Mayer N. Zald. 1973. *The Trend of Social Movements in America: Professionalization and Resource Mobilization.* Morristown, N.J.: General Learning Press.

Meier, August. 1971. "Negro Protest Movements and Organizations." In *Conflict and Competition: Studies in the Recent Black Protest Movement,* ed. John H. Bracery Jr., August Meier, and Elliott Rudwick. Belmont, Calif.: Wadsworth, 20–33.

Meier, August, and Elliot Rudwick. 1973. *CORE, A Study in the Civil Rights Movement, 1942–1968.* New York: Oxford University Press.

Messinger, Sheldon L. 1955. "Organizational Transformation: A Case Study of a Declining Social Movement." *American Sociological Review* 20: 3–10.

Michels, Robert. 1959. *Political Parties.* New York: Dover.

Muse, Benjamin. 1968. *The American Negro Revolution.* Bloomington: Indiana University Press.

National Association for the Advancement of Colored People. 1948–70. *Annual Report of the National Association for the Advancement of Colored People.* New York: NAACP.

New York Times. 1948–70. *The New York Times Index.* New York: New York Times.

Oberschall, Anthony. 1968. "The Los Angeles Riot of August 1965. " In *The Black Revolt,* ed. James A. Geschwender. Englewood Cliffs, N.J.: Prentice-Hall, 264–84.

———. 1973. *Social Conflict and Social Movements.* Englewood Cliffs, N.J.: Prentice-Hall.

———. 1978. "The Decline of the 1960's Social Movements." In *Research in Social Movements, Conflicts, and Change,* vol. 1., ed. Louis Kriesberg. Greenwich, Conn.: JAI Press, 257–89.

Perrow, Charles. 1979. "The Sixties Observed." In *The Dynamics of Social Movements: Resource Mobilization, Social Control, and Tactics,* ed. Mayer N. Zald and John McCarthy. Cambridge, Mass.: Winthrop.

Rustin, Bayard. 1965. "From Protest to Politics: The Future of the Civil Rights Movement." *Commentary* (February): 27–32.

Senate Select Committee to Study Governmental Operations with Respect to Intelligence Activities. 1976. *Final Report. Hearings,* vols. 1–7. Washington, D.C.: U.S. Government Printing Office.

Skolnick, Jerome H. 1969. *The Politics of Protest.* New York: Simon and Schuster.

Smith, Tom W. 1980. "America's Most Important Problem—A Trend Analysis, 1946–1976." *Public Opinion Quarterly* 44, no. 2: 164–80.

Webb, Horace. 1969. "Police Preparedness for Control of Civil Disorders." *Municipal Yearbook, 1969.* Washington, D.C.: International City Management Association.

Weiss, Nancy J. 1970. "The Negro and the New Freedom." In *The Segregation Era 1863–1954,* ed. Allen Weinstein and Frank Otto Gatell. New York: Oxford University Press, 129–42.

Wilson, James Q. 1965. "The Negro in Politics." In *The Negro American,* ed. Talcott Parsons and Kenneth B. Clark. Boston: Houghton Mifflin, 423–47.

———. 1966. "The Negro in American Politics: The Present." In *The American Negro Reference Book,* ed. John P. Davis. Englewood Cliffs, N.J.: Prentice-Hall, 431–57.

Zinn, Howard. 1965. *SNCC.* Boston: Beacon Press.

17

The Student Nonviolent Coordinating Committee: Rise and Fall of a Redemptive Organization

Emily Stoper

The Student Nonviolent Coordinating Committee (SNCC) presents an enigma to the political analyst, an enigma left unsolved in descriptive histories by former members (Zinn 1964, Lester 1968, Forman 1972, Sellers with Terrell 1973). SNCC was founded in 1960 for the purpose of coordinating the sit-in movement then sweeping the South in an attempt to integrate bus stations, lunch counters, and the like. The following year, with the integration of public facilities largely achieved, SNCC moved into voter registration work among poor blacks in the rural Deep South. Most of its members in this period from 1960 to 1963 were black southern college dropouts. After several years of almost total frustration in this effort, SNCC decided to bring its case to the nation. In order to dramatize the disenfranchisement of blacks in the Deep South, it threw all its efforts behind a challenge to the seating of the all-white Mississippi delegation at the 1964 Democratic National Convention.

Here was the beginning of SNCC's seeming success. The convention offered a compromise that had the effect of expelling the white Mississippi delegates and seating some of the black challengers. The following year, a federal Voting Rights Act was passed, which sent federal registrars to the southern states, something SNCC had been demanding for years. The registrars effectively ended the mass disenfranchisement of blacks.

Meanwhile, in 1964 SNCC had gained a large number of new, highly capable, and enthusiastic members. Then in 1966 it achieved national fame when its chairman, Stokely Carmichael, enunciated the slogan "Black Power."

After this cavalcade of apparent successes, what did SNCC do? It rapidly faded out of existence! In-depth interviews with about fifty former SNCC members suggest to me that the solution to this enigma (success leading to failure) lies in SNCC's almost unique organizational ethos and in the tension between that ethos and SNCC's pursuit of purposive goals.

SNCC's ethos was a product of its unusual incentive structure, which made it a "redemptive organization," one type of purposive organization in the typology that includes purposive, solidary, and material organizations (according to their incentive structure). This typology was developed by Clark and Wilson (1961) and refined by Wilson (1973). Wilson (1973) describes a redemptive organization as one that

> seeks not only to change society and its institutions, but also to change its members by requiring them to exemplify in their own lives the new order. The way in which goals are sought is as important as their substance. Moral and political enthusiasm are to be made evident in the routine activities of the members and in all organizational meetings. (47)

SNCC fits this description very well. This study of SNCC extends and elaborates on the characteristics of redemptive organizations. First, I discuss what SNCC as a redemptive organization was *not*.

SNCC's members (who were all full-time activists) certainly did not join because of material incentives. Their salaries, which were paid very irregularly, ranged from $10 to $60 a week, with the mode about $10.

Nor did they join out of a belief in SNCC's ideological correctness, as did members of the Socialist and Communist parties. SNCC had no formal ideology. Its members plucked ideas from the works of Albert Camus, Karl Marx, Mao Tse-tung, Malcolm X, Frantz Fanon, and others, but there were no basic SNCC principles on which they all agreed.

SNCC does not fit Max Weber's famous classification of organizations as either bureaucratic, charismatic, or traditional (Gerth and Mills 1958). SNCC was obviously not held together by a bureaucracy or bureaucratic incentives. Almost all of its members were activists in the field, and the office staff was kept to a bare minimum.

Nor were SNCC's members drawn together by a few charismatic leaders at the top. Leadership in SNCC tended to be decentralized at the level of a state or local project. No one controlled the organization from the national office in Atlanta. Even at the project level, SNCC members rejected leadership. In many interviews activists actually denied that there were leaders in SNCC at all—because the word "leader" connoted to them a person who manipulated others, thus distorting the purpose of an organization.

SNCC did, of course, have leaders, and they were an important source of its redemptive ethos. Such men as Bob Moses in Mississippi, Charles Sherrod in southwest Georgia, and Bill Hansen in Arkansas were highly effective leaders not so much because of their intellectual acumen or organizing skills as because of their moral courage, a quality that gave others a sense of hope for personal and social redemption. They were praised for this quality again and again in interviews.

SNCC's redemptive ethos consisted partly of a set of attitudes toward the world that were exemplified by the lives of these leaders. These attitudes constituted both more than and less than an ideology. They were both broader and deeper than ideology in the sense that they embraced life style as well as political ideas and in that they called for a commitment in action as well as a mere affirmation of belief. They were also less explicit than ideology. Nowhere was there a pamphlet stating authoritatively that "this is what you must believe to be a SNCC member." One would have been hard put between 1961 and 1965 to say precisely which ideas were basic to the SNCC worldview. There was a high level of agreement among members about many things, but no clearly stated central tenets.

The redemptive ethos was more than a set of attitudes. It was also a strong sense of intimacy, solidarity, and loyalty among SNCC members in the face of what was increasingly seen as an implacably hostile world. The world was also seen in highly moral terms, more and more as time passed. SNCC was good; those who were not with it were against it, so were evil. One did not make compromises because one does not negotiate about matters of good and evil.

To sum up, SNCC was a redemptive organization because it had

1. A moral ethos, consisting of a set of broad attitudes, shared by almost all members, involving a rejection of ideology (formal sets of beliefs)
2. A sense of superiority of other institutions and to individual nonmembers
3. A very high rate of activism among members
4. Pervasiveness, that is, an important influence on all or almost all aspects of its members' lives
5. A belief in the equality of all members, which leads to the rejection of bureaucracy and of all formal leadership structures

A redemptive political organization is in many ways analogous to a religious sect, as distinguished from a church, in the work of Ernst Troeltsch

(1958) and others. For example, it possesses a total rather than a segmental hold over its members. Virtually all SNCC members were totally absorbed in SNCC work at all times. In sects, too, spirituality or grace is something to be lived or at least sought at every moment, not merely occasionally or one day a week (see Knox 1950). Like a sect, SNCC practiced the "priesthood of all believers"; every member was actively engaged in spreading its message.

SNCC's redemptive ethos gave its members the feeling, common in sects, of belonging to an elect group with special enlightenment. It played a role analogous to that of faith or "inner light" in sects; the members considered it superior to mere doctrine. For SNCC, moral impatience took the place of a systematic body of ideas, just as for sects millennialism takes the place of theology.

In sects, the "inner light" perceived by a member is expressed in spontaneous displays of religious feeling ("holy rolling"). Similarly, SNCC expected its members' moral and political enthusiasm to help them initiate new projects and experimental tactics. Going even further in a religious direction, the members of the Freedom High, a small, mostly white group within SNCC in 1963 and 1964, thought that SNCC members should strive chiefly for personal perfection (salvation). All of these are characteristics of sects as described by Wilson (1959).

But the Freedom High was short-lived; most of its adherents were soon driven out of SNCC. For SNCC was not a sect; it was a political organization, and its political goal (racial justice) was central to its existence. My thesis is that it was the tension between its sectlike qualities and its political purposiveness that eventually destroyed SNCC.

A number of factors made SNCC a redemptive organization. The first of these was its origin in the sit-in movement, with that movement's emphasis on moral confrontation with the evil of segregation and its quasi-religious tone (supplied by the many divinity students who helped lead it).

The second factor was the youthfulness of the membership. Zinn (1964) found that most Mississippi SNCC members in 1963 were 15 to 22 years old. Only the very young had the freedom from family responsibilities, the energy, and the physical stamina necessary for SNCC work. And the very young are also often very moralistic. As Keniston (1968) and Fishman and Solomon (1963) show, the young see with fresh eyes the rampant injustice and suffering to which their parents have become calloused. And they have a shorter time perspective for the correction of these injustices than even those adults who perceive that they do exist. Moreover, they are less forgiving of those who cooperate in perpetuating the evils of the world.

For many reasons, these young people chose to concentrate their crusade against injustice in the rural counties of the Deep South, especially Mississippi. One of these reasons was that Mississippi, which had a reputation as the most racist state in the Union, had some of the appeal of the conversion of the worst sinner. Also, little work was being done there by other black groups, mainly because of the white terror. In tackling the rural Deep South, SNCC could enjoy a sense of a special and superior mission, which proved to be an important source of solidarity.

SNCC's choice of locale became the chief cause of its difficulties in the next few years. Almost every SNCC member was jailed at least once in the next few years on such charges as "disturbing the peace" or "parading without a permit." Going to jail became almost an initiation rite. Nearly every male SNCC member (and many females) had been beaten, either in jail or on the street. SNCC offices were fire-bombed, its members were shot at (and sometimes hit), many of its close associates were actually murdered. Through all this, SNCC was almost entirely nonviolent (not in principle, but out of tactical necessity). This experience of persecution was probably the most important factor in shaping SNCC's moral ethos. It made SNCC righteously angry, defiant, uncompromising, and filled with suspicion as to the goodwill and sincerity of those who had never faced the terror. Until the beginning of 1964 most of SNCC's efforts were devoted to surviving in the face of fear and to helping its clientele, the poor blacks of the Deep South, overcome that fear and achieve political freedom.

After the spring of 1964 SNCC began to experience the tension between its ethos and its political effectiveness. Five crises in rapid succession destroyed it: (1) the challenge to Mississippi's delegation to the Democratic National Convention, (2) the sudden influx of several hundred whites into the organization, (3) the bad results of SNCC's inability to get along with other civil rights groups, (4) the loss of a financial base, and (5) an attempt to shift the base of operations from South to North. I shall describe these one by one.

The Convention Challenge

In August 1964 a SNCC-founded and SNCC-backed organization called the Mississippi Freedom Democratic Party (FDP) attempted to have its delegates seated as representatives of Mississippi in place of the regular delegates at the Democratic National Convention. The narrative that follows comes from various reports in the *New York Times* (1964) and from interviews. The FDP delegates had been selected in a political process that paralleled the regular method of delegate selection in Mississippi but (unlike the regular Mississippi Democratic Party's practice) excluded no one on grounds of race. (Of course, almost no whites had chosen to participate in the FDP conventions.)

There was a further basis for the FDP challenge—that the regulars were unwilling to pledge support for the nominees of the convention, as required by a convention rule. (Most of the regulars later publicly endorsed Barry Goldwater, the Republican candidate for president.)

Ultimately, after a great deal of backroom negotiations, demonstrations, and impassioned pleas, the Credentials Committee of the convention offered the following compromise, which was approved by a voice vote of the convention: all of the regulars who signed the loyalty oath would be seated, plus two delegates-at-large from the FDP, with voting rights but without the right to sit in the Mississippi seating section. The rest of the FDP delegates were welcomed as honored guests of the convention. Moreover, it was promised that the call to the 1968 convention would announce that states that practiced racial discrimination in the selection of their delegates would be denied seating.

All the 1964 regulars did eventually withdraw from the convention; almost the entire FDP delegation did take the regulars' seats on the floor (but only two of their votes); and four years later, in 1968, the regulars (as well as half the regulars from Georgia) were denied their seats because of racial discrimination in the selection procedure.

However, to SNCC the compromise was totally unacceptable and was taken as evidence of pervasive racism and hypocrisy within the Democratic Party. First, the regulars lost their seats not as a penalty for racial discrimination but because they themselves chose to protest against the offering of the compromise by leaving and also to refuse to sign the loyalty oath to the convention's nominees. So the principle that delegates chosen in Jim Crow elections were unacceptable was not established. The change in the call to the 1968 convention was considered meaningless because it forbade discrimination against voters and most of Mississippi's blacks were not voters and had little prospect of registering. (This was before the passage of the 1965 Voting Rights Act.) Moreover, the FDP's right to represent Mississippi was not acknowledged since its delegates were designated "at large"; nor was its right even to choose its own delegates, since the two with voting rights were specified by the convention.

SNCC thought it had gone quite far by expressing its willingness to accept another compromise (suggested by Representative Edith Green of Oregon) that treated FDP equally with the regulars. And it was deeply insulted at being treated worse than people whom it considered totally immoral.

Despite all this, white and black liberals generally thought the compromise was generous and were puzzled at SNCC's rejection of it. The FDP delegates themselves (who were almost all local Mississippi blacks) seemed much more inclined to accept the compromise than were their SNCC advisers. SNCC's rejection of the compromise meant that it defined the convention challenge as a failure. This felt failure was in turn an important factor in causing the period of depression and turmoil that SNCC went through during the following year, and also in the fact that the FDP never again regained the organizing momentum of the heady summer of 1964.

Almost any other organization, recognizing the slowness with which so vast and decentralized an institution as the Democratic Party shifts its commitments, would have seen the proffered compromise as a victory. In fact, the Southern Christian Leadership Conference (SCLC, Dr. Martin Luther King's group), the NAACP, the AFL-CIO, and most of SNCC's other allies urged SNCC to accept the compromise.

But SNCC by its nature as a redemptive organization could not accept the kind of partial commitment implied in the compromise. In discussing the convention in the interviews, SNCC members often spoke of backroom negotiations, of deals, of pressure, and of betrayals. It apparently shocked them that the Democratic Party operated so amorally that it seemed to regard the FDP and the Mississippi regulars chiefly as political rivals who must both be at least partly accommodated, rather than as the forces of right and justice fighting against the forces of evil and racism. The fact that the northern liberals in the party had important links to the southern conservatives (on whom they depended for votes in presidential elections) indicated to SNCC that these liberals were totally useless as allies of SNCC. A partial commitment was worse than no commitment at all, because it opened the door to betrayal (see Carmichael and Hamilton 1967). Moreover, concessions in practice were meaningless without concessions in principle. Having been immersed in its own moral universe for several years, SNCC simply could not accept the moral universe of the mainstream of the American political system, in which "compromise" is not a dirty word but the very basis of all activity.

The Influx of Whites

Simultaneously with the crisis created by the convention challenge, SNCC was undergoing another deep struggle. This one concerned the aftermath of the Mississippi Freedom Summer project, in which more than eight hundred whites, mostly northern students, came into Mississippi in the summer of 1964 to work with SNCC in organizing the blacks of Mississippi around the convention challenge, and also to draw national attention to the persecution of civil rights workers in that state. Over a hundred of these whites stayed on to work in Mississippi after the summer. Since before this SNCC had rarely numbered more than one hundred members (and only about sixty in late 1963), the increase in numbers alone meant a transformation of the organization. These mostly intelligent and aggressive new members could have provided the basis for a vastly expanded and far better publicized organizing effort. Instead, SNCC in Mississippi in the fall of 1964 and winter and spring of 1965 was almost paralyzed. The situation in Mississippi affected the entire organization profoundly. In almost every month in that period, there was a national SNCC staff meeting (membership meeting) lasting a week to ten days. The sessions were stormy and often lasted far into the night. The major disputes were (1) how to socialize so many new members into the organization at once, especially since they differed from the old members in social class, race, and level of education; (2) whether whites could ever organize black people effectively; and (3) how SNCC should be structured and where its centers of power should be.

The meetings were a sign of the fact that SNCC was no longer functioning as a redemptive organization. It was too big, it was too diverse, and it had too many members who had never shared the unifying experience of the terror (and since they were white, never fully would). SNCC met the problem by tightening its structure, driving out the newcomers (and those old-timers who were white or were closely associated with whites), and thus trying to restore the old SNCC. But this proved futile. Too much talent was lost, too many people were left disoriented by the long internal struggle, and for too many people the tension between SNCC's redemptive ethos and their personal desire to be effective opponents of racial injustice became painfully manifest. Many of those who left SNCC in early 1965 joined more moderate civil rights groups or Lyndon Johnson's War on Poverty. Many others, unwilling to dilute their principles, dropped out of politics entirely.

The expulsion of the whites pointed up a major problem: racism within SNCC. Before 1964, when there were only a small number of highly dedicated whites in SNCC, their presence had not created serious problems. After the summer project and convention challenge, however, some blacks in SNCC began to question both the effectiveness and the motives of the large number of new white members. The new whites were enthusiastic, self-confident, mostly better educated than the blacks, and often more skilled at typing, expressing their ideas at meetings, putting out newsletters, and other organizing abilities. Therefore, in many places they began to take over the day-to-day and week-to-week decision-making. This angered the blacks who had been working in SNCC for several years and were really much better at the essential work of communicating with and encouraging local black people. The whites, in fact, tended to reinforce the tendency of local blacks to defer to white people. For example, a white volunteer who asked a local black person to vote might receive the reply "Yessir, boss!"

Blacks in SNCC also began to question the motives of the whites for coming to work in the Deep South. The whites seemed to have come to learn about life or to find themselves, to help the poor benighted black people and earn their gratitude, to act on an ideology, to satisfy a need for engagement or political activity, to play the political game, to atone for guilt, to escape themselves, and for any number of other reasons that did not seem legitimate to the blacks. None of these motives could form a satisfactory basis for a redemptive commitment.

Probably the blacks in SNCC also had motives that were not totally altruistic, but they were right in believing that the whites' commitment would never have the same meaning as their commitment. The blacks, after all, were fighting in their own cause, whose outcome would directly affect their personal destinies. The whites were merely giving a little of their time to somebody else's cause. (On the whole question of white-black relations within SNCC, see also Poussaint 1966.)

If SNCC had not been a redemptive organization, it could probably have dealt with the fact that different members had different levels and types of commitment. But the complete egalitarianism and the complete unity of sentiment necessary to sustain the redemptive ethos were incompatible with different types of membership. After all, a redemptive ethos involves seeing everyone in the world as either "sinners" or "saved." Partial salvation, partial commitment, is not possible.

For almost any organization, the absorption of so many new members, especially new members who were different in important ways from the old members, would be a serious problem—but few would have been so crippled by the crisis as SNCC. Most would have been sustained by the tremendous opportunities for renewal and expansion of activity presented by the new members. In fact, it would be difficult to think of another example of an ongoing voluntary organization that went into a rapid decline a few months after tripling its membership.

Problems with Other Civil Rights Groups

At about this time (the spring of 1965), SNCC faced another serious problem. It began to reap the consequences of its long-term bad relations with other civil rights organizations. SNCC people had always despised the NAACP, regarding it as a corrupt group concerned chiefly with gaining advantages for the black middle class. (SNCC's clientele had, with few exceptions, always been the poorest of the poor.) However, SNCC had a policy of never publicly attacking the NAACP or any other black group, a policy it almost always adhered to.

By the spring of 1965, the national leadership of the NAACP had become very concerned about Communists in SNCC. A few white conservatives had been saying for some time that SNCC was Communist-infiltrated, but now the NAACP became one of the most zealous participants in a broad attack by liberals and liberal groups on alleged Communist influence in SNCC (see Kopkind 1965a, Evans and Novak 1966).

The NAACP has always been meticulous in maintaining the "purity" of its own membership and associates, so as not to antagonize powerful anticommunist liberals or give its racist enemies extra fuel for attacking it. SNCC could not understand such toadying to one's enemies and to doubtful allies at the expense of one's own people. SNCC refused even to reply to the charges. Its leaders would say only that SNCC did not require a loyalty oath and that they personally were unconcerned about fighting the battles of the 1930s, 1940s, and 1950s. They might have added that SNCC's redemptive ethos was totally incompatible with that of the Communist Party and that a person who joined SNCC either adapted to that ethos or left. What SNCC did, instead, was to take a moral stand against McCarthyism. Its failure to deny the charges explicitly hurt it a good deal with the liberals who were its chief financial backers. But the last thing SNCC would do would be to compromise its principles by yielding to McCarthyistic (or any other external) pressures. After the 1964 Democratic National Convention, it was extremely suspicious of the commitment of liberals and the NAACP anyway—and when they began to attack it publicly, SNCC became even more alienated from them.

The spring of 1965 also saw SNCC come into conflict with SCLC and Dr. Martin Luther King Jr., this time far more dramatically than ever before. Both SNCC and SCLC had been working in Selma, Alabama, on voter registration—SNCC for two years, SCLC for a few months. Progress was very slow, and therefore SCLC decided to sponsor a march to the state capital at Montgomery 50 miles away to demand voting rights for black people. The march would be in defiance of an order by Governor George Wallace. SNCC opposed the march as yet another one of Dr. King's tactics that (in SNCC's view) would give him a lot of glory overnight and undermine the long-term efforts to develop local people's confidence in their ability to achieve political goals on their own. The SNCC project in Selma decided not to participate officially in the march. The march eventually became three marches: the first one, in which the nonviolent marchers were turned back at a bridge near Selma by police led by Sheriff James Clark and using whips, guns, horses, and tear gas; the second march, two days later, in which by prior agreement with the police the marchers turned back at the same bridge ("making secret deals with

Jim Clark" was the way SNCC members described this, since neither SNCC nor the public had been told of the agreement); and a third march, two weeks after the first, in which an estimated 3,200 people participated, including hundreds of northern whites, protected by almost 4,000 federal soldiers. This march provided the push necessary to bring the Voting Rights bill, which had been languishing in committee, up to the floor of Congress and get it passed. The Voting Rights Act sent large numbers of federal registrars to the Deep South, who quickly accomplished what SNCC and other black groups had been vainly attempting for years: the mass registration of black voters in the South.

So Dr. King's "glory-seeking" had resulted in an enormous success for the entire civil rights movement—but not a success for SNCC. SNCC defined its goal not as the passage of specific laws but as teaching people (which did not mean federal registrars) to act politically on their own behalf. Of course, the Voting Rights Act opened up previously undreamed-of possibilities for the self-organization of black people in the South—but not at all in the way SNCC had been hoping. SNCC envisioned its followers as developing a kind of "alternative politics" for America—a politics that was more decentralized, idealistic, intimate, noncoercive—in short, more redemptive. The Voting Rights Act in effect co-opted the people whom SNCC had been counting on to build the new politics by luring them into standard two-party politics.

In the year that followed passage of the Voting Rights Act, most of SNCC's projects in the Deep South (with the notable exception of Stokely Carmichael's Lowndes County Freedom Organization) were either dead or dying. It was clear that SNCC was going to have to change if it was to continue to exist.

The Move North

The logical direction for SNCC to look at this point was North and to the cities. By 1966 the political awakening of black urban youth that had begun with the 1964 and 1965 riots had become quite widespread. Moreover, the continuing mechanization of southern agriculture was driving increasing numbers of blacks northward and cityward. There were fewer and fewer southern counties with black majorities, and two northern cities (Washington and Newark) by then had populations more than half black.

But SNCC faced severe problems in moving. Its membership (staff) had been decimated, and it faced strong competition in the North with other groups in recruiting new members.

Loss of a Financial Base

Moreover, its financial base had all but disappeared, partly because of its own behavior (such as sending Stokely Carmichael to Havana and Hanoi, and also issuing a strongly anti-Israeli pamphlet, thus alienating its anti-communist and Jewish supporters). No doubt it was also the case that white liberals were becoming chary of supporting blacks now that they were getting so militant.

SNCC's only hope at this point seemed to be to form alliances with other groups. It had always been able to work harmoniously with the Congress of Racial Equality (CORE) in the South because CORE's southern chapters had a redemptive ethos similar to SNCC's. But now, in 1967, a planned alliance with national CORE for the purpose of forming a new political apparatus for black people never got off the ground. And a working alliance with the Black Panthers in 1968 lasted only five months, ending in bitterness and violence. It would have been very surprising, in the light of the explanation offered here, if SNCC had been able to maintain an alliance with the urban-bred Panther party, which had such a different ethos.

So SNCC never took hold in the North. Its redemptive ethos, so dependent on a particular mix of circumstance, belief, and background, was like a delicate plant. It was not easily transplanted into new soil— nor could it survive, under changing conditions, in the old soil. SNCC could not change its ethos, and given that ethos, it was capable only of limited responses to political opportunities— and mosty self-destructive ones. So SNCC flowered and died in a very brief span of years.

What can be concluded from this strange tale of success through failure and failure through success? I say success through failure because during the 1961–63 period when SNCC was encountering almost total frustration in its voter registration campaigns, its members described it as the most "meaningful" and "beautiful" group they had ever known. I say success also because despite the hardships, danger, and frustration of SNCC life, SNCC in that period always had a stream of new members to replace the old. And the old members left not in disillusion but in exhaustion (they usually lasted no more than a year). The many ex-SNCC members interviewed were almost universally very positive in their feelings toward SNCC. This was true even of the whites who were forced out in the spring of 1965.

SNCC's failure through success is more obvious. The compromise offered at the 1964 Democratic convention, the advent of so many talented new members, the passage of the Voting Rights Act, the national fame that Stokely Carmichael brought with his "Black Power" slogan—these look, to the outsider, like successes and opportunities for more success.

Yet within SNCC they were experienced as failures and portents of greater failure.

That SNCC was a strange kind of organization is clear. Very few other political organizations have resembled it, even radical ones. For example, the Socialist and Communist parties in America, far from being redemptive, have been basically ideological organizations.

SNCC has sometimes been compared with the Industrial Workers of the World (IWW), also know as the Wobblies. As Renshaw (1967) relates, in the 1905–20 period, the IWW challenged the conservative, bread-and-butter unions of the day by being radical and visionary. Yet the IWW was very different from SNCC. It was bureaucratic and large, with a peak membership of about one hundred thousand. Its disputes over strategy and structure were fought out among the top leaders in the language of European radical ideologies (Marxism and syndicalism), whereas SNCC's disputes directly involved the entire organization and had little to do with any ideologies.

SNCC has also been compared with the Students for a Democratic Society (SDS), and there are a number of similarities in values and attitudes between members of the two groups. In fact, before 1965, when it was engaged in small-scale community organizing, SDS did seem to have a redemptive organization. But SDS then began organizing students around the issues of the Vietnam War, the draft, and student power. It became a large organization with thousands of members, some very active, most of them almost entirely inactive. Moreover, some of the leaders began a serious effort to develop an ideology, in order to explain to people how their problems were caused by deep-rooted failures of the American system. Other leaders continued to hold the more redemptive viewpoint that to explain this to people was to preclude their discovering it through experience, which was the only way to gain real knowledge. So SDS after 1965 retained some redemptive characteristics but was too large and diffuse to be really a redemptive organization (on SDS, see Kopkind 1965b, Blumenthal 1967, Jacobs 1968, Brooks 1965).

The Weather Underground, which split off from SDS, does seem to have been redemptive. Its members lived together in collectives of ten to thirty people in which they studied revolutionary doctrine, wrote, organized, and participated in Maoist-style self-criticism sessions. Kifner (1970) describes them as having a "quality approaching religious fanaticism." The result of its redemptive spirit was a burning moral outrage that led it to commit acts of violence, which in turn resulted in its being driven underground and eventually into virtual extinction.

No wonder SNCC did not have the instinct for staying alive in a political world. It was held together almost entirely by incentives that are atypical of political organizations. Just as SNCC's incentive structure was non-political, so its contribution was also nonpolitical, or rather prepolitical.

That contribution was a challenge to the extreme rationality and individualism of the American system. This challenge came not through anything SNCC taught but precisely through its redemptive nature. SNCC offered its members a kind of total universe that made possible a full commitment, an unmediated caring about the values and the people in that universe. Many of its members report that before 1964, they often experienced a sense of harmony and certainty that is rarely felt by other Americans. Their lives were not fragmented. Instead of filling a series of largely unrelated roles (parent, employee, citizen), they filled only one role: SNCC worker. Instead of balancing in their heads a multiplicity of values, all of them tentative, they had one certain, absolute set of beliefs. The group provided a world order that is far more complete and stable than any that individuals could assemble for themselves.

The SNCC outlook stands most sharply in contrast to that of the liberal—the person who makes a point of seeing every issue from all perspectives and of being always prepared to trade off his or her values for each other. The liberal is a specialist in living with a minimum of conflict in a complex, atomized, shifting world. Without the liberal, the American system could hardly exist. The liberal makes possible the relatively peaceful coexistence of many highly diverse groups. The liberal is the keystone of a society that fails to give its members any sort of total viewpoint or meaning.

It was to this society that the early SNCC offered an alternative. But the pressures and the temptations proved too great for that alternative to last. The history of SNCC after 1964 is the history of the gradual breakdown of the earlier total universe leading to its dissolution.

But the SNCC experience offered a kind of model, a definition, a direction to the rest of the New Left. Some of SNCC's members became prominent in other New Left groups. Tom Hayden, after working in SNCC during 1961, went on to become one of the founders of SDS in 1962. Mario Savio, a 1964 summer volunteer, that fall became the best-known leader of Berkeley's Free Speech Movement. The Black Panther Party took its name from the nickname of a SNCC project, Stokely Carmichael's Lowndes County Freedom Organization. SNCC's ethos served a kind of prepolitical role by presenting a model of an alternative politics to the New Left and a critique of America's values that is of potential interest to many more people—though very few outside the New Left heard the message. It was very hard to understand, and it got mixed up with the more frightening simultaneous Black Power message coming from SNCC.

In short, SNCC's contribution was precisely that it was a redemptive political organization. There are probably thousands of redemptive organizations, from motorcycle gangs to religious sects. They are rarely explicitly political. (Those that are political, like SNCC and also CORE in the South in the early 1960s, tend to be very short-lived or to have a very short redemptive phase.) Those Americans who feel the need for the rewards of intimacy and moral certainty offered by a redemptive ethos do not generally seek them in politics. SNCC is of interest because it attempted to do both things: to be political and to offer its members the satisfactions of a redemptive ethos. The story of how it failed provides an illustration of the reason the American political system is not likely to provide its citizens with a sense of community or meaning for their lives.

SNCC's story also shows the limitations of compromises, concessions, and reforms as a government strategy for dealing with dissident groups. Most groups, even radical ones, can be influenced to some extent by these three basic techniques of American government and can even work temporarily with reformist groups for reformist ends, as the Communist Party did during the Popular Front (Howe and Coser 1957) and as the Black Panthers did in the 1980s. But to a redemptive group a compromise is always an implied insult (because it denies the absoluteness of the group's moral right); a concession is always a trick (because it is never given in a redemptive spirit but may sway people from the redemptive group's position); and a reform is always a sham (because it does not change the underlying immoral or amoral system). The rejection of the convention compromise makes perfect sense in these terms. If the government is faced with further redemptive political challenges—by the remnants of the New Left, by young people, by black people, by women—it can expect further rebuffs to any concessions it offers.

But in another way a redemptive group is extremely vulnerable to offers of reform. Its lack of adaptability means that its base—of both financial supporters (white liberals, for SNCC) and active followers (poor rural southern blacks, for SNCC)—can easily be stolen. The redemption-oriented core of active members is then left impotent and frustrated and more morally offended than ever. I do not know what effect this usually has—whether it stimulates other, even more angry redemptive challenges like the Weatherman; whether it reinforces the determination of nonredemptive reformist groups like SCLC to continue "working within the system"; whether it encourages redemptive groups like SDS to transform themselves into something else; or whether it merely increases apathy and cynicism and a kind of simmering anger among the excluded groups (like blacks and youth) to which redemptive organizations seem to appeal. Probably all four to different degrees. In any case, this will have to be the subject of further research.

References

Blumenthal, R. 1967. "SDS: Protest Is Not Enough." *Nation* 204 (22 May): 656–60.

Brooks, T. R. 1965. "Voice of the New Campus Underclass." *New York Times Magazine* (7 November): 25–27.

Carmichael, S., and C. V. Hamilton. 1967. *Black Power*. New York: Vintage.

Clark, P. B., and J. Q. Wilson. 1961. "Incentive Systems: A Theory of Organizations." *Administrative Science Quarterly* 46 (September): 129–66.

Evans, R., and R. Novak. 1966. *Boston Globe*, 7 September.

Fishman, J. R., and F. Solomon. 1963. "Youth and Social Action, 1: Perspectives on the Student Sit-in Movement." *American Journal of Orthopsychiatry* 33 (October): 872–82.

Forman, J. 1972. *The Making of Black Revolutionaries: A Personal Account.* New York: Macmillan.

Gerth, H. H., and C. W. Mills, eds. 1958. *From Max Weber.* New York: Oxford University Press.

Howe, I., and L. Coser. 1957. *The American Communist Party: A Critical History, 1917–57.* Boston: Beacon Press.

Jacobs, J. 1968. "SDS: Between Reform and Revolution." *Nation* 206 (10 June): 753–57.

Keniston, K. 1968. *Young Radicals.* New York: Harcourt, Brace and World.

Kifner, J. 1970. "Vandals in the Mother Country." *New York Times Magazine* (4 January): 14–16.

Knox, R. A. 1950. *Enthusiasm: A Chapter in the History of Religion.* Oxford: Clarendon Press.

Kopkind, A. 1965a. "Of, by, and for the Poor." *New Republic* 152 (19 June): 15–19.

———. 1965b. "New Radicals in Dixie: Those Subversive Civil Rights Workers." *New Republic* 152 (10 April): 13–16.

Lester, J. 1968. *Look Out, Whitey! Black Power's Gon' Get Your Mama!* New York: Dial.

Poussaint, A. F. 1966. "The Stresses of the White Female Worker in the Civil Rights Movement in the South." *American Journal of Psychiatry* 123 (October): 401–7.

Renshaw, P. 1967. *The Wobblies: The Story of Syndicalism in the United States.* Garden City, N.Y.: Doubleday.

Sellers, C., with R. Terrell. 1973. *The River of No Return.* New York: Morrow.

Troeltsch, E. 1958. *Protestantism and Progress.* Boston: Beacon Press.

Student Nonviolent Coordinating Committee. n.d. "Some Aspects of Black-White Problems as Seen by Field Staff." SNCC. Mimeographed.

Wilson, B. 1959. "An Analysis of Sect Development." *American Sociological Review* 24 (February): 3–15.

Wilson, J. Q. 1973. *Political Organizations.* New York: Basic Books.

Zinn, H. 1964. *SNCC: The New Abolitionists.* Boston: Beacon Press.

Index

Education Research Action Project, 309
Eizenstat, Stuart, 32
elites, 6, 61, 129
Ellsberg, Robert, 270
emancipation, 9
emotion, 6, 68, 94
employment discrimination, 226, 340
encapsulation, 307–8
Endangered Species Act, 88
entrepreneurs (movement), 99, 107, 110, 111, 128
Environmental Defense Fund, 86
environmental movement, 73, 85; characteristics, 86–93
Environmental Protection Information Center, 88
Equal Employment Opportunity Commission (EEOC), 18, 21, 22, 230, 231
Equal Rights Amendment (ERA), 16, 67, 115, 223, 235, 244
Erhard, Werner, 30, 37
est, 30, 37
expressive movements and goals, 136, 137, 148

FACE. *See* Freedom of Access to Clinic Entrances Act
factionalism, 307–8
Fair Play for Cuba, 13
Falkenberg, Nanette, 107
Falwell, Jerry, 158, 163, 244, 253
family planning, 107, 111
Family Research Councils, 161
Fanon, Frantz, 350
farm bloc, 289
farm worker movement: dual strategy of, 295–96; ethnic composition of, 278–80, 284, 289, 290, 296; mobilization of, 278, 279, 284, 286–89; opponent tactics, 280, 295; recruitment and incentives, 283, 287–88, 293; resources and elite support of, 280, 291–93; structural powerlessness of, 220, 278–81
fascism, 3
Federal Bureau of Investigaton, 71, 140, 311, 341, 342

Federal Election Commission, 162
Federal Workers Union, 30
Federation of Business and Professional Women's Clubs, 16
Fellowship of Reconciliation, 10, 270
Feminine Mystique, The, 17
feminism. *See* women's movement
Firestone, Shulamith, 19
Focus on the Family, 161
Food and Drug Administration (FDA), 143
Food Conspiracy, 86
Foreman, Dave, 89
formalized social movement organizations, 2, 103, 106, 110–14, 124–25, 130n3
frames and framing: definition, 67; resonance for, 68; types, 68
free speech movement, 61
Freedom Council, 158
Freedom Democratic Party (FDP), 354
Freedom High, 352
Freedom of Access to Clinic Entrances Act (FACE), 251–52, 260, 273
Freedom Rides, 269, 275
Friedan, Betty, 17, 173
Friends of the Earth, 86
Fundamentals, The, 155
Furies, founding of, 173

Galarza, Ernesto, 281
Gandhi, Mahatma, 249, 256, 257
Gandhian techniques. *See* civil disobedience, nonviolent strategies and tactics
gay and lesbian community, x, 30, 135, 137, 139, 142, 144, 145, 156; coalitions within, 187; leadership, 139, 140; mobilization of, 138
Gay Men's Health Crisis (GMHC), 139
Gay Rights Lobby, 138
General Federation of Women's Clubs, 16
General Services Administration, 28
generation gap, 9, 16
Gill, Gary, 36, 37
Glassblowers Union, 293

About the Contributors

Jo Freeman holds a Ph.D. from the University of Chicago (1973) and a J.D. from New York University Law School (1982). She is author of *The Politics of Women's Liberation: A Case Study of an Emerging Social Movement and Its Relation to the Policy Social Process* (1975) and winner of a prize from the American Political Science Association for the Best Scholarly Work on Women in Politics. She has written numerous articles on women, social movements, law, and public policy. She edited *Women: A Feminist Perspective* (1975, 1979, 1983, 1989, 1995) and *Social Movements of the Sixties and Seventies* (1983). Among her works in progress is *A Room at a Time: Women's Entry into Party Politics from the Mid-Nineteenth Century to the Mid-1960s*. She practices law in New York City.

Victoria Johnson received her B.A. from San Francisco State University and her Ph.D. from the University of California, Davis. From 1993 to 1997 she was an editorial associate in the journal *Theory & Society: Renewal and Critique in Social Theory*, at the University of California, Davis. Her areas of interest include collective behavior and social movements, historical and comparative methods, social theory, political sociology, cultural sociology, and labor history. She has authored and co-authored several articles about social movements and is currently working on a book comparing the emergence, dynamics, and outcomes of general strikes in Seattle in 1919 and San Francisco in 1934. She is assistant professor of sociology at Bates College in Lewiston, Maine.

David G. Bromley is professor of sociology and affiliate professor in the Department of Religious Studies at Virginia Commonwealth University in Richmond. Among his recent books are *The Politics of Religious Apostasy* (1998), *The Handbook on Cults and Sects in America* (1993, edited with Jeffrey Hadden), and *The Satanism Scare* (1991, edited with James Richardson and Joel Best). He is currently working on *Religion As Resistance: Prophetic*

Religion in a Secular Age. His research interests include sociology of religion, social movements, deviance, and political sociology. He is former president of the Association for the Sociology of Religion, founding editor of the annual series *Religion and the Social Order,* and former editor of the *Journal for the Scientific Study of Religion.*

Diana Gay Cutchin is affiliate professor in the Department of Sociology and Anthropology and coordinator of the Sexual Assault Program in the Division of Student Affairs at the Virginia Commonwealth University in Richmond. She received her M.S. degree in sociology in 1995. Her primary professional interests are in sexual assault, human sexuality, and marriage and family.

Luther P. Gerlach is professor of anthropology and member of the graduate faculties in conservation biology and water resources at the University of Minnesota. He is co-author of *People, Power, Change: Movements of Social Transformation* (1970), *Lifeway Leap: Dynamics of Change in America* (1973), and numerous articles. He also produces educational films based on his research. After receiving his Ph.D. from the University of London (1960), he studied social, religious, and environmental movements in Kenya, the United States, Europe, and the Caribbean. The National Science Foundation and the Environmental Protection Agency are funding his current research on human/environment interactions.

John C. Green is director of the Ray C. Bliss Institute and professor of political science at the University of Akron. His research interests include political parties, social movements, religion, and politics. He is co-author of *The Bully Pulpit: The Politics of the Protestant Clergy* (1997) and *Religion and the Culture Wars* (1996).

Abigail Halcli is lecturer in sociology at Oxford Brookes University, UK. Her research interests are in the areas of social movements, gender, and politics. She is co-editor (with Gary Browning and Frank Webster) of *Theory and Society: Understanding the Present* (1999). She has also published research on the gendered experiences of female politicians and on foundation funding of American social movements.

Eric L. Hirsch is associate professor of sociology at Providence College in Rhode Island. His publications include *Urban Revolt: Ethnic Politics in the Nineteenth-Century Chicago Labor Movement* (1990) as well as a variety of articles on social movements and homelessness. His research interests include homelessness, poverty, race and ethnic relations as well as social conflict and social movements. Politically, he is working with homeless Rhode Islanders to try to end homelessness in the state.

James M. Jasper received his B.A. in economics from Harvard and his Ph.D. in sociology from the University of California, Berkeley. He has taught at Berkeley, Columbia, Princeton, and New York University. His books include *Nuclear Politics* (1990), *The Animal Rights Crusade* (1992), and most recently *The Art of Moral Protest* (1997), a synthetic effort to outline a cultural and psychological approach to social movements. He is currently co-editing a volume on emotions and social movements (with Jeff Goodwin and Francesca Polletta) and completing *Restless Nation*, a book about the cultural effects of immigration and mobility in the United States. His research has been funded by the MacArthur Foundation and the National Science Foundation, among others. He writes from his home in New York City about politics and culture.

J. Craig Jenkins is professor of sociology and faculty associate at the Mershon Center for International Security Studies at Ohio State University in Columbus. His work on the farm worker movement includes a book on *The Politics of Insurgency: The Farm Worker Movement of the 1960s* (1986). He is co-editor of *The Politics of Social Protest* (1996) and numerous articles on social movement theory and political change. He is currently studying international civil conflict and violence, the sources and early warning of humanitarian disaster, famine and refugee problems, and with funding from the National Science Foundation and Ameritech Foundation he is working with Charles Taylor and Doug Bond to update the *World Handbook of Political and Social Indicators*.

Roberta Ann Johnson is professor of politics and chair of the Public Service Program at the University of San Francisco. Her Ph.D. is from Harvard. From 1980 to 1985 she was a technical assistance specialist and an investigator for the Office for Civil Rights, U.S. Department of Education. She is the author of *Puerto Rico: Commonwealth or Colony?* (1980) and numerous articles on minorities, women, the disabled, and civil rights. She is currently editing a book on international whistleblowing.

Doug McAdam is professor of sociology at Stanford University and author of numerous books and articles on social movements and the dynamics of collective action. His books include *Political Process and the Development of Black Insurgency, 1930–1970* (1982), *Freedom Summer* (1988), and with John McCarthy and Mayer Zald (eds.), *Social Movements in Comparative Perspective* (1996).

Davis S. Meyer is associate professor of political science at the City College of New York and the City University Graduate Center. He is author of *A Winter of Discontent: The Nuclear Freeze and American Politics* (1990) and many articles on social movements, public policy, and institutional politics. He is currently studying, with Suzanne Staggenborg, the abortion conflict in the United States.

Frederick D. Miller observed the transformation of SDS into Weatherman while working for a left-wing undergraduate newspaper at the City College of New York. He studied social movements and psychological issues in social perception while pursuing his Ph.D. in social psychology from the Department of Psychology and Social Relations at Harvard. He is currently a director in the Strategic and Organizational Change Practice of Price Waterhouse Coopers where his work focuses on the transformational impacts of large-scale technology deployment. He taught in the Psychology Department at New York University, did applied research and software development at AT&T Bell Laboratories, and occasionally lectures on technology and strategy at Columbia University School of Business.

Suzanne Staggenborg is associate professor of sociology at McGill University in Montreal. She is author of two books on social movements, *The Pro-Choice Movement: Organization and Activism in the Abortion Conflict* (1991) and *Gender, Family, and Social Movements* (1998). Her current research includes a study of changes in the women's movement from the 1960s to the present and a study with David S. Meyer of movements and countermovements, focusing on the abortion conflict.

Emily Stoper is professor of political science at California State University, Hayward. She received her Ph.D. from Harvard. She is author of a history of *The Student Nonviolent Coordinating Committee* (1989) and co-editor (with Ellen Boneparth) of *Women, Power, and Policy: Toward the Year 2000* (1988). She has published many articles on women in American politics and public policy. She spent a year (1977) in Washington as legislative assistant to Representative Stephen J. Solarz of New York.

Verta Tayor is professor of sociology and member of the graduate faculty of women's studies at Ohio State University in Columbus. She is co-author with Leila J. Rupp of *Survival in the Doldrums: The American Women's Rights Movement, 1945 to the 1960s* (1987), co-editor with Laurel Richardson and Nancy Whittier of *Feminist Frontiers* (1986, 1989, 1993), and author of *Rock-a-By Baby: Feminism, Self-Help, and Postpartum Depression* (1996). She has published on social movement theory, women's movements, and the gay and lesbian movement. She is currently completing an edited volume with Nancy Whittier on *Gender and Social Movements,* collaborating with Leila Rupp and Josh Gamson on a historical and ethnographic study of cross-dressing as a collective action repertoire, and working with Nicole Raeburn on a study of the role of social movements in winning domestic partnership benefits in Fortune One Thousand corporations.

Nancy E. Whittier is assistant professor of sociology and member of the Women's Studies Program Committee at Smith College, where she teaches courses on gender and social movements. She holds a Ph.D. from Ohio State University. She is the author of *Feminist Generations: The Persistence of the Radical Women's Movement* (1995) and has published articles on the women's movement, collective identity and culture in social movements, and political generations. She is currently working on a study of the gender politics of social movements against child sexual abuse.